# English Literature before Chaucer

Longman Literature in English Series

**General Editors: David Carroll and Michael Wheeler**
**University of Lancaster**

For a complete list of titles see pages viii and ix

# English Literature before Chaucer

## Michael Swanton

**Longman**
London and New York

81-0993

$32.95

**Longman Group UK Limited**
Longman House, Burnt Mill, Harlow
Essex CM20 2JE, England
*Associated companies throughout the world*

*Published in the United States of America
by Longman Inc., New York*

© Longman Group UK Limited 1987

First published 1987

BRITISH LIBRARY CATALOGUING IN PUBLICATION DATA
Swanton, Michael
 English literature before Chaucer.—(Longman
 literature in English series)
 1. English poetry—Middle English, 1100–1500—
 History and criticism   2. Anglo-Saxon poetry
 —History and criticism
 I. Title
 821'.1'09      PR311
 ISBN 0-582-49241-6 CSD
 ISBN 0-582-49242-4 PPR

LIBRARY OF CONGRESS CATALOGING IN PUBLICATION DATA
Swanton, Michael James.
 English literature before Chaucer.

 (Longman literature in English series)
 Bibliography: p.
 Includes index.
  1. Anglo-Saxon literature—History and criticism.
 2. English literature—Middle English, 1100–1500—
 History and criticism.  I. Title.  II. Series.
 PR166.S96   1986      829'.09      85–20984
 ISBN 0–582–49241–6
 ISBN 0–582–49242–4 (pbk.)

Set in 9½/11pt Bembo (Linotron 202)
Produced by Longman Singapore Publishers (Pte) Ltd.
Printed in Singapore.

# Contents

# Editors' Preface

The multi-volume Longman Literature in English Series provides students of literature with a critical introduction to the major genres in their historical and cultural context. Each volume gives a coherent account of a clearly defined area, and the series, when complete, will offer a practical and comprehensive guide to literature written in English from Anglo-Saxon times to the present. The aim of the series as a whole is to show that the most valuable and stimulating approach to literature is that based upon an awareness of the relations between literary forms and their historical context. Thus the areas covered by most of the separate volumes are defined by period and genre. Each volume offers new and informed ways of reading literary works, and provides guidance to further reading in an extensive reference section.

As well as studies on all periods of English and American literature, the series includes books on criticism and literary theory, and on the intellectual and cultural context. A comprehensive series of this kind must of course include other literatures written in English, and therefore a group of volumes deals with Irish and Scottish literature, and the literatures of India, Africa, the Caribbean, Australia and Canada. The forty-six volumes of the series cover the following areas: Pre-Renaissance English Literature, English Poetry, English Drama, English Fiction, English Prose, Criticism and Literary Theory, Intellectual and Cultural Context, American Literature, Other Literatures in English.

David Carroll
Michael Wheeler

# Longman Literature in English Series

**General Editors: David Carroll and Michael Wheeler**
**University of Lancaster**

## Pre-Renaissance English Literature

*English Literature before Chaucer    *Michael Swanton*
English Literature in the Age of Chaucer
English Medieval Romance

## English Poetry

*English Poetry of the Sixteenth Century    *Gary Waller*
*English Poetry of the Seventeenth Century    *George Parfitt*
English Poetry of the Eighteenth Century, 1700–1789
*English Poetry of the Romantic Period, 1789–1830    *J.R. Watson*
English Poetry of the Victorian Period, 1830–1890
English Poetry of the Early Modern Period, 1890–1940
English Poetry since 1940

## English Drama

English Drama before Shakespeare
English Drama: Shakespeare to the Restoration, 1590–1660
English Drama: Restoration and Eighteenth Century, 1660–1789
English Drama: Romantic and Victorian, 1789–1890
English Drama of the Early Modern Period, 1890–1940
English Drama since 1940

## English Fiction

English Fiction of the Eighteenth Century, 1700–1789
English Fiction of the Romantic Period, 1789–1830
*English Fiction of the Victorian Period, 1830–1890    *Michael Wheeler*
English Fiction of the Early Modern Period, 1890–1940
English Fiction since 1940

## English Prose

English Prose of the Seventeenth Century, 1590–1700
English Prose of the Eighteenth Century
English Prose of the Nineteenth Century

## Criticism and Literary Theory

Criticism and Literary Theory from Sidney to Johnson
Criticism and Literary Theory from Wordsworth to Arnold
Criticism and Literary Theory from 1890 to the Present

## The Intellectual and Cultural Context

The Sixteenth Century
The Seventeenth Century
★The Eighteenth Century, 1700–1789    *James Sambrook*
The Romantic Period, 1789–1830
The Victorian Period, 1830–1890
The Twentieth Century: 1890 to the Present

## American Literature

American Literature before 1880
American Poetry of the Twentieth Century
American Drama of the Twentieth Century
American Fiction, 1865–1940
American Fiction since 1940
Twentieth-Century America

## Other Literatures

Irish Literature since 1800
Scottish Literature since 1700

Australian Literature
Indian Literature in English
African Literature in English
Caribbean Literature in English
★Canadian Literature in English    *W.J. Keith*

★*Already published*

# Author's Preface

The period covered by this volume is large. Spanning the seventh to the thirteenth centuries, it stretches from the emergence of English literature in the earliest surviving records to the eve of the Chaucerian Age – six centuries full of social and intellectual change, their shifting aspirations and constraints, successes, and inadequacies naturally reflected in the literature they provoked.

The centuries in question are rarely thought to form a natural or coherent 'period' in conventional historical terms; they are traditionally divided, albeit with caveats enjoined, into two phases, politically and culturally separated by the Norman Conquest and conveniently corroborated by the linguistic distinction between Old English on the one hand and early Middle English on the other. But chronological divisions are at best arbitrary conveniences. Too often they distort our thinking. No one date provides any kind of reliable diagnostic turning-point, of uniform importance marking off all aspects of life. No mere event breaks all the multitudinous threads connecting the past with the future. Any dissection of the continuous and complex web, composed of the most diverse elements – political, economic, intellectual, moral – is manageable only at the cost of artificiality. Current reassessment of documentary sources, together with cognate disciplines such as archaeology, philology, and the history of ideas, emphasizes the evolutionary rather than the revolutionary aspects of this period, recognizing the resemblance rather than the dissimilarity between contiguous cultures. An evolutionary development does not produce all its effects at once, nor proceed at the same rate in every field. No diagnosis will prove universally applicable. We may identify a preponderance or trend, but at all times individually precocious and archaizing elements may be found to co–exist, albeit uneasily. Analytical exposition of literary history rarely reveals a simple linear pattern. What we might prefer to suppose a necessarily sequential development, is often more realistically visualized as pleated or helicoidal. This is the more so in the early medieval period where it is impossible to ascribe more than very approximate dates, or even provenance, to many works.

In view of the very considerable literary production that must have taken place over this period of time, it is important to remember that the surviving remains are both exceedingly fragmentary and for the most part quite arbitrary. It is clear that certain of our conclusions might require substantial modification if we were permitted larger access to the vast body of original material of which we must necessarily regard our isolated examples as representative.

The centuries under review, if not commonly thought of as a unity, are unified in sharing one important common factor with significant literary consequence. In a period when both literacy and privacy were rare, the substance of all literature, whether originating in oral or manuscript form, was conceived with a public dimension in mind, and received by a relatively homogeneous audience without, as yet, fragmented concerns. But if social aspirations and ideals were not yet clearly stratified, the levels of response, dependent on personal context, ability, and expectation, can scarcely have been uniform. In matters of interpretation it may be assumed without hesitation that, in this period at least, plural accessibility allows, even demands, the possibility of multiple response. This in turn implies an exceptionally high degree of sophistication on the part of the author. His was an open language, without dictionaries or formal grammars: a flexible, multidimensional medium eminently suited to the communication of complex experience. Each word might accommodate several layers of meaning, often of great ambivalence, a fact which, depending on our temperament, we will be predisposed either to condemn as imprecise or to celebrate as intellectually and aesthetically provocative. The instability of the 'text' merely endorses the plural possibilities. We are not only permitted, but obliged, to deny the absolutism of over-determinate 'meanings' demanded by any of the more obscurantist schools of literary criticism. Too often poetry disappears beneath a welter of patristic reference scarcely accessible to Alcuin or Aquinas, let alone lesser mortals; or any possibility of personal appreciation seems pre-empted by the statistical tyranny of formulaicism. If the experience of present-day authors provides any sort of measure, then their earlier medieval counterparts might well be both amused and shocked by the exclusive posture of much recent criticism – delighted to find their work so greatly developed, however bizarre the reaches of scholastic fancy may seem, but undoubtedly dismayed at any self-righteous denial of alternative validity. The intelligent reader will, of course, pursue whatever avenue seems likely to prove most stimulating at any one time, irrespective of the false claims of blinkered consistency. The most fortunate might hope to hold in simultaneous suspension the variable responses of different parts of the original audience, each coloured by the others. If this is perhaps an over-academic proposition, and one unlikely to reflect any kind of individual original response, it does at least have the virtue of acknowledging the inevitability of temporal perspective. We stand where we are, and can do no other than see through unashamedly twentieth-century eyes.

These chapters do not, could not, nor should not, pretend a definitive view, but offer merely a series of starting-points from which it is assumed the reader will wish to advance, perhaps along very divergent avenues. Adequate documentary surveys of the period already exist in plenty; but these allow for little more than a passing glance at each piece in turn, and tend to degenerate into mere listings. Within the limited space available, I have tried to provide a sufficiently synoptic view combined with an appreciation of individual texts. This is attempted by way of introducing a limited number of representative works, but without swamping the reader in qualifying minutiae which only a full apparatal reading of each piece would warrant. Quite obviously, not all that is of interest can be considered. Given the necessity for selection, I have thought it most fruitful to avoid what the modern librarian would classify as 'non-fiction', to concentrate on creative or imaginative writings rather than primarily didactic or official genres such as sermons, hagiography, or chronicle which, although often of un-doubted linguistic interest and often displaying stylish 'literary' qual-ities, remain essentially the province of the historian or theologian. The boundary between 'literature' and anything that happens to be written down is notoriously imprecise; it is unfortunate that the use of the term *litterae* is apparently indeterminate between Classical times and the Ren-aissance.

Traditionalists standing four-square on different ground may claim that, like Byrhtnoth, I have allowed *landes to fela*. Well then, so be it – *hloh þa . . .!*

Michael Swanton
Exeter and Lausanne, 1985.

Haec quicunque legis, stridenti ignosce cicadae
Raucellam nec adhuc vocem perpende, sed aevum,
Utpote quae nidis nondum petit alta relictis.

# Chapter 1
# Introduction : Anxiety and Assertion

Changing perspectives in our understanding of the period no longer permit us to think of the fall of Rome as a radical divide, a cultural watershed separating order and chaos, civilization and barbarism, urban sophistication and 'dark age' superstition. Although undeniably burdened by troubles of all kinds, economic uncertainty and locally internecine warfare bringing temporary cultural regression, the post-Roman scene was by no means the total dereliction of popular imagination. In several respects the Germanic groups colonizing the western provinces of the Empire would consider themselves natural heirs to many features of Roman provincial life. A degree of continuity was in their very real interest. Not only the network of major roads and the principal cities, but a considerable amount of detail in the English landscape, are Romano-British in origin.

In conformity with imperial policy throughout the north-western provinces, it was mercenary troops who maintained the effective defence of Roman Britain during the later phase of direct imperial administration. Groups of semi-organized Germanic *foederati* settled in the north and east of the province, providing both land-based military units and sea-borne coastal patrols, ensured such security as was possible in face of the persistent threat of incursion by Pict and Scot. When Constantine was proclaimed emperor during a visit to York in 337, it was Germanic tribesmen who led the cheering in the streets.[1] Other federate groups lodged in the south-east around what was already described officially as 'the Saxon Shore' provided defence from piratical raids across the North Sea, protecting the Channel ports and thus direct links with the Continent. This policy of Germanic settlement, introduced first by imperial administrators, was naturally maintained by the British princelings like Vortigern upon whom power devolved after the formal abandonment of the province early in the fifth century. The story of Hengest and Horsa as related by Bede, the *Anglo-Saxon Chronicle* and, more dramatically, Nennius, supplies a narrative paradigm reflecting much of the historical truth.[2] Refused further military assistance from the imperial administration, Vortigern, *c.* 450, invites assistance from the successful Germanic mercenary leaders Hengest and Horsa – an arrangement which appears to have proved eminently satisfactory until, demanding more substantial control, the hired men turn to rend their former employers whom they have learned to despise. Calling for reinforcements from their homeland, they speak of the richness of the province and the worthlessness of its inhabitants: *Brytwalana nahtscipe and ðæs landes cysta*.[3] For the next century and a half reinforcements were to come in such numbers that the Angeln peninsula (Schleswig-Holstein), from where the Anglian element was drawn, was said to be still deserted in Bede's day.[4] In one significant respect the circumstances governing the Anglo-Saxon settlement of Britain differed from those on the continent of Europe, where Frankish armies in Gaul, Lombards in Italy, Visigoths in Spain, were simultaneously carving new Germanic kingdoms out of the remaining western provinces of Rome. There the invading armies seem to have formed merely a sparse tenurial military élite, soon assimilated and so susceptible to the cultural expectations of the mass of the native population as to abandon even their native language in favour of the regional Romanic dialect of those among whom they settled. Those who colonized Britain, on the other hand, seem to have done so not merely as an invading army but in coherent familial groups, with women and children, and in numbers large enough eventually to swamp the indigenous population, maintaining their own distinctive linguistic identity and, implicitly, albeit as yet undocumented, distinctive literature. Here it was the native British element who would eventually find it expedient to adopt the language of their powerful new neighbours.

There is now good reason to suppose a considerable degree of native survival in what had been, after all, one of the richest provinces of the Empire, well populated and intensively farmed. Of course there were sections of native society, especially perhaps the great estate owners, who could anticipate only a bleak future with the land-hungry incomers, and these fled as refugees into the hinterland, their resentment reflected in Gildas's *Liber de Excidio et Conquestu Britanniae*.[5] Others, however, might come to terms with the new conditions, even finding them a stimulus to personal advancement. The Anglo-Saxon settlement of what was to become known as England was a long-drawn-out process, only partially completed in some areas. It was well into the seventh century before the English took political control of the west country or the Welsh marches. They moved slowly westwards against the native princedoms of Cumbria in the north-west and Dumnonia in the south-west, leaving residual British enclaves in, for example, south Yorkshire, the Fenland, and the Chilterns. Throughout the country, however, regardless of military disasters and economic uncertainties, the native population lived on and farmed the land – the English eventually assuming political and tenurial control over an ancient economic substructure which would permit only gradual change. If the English colonists usually chose to set up their substantial mead-halls – the social and administrative centres of their new society – on sites away from the great Roman country villas, the estates these governed seem to have survived as economic units regardless of any change in ownership. The study of local boundaries suggests that the parish – the basic unit of late Saxon, and hence medieval, farming – frequently originated in estates taken over more or less intact from Romano-British landlords. However, population pressures now were such that, having occupied nearly the entire area utilized in Roman times, settlers began to penetrate whatever wasteland the Romans had left uninhabited. Pollen analysis shows that at this time, perhaps stimulated by a dispossessed element from the east, demand for land was such that it was found profitable to clear even marginal hill-country in the north and west. There is no doubt but that, despite temporary local regression, the economy continued to prosper, and that Britain remained a rich and productive province, an attractive prize to Viking and Norman in turn. If the cities of Roman Britain no longer exercised any governmental function, their commercial and industrial importance survived. London especially remained a thriving port: *multorum emporium populorum terra marique venientium*, 'a mart for many nations coming by land and sea'.[6] And in one respect at least, certain towns would regain even a degree of administrative importance since, following continental practice, many missionary bishops from the early seventh century onwards would choose to establish their seats in ancient Roman urban centres such as Canterbury, Rochester, Leicester, or York.

If the Ostrogothic Emperor Theodoric explicitly considered himself the direct heir of Rome, we cannot suppose a totally barbarian rejection of imperial dignity on the part of his English contemporaries. Hengest's great-great-grandson Æthelberht, now established as king of Kent, claiming the high-sounding title *Bretwalda* and with it at least nominal suzerainty extending as far as the Humber and the Severn, held court in the Roman city of Canterbury, presumably in one of the grander buildings in the town, while his Christian queen, the Frankish princess Bertha, worshipped in an already extant Roman church on the immediate outskirts of the city. When in 625 at the invitation of the new Bretwalda (the Northumbrian King Edwin) the Roman missionary Paulinus travelled northwards from Kent, eventually reaching Bernicia, a genuinely Celto-Germanic province in the foothills of the Cheviots, he would encounter a highly dignified court procedure, whose ceremonial and setting owed much to the inherited Roman idiom. Edwin's country seat at Yeavering was elaborately provided with a series of impressive formal buildings associated with sophisticated ceremonial and regal administration: substantial reception-halls with white-plastered walls, raised dais and throne, pagan temple – soon to be refurbished as a Christian chapel – and an amphitheatre-like assembly-place capable of seating a large audience for public debate or proclamation, focusing the attention of a large concourse on a single speaker at the centre of the stage. Long-established and confidently undefended, this impressive *palatium* was destroyed within a year or two of Paulinus's visit when Edwin's kingdom was savagely laid waste by an old enemy, Cadwallon, king of Gwynedd. Yeavering was probably the scene of only occasional visits by Edwin and his entourage during the course of royal progresses or the occasional great council or assembly like that addressed by Paulinus – and otherwise left in charge of a resident bailiff. It is in the light of such a picture of life in a royal country seat that we may visualize the probably yet more formal circumstances of Edwin in his chief stronghold – the Roman city of York, or of Æthelberht at Canterbury.

From its foundations, archaeology can construct merely the shell of Edwin's Yeavering, and Bede's incidental account,[7] written for near-contemporaries, could take so much of its trappings for granted. But it is possible for us to clothe our picture of Edwin's regal state from a remarkable contemporary East Anglian royal funeral deposit at Sutton Hoo in Suffolk. Before coming to the Northumbrian throne Edwin, as the ambitious heir of a rival line, had spent many years in exile, finding refuge first with various British princes and latterly with the semi-pagan Rædwald of East Anglia, to whom the title of Bretwalda had recently passed. Although archaeology has yet to reveal Rædwald's palace buildings at Rendlesham, investigation of the royal cemetery near by at Sutton Hoo demonstrates the wealth, cosmopolitan tastes, and wide contacts at the command of an Anglo-Saxon prince. The funeral ship of Rædwald himself, who died at just about the time of Paulinus's visit to Yeavering, contained, in addition to various emblems of state, fine arms and armour (heirlooms from his Swedish forebears), a quantity of Byzantine silverware, ornamental Celtic metalwork, a presentation purse containing a representative collection of coinage from the royal mints of Merovingian Europe, and a wealth of superb jewels, unsurpassed in the western world for technical sophistication and artistic originality, incorporating masses of blood-red garnets imported from the East, and ingenious miniature artificial glass mosaic gemstones. But these were merely some of the more portable, and disposable, trappings of regality. The decor of Rædwald's Rendlesham hall, sculpted and painted, hung with silks and embroideries, must have presented a very remarkable picture indeed.

The great land-takings of the Migration Age had merely confirmed and accelerated tendencies long present in European society: its political and economic fragmentation and consequent social and intellectual turmoil. With decay of central government the great households, already

self-sufficient economically, assumed increasing localized military responsibility. As the disaffected flocked to the local *potentiores* for protection, there had developed within Roman Britain a pattern of *patronatus*
and *clientela* not markedly dissimilar from the familiar Anglo–Saxon war-
band or comitatus. Shadowy kingdóms of a pre–Roman type had begun
to emerge at least a generation before the official end of central
administration: relatively small sovereign states, their size largely determined by the configuration of the landscape; ephemeral institutions
depending for their existence on the reputation of a single man, described
variously as *rex, tyrannus, princeps, dux,* etc. This period is characterized
by the reoccupation of ancient pre–Roman hilltop strongholds, some
built entirely new, most refurbished, modified, and reduced in size. The
massive fortification of Cadbury-Camelot in Somerset implies the existence of concerted regional organization during at least part of this
phase, and must represent the base for an army that was large by the
standards of the time, and the court of a military leader of some status – if
not the historical Arthur, then an Arthur figure of some kind. But most,
like Castle Dore in Cornwall, the abode of Mark/Cunomorus and the
original locale for the Tristan and Iseult story, were much smaller,
designed to be easily defended by a comitatus of, say, between thirty and
a hundred men. No doubt such forts would serve not only to defend the
local population, but also ensure the personal protection of the tyrannus
and his retinue from their 'subjects'. They represent the strongholds of a
local military and political élite, at least some of whom seem to have
sponsored a revival of paganism at this time. Almost all exhibit aristocratic material tastes, marked by a variety of luxury goods imported from
Gaul and the Mediterranean. But if the occasion of this development is
clear, the origins of those who set themselves up as local tyranni are
shrouded in mystery. They may have come from the last of the 'Roman'
aristocracy, rich landowners, or urban gentry. Dispossessed noblemen
from any part of the province, immigrant Irish, or even Picts may have
taken advantage of the final collapse of centralized administration to seize
lands and power. If Rædwald's immediate forebears had come from
southern Sweden, Edwin's from Schleswig-Holstein, Æthelberht's from
Jutland via Frisia, the Welsh Cadwallon's were no less recent immigrants
– in his case from Lothian – descended from one of the heroes com-
memorated in the *Gododdin*, who had come with eight sons from central
Scotland, glorying in fine-sounding Roman military titles, to found a
dynasty in North Wales.

The Celtic interior of Britain was in as considerable a state of ethnic
and social turmoil as the Teutonic-settled East. Originating *in
peregrinatione*, the *gens* of the Heroic Age did not correspond to any fixed
territorial unit, nor boast any closed ethnic identity. The flux of the
*Völkerwanderung* allowed an enormous degree of social mobility. Who-

ever joined the comitatus of a particular leader might share its fortunes irrespective of social or racial origins. The extreme polyethnic composition of certain of the great European armies of the Migration Age is well attested. The 'Ostrogothic' army of the great Eormenric, for example, incorporated not only various Teutonic groups but also non-Germanic Huns, Slavs, Finns, Sarmatians, and even Romans who would serve 'with Gothic hearts'. But any Roman who 'went native' would depend for personal advancement on his assimilation into the warrior ethos of this open society, as witness the contrasting fortunes of two Romans whom Priscus encountered at the court of Attila.[8] One, a former merchant, had distinguished himself in Hunnish military service and now considered his present life infinitely preferable to his past; the other, a master builder who sought to impress by the construction of a magnificent bath-suite, found himself reduced to slavery as a permanent bath-attendant for his pains.

In devolution first local and then personal loyalties assume paramount importance. During the phase of British recovery following their victory at Mons Badonicus, the founding West Saxon war-leader Cerdic bore a Celtic name; and at least one of his successors, Cædwalla, who came out of obscurity at the head of his comitatus to fight for the kingdom, also bore a Celtic name. As late as 784 a British hostage attached to the comitatus of Cynewulf was prepared to fight to the death if necessary to avenge his Saxon patron's murder, rather than take the opportunity to escape when it was offered him.[9] The war-band of a Hengest or Cerdic may have contained a host of warriors who shared little in common save a deep personal commitment to their leader and mutual dependence on his prowess. It is not insignificant that the first English poet we can identify, Cædmon, also had a Celtic name. Ethnic blurring was a natural consequence of the *Völkerwanderung*, as nations shifted, driven by economic and political necessities, absorbing and absorbed by others. Archaeological evidence suggests that on the eve of the great land-takings, the Anglo-Saxons were already a mixed and mongrel people. The confusion of the documentary record merely reflects actuality. It should not have puzzled the Beowulfian critics that the Geatish Weohstan could be regarded as a Scylfing prince, fighting on behalf of the Swedish Onela, the Geat's implacable enemy, or that at the end of his life the Geatish king Beowulf should be described as a Danish champion. The ethnic dissociation of European heroic society is reflected in the non-national subject-matter of its literature. It is significant that the hero of the first great English poem is not an Englishman but a Geat who undertakes adventures in Denmark, while the Arthurian 'matter of Britain' was most enthusiastically preserved in France. In the far North the oldest stories are not those of Scandinavian heroes but Goths, Burgundians, and Huns.

Just as the open society which allowed for the rise of a heroic age emerged in the hiatus of authority which yawned between the breakdown of imperial administration and its restoration in feudal form at the close of the eighth century, so it lay geographically in the broad band either side of the old *limes*: a region of fluid social movement in the frontier provinces of northern and western Europe, rather than deep in the heartlands either of Mediterranean empire or Germano-Slavic barbarism. Heroic society properly speaking is not characteristic of the relatively stable agrarian communities of the interior. Neither the Finno-Ugric furthest north nor isolated Ireland would develop a meaningful heroic literature, scarcely evolving beyond the sacral epic where ultimate human motives rise above the peasant interests of abduction or cattle-stealing only to be distorted by myth and magic.

It is hardly surprising that the unstable conditions which allowed such considerable social mobility, should also give rise to the strongly active Pelagian ethic of self-reliance, with its insistence on the exercise of independent will, its belief that ultimately all men would be judged strictly on their merits. The stability of the old Empire may have gone for ever – no matter; individuals might look to their own salvation; vigorous local resistance was both possible and desirable; it was evident that by his own exertions a man might save himself in this world – and the next. The general nature of the open society which fostered the heroic values of self-reliance and active initiative is well known: a warfare society in which a man might rise to prominence by wisdom or courage, but would retain his position by example rather than by authority *de jure*. At the same time freedom from traditional external restraints, whether those of imperial bureaucracy or tribal authority, meant that the only source of censure or approval is reduced to the *comites*, who in turn exist only in their estimation of the *dux*. Power consists in the ability to attract and maintain a large and enthusiastic following. In consequence the mere weight of a leader's reputation could of itself often virtually decide the issue of war. The *dux* both generates and confirms his reputation by openhanded generosity of an order which degrades neither the giver nor the recipient, and by ostentatious hospitality, a prominent part of which included the entertainment of poets. It is significant that, along with all the costly goods which were to accompany Rædwald to Valhalla, the royal funeral deposit at Sutton Hoo should contain, carefully packed in a beaver-skin bag, a six-stringed lyre – the necessary accompaniment to the recital of verse – a characteristic feature of social life in the hall which might be anticipated in the halls of the afterlife. The performance of poetry was a mode of entertainment which the greatest as well as the humblest might be expected both to enjoy and join – reflecting the public dimension of their manner of life. The lyre passed from hand to hand round the hall: an intimate context in which, as in some contemporary eastern societies, virtuosity might be admired but willing participation was obligatory.

The songs they sang may well have been appreciated as literary constructs on very different levels depending on the degree of sophistication of the individual listener, but as yet the general concerns, aims, and aspirations of hall-society were undivided; coterie literature belongs to a later age.

The role of the poet is central to heroic society, recording and re-hearsing its ideology, his professional status guaranteed by early legal codes. Some attached themselves to a particular hero, others were peripatetic, of which the types are Deor and Widsith respectively (see below, p. 32f). It is not insignificant that these are mere pseudonyms. Their verse is necessarily anonymous since its function is to serve their patrons' reputation rather than their own. The client's urgent priority was for fame in his own lifetime. Like Hrothgar's scop, the poet will speak of heroes of the present as well as the past; in due course, if his song is successful, it will enter the popular repertoire and its subject will become part of the traditional stock of heroic legends. Because heroic poetry originates in the need to celebrate men at a purely local level, it is understandable that so many heroes of this literature are unknown to history. It is presumably a matter of chance that the Frankish war-leader Clovis, whose picturesque exploits occupy so many pages of con-temporary chronicles, should be unremembered in verse. But the poet did not choose his subject necessarily because he was an effective figure on the world stage, but for what he quite personally achieved or endured. Historical verse as such belongs to a later age. The most momentous events of the age – the fall of Rome or the defeat of Attila – may never have caught the poetic imagination.

The creative stimulus of political fragmentation is well known: a social dynamism generated by tension between small states administratively independent but sharing a common culture; multiplicity permitting variation, competition encouraging emulation. But any cultural dividend earned by disunity would be drastically undermined by social losses. The poet's idealized fiction concealed and transformed a sordid proclivity for mutual extermination, exemplified by the heroic but dismal facts of the *coup d'état* at Merton recorded in the *Anglo-Saxon Chronicle s.a.* 755. The courageous vigour so respected by classical commentators like Tacitus, could assume less admirable qualities when unconstrained. The fact that, far from seeming merely despicable, the great men of this society can still arouse our admiration and awe, is due to the nature of the heroic ethic. Warfare society is savagely self-consuming, needing a constant flow of loot on which to feed. The premium placed on personal success meant that conspiracy, delation, and fractricidal warfare were inevitable. And, when stability depended on the survival of a single charismatic individual, it is hardly surprising that kingdoms should rise and fall in quick succession, whole nations often disappearing without trace. The liter-ature of this age celebrates the lives of men caught up in a constant process of disintegration and dissolution – a universally entropic supposition reflected in the *disjecta membra* of contemporary Germanic zoomorphic art, or the introverted geometrism of its Celtic counterpart; both of which are composed of motifs designed to deceive the eye and incorporate images which have more than one meaning.[10]

The patent attraction of alternative Christian values introduced with the opening of the seventh century, is clear. Paulinus's encounter with the traditional order at the court of Edwin – if not over-coloured by Bede's informant – is at once graphic and diagnostic. The traditional voice betrays a fundamental scepticism as to any final purpose human life may have, questioning even the most heroic secular activity. Man's sole assurance limited to the uniform inevitability of the natural process of mutability held little to sustain him in the face of adversity. The lot of individual men, or of mankind as a whole, was merely to struggle in the face of adversity, to do what he can – until the dragon comes. No appeal to supernatural power or to any alternative code of spiritual values would soften the bewildered negativism of such a world-view. The traditional voice of the old order reveals itself in one of the most elegant and potent similes of English history, from the lips of one of Edwin's anonymous counsellors:

> This present life of men on earth seems to me like this. It is as if
> you are sitting to a feast with your chief men and thegns in
> wintertime; the fire is burning on the hearth in the middle of
> the hall and all is warm inside, while outside the wintry storms
> of rain and snow are raging; and there comes a sparrow flying
> swiftly through the hall. It comes in at one door and quickly
> goes out through the other. For the time it is inside it is not
> touched by the winter's tempest, but after the barest moment
> of calm it is lost to sight; straightway it passes from winter, and
> to winter returns. In the same way man's life appears but a
> moment; what follows, or what went before, we don't know.
> So if this new teaching brings any greater assurance, it's worth
> our attention.[11]

The advent of Christianity was clearly welcome, even to a self-confessed time-serving materialist like Edwin's pagan high priest, Coifi. Nevertheless, perhaps due partly to the conciliatory nature of the Augustinian mission, heathenism was never far below the surface, and for centuries to come the English readily lapsed into paganism at the slightest loss of confidence, in times of national disaster, famine, or invasion.

It is unlikely that either party to the agreement, Edwin or Paulinus, could have foreseen the long-term implications of the new amalgam – a catalyst which would eventually bring feudalism to the northern world. The intrusion of Christian dogma into the Germanic character of early Anglo-Saxon society inevitably unsettled the traditional structure once it was discovered that the new faith, nominally accepted, logically required practical corollaries in the conduct of affairs. While it is true that certain sins were in some senses heroic sins too – arrogance for instance leading to carelessness for others – much Christian teaching would be found sadly at odds with accepted tenets of the heroic ethos. The heroic *beot* 'assertion' was central to Germanic virtue, leading directly to the action which merits *lof*, the praise of one's peers, and *dom*, their esteem. But now such drunken boasts as Tacitus described[12] would be ascribed to the prompting of Satan himself. The *lof* of a Christian God and the *dom* of his heaven were to be gained by different means. The particular stumbling-block for the heroic prince, as Paulinus remarked of Edwin, seems to have been that *superbia* which was the inevitable accompaniment of heroic life and irreducibly hostile to Christian *humilitas*.

No doubt we might ascribe to this conflict between pagan and Christian ideals many of the violent fluctuations of fortune which came upon Anglo-Saxon rulers during the early missions. Few seem to have enjoyed uninterrupted reigns. Some, like Rædwald, continued to subscribe to pagan customs side by side with their nominal acceptance of Christianity; others, like Ceolwulf or Eadberht, gave up the struggle and retired to monastic seclusion or simply disappeared as *peregrini pro amore deo*. This phase in the insular church was characterized by a lengthy catalogue of princely saints, both British and Saxon. Although the initial effect of organized Christianity was to impoverish the prestige of the heroic leader, princes in need of authoritarian support and prepared to grant reciprocal privileges contrived to enhance their kingly office with the lustre of a special relationship. The Roman clergy brought with them a traditional sympathy between Church and Crown, aware since imperial days of the practical value of a strong earthly king in extending the kingdom of God. The aristocratic Pope Gregory, initiating the mission to England, could flatter Æthelberht by comparing him with the Emperor Constantine and suggesting that similar honours might also await the Kentish Bretwalda as the recipient of a heavenly as well as secular *dom*. Pragmatists like Æthelberht, overcoming any initial difficulties, would find in the organized Church a ready-fashioned secretariat to serve the increasing administrative requirements of a developing state. Once established within the courts of converted kings, the Church would not accept without closer scrutiny the traditional assumptions of power, eventually formulating a new assessment of the role of kingship and the source of its authority. Already in the pages of Bede we find a tacit assumption that kingly power, like that of the Church, derives not from the people but from God. Once this came to be recognized not only by ecclesiastical dignitaries but by kings themselves, then the relationship between governor and governed needs must radically change, with the descending rather than ascending scheme of authority resulting in an entire reversal of the structure of society.

By the later eighth century in England, as in Merovingian France, there were to arise those who could seize upon the potential nexus of Church and State as a means of practical power. During the anarchic middle decades of the eighth century, with Wessex, Kent, and Northumbria in chaos, the strong and ambitious Mercian nobleman Æthelbald rapidly extended his suzerainty over the greater part of the country – an imperium which clearly required some supra-national formula of authority. Æthelbald was the first to claim the overlordship of conquered peoples in his title: 'King not only of the Mercians but those neighbouring peoples over whom God has set me', signing 'by divine dispensation'.[13] But when in 754 Æthelbald was finally slain as a tyrant by his own comitatus, his confederacy collapsed, with civil war in Mercia, until a new strong man, Offa, would reestablish his predecessor's hegemony with yet greater firmness. Whereas Æthelbald sought only at the very end of his reign to justify his ambition in terms of the new theory of government awarded by God, Offa resorted to this from the outset, granting conquered estates 'in the name of Jesus Christ . . . through whom sovereigns reign and divide the kingdoms of the earth'. He is the first to sink the identities of all the southern settlements in a single 'Kingdom of the English', taking to himself the title Rex Anglorum and even Rex Britanniae.[14]

However, while overlordship by conquest might be justified by reference to divine dispensation, some meaningful act was required to seal the assumption. Like his Continental contemporaries, Offa was quite prepared to appeal to ecclesiastical institutions for spiritual authority to confirm an irregular or insecure position; and he sought to secure his family's position by means of religious consecration (specifically unction) having his son Ecgfrith gehalgod[15] – a ceremony previously reserved for the consecration of bishops. From this time onwards the style rex dei gratia was introduced as a regular formula, implying the independence of monarchial power from popular will, and conversely the sinfulness of disobedience to one who was considered vicarius dei, Christ's substitute on earth. Thereafter religious consecration came to be regarded as a necessary outward sign of the realization of power. The practical implications of this newly adopted descending pattern of kingship are mirrored in the developing coronation ordines of the following century, the central ceremonial thrust of which is a repeated insistence upon the people's necessary subordination to a ruler made distinct in kind from themselves by divine grace, Christus domini, 'the Lord's anointed'. A distinct new 'regal' persona had been laid on the Germanic war-leader, demanding as its corollary the sacredness of both his person and his enactments. Offa, no less than Charlemagne, would look to the regal ideologue Alcuin of York to justify the authority he instinctively wore. The rights of lineal succession were defined, if not secured; and there was required the immediate codification of a new law of treason to accommodate opposition to the sovereign's role as Christ's 'vicar on earth'.

This new conception of kingship resulted in a general augmentation of not only the titles but the materials of dignity. The king's position now demands the majesty of possession, gathering both territorial and material wealth to his person – a persona which can no longer be identified with the *folc*. The progressive association of regal authority with that of God results in a proportional detachment of the king from his people. The traditional web of individual relationships founded on personal loyalties proved insufficiently firm a basis for this wider conception of regal state. Mere loyalty is no longer adequate; obedience is required. And society subsequently hardens into this posture throughout all its ranks.

What began as a simple pact of mutual benefit between Church and State at a time of crisis, developed into an increasingly rigid interdependence, ceremonial elaboration and practical power evolving side by side. Henceforth the interests of Church and State would remain one and the same, moving in the direction of a strong central authority. Administration both legal and territorial becomes increasingly centred in the king's hands. *Folc-land* changes to royal demesne and there is a consequent growth of territorial patronage, the older comitatus turning into a landed nobility, while the *ceorlisc* class gradually sank into the position described in the *Rectitudines*.[16] Well before the end of the Anglo-Saxon period a fully fledged feudal state existed. By the mid-eleventh century Edward the Confessor can refer to a widowed female landowner as his 'man', or can demand that the thegns of a rebellious earl be transferred to himself, while the term *þegn* itself has so far lost its warrior overtones as to be applicable to either male or female servants.[17] The isolative effect of later Anglo-Saxon tenurial aristocracy was merely exacerbated by the linguistic separation which followed on the Norman Conquest. Territorial apportionment ultimately carried with it the right to set up manorial courts, but the laws they executed were no longer those of the *folc*, the ancient customs of the community, but those of a feudal king. Obedience to the law is considered a religious duty. As a logical consequence of the claim to divine succession from Old Testament kingship represented by David, royal genealogies now show Woden to have descended from Adam, while by the same token customary English law is prefaced by the Mosaic. The rise and easy acceptance of this attitude towards the rule of kings, together with a reverence for their enactments, betokens no less than the arrival of a feudal state of mind. Already by the

940s Edmund, with a consciousness of his sacerdotal office verging on the god-like, can decree that no man guilty of shedding blood should presume to come into his presence until the guilt had been fully expiated. The same king is the first in England on record as demanding an explicit oath of allegiance from all his 'subjects' which is in most respects identical with those of later feudal 'vassalage'. The sanctity of kingship is now so far attached to the office rather than its holder that Wulfstan can introduce his *Institutes of Polity* with the injunction that even Æthelred's person is inviolable, being Christ's substitute on earth.[18] Ultimately the twelfth-century 'Anonymous of York' would insist that an anointed king could even save souls and absolve sinners.

During the course of the Anglo-Saxon period the open amorphous social structure based on personal relationships was transformed into one with a territorial base, the inherent *folc-riht* of the settlement increasingly invaded by the forces of lordship justified by the words of the Church. Local lordship founded on an open contract with the *folc* altered rapidly under the influence of antithetical authoritarian notions which derived ultimately from the Mediterranean, towards the nationally integrated State, with the regal direction from a strong administrative centre; there was a consequent shift in the function of the *folc-moot* from motivation to execution; laws ceased to be issued in the name of the *folc*, and were replaced by the promulgation of an individual ruler, with government logically enforced through the medium of officers appointed by and responsible to himself alone.

The Church was no less accommodating in its attitude to the military aspects of heroic society. Just as it sought to mould the government of society to its own, ultimately feudal, ends, so it would eventually turn the warrior's role to its own advantage. The attitude of the Church towards war was perennially equivocal; while violence was of itself clearly culpable, many would concede the legitimacy of the 'just war' – an ambivalence developed from Christ's reference to two kinds of peace, earthly and spiritual (John 14. 27). From earliest times Christian thinkers had promoted the concept of the 'Church Militant'. The individual believer, like the Church as a whole, was engaged in a struggle – to the death even – but in a warfare fought with spiritual arms and armour (II Corinthians 10. 3–4; II Peter 1. 5–7; II Timothy 2. 3). Since suffering was man's lot, and death no finality, worldly aggression, even self-defence, was discountenanced, in theory, and martyrdom a high ideal at a period when violence and destruction were commonplace. The heroic Pelagian ideal of active Christianity was naturally attractive in aristocratic circles. The saint stepped easily into the hero's niche; the warfare of the *miles spiriti* was conducted with heroic determination. The universality of sin and its inevitability – an inevitability which cannot be conceded – ensure that the life of the *integri Christiani* was a heroic assertion, his commitment a moment of *beot* affirming the moral progression: *posse, velle, esse*. Men like Guthlac who wearied of the warrior life might carry their warfare into another, no less real, dimension in which conflict may still be physically perceived – a virile counterpart to the feminine obsession with militant virginity which was the formative ideal of the aristocratic nunnery which flourished at this time. The secular repository of heroic ideals: generosity, courage, and loyalty, might readily be transferred to the comitatus of a new leader – Christ – assembling its own supplemental constellation of values and code of behaviour, and allowing a no less personal relationship.

Taking up the Pauline image of *miles Christi*, military metaphors abound in patristic writings. But actual military service was shunned by the early Church, deprecating the shedding of blood on scriptural grounds; the prohibition on bloodshed precluding even the practice of surgery, so far as the clergy were concerned. But the new contract between Church and State would require some pragmatic accommodation of principle, however uncomfortable. At least twice during the eighth century successive popes would seek military intervention to secure their secular independence from Lombard encroachment. But when in 849 Islamic armies, which had already established bridgeheads along the northern shore of the Mediterranean from Spain to Sicily, now approached the very gates of Rome, Leo IV himself took the field, calling on all Christian warriors to defend the city. During the following centuries the former distinction between earthly and spiritual arms was to become increasingly blurred as the Church gradually shifted its position to become the exponent of a 'holy war' directed specifically against infidels and heretics, whether Islamic, Viking, or Slav. The earthly reality of the Church Militant culminated in 1095 when, by the Edict of Clermont, Pope Urban II proclaimed the first crusade, declaring that war against non-Christians was not only justified but sanctified, service to God in arms guaranteeing salvation. Although canon law continued to forbid any cleric to take up arms on pain of excommunication, there were continual exceptions. No small power in the land, bishops and abbots were now recruited mainly from the middle ranks of the nobility, landowners in their own right, surrounded by military bodyguards. Not untypical perhaps was Leofgar, Harold Godwinson's moustachioed chaplain who, immediately after consecration as Bishop of Hereford in 1056

> forsook his chrism and his cross, his spiritual weapons, seized his
> spear and his sword, and thus armed joined the levies against
> Gruffydd, the Welsh king; and there he was slain, together with
> the priests who were with him.[19]

The Abbots of Winchester and Peterborough both apparently died of wounds received at Hastings. During the anarchy of Stephen's reign the

Bishops of Lincoln, Salisbury, and Ely, it was said, 'devoted themselves utterly to warfare',[20] while Thomas Becket, Archbishop of Canterbury, was accustomed to fight at the head of a troop of 700 knights.

The image of the fighting man had undergone a gradual metamorphosis as warfare was channelled to ecclesiastically acceptable ends. The internecine warfare of the heroic age was curbed by a new ideology in which gratuitous violence was disallowed, but sanctioned, even sanctified, provided the Church might determine its aims. The profession of arms was no longer a source of independent pride but a means to an end, its acceptability directly related to its application. Metamorphosed by ecclesiastical sanction, the former despoiler is made the guardian of society, entrusted with a duty to defend the poor, widows, and orphans. By the end of the eleventh century at least, even the seigneurial bestowal of arms had been brought into the context of religion, enduing it with contemplative and ritual aspects, blessing the symbols of knighthood: sword and pennoned lance, helm, and spurs, the ceremony of *adoubement* spoken of as a second baptism. The vocation *miles Christiani* found its most profound expression in the various crusading military orders, most remarkably of all, that of the Knights Templar, a unique aristocratic contribution to the realm of ideology, a mystic amalgam of puritanical monasticism and chivalry with the avowed purpose: 'that knighthood should be admitted to religion, and religion thus armed by knighthood should proceed and kill the enemy without guilt'.[21] Sensationally successful, it would receive the enthusiastic support of no less a spiritual authority than Bernard of Clairvaux in his tract *De Laude Novae Militiae*.

Understandably the gap between ideal and actuality was often large. As one detached contemporary observed, 'the sword creates more widows and orphans than it protects'.[22] The recognized inadequacy of feudal military obligations encouraged financial commutation allowing the more reliable substitution of mercenaries. These soldiers of fortune – the knights errant – not unnaturally exacerbated the more vicious aspects of warfare, especially when operating in country to which they had no personal commitment. To those for whom the knightly way of life was simply a matter of commercial enterprise, mere peace was profitless. But the view of those knights who, full of greed and violence, hated King Henry's peace because then they earned only a scanty livelihood[23] was not without feudal rationale. Knights harrying a provincial town could excuse their oppression of the poor thus: 'What we are doing is not pillage and violence but peace and obedience; the land is our lord the king's; we are his instruments and this is our reward'.[24] Horrific tortures were witnessed in the baronial castles which proliferated during the anarchic years of Stephen's reign; they were graphically described by the Peterborough Chronicler, *s.a.* 1137, as so truly appalling that 'men said openly that Christ and all his saints were asleep'.[25] The large amount of portable wealth accumulated in medieval churches made them a natural prey to predatory mercenaries; fighting was often carried into the body of the church – often at the behest of contending clergymen and regardless of any claim to sanctuary; Becket was not the only cleric to be cut down before the altar. It might even prove expedient to burn down a church, cremating those inside. The tensions provoked between secular lordship and the claims of an increasingly independent Church, of which the so-called 'investiture context' was a political symptom, were the inevitable converse of the chivalric ideal. Even the Crusades, never totally free from contemporary criticism, had their darker side. For some elements in society the Crusade may have revived wholesale the concept of a penitential pilgrimage, albeit armed, *deo duce*, at a time of millennial sentiment. But in Europe the Teutonic Knights' cynical *Drang nach Osten* was a scarcely cloaked wholesale economic exploitation of Slavonic lands. And events surrounding the foundation of new crusader kingdoms in Palestine gave no less rein to individual lust and greed. The mass psychosis which followed in the wake of crusading armies was marked by massacres of Jews throughout Europe and most of the major towns in England. Voices raised in doubt of the crusaders' divine inspiration increased in pitch following military failure, and the more so when the leaders of the Fourth Crusade (1202–04) abandoned any intention of reaching its Palestinian objective, turning aside to subjugate Christian Constantinople instead.[26] The Messianic vision of an earthly and heavenly Jerusalem, always hopelessly confused in the popular mind, was finally forgotten.

Despite regular ecclesiastical and at least sporadic regal prohibition, periods of prolonged peace might be enlivened by attendance at tournaments – not yet a leisurely series of individual jousts, but a mass mêlée which differed little from real war. There was little that a modern Englishman might recognize as 'fair play', let alone chivalry, with sides often unevenly matched and a high premium on low cunning. The stakes were high; large ransoms might be raised; at times the vanquished lost all they possessed, while those fatally wounded were, theoretically at least, denied a Christian burial. With a notoriously hooligan element present among the supporters, events were always liable to turn nasty.

But the validating myth of feudal knighthood was preserved, if not wholly unquestioned, by the ministrel-poet. The feudal hall, no less than the heroic, would celebrate the ideals and aspirations of its age and the circumstances which would lead men to die for a cause. Now battle literature could no longer ignore national and ethnic boundaries. Unlike the heroes of old, knightly protagonists fight not for themselves but for larger concerns, a patriotic or religious cause and not merely their own: Alfred or Byrhtnoth versus Vikings, Hereward or Eadric versus

Normans, Roland or Richard versus Saracens. The patriotic sentiment which described Edgar Ætheling as willing to lose all for the chance to live and die in England[27] would have seemed inexplicable to his immigrant forebears. Although these later protagonists sometimes seem to strike the old heroic postures, and their exploits are indubitably valorous, theirs is not the individual heroic ideal that led Beowulf or Hengest to their deaths. The restoration of confidence that the closed society brought about muted and channelled notions of mutability into ready-made millennial beliefs like those portrayed in Wulfstan's *Sermo Lupi ad Anglos*.[28] Such literary materials of the Migration Age which survived to be used anew, did so only in so far as they could be adapted to conform with the social truths of a feudal age – resulting in the strangely ambiguous world of Tristan and Havelok, while Arthur takes on a guise which Nennius could scarcely have recognized. When genuinely new war literature emerges, it will present aspects of both social realism and authentic historical perspective (see below, p. 155ff).

Feudal society was fundamentally militaristic, chivalry the emotive bond which secured its cohesion in a turbulent world. As the open society of the heroic age gradually gave way to the tenurial stratification that marked the closed *feudum*, warfare became increasingly the purview of a limited class divorced from the mass of common people – its ideals confined to a military élite which by the end of the tenth century had become almost universally hereditary. 'Chivalry' evokes an entire ethos: castle-base, lineage, and social framework – and yet technically the term denotes merely the possession of a horse – a term reserved for the mounted élite as distinct from the mass of soldiers who of necessity fought on foot. The profession of chivalry, requiring considerable investment – not merely in a horse but a variety of expensive equipment and training – is simply not accessible to all classes. Consequently, social esteem is determined less by personal merit than by the incidental accessories of tenure: lineage and heraldic blazon. This development is reinforced during the eleventh and twelfth centuries by the growth of hereditary, and especially toponymic, surnames attaching the family, its history, and its fortunes to its estates. Lineage, particularly that of an *arriviste* family, was often dependent on fiction, often absorbing recent dramatic events and sometimes, at its most extreme, taking them back to legends of Troy.

Despite the proliferation of early feudal noble houses, during the eleventh and twelfth centuries the available supply of aristocratic women seems to have greatly exceeded the supply of eligible men. Many men therefore married 'above themselves', acquiring desirable family connections. Many of the Conqueror's knights could establish family links with their new-found estates by marrying English heiresses now widowed or left without hope of marrying into their own class. These demographic trends coincided with, and perhaps related to, changing attitudes towards marriage and the status of women in general. There was a corresponding rise in matronymics, with importance attached – in 'Anglo-Norman genealogies specially – to noble ancestors in the female line. The fragmentation of society extended also to the female role – certainly in an aristocratic context where, more individuated domestic arrangements would permit the lady of a wealthy house to withdraw to a separate chamber in the company of her intimates. Such a courtly coterie might provide a ready audience for such refined notions as that of *fin' amor*, condemned by the Church but flourishing under the patronage of the highest in the land.

The Angevin Empire stretched from the Cheviots to the Pyrenees, linked not only geographically but by treaty and marriage with the Mediterranean world. At its centre the most powerful man in Europe, Henry II, patron of all the arts and probably the most scholarly man ever to occupy the throne of England, presided over an immensely influential and necessarily cosmopolitan court where, according to Peter of Blois, it was as if 'there is school every day, constant conversation of the best scholars and the discussion of ideas'.[29] Literary activity of all kinds flourished, but in a closed French circle from which English vernacular sensibility was by definition excluded. The courtly context formed a fine seed-bed for the more exotic themes of Hispano-Arabic art and literature, and most notably for an ideology of love which, originating in the language of the Sufis, proximated agape and eros, divine and human love, presenting eroticism as a fundamentally ennobling experience. Extravagantly codified in terms of a refined and leisured aristocratic society, what we have come to term 'courtly love' would find a receptive feminine audience, of which the *grande dame* was no less than the Queen herself, Eleanor of Aquitaine. As cultivated as her husband, she was also beautiful, desirable, scandalous, and provocative; her romantic *affaires* were the topic of envious gossip, and she herself both the object and subject of passionate love-poems. The codification of natural or 'romantic' love (i.e. sexual liaison outside the confines of marriages which were often contracted for tenurial, political, or economic reasons), probably represents a genuine reflection, albeit imaginative, of familiar conditions: unloved and frequently absent husbands replaced in the affections by any one of a host of attractive and available squires, all owing homage to their superior, and theoretically untouchable, mistress.[30] As the ideologue Andreas Capellanus's celebratory and admonitory tract *De Arte Honeste Amandi* makes clear, the concept of *fin' amor* had essentially aristocratic parameters deriving from the real world of the feudal estate. Love, rather than brute sex, is not considered natural to the peasant – neither should it be encouraged, 'since it makes them lazy and unproductive in our interests'. It is for this reason that the rape of a peasant girl by the knight is to be deprecated; on any other grounds it was apparently quite understandable.[31] However, the exotic, colourful, leisured world of the southern courts may have permitted, even encouraged, such fictive games as *fin' amor*, the feudal households of Norman England, albeit courtly and requiring the guidance of books of etiquette such as that written by Daniel of Beccles in the later twelfth century[32] were essentially workaday, less exclusively leisured, the knightly class involved in the pedestrian administration of what was still a new colony. The courtly themes of Anjou and Provence underwent something of a sea-change, and are depicted by an Anglo-Norman poet like Hugh de Roteland with at least a degree of ironic detachment.[33] Nevertheless they remained French, not English.

After the Norman Conquest, what was an already élite class of knighthood, was now an overwhelmingly alien one; the occupying power made the more secure by a ruthlessly efficient administration led by the most able military commander of the age. While no section of English society remained unaffected by the Conquest, it was felt most by the upper and middle land-owning classes. Some resisted; some actively collaborated; the vast majority had little option but to acquiesce, albeit with bad grace. Wishing to be regarded as the Confessor's legitimate heir, William at first maintained a continuity of administration, governing England extensively through English magnates who had formerly held high office but had taken no part against him at Hastings. For a year or two at least local administration would change little. Most local sheriffs remained Englishmen; and in general the law remained traditional English law. Despite his preoccupations William himself is even said to have attempted to learn English in order to serve justice the better. The Conqueror's policies were by no means racialist. He was prepared to take into his service any Englishmen on whose loyalty he could depend. Many are known to have served under his command in Continental wars; one of them, Tokig Wigotson of Wallingford, would gallantly give his life to save William's at the siege of Gerberoi. It was a largely English army, albeit under Norman command, that subdued the rebellious citizens of Exeter. It was Somerset squires who led local militia to repel an exploratory coastal raid by the sons of Harold's mistress, Edith Swan's-neck, in 1068. But it is important to recognize the extent to which the squirely class had been reduced. Many, perhaps most, leading English families were decimated during the course of the Conquest.

The year 1066 had seen three large-scale engagements, in two of which an English army was destroyed. The flower of Northumbria and Mercia had been annihilated trying to defend York against the Viking invader, while subsequently Wessex and East Anglia must have sustained heavy losses at Stamfordbridge before rushing to be slaughtered in the protracted and desperate resistance to the Normans at Hastings. Reparations were widely imposed. All who had fought by

William's side might now expect to be rewarded with lands confiscated from those English families who had taken an active part in resisting the Conquest. For the English landed gentry the Norman occupation came as a catastrophe from which it never fully recovered. Many dispossessed Englishmen simply left to seek their fortune elsewhere, finding refuge in Flanders or in Scotland. Others more adventurous still would take service with the Varangian Guard, a northern *corps d'élite* of the Emperor at Constantinople. For the remainder it was by no means impossible to come to terms with the Conqueror. Only those who disputed his suzerainty were at risk. Those who had not personally borne arms against William might, at a price, be confirmed in possession of their estates. But however smooth a transition of administration was intended, the situation on the ground was less ambiguous. Uprisings, although piecemeal and ineffectual, were an embarrassment to the administration and were invariably suppressed with ferocity, the land laid waste in the fashion of the time, leaving a legacy of bitterness which would last for generations. There followed further punitive confiscations and a considerable intensification of the Norman plantation. Eventually only two Englishmen, Thurkill of Arden and Colswein of Lincoln, held tenancies of any size directly from the king – and even Thurkill's son would soon lose his inheritance. And since tenancy was now given in exchange for military duties, all Englishmen were now effectively excluded from any kind of political or military influence. There was a thoroughgoing overhaul of administration and replacements at local level. French sheriffs, many notoriously rapacious, were appointed to all but a few insignificant country areas.

The Normans, if not noted for their artistic taste, had an undoubted genius for order and administration, which was to be exemplified in the great Domesday survey, an unprecedented investigation into the lands of England carried through with ruthless efficiency and energy by the king's commissioners. It was so shamelessly thorough, remarked one shocked Englishman, that not a yard of land, not one cow or pig escaped notice.[34] He was right to be dismayed. Central authority would not now lose its grip. It was inevitable that William should turn his attention also to the native Church which, cherishing independent traditions, was an obvious focus for national identity and cause for discontent. In any case, its unfamiliar liturgies and numerous obscure saints could scarcely meet with the approval of William's Continental chaplains. English churches were stripped of enormous quantities of treasure, their crosses, shrines, and statues melted down or dispatched to deck a thousand churches throughout all parts of France, while the highly admired English embroideries and plate were sent to adorn Norman dining-tables. With ecclesiastical as well as secular authority firmly in William's hand, the English Church was soon ruled by men of Continental birth and training.

Within ten years of the Conquest the only English bishop to remain was Wulfstan of Worcester, and only two important abbeys, Bath and Ramsey, were still governed by Englishmen. Within seven or eight years of Hastings, with all pretence at anything other than outright investment now abandoned, Willam felt sufficiently secure in his conquest to be able to spend most of his time in Normandy. He died and was buried at home in Rouen. It would be another three and a half centuries before a king of England would speak English as his native language.

Very many aspects of English social life changed as a result of the Norman occupation. Those landowners who could come to terms found themselves living in a strange and unfriendly environment. The English free peasant steadily declined yet further in the economic scale, sinking to the status of the unfree medieval villein. But despite wholesale political disruption the economy continued to flourish. A period of European stability, free for the first time in centuries from the threat of invasion from either the Islamic East or Viking North, coinciding with an unprecedented growth in population, resulted in a great wave of internal colonization, facilitated by a new agricultural technology: improved animal harnesses and heavier ploughs. For two centuries from *c.* 1000 forests were cleared, swamps drained, and thousands of new villages founded, permitting yet more intensive cultivation. The consequent rural surpluses served to facilitate a significant growth in urban populations, resulting in the expansion of existing towns and the foundation of very many more. Although falling off somewhat during the troubled years of Stephen's reign, new-town colonization continued unabated into the thirteenth century, after which the country seems to have become more or less saturated with borough foundations. The urban economy burgeoned *pari passu* technological innovation, affecting not only the lives of men but the way they perceived the world. Improved harnesses not only enhanced agriculture but drastically improved inland transport. The twelfth-century introduction of keel and rudder, together with the compass, enabled merchant seamen to voyage further afield and with greater security. Urban renewal was thus accompanied by a significant growth in commerce, especially now that Christian Europe had shifted from a defensive to a confidently aggressive posture in relation to its pagan neighbours. Merchants both preceded and followed the Teutonic Knights' drive towards the Baltic and the crusaders' adventurous investment in the Near East, resurrecting an international luxury trade on a scale unknown since Roman times. Energy-productive machines were perfected: first hydraulic- then wind-mills, which would enable one man, or horse, to do work that formerly required two dozen. Henceforth the future of European culture would lie predominantly with the towns and the citizen class.

Already by later Saxon times the town was more than merely a commercial centre; its fortification, with communal responsibility for manning and maintenance, marked the development of the 'borough'. A distinct sense of borough identity emerged, with special courts required to handle the affairs of townspeople, self-governing craft and trade associations controlling standards, and socio-religious confraternities or guilds of mutual benefit. The Crown, in seeking to free itself from undue baronial influence, would find ready sympathy in the towns, now the sites of regal, as distinct from baronial, castles and courts. The increasing wealth of the towns meant influence and authority, their power growing hand in hand with that of the Crown – natural allies in their mutual struggle with the feudal aristocracy. Lying adjacent to, but outside, the feudal structure associated with land-tenure, their spirited independence exacted increasingly distinct freedoms – their charters incorporating, for instance, the exemption of citizens from such pernicious practices as trial by battle or duel. By the thirteenth century the tradition of borough privilege was well established, the use of independent corporate seals marking the machinery of self-government. The important townsman is as well known from the archives as the knight of the shires. And archaeology is beginning to reveal their sophisticated tastes. The backyard rubbish-dump of Richard de Southwick who lived in thirteenth-century Southampton suggests that, among other things, he appreciated: finely painted Angevin claret-jugs, Spanish lustre-ware, Venetian glass, Persian silks, and wooden specialities imported from the Baltic and the Netherlands; and his family kept a pet Barbary ape.[35]

With the great fortunes that men of ability and ambition might now make in the towns, borough society attracted, as always, the best talents from far afield. The percentage of newcomers was always high – the antecedents of Dick Whittington recruited to commercial and administrative roles of all kinds. If access to the feudal élite by way of martial prowess was now denied him, the social aspirant might look to the towns – and education. In any case the careers of knight and burgess were incompatible. The mounting pressures of commercial expertise, no less than the urban specialisms of law and medicine, required an increasing professionalism which was served and fostered by the flourishing town schools. The old ecclesiastical orders were unsuited both spiritually and academically to meet these newer urban requirements. Traditional monasteries were typically located in rural areas, both temperamentally and economically dependent on the feudal structure of country estates. If the isolative requirements of their spiritual life discouraged settlement in towns, their position among the greatest landowners linked them intimately with the feudal institutions, their ideals as well as their administrative structures shaped by the life of the agricultural domain, demanding the stability of both place and people, obedience within the cloister and serfdom without. There had been an enormous increase in the number of new monastic foundations from the tenth century onwards, but none – even among the reformed orders – sought to serve the needs of the market-place. Either, like the Cluniacs, they overburdened their members with yet more liturgical demands, or like the Cistercians sought yet deeper isolation from the dangers of social or intellectual stimulus. Scorning secular society, neither of these approaches would attract the patronage of the rising citizen class.

By the early thirteenth century, however, there was a more amenable, more accessible alternative. Rejecting the socially obsolescent monastic attitude, there were those less prepared to concede the worthlessness of secular society. New brotherhoods of mendicant friars – Franciscans, Dominicans, and a host of lesser groups – carried their mission direct to the market-place, ministering to, and in turn recruiting from, new generations of city-dwellers, to whom they offered a wide variety of spiritual and charitable services. Many of them secured teaching positions in urban schools. The progressive ideal of service to others found natural sympathies with the socially concerned guilds and religious confraternities. As the thirteenth century advanced, they established houses in every major centre of population in the land, their enormous popularity with the townspeople often bitterly resented by establishment clergy. The friar's sympathetic image is well reflected in the popular tales of Robin Hood where the rich abbot is the object of verbal and physical abuse while Friar Tuck is depicted with affection, playing an active role in the socially concerned outlaw band. This is not to say that certain members of the mendicant orders were not highly influential in Church and State, like the Franciscan Adam Marsh (*ob.* 1257), Oxford lecturer, friend of both Grosseteste and Simon de Montfort, or John of Peckham who became Archbishop of Canterbury (1279–92).

By the same token, systematic education, hitherto the preserve of monasteries and directed to solely religious ends since conceived to serve an ecclesiastical framework, now passed via cathedral schools into the world of the towns, bringing education more into accord with the needs of secular society. By the twelfth century schools had been established in a wide variety of urban centres. Some acquired a reputation for relatively specialist studies: e.g. Exeter for theology or Lincoln for law. Others maintained a much broader curriculum: Hereford for example, according to a celebratory poem by Simon du Fresne (*c.* 1195–97), offering not only law but all seven liberal arts, along with the more recondite oriental subject of geomancy.[36] The schools at London and York were prominent; but, although strongly rivalled by that at Northampton for a while, only the school at Oxford seems to have maintained the complete *studium generale* which would allow it to evolve a nascent university. Despite their technically clerical status, the students of the cathedral schools had primarily secular, vocational interests requiring precise curricular programmes. Their sponsorship by dignitaries of the proudly independent urban secular cathedrals determined to preserve their liberal unregulated way of life in sharp distinction from that of the regular monastic foundations, fostered persistent individuality in many aspects of their institutional life. But all schools now pursued a vigorous mode of enquiry along dialectical lines, training their students in the art of disputation, required not only of the active theologian but of all legal and diplomatic professions. Mercantile society came to depend on a network of highly trained clerks, expert in increasingly exacting business methods. The administration of State similarly now relied on graduate recruitment, opening a clear avenue of advancement for the talented. By way of education men of humble rank like John of Salisbury, proud of his plebeian origins, might rise to positions of high dignity and wealth. At the same time, of course, the schools would not fail to attract those members of the knightly class like Peter of Blois who displayed intellectual interests.

Although the schools evolved to meet professional needs, legal, medical, and clerical, they served to promote educational and literary ideas beyond the merely utilitarian. The strength and momentum of this new development was stimulated by a renewed access to the corpus of classical materials – a process of discovery reaching its zenith between 1000 and 1150. Of course the Anglo-Saxon world had long been well acquainted with the classics, their monastic libraries forming a cultural reservoir of European literary heritage. During the seventh century Greek or Hebrew might be studied at Canterbury under the Syrian Theodore of Tarsus or the Byzanto-African Hadrian, or at Malmesbury under the Irishman Maeldubh. Aldhelm, pupil in turn of both Maeldubh and Hadrian, and later Bishop of Sherborne (*ob*. 709), could quote from more than two dozen classical sources in the course of his *Epistola ad Acircium*.[37] Bede's extraordinary breadth of learning reflects what must have been very extensive library resources at Jarrow. Alcuin celebrated the remarkable range of his later eighth-century library at York; before going on to enumerate an impressive list of specific authors, remarking in general that:

> There gathered over the years
> you will find the ancient fathers' legacy:
> all that Rome possessed in the west,
> all that glorious Greece passed on to Rome,
> refreshing draughts from Hebrew sources,
> illumination spread from Africa.[38]

So far as the classics were concerned, however, they figured prominently in the library of the monastic school, rather than in that of the devotional community itself. The monastic world maintained a persistently ambiguous attitude towards pagan *auctoritates*, while acknowledging their classical *auctoritate*. Aldhelm repeatedly questions his own pupils' motives in travelling afield to study secular letters, urging them to avoid the allure not only of whores but of philosophers: 'The polluted waters and muddy liquid in which a black hoard of toads abounds and the croaking of frogs resounds'.[39] Alcuin not only questioned the Lindisfarne monks' interest in native heroic stories in the querulous: 'What has Ingeld to do with Christ?'[40] but also the usefulness of Virgil – although ironically in the course of his erudite denunciation he displays his own easy familiarity with the *Aeneid*; and of course his own writings are full of Virgilian reminiscences.[41] Despite distrust and disparagement, the cult of classical *auctoritate* went some way to alleviate natural concern as to the effects of pagan literature. The often-repeated dictum attributed by John of Salisbury to his old teacher Bernard of Chartres: 'We are like dwarves perched on the shoulders of giants; we see more and further than our predecessors, not because we have keener vision or great height, but because we are lifted up and borne aloft on their gigantic stature',[42] was in fact a commonplace of the age, acknowledging a clear moral tendency in classical studies. After all, medieval scholars recognized no break in continuity between the classical world and their own; antique culture might be distant in time, but not in significance.

*Rapprochement* with the eastern world brought not merely commercial but additional intellectual rewards, as western scholars came into contact with a coherent educational network stretching from Samarkand to Toledo. Direct inheritors of the Byzantine, and therefore Hellenistic, world, they had access not only to the genuine Plato (hitherto available to the West only as transmitted via the fathers), but also to Aristotle. The study of Arabo-Greek science drew many Englishmen to the schools of Islamic Spain and Sicily during the twelfth century. Adelard of Bath (1126) and Robert of Chester (1145) translated algebraic, trigono-metrical, and astronomical treatises by al Khwarizmi; Adelard's access to Euclid was through the medium of Arabic, but others like John of Basingstoke (*ob.* 1252) would demand more direct access, studying Greek with a young female teacher at Athens. Walcher of Malvern (1092–1120), using the method of reckoning in degrees, minutes, and seconds he learned from a Spanish Jew, Peter Alfonsus, and by experimental verification, established time-lapses between different countries. In many ways men were becoming more aware of the realities of their environment, coming to a new appreciation of the world of nature in all its variety – its beauty and its dangers. All promoted a mode of objective observation, hypothesis, and experimental verification allowing a new perception of the world and of human experience very different from the static picture proposed by traditional Augustinian Platonism. Systematic arrangement and analysis revealed new relationships and brought new meaning into the apparently chaotic world of experience.

To logicians like William of Sherwood (*ob.* 1279) or the Franciscan Alexander of Hales (*ob.* 1245) the possibilities of human knowledge must have seemed boundless. What had begun as a logical enquiry soon adopted a fundamental epistemological stance: the neo-Aristotelian one that the intellect is dependent on the senses, that the individual alone has real existence and that we come to knowledge only by mental abstraction. This radically questioned assumptions fundamental to all educated men since the introduction of Christianity into these islands – the conservative Platonic notion of a world of ideas continuously present with God – the archetypal world of universal forms in which the intelligible and the visible symbol, word, idea and actuality, all merge. The unique basis of Romanesque imagination, such dramatic but highly conceptualized figural forms lacked individuation, whether substantial like the palace Heorot, or personal like the figure of Deor (see below, pp. 39, 53). The kind of literary or intellectual construction Platonic symbolism promotes (irrespective of analytical awkwardness – the avoidance of which results in over-elaborated allegorization), predicates an accessible and dramatic empathy drawn from the sacramental character of a universe comprehended by God; thus symbolism is the means of approaching that which remains mysterious – a system whose values arise from a presumed parallel between the soul of man and the cosmic order. But lacking individual character or singularity, mere universality must now have seemed monotonous, lifeless, even barren. And the new natural science would necessarily question the value of any symbolic presentation of reality. Not that the new scholar was entirely lacking in devotional sentiment; indeed, he was possibly the more devout in consequence of deep learning. As the natural historian Alexander Neckham complains of his zealous students:

> Oh that they would employ such effort in the improvement of their lives as they spend in studying far into the night! Oh that they would grow as pale from desire for their heavenly home as they do from intellectual effort, wasting as they do both time and youth in altercations over words! Subtleties which they cannot encompass they wish wholly to comprehend. Oh vanity of vainglory! Oh snare of praise! Oh useless curiosity![43]

But the very success of the new curriculum resulted in nervous opposition as materials flooded the schools far more rapidly than they could be assimilated by the educational establishment. Conservative theologians would question the value of bombarding society with ideas whose validity in terms of traditional Church ethics was not yet assessed.

Many felt that Christendom was being insidiously and systematically undermined by pagan morality: if not by the rhetorical excesses of individual dialectical wild men, then by the all-pervasive influences of classical erotica. Essentially, however, the humanistic movement of the eleventh and twelfth centuries predicated a belief in the fundamental dignity of mankind, albeit fallen from grace, and in the comprehensibility of a sensible universe accessible to systematic enquiry. Divine revelation apart, observation would now replace textual authority as the source of truth, supported by the use of logic as a tool of creative enquiry. This new-found confidence in man's power of reason brought with it not only an exciting intellectual reorientation, but a new sense of redemption in the human condition. Once begun, the process of rational enquiry would extend into every area of human existence. In the field of political philosophy, for example, where Gerald of Wales's *De Principis Instructione*, written in the Carolingian tradition, cited solely classical, biblical, and patristic authorities, John of Salisbury's *Policratus* now not only displays the expected classical erudition but draws extensively on his personal experience as Chancellor of England to propound a systematic political view.[44]

As the enquiry into natural phenomena gained momentum, the frontiers of the supernatural were progressively pushed back. The symbolic Romanesque bestiary gives way to the objectivity of Alexander Neckham's scientific descriptions or the closely observed detail of the zoological drawings of Matthew Paris. The consequent desacralizing of natural phenomena put inevitable stress on traditional symbolist interpretation. It certainly conflicted with the persistent attraction that the mysterious and miraculous exercises on the human mind, although for the time being at least, the logical hostility of the irreconcilable might be contained within an individual thinker's response. For example, the Aristotelian John of Salisbury, who knew very well that 'all knowledge originates in the senses while judgement lies in reason', feels it necessary to question the motives of those who would describe the miracles attributed to Becket as merely 'men's fancies'.[45] But it was no longer sufficient to declare with Isaiah (7. 9) 'Unless you believe you shall not understand'. The twelfth-century conflict between conservative faith and the new reason, the fundamental questioning of traditional sources of authority, the feigned and sometimes unfeigned coexistence of old and new, was not only recognizably present in society, but intellectually systematized in the methods of the schools. The scholastic disputation, a mode of enquiry examining the interaction of opposites, might in theory seek to establish a truth or resolve the point of balance inherent in a supposition of universal order. But more often than not it was employed to expose opposing viewpoints rather than to come to clear-cut conclusions: an intellectual consideration of how far man's expectation of universal order might square with his personal experience of disorder and inadequacy. Diagnostic was the logical mode *sic et non* popularized by Abelard – the tendency to think in terms of irreconcilable but edifying opposition, a mode of enquiry intimately concerned with tension and conflict, and therefore wholly suited to a society in change and under stress.

Students played an active intermediary role in the intellectual and social ferment of the age. The progressive atmosphere of the schools sponsored a floating population of youthful intelligentsia. The wandering scholar or *vagante* was now as familiar a part of the European scene as the *peregrinus* had been in former times – numerous enough to form a recognizable class by themselves and influential enough (voting with their feet more often than not) to determine the success or even existence of particular schools. The attractions of education were such that the supply of graduates soon came to exceed the rate at which they could be absorbed by the professions. Consequently there emerged a kind of intellectual proletariat of unemployed 'clerks', educated and resentful, frustrated by their lack of social acceptance, eager to recognize dissipation and degeneration in the civil and ecclesiastical establishment to which they could gain no entrée. Expert in satire and irony, their observation of social and literary convention was radical and unrestrained. They formed a receptive audience for the numerous religious heresies which proliferated from the eleventh century onwards, and were responsible for the dissemination of unorthodox views on the nature of love and society. Concern with the experience of the individual found ready sympathy with townsmen, no less alienated from established order and sensitive to the paradox and incongruity of convention.

The twelfth century, increasingly accustomed to view the book as a tool rather than an object of authority *per se*, witnessed a significant increase in the reading public, demanding materials not merely of edification but entertainment – one of the attendant benefits of increased leisure. Urbane literature, whether weightily Latinate, like the *Nugis Curialium* of Walter Map,[46] or lighter in tone like the *fabliaux* or the songs of the *vagantes*, spared no one and no subject, whether sacred or profane, displaying a mocking contempt for the self-satisfied of whatever background. However, while many men called for *thynges þat fallyd to ribaudy*,[47] there was no lack of devotion on the part of the citizen class. Indeed, it was now that the great urban cathedrals arose. But while their Romanesque predecessors may have recognized in their sculptural ornament the presence of devils, monstrous races, and worldly forces around these ecclesiastical fortresses of God, Early English Gothicism, as at Wells, now incorporated the most realistic scenes from contemporary life, and a wealth of highly individualized portrait heads. At Exeter the later thirteenth-century religious sensibility could admit at least an element of human tension in its representation of a sympathetic, humane God. Facing the Lady Chapel altar a youthful attendant insolently pokes out his tongue at pontifical dignity, while a lazy hound prefers to scratch itself rather than attend a huntsman's furious summons. Slowly but surely, confidence was reasserting itself.

\*\*\*

As it began, so it continued. From Migration to Crusade there was a restlessness in the age; men seem constantly to have been in motion, physically, socially, and intellectually mobile. Only for a limited period, and for a limited class, was any part of the population static. Whether *peregrinus* or *vagante*, journeyman-mason, merchant, hero in exile, or knight errant, there could be none, whatever his condition, who would not experience the anxiety of the journey spoken of by the Old English poet: *pæt he a his sæfore sorge næbbe* (see below, p. 116). From the fifth-century collapse of the Roman Empire in the West to the progressive disengagement of belief from natural experience at the end of the thirteenth century stretches an age susceptible to social and intellectual stress in which men were constantly obliged to adjust their perception of experience to received notions of order. The social and intellectual development of early medieval England progresses in a constant series of resolved contradictions, redefinitions to accommodate changing economic and political conditions, its literary reflex marking the hiatus between aspiration and achievement, individual or communal. Such a period of social transition is marked by enhanced vitality among ordinary people simply because the reassessment of habitual custom necessitates individual reassertion. The landscape, both inner and outer, is rearranged: the heroic warrior ideal is internalized and sanctified in the service of God; the Crusade turned to cynical self-aggrandisement. Sexual love is pressed into the service of divine worship – yet escapes. The dismal facts of lust and power promote and are in turn transformed by the world of romance. Intellectually seminal, such an age would generate compelling materials and themes, the significance of which persist to the present time.

## Notes

1. Ammianus Marcellinus, *Rerum Gestarum*, edited by W. Seyfarth (Leipzig, 1978), II, p. 114; Sextus Aurelius Victor, *Epitome de Caesaribus,* edited by F. Pichlmayr, revised by R. Gruendel (Leipzig, 1966), p. 166.

2. *Bede's Ecclesiastical History of the English People,* edited by B. Colgrave and R. A. B. Mynors (Oxford, 1969), pp. 48–53; *Two of the Saxon Chronicles Parallel,* edited by J. Earle and C. Plummer (Oxford, 1892–99), I, pp. 12–15; Nennius, *Historia Brittonum,*

edited by T. Mommsen *Monumenta Germaniae Historica, Auctorum Antiquissimorum,* XIII (Berlin, 1898), pp. 177–89.

3. *Two Saxon Chron.,* edited by Earle and Plummer, I, pp. 12–13.

4. *Bede's Eccles. Hist.,* edited by Colgrave and Mynors, pp. 50–51.

5. Edited by Mommsen, *Monumenta Germaniae Historica, Auctorum Antiquissimorum,* XIII (Berlin, 1898), pp. 25–85.

6. *Bede's Eccles. Hist.,* edited by Colgrave and Mynors, pp. 142–43.

7. Ibid., pp. 188–89.

8. *Historici Graeci Minores,* edited by L. Dindorf (Leipzig, 1870), I, p. 303f.

9. *Two Saxon Chron.,* edited by Earle and Plummer, I, pp. 48–49.

10. See D. Leigh, 'Ambiguity in Anglo-Saxon Style I Art', *Antiquaries Journal,* 64 (1984), 34–42.

11. *Bede's Eccl. Hist.,* edited by Colgrave and Mynors, pp. 182–85.

12. *Cornelii Taciti Opera Minora,* edited by M. Winterbottom and R. M. Ogilvie (Oxford, 1975), pp. 48–49.

13. *Cartularium Saxonicum: A Collection of Charters Relating to Anglo-Saxon History,* edited by W. de G. Birch (London, 1885–99), I, pp. 222, 236, 256.

14. Ibid., I, pp. 300–03, 369, 409, etc.

15. *Two Saxon Chron.,* edited by Earle and Plummer, I, pp. 52–55.

16. *Die Gesetze der Angelsachsen,* edited by F. Liebermann (Halle, 1898–1916), I, pp.444–53

17. *Two Saxon Chron.,* edited by Earle and Plummer, I, pp. 174–75; *Codex Diplomaticus Aevi Saxonici,* edited by J. M. Kemble (London, 1839–48), IV, p. 200.

18. *Die 'Institutes of Polity, Civil and Ecclesiastical',* edited by K. Jost (Berne, 1959), pp. 40ff.

19. *Two Saxon Chron.,* edited by Earle and Plummer, I, pp. 186–87.

20. William of Malmesbury, *Historia Novella,* edited by K. R. Potter (London, 1955), pp. 48, 104.

21. *La Règle du Temple,* edited by H. de Curzon (Paris, 1886), p. 58.

22. Peter Damian, *Epistolarum Libri Octo,* in *Patrologia Latina,* edited by J.-P. Migne (Paris, 1844–90), CXLIV, col. 313.

23. William of Malmesbury, *Historia Novella,* edited by Potter, p. 17.

24. Walter Map, *De Nugis Curialium: Courtiers' Trifles,* edited by M. R. James, second edition, revised by C. N. L. Brooke and R. A. B. Mynors (Oxford, 1983), pp. 96–97.

25. *Two Saxon Chron.,* edited by Earle and Plummer, I, p. 265.

26. See generally E. Siberry, *Criticism of Crusading, 1095–1274* (Oxford, 1985).

27. William of Malmesbury, *De Gestis Regum Anglorum*, edited by W. Stubbs, Rolls Series, 90 (London, 1887–89), II, p. 310.

28. *Sermo Lupi ad Anglos*, edited by D. Whitelock, third edition (Exeter, 1976).

29. Peter of Blois, *Opera Omnia*, edited by J. A. Giles (London, 1846–47), I, p. 194.

30. For a general survey of critical attitudes to this difficult subject, see R. Boase, *The Origin and Meaning of Courtly Love* (Manchester 1977); the collection of conference papers, *The Meaning of Courtly Love*, edited by F. X. Newman (Albany, NY, 1968) remains stimulating.

31. Andreas Capellanus, *De Amore*, edited by E. Trojel (Copenhagen, 1892), pp.235–6

32. Daniel of Beccles, *Urbanus Magnus*, edited by J. G. Smyly (Dublin, 1939).

33. See M. D. Legge, *Anglo-Norman Literature and its Background* (Oxford, 1963), pp. 85–96 *et passim*.

34. *Two Saxon Chron.*, edited by Earle and Plummer, I, p. 216.

35. C. Platt and R. Coleman-Smith, *Excavations in Medieval Southampton, 1953–1969* (Leicester, 1975), I, pp. 32, 293–94.

36. See R. W. Hunt, 'English Learning in the Late Twelfth Century', *Transactions of the Royal Historical Society*, Fourth Series, 19 (1936), 19–42 (pp. 36–37).

37. *Aldhelmi Opera*, edited by R. Ehwald *Monumenta Germaniae Historica, Auctorum Antiquissimorum*, XV (Berlin, 1919), p. 61ff.

38. Alcuin, *The Bishops, Kings, and Saints of York*, edited by P. Godman (Oxford, 1982), pp. 122–23.

39. *Aldhelmi Opera*, edited by Ehwald, p. 479.

40. Alcuin, *Epistolae*, edited by E. Dümmler, *Monumenta Germaniae Historica, Epistolae*, IV (Berlin, 1895), p. 183.

41. Ibid., pp. 39, 233, 235, 290, 294 etc.

42. Joannis Saresberiensis Episcopi Carnotensis, *Metalogicon*, edited by C. C. J. Webb (Oxford, 1929), p. 136.

43. Alexander Neckham, *De Naturis Rerum*, edited by T. Wright, Rolls Series, 34 (London, 1863), p. 311.

44. *De Principis Instructione Liber*, in *Giraldi Cambrensis Opera*, edited by J. S. Brewer *et al.*, Rolls Series, 21 (London, 1861–91), VIII; Joannis Saresberiensis Episcopi Carnotensis, *Policratici*, edited by C. C. J. Webb (Oxford, 1909).

45. R. Foreville, 'Une lettre inédite de Jean de Salisbury, évêque de Chartres', *Revue d'Histoire de l'Église de France*, 22 (1936), 179–85 (pp. 181–82).

46. Map, *De Nugis Curialium*, edited by James.

47. *Octovian Imperator*, edited by F. McSparron (Heidelberg, 1979), p. 61.

Chapter 2
# Until the Dragon Comes

*Widsith, Deor, Waldere, The Fight at Finnsburh,* and *Beowulf*

In their social origins, history and literature are indistinguishable. Early Germanic peoples would probably have recognized three occasions as most fitting the recitation of verse: the recollection of national history, the praise of individual exploits of bravery, and lament at the death of a hero. Such poetry had a clear mnemonic function; it dealt with the genealogies of their people, the original homes of their race, and the historic events which led to their migration.[1] The recital of these events almost certainly involved accounts of heroic deeds: 'What is history', remarks Jordanes in concluding his history of the Goths, 'but an account of the actions of brave men',[2] affirming the unique importance of the heroic act, and clearly impinging on a further poetic category – the war-songs. All such literary occasions will have been present in early Anglo-Saxon times. We must surely have the material reference, if not the structures, of ancient mnemonic songs recorded in the oldest parts of the *Anglo-Saxon Chronicle*, incorporating onomastic and other information that antedates literacy by many generations. Like those of the Germani, early Anglo-Saxon genealogies have all the appearance of mnemonic origins; although they begin with the genuine names of credible kings, the further back they go into remote antiquity, the more they invite guesswork and incorporate clearly mythological figures. The courts of early Anglo-Saxon kings, both collectively and individually, must have formed reservoirs of orally trans-mitted information. And indeed many kings themselves, aware of the historic proprieties, will have taken an interest in the ancient songs.[3]

English literary history begins, not inappropriately, with two poems dealing directly or indirectly with the function of the poet and the nature of poetry. In *Widsith* certainly, and in *Deor* in all probability, we have the words of two early court scops themselves. But neither can properly be considered lays as such. They are in one sense more valuable: cleverly constructed catalogues, as it were, of the scop's materials of trade. The poem we call *Widsith* takes its title from the very first word:

Widsið, maðolade,    wordhord onleac,
se þe monna mæst    mægþa ofer eorþan,
folca geondferde;    oft he on flette geþah
mynelicne maþþum.    Him from Myrgingum
æþele onwocon.    He mid Ealhhilde,
fælre freoþuwebban,    forman siþe
Hreðcyninges    ham gesohte
eastan of Ongle,    Eormanrices,
wraþes wærlogan.    Ongon þa worn sprecan:
'Fela ic monna gefrægn    mægþum wealdan!
Sceal þeodna gehwylc    þeawum lifgan,
eorl æfter oþrum    eðle rædan,
se þe his þeodenstol    geþeon wile'.    (ll. 1–13)

[Widsith spoke, unlocked his treasury of words, he who of all men had
travelled most widely among all the nations and peoples of earth; often he
had received on the floor of the hall some memorable jewel. His race sprang
from the Myrgings. First of all, he had gone with Ealhild the beloved peace-
weaver, east from Angeln, to seek out the abode of the Ostrogothic king,
Eormenric, savage violator of treaties. He began then to speak of many
things: 'I have learned much of men who ruled over nations. Every leader
should live according to custom, governing the homeland, one warrior after
another, if he wishes his throne to prosper'.]

There follows a long list of such early heroic rulers. At first sight this
seems a jumble of apparently heterogeneous material, a geographical
sweep from Burgundians in the west to the Huns in the east, embracing
in one bewildering movement the whole ethnic melting-pot of Migration
Age Europe. But as with the *disjecta membra* of contemporary applied art
where only close and sympathetic examination reveals rhythm and
meaning, the poet's presentation is by no means as disorganized as it
might at first appear. We can recognize a coherent syntactic and thematic
structure, a generically balanced sequence of two-line formulae of the
kind: 'X ruled Y, PQ, ST, and UV', accelerating and intensified by
omission of the verb after the first hemistich. Repeated over and over
again, with variations, this formula patently represents an ancient form of
mnemonic name-list, or *thula*. The cumulative effect of the progression is
to evoke the vast panorama of the *Völkerwanderungzeit* – a tense sequence
of separable moving elements. Any attempt to unravel a precise
geographical or historical programme is unprofitable and irrelevant; the
list serves merely to whet the appetite by its very variety, displaying the
rich wares of the minstrel's repertoire – a mnemonic interspersed with
brief but tantalizing narrative expansions, any of which might be enlarged upon at the request of a patron.

The bulk of references are to heroes who flourished between the
opening of the fourth century and the third quarter of the sixth, that is to

say the immediate cultural hinterland of Migration Age Europe, so that it was probably composed during the migrations or at a time when the traditions of the Continental homelands were still relatively fresh. But to suppose that it represents anything other than an imaginative interpretation of the historical circumstances would be mistaken. The purportedly autobiographical details of Widsith's journey to the court of the Gothic king Eormenric are given a legendary rather than factual framework, reflecting a situation which had passed away even in the fourth century. The localization of the struggle between Goths and Huns is certainly unhistoric. In Eormenric's day the Goths were dwelling in the Black Sea plains, fighting their battles between the Sea of Azov and the Danube, rather than in the northern Vistula Wood which they had left some generations earlier. The poet's story materials may also have been at a relatively pristine stage of development: his Burgundian patron Gunter (Guðhere, l.66) not yet joined with the mythical story of Sigemund Volsung and the Nibelungs.

The poet's range of reference is remarkable, covering some seventy races and as many named heroes. It includes memorable Germanic warrior-kings with well-attested historical contexts, such as the Gothic Eormenric or Theodoric of the Franks, others like Widia or Ingeld whom we now know of only through legend, and a host whose identity and significance are now quite lost to us. Some are not Germanic at all. References like that to Alexander (ll.15–17) were presumably incorporated at a somewhat later stage in the poem's transmission, perhaps deriving second hand from one or other of the small encyclopaedic manuals which circulated in early Anglo-Saxon England.[4] No insular Anglo-Saxon references occur – naturally enough since the entire panorama is that of the antique age of Continental turmoil which preceded the English settlement of Britain. But there are certainly characters mentioned who are familiar from elsewhere in early Anglo-Saxon literature. Finn Folcwalding, we are told, ruled the race of the Frisians, Hnæf the Hocings, and Sæferth the Secgan (ll.27–31). In the epic fragment known as The Fight at Finnsburh (see below, p. 45f), we will meet these three tragic figures again. It is on a visit to his sister married to Finn Folcwalding, that Hnæf is slain and Sæferth, for the time being part of Hnæf's comitatus, plays such a heroic part in the defence of the hall at Finnsburh. This review of heroic kings is no mere list; it includes tantalizing hints of some of the story materials that lay behind the scop's allusions. The story of Finnsburh is not told, but the outline plots of others are – two in particular that link significantly with the Beowulf story. The first thula concludes by turning from a welter of obscure referents to the well-known figure of Offa, temporarily releasing the staccato pressure of formulae in a more expansive mode, the sense no longer tensely confined within the hemistich:

Offa weold Ongle,    Alewih Denum;
se wæs þara manna    modgast ealra,
no hwæþre he ofer Offan    eorlscype fremede,
ac Offa geslog    ærest monna,
cnihtwesende,    cynerica mæst.
Nænig efeneald him    eorlscipe maran
on orette.  Ane sweorde
merce gemærde    wið Myrgingum
bi Fifeldore;    heoldon forð siþþan
Engle ond Swæfe,    swa hit Offa geslog.    (ll. 35–44)

[Offa ruled Angeln, Alewih the Danes: he was the bravest of all these
men, yet he did not perform deeds of heroism mightier than those of Offa,
for Offa, foremost among men while still a youth, won the greatest of
kingdoms. No one of the same age performed greater deeds of heroism in
battle. With his sword alone he fixed the boundary against the Myrgings
at the River Eider; thereafter the Angles and Swabians maintained it just
as Offa had won it.]

This same Offa, whose story was utilized by the *Beowulf*-poet in similar
terms, was the renowned leader of the Continental Angles shortly before
their wholesale migration to Britain, and ancestor and namesake of the
later Anglian king, Offa of Mercia, whose career bore so remarkable a
resemblance to that of his forebear. Certainly we may assume that
flattering dynastic lays dealing with the exploits of his namesake will have
been common in Offa's court at Tamworth.

Widsith's recital continues:

Hroþwulf ond Hroðgar    heoldon lengest
sibbe ætsomne    suhtorfædran,
siþþan hy forwræcon    Wicinga cynn
ond Ingeldes    ord forbigdan,
forheowan æt Heorote    Heaðobeardna þrym.    (ll. 45–49)

[Hrothwulf and Hrothgar, nephew and uncle, kept peace together for a very
long time, after they had driven away the tribe of the Wicings, and
humiliated the vanguard of Ingeld, cut down the power of the Heathobards
at Heorot.]

Heorot is of course the Danish palace that Beowulf went to deliver from
the ravages of Grendel – and Hrothgar its once great but now old and
failing king. Hrothwulf his nephew, who plays a sinister role throughout
the *Beowulf* poem, will succeed to the Danish throne only after disposing
of Hrothgar's own sons, whose claims ironically Beowulf had promised to
support. It is the feud with Ingeld's Heathobards – tragic sequel to
Hrothgar's hopes of securing peace by a marriage alliance – that will

ultimately lead to the final destruction of Heorot by fire, and the end of that national prosperity which Hrothgar, Beowulf, and Hrothwulf all in turn fought to save (see generally below, pp. 49–66).

Widsith goes on to tell how he came by his repertoire: he has travelled through many foreign lands throughout this wide world; good and evil he has suffered there, cut off from kinsmen, far from others of his blood, serving far and wide.

> Forþon ic mæg singan    ond secgan spell,
> mænan fore mengo    in meoduhealle
> hu me cynegode    cystum dohten.    (ll. 54–56)

[Therefore I can sing and tell a tale, describe before the company in the mead-hall how noble men have been generous to me with gifts.]

It is specifically this experience – the fact that he has known adversity and fluctuating fortunes, estate and exile, good company and the loss of friends – which he cites as qualifications for his role as poet. This autobiographical interlude soon absorbs and is superseded by the fictional persona. The mnemonic formula 'X ruled Y' is replaced by a personal statement 'I was with Y' or 'I sought out X'. The claims now made by the poetic voice are remarkable both historically and geographically. Widsith claims to have been with: Angles, Danes, Thuringians, Langobards, Burgundians, and Franks – any or all of whom might have been well known to an experienced traveller. Indeed in some repsects the list is very credible – in what it omits, for example. The poet evinces no knowledge of the interior of Scandinavia or of German peoples south of the Ruhr and west of the Elbe; he has apparently never heard of either Vandals or Visigoths. But however the poet of *Widsith* may have gained his information as to contemporary Europe, the claims of his persona by no means end there. 'With the Scots I was', he continues, 'and with the Picts, and with the Lapps, and in the land of the Welsh', and then proceeds with exuberance to embrace even oriental regions:

> Mid Sercingum ic wæs    ond mid Seringum;
> mid Creacum ic wæs ond mid Finnum,    ond mid Casere,
> se þe winburga    geweald ahte,
> wiolena ond wilna,    ond Wala rices.
> . . .
> Mid Israhelum ic wæs    ond mid Exsyringum,
> mid Ebreum ond mid Indeum    ond mid Egyptum.
> Mid Moidum ic wæs ond mid Persum . . .    (ll. 75–84)

[I have been with Saracens and with Scythians; I have been with Greeks and with Finns, and with Caesar who had possession of festive cities, of riches

[and desirable things, and the kingdom of the Romans. . . . I have been with
Israelites and with Assyrians, with Jews and with Indians, and with
Egyptians. I have been with Medes and with Persians . . .]

and then in just a line or two more this galloping, kaleidoscopic and most
exotic of lists focuses suddenly and dramatically in shocking paradox:

Ond ic wæs mid Eormanrice    ealle þrage;
þær me Gotena cyning    gode dohte.    (ll. 88–89)

[And I was with Eormenric all that time: the King of the Goths treated me
generously.]

Just as Offa had provided a dramatic culmination for the earlier *thula*, so
the known figure of Eormenric absorbs the accelerating force of this
second list. But it provides much more than fine oral effect. Clearly either
our poet is mad – a liar of heroic proportions – or he does not expect his
words to be taken at quite their face value.

The poet modulates from the individualized narrative voice of credible
autobiography to a fictional, universal poet-figure. The rhetorical precipitate
forms a celebratory definition of the role of the scop in embracing and
transcending his world. If he has in fact been with all these people – Medes
and Persians, Picts and Scots – or possibly even with Eormenric at the court
of the Goths – then it is by way of poetic licence only. If he has never
actually made the journey north to Pictland, he certainly has stories enough
about them, their kings and the monsters they fought, if only you will listen.
If he can tell of such, it is by virtue of his role as the scop – poetic licence *per
se*. In this sense it is uncertain which journey has the greater imaginative
validity, that in actuality or that in song. In oral delivery the synthesis of the
two poetic identities would be even less defined; it would be less possible to
distinguish between Widsith's own claims and those of 'poetry' – the eclectic
wares of his trade that he lays out before you.

The poet's *envoi* returns to the opening theme – the necessary
celebration of liberal patronage; an expansive lyrical climax defining the
symbiotic relationship of poet and patron:

Swa scriþende    gesceapum hweorfa
gleomen gumena    geond grunda fela;
þearfe secgað    – þoncword sprecaþ.
Simle suð oþþe norð    sumne gemetað
gydda gleawne,    geofum unhneawne,
se þe fore duguþe wile    dom aræran,
eorlscipe æfnan,    oþþæt eal scæceð,
leoht ond lif somod.    Lof se gewyrcað;
hafað under heofonum    heahfæstne dom.    (ll. 135–43)

[Thus the peoples' minstrels go wandering, as fate directs, through many lands; they tell their need – speak words of thanks. South or north, they will always meet someone appreciative of songs, unniggardly with gifts, who wishes to enhance his reputation in front of the comitatus, confirm his heroism, until everything falls into ruin, light and life together. Such a man gains praise; he will have a great and secure reputation beneath the heavens.]

And so, he implies, may *you*; and I'm the man to do it – at a price of course. The implicit hiatus between the two half-lines 137a and b, will be filled by the hoped-for patron. The link is an openly practical one, a potential sequence: gift, song, and glory – praise in direct proportion to generosity.

Despite its first-person air of directness and actuality, we cannot take this persona at face value; it has too much in common with other types of the early minstrel tradition. His name Widsith is, after all, merely a term denoting 'the widely travelled one'. The same epithet, 'wide-journied', *vidfœrull*, is applied to later Viking skalds who claim to have travelled in search of songs almost as widely as our earlier English scop.[5] And they too, if we are to credit them, seem to have had a sufficiently long life-span to have witnessed events which actually took place centuries apart. The same longevity was claimed for Widsith's own Celtic contemporary, the legendary Welsh bard Taliesin.[6] Widsith is not simply a poetic compendium, but an oblique portrait of the Anglo-Saxon scop himself – of course much larger than life. If any man could actually have visited as many nations as Widsith claims to have done, he certainly did not live so long as to sing in the presence of both Eormenric, who died in 375, and the Langobard Ælfwine when he invaded Italy in 568. This figure is none other than the archetypal poet – the omniscient, semi-divine Orpheus figure – his role at once glamorous and poignant, the most welcome of guests and yet the loneliest, both teacher and servant.

But the *Widsith*-poet was not prepared to leave his mouthpiece a mere faceless persona of the kind we will find introducing early Old English elegies (see below, p. 107). He gives him some substance, a name and the corroborative details of specific context. He belongs to the tribe of the Myrgings, a small Saxon group living in Schleswig-Holstein just south of Offa's border in Angeln. His immediate lord is called Eadgils, and it is from him that he holds the estate his father held before him. He has in addition a well-defined professional career, the experiential nucleus of which is his journey to the Gothic court of Eormenric accompanying the 'peace-weaver' Princess Ealhild (ll. 5–8, 109f) and his subsequent experience in the Hunnish Wars with members of Eormenric's legendary comitatus, like Wudga and Hama (ll. 119ff). But he is no mere sycophant; if he has served the Goth Eormenric and found him a generous patron – and admits as much in honest appraisal, he does not fail to acknowledge that king's hostile reputation as a savage violator of treaties (*wrapes wærlogan*, l.9); but there is no need to mention Eormenric's overthrow by the Huns, let alone his suicide. It is lasting *dom* the poet offers. By the same token, his view of Ælfwine is no less favourable, diplomatically remembered as the most generous of patrons, rather than as the savage who was murdered by his wife after forcing her to drink from a cup made from her father's skull.[7] The design and effect of the poem would not be enhanced by any explicit allusion to ruthlessness on the part of a supposed patron. Widsith remains a persona – the perfect scop; not only one who has for himself been and seen – no second- or third-hand accounts from him – but one who has sufficient fund of wisdom to use his wide range of materials to present contemporary rulers with considered advice – the lessons of history.

In *Deor* we are presented with just such a piece of gnomic wisdom, delivered through the mouth of a similarly actualized persona – this time a scop called Deor – a name that proves to be no less significant than that of Widsith – who for the sake of the poem's argument claims for himself no less authentic a context, no less specific a career. But whereas the figure of Widsith is introduced from the very beginning of that poem, Deor dramatically and effectively delays his personal appearance until the poem's end. The particular advice implicitly urged by this persona is that those in adversity, like heroes of the past – and like himself we eventually learn – might bear misfortune with greater fortitude in the light of historical experience. This advice is presented in the form of a catalogue of references to figures who in one way or another were renowned for having endured and overcome misery. This has much in common with the allusive, and too often elusive, lists of *Widsith*, but poses less difficulty to the modern reader in consequence of its more visible structure, carefully marshalled into six, albeit unequal, stanzas, each developing its own theme and punctuated by a refrain: a highly organized sequence of allusions to various calamitous circumstances – self-induced or brought about by others, which, however dire they might have seemed to those individuals concerned, in fact proved temporary. Not content merely to list, the *Deor*-poet presents a rhythmic, cyclic, dramatic, and sequential progression of thought by example and application, regularly punctuated by the strophic refrain:

þæs ofereode:   þisses swa mæg.

[That passed over: so can this.]

which provides both structural link and leitmotif, the only genuine refrain known in Old English poetry. We are never quite sure what 'this' should refer to; it links and leads on from one allusion to the next, anticipating every next statement, and then in the end is left in abeyance, directed solely at the poet's audience.

The opening sequence of three stanzas alludes to the legend of Weland the Smith, well known to the early Anglo-Saxons as its depiction on the seventh- or eighth-century Franks Casket suggests,[8] but recorded in its fullest form in the Old Norse *Vǫlundarkvitha* (Lay of Weland).[9] Three narrative elements, organically related, allow for the development of different modes of misery. The opening stanza establishes the frame of reference by alluding directly to Weland himself: the legendary weapon-smith, captured and crippled, forced to work for the Geatish king Nithad, enduring irksome and humiliating captivity although, as the audience would have been well aware, eventually escaping – but not before taking vengeance by way of raping Nithad's daughter Beadohild, and slaying his two sons. The second stanza derives directly from this understood information:

> Beadohilde ne wæs    hyre broþra deaþ
> on sefan swa sar    swa hyre sylfre þing,
> þæt heo gearolice    ongieten hæfde
> þæt heo eacen wæs;    æfre ne meahte
> þriste geþencan,    hu ymb þæt sceolde.
> þæs ofereode:    þisses swa mæg.    (ll.8–13)

[For Beadohild the death of her brothers was not such an aggravation to her spirit as her own condition was, in that she had clearly realized that she was pregnant; she could never with confidence think about what needs must come of that.
        That passed over: so can this.]

Weland's misery becomes the cause of misery in others, his physical humiliation breeding violence, the hero's revenge achieved at the expense of the wholly innocent girl, who suffers not merely in the act of rape itself but in its debilitating consequences, sapping the will. Again as the audience was well aware, the issue – if unstated – was not totally unwelcome, inasmuch as Beadohild was known to have given birth to a notable hero, Widia (the Wudga of *Widsith*). The incidents outlined in the second stanza lead directly to the circumstances of the third, redounding to the psychological if not physical distress of 'the Geat' (whom the *Vǫlundarkvitha* allows us to identify with Nithad),[10] the original instigator himself, whose rage growing beyond all bounds, becomes a neurotic insomniac. It is clear that the cycle of misery can be self-generating, ultimately impinging not least on those responsible for the distress of others.

The poet now turns from a legendary context to one of historical actuality, drawing on some part of the Eormenric cycle employed by

Widsith, referring to the unhappy circumstances of two known kings, no less carefully linked. Whereas Widsith's theme could scarcely admit more than a hint of his patron's less acceptable face, here no punches are pulled; Eormenric is remembered solely for his savage and tyrannical rule, and in particular for his treachery towards his nephew Theodoric (Dietrich von Bern), represented in legend as a fugitive, the type of endurance under constant and undeserved misfortune.[11] We follow the same movement as in the Weland sequence, turning from sufferer to instigator. After a two-line allusion to Theodoric (ll.18–19), brief but apparently sufficient for a contemporary audience, we move by natural conversion to the cause of his, and so many others', misery: *Eormanrices wylfenne geþoht,* [Eormenric's wolf-like disposition] (ll. 21–22), the calamitous nature of his rule summarized in a single, self-contained hemistich: *Þæt wæs grim cyning,* [That was a cruel king!] (l.23b). So harsh was his rule indeed, says the poet, that many, sitting bound with sorrow, wished for nothing but the overthrow of his kingdom – which of course, happened; there is no need for the poet to specify the nature of Eormenric's own precipitate downfall at the approach of the Huns.

The poet has already begun to shift his focus from the specific to the universal, from the known cases of named individuals to the general distress of 'many a man'. There follows a more expansive general reflection on the nature of adversity:

> Siteð sorgcearig, sælum bidæled,
> on sefan sweorceð; sylfum þinceð
> þæt sy endeleas earfoða dæl. (ll.28–30)

[He who sits in sorrowful anxiety, severed from prosperity, grows dark in spirit; it seems to him that his share of miseries is endless.]

Such a man may meditate on how throughout this world God in his wisdom will frequently allow fortunes to fluctuate, enduing many with assured prosperity but to certain others a share of woes, the truth of which is self-evident and calls for no refrain. Finally the poet turns to speak for himself, setting against old legends and figures of world history, his own misfortune – domestic in scale by comparison, but no less intense for all that, proffering a sympathetic personal perspective. With a sudden striking use of the first person and present tense we are made aware of the human personality behind the consolatory aphorism. Psychologically adroit, the minstrel's own voice adds both immediacy and sympathetic relevance to the whole historical parade of woes endured and overcome by citing his own case – the effective consolatory posture of 'I too . . .', personal experience validating the moral aphorism:

Þæt ic bi me sylfum    secgan wille,
þæt ic hwile wæs    Heodeninga scop,
dryhtne dyre   – me wæs Deor noma!   (ll. 35–37)

[I'll say this for my part, that I was once the Heodenings' minstrel, dear to my leader – 'Dear' was my name!]

As a professional minstrel he has been ousted from his well-established and lucrative position with the Heodenings in favour of a more attractive rival – the famed poet Heorrenda[12] who has taken his place and his living. No matter whether or not this was a fictitious event, it has the authority of a realistically portrayed persona. He puns wistfully, perhaps bitterly, on the significance of his own name of favoured poet,[13] but remains apparently stoically unresentful at the fact of his displacement, acknowledging both the competence of his rival, 'an expert poet', *leoðcræftig monn* and the propriety of his former patron's role, whether ironically or honestly understood, as 'protector of men', *eorla hleo*, in transferring to Heorrenda the estate and stipend the poet had himself formerly enjoyed (ll. 40–41). His words have the ring of truth. Curiously, indeed, Deor actually contrives to gain respectful attention from the very fact of having been the precursor of so famous a poet. A lifelike, if perhaps imaginary creation, Deor like Widsith appears to be engaged in the wandering minstrel's perpetual search for patronage. Whether or not given fictive dress, he must appear credible if his words are to have value. His reduced circumstances are aggravated by no expression of injustice; it is merely the fact of mutability: nothing lasts for ever – and it may well be that his present reduced circumstances will change for the better.

It is significant that the poet chooses to end with the words: 'That passed, so can this', leaving it quite uncertain what this the final 'this' may be, pushing the response and responsibility firmly in the direction of the listener. This refrain is critically important to the understanding of the poem, thought-provoking, the more emphatically so because always unexpected, coming as it does after 'stanzas' of unequal length and character. Its import, although meaningful throughout, is unstable, shifting its sense according to the perceived situation. If the recital has been solicited in response to a set of known circumstances requiring consolation, then the 'this' may have a readily perceived referent; otherwise it must necessarily anticipate every next allusion through to the end, when the poet describes his own climactic distress – position, rank, possessions, even his very name, all gone at a stroke – endurable only by philosophic reflection on the mutability of the world, and not a cause of despair but of resignation and quietude. But the fact is that the refrain occurs one more time – the incremental process left deliberately open-ended, its recurrence marking a progression of increasingly focused re-

ferents: legend, history, mankind, me – now *you*. The words of the refrain are appropriate not only structurally but thematically, directed at
our own condition, since generally applicable to the human lot, accepting, as at the end of *Widsith*, the prophylactic function of poetic form in
the face of universal entropy.

Certain of the names already mentioned recur in the *Waldere* fragments
– short sequences of dialogue found on two manuscript leaves which is all
that remains of a once-fine epic drawing on the now familiar material of
the seminal 'Eormenric' cycle emerging from the early-fifth-century
Hunnish Wars. The main lines of the story can be reconstructed from a
Germano-Latin version, the *Waltharius Poesis* – possibly Carolingian in
date, and certainly very classical in its sentiment.[14] With the advent of
the Huns in western Europe, noble hostages had been taken to ensure the
continuing submission of certain major tribes. The Frankish nobleman
Hagen(a), a Burgundian princess, Hildegund (Hildegyth), and her
betrothed, Walter (Waldere), the son of another western race – perhaps
Visigothic or Romano-Gallic – were taken east to live as enforced, if
honoured, guests at the court of Attila the Hun. As conventionally in
heroic society (see above, p. 6) the young men join Attila's *comitatus*,
performing noteworthy deeds in battle on his behalf, while Hildegund is
given special responsibility for the Hunnish queen's jewels. Hagena,
upon learning of changed political circumstances at home among the
Franks, flees to the West. Eventually Waldere and Hildegyth flee
together, taking with them quantities of Hunnish treasure. Having
crossed the Rhine, however, their danger comes now not from pursuing
Huns, but from the new Frankish king, Gunther (Guthhere) and his
*comitatus*, who seek to seize both treasure and girl. Waldere and
Hildegyth are cornered in a defile in the Vosges mountains. Hagena, now
a member of Guthhere's *comitatus*, tries in vain to dissuade his leader
from attacking his former friend; Waldere for his part tries to buy him off,
offering the gift of a valuable sword and part of the treasure – but without
success. A running fight ensues in which these three named warriors are
the main, perhaps the sole, protagonists. Finally Waldere is cornered and
attacked by Guthhere and Hagena together. Their long-drawn-out encounter was eventually fought to a standstill, all three warriors suffering
extensive, crippling wounds. In the later Latin version Hildegyth, at
Waldere's suggestion, binds their wounds and offers refreshment to all,
before the bethrothed couple continue their journey, rejoin their families,
and are married; but there is no reason to suppose that this happy ending
formed part of the original scheme.

If the entire Waldere story was told in the same leisurely, expansive
style as that of the surviving fragments, then it might have formed a fine
epic of some two or three thousand lines, comparing in length with
*Beowulf*. All that remains, however, is small parts of three speeches

belonging to some stage in the final encounter in the Vosges. Although fragmentary, the sequence usefully illustrates the nature of heroic dialogue: dramatic, intense, yet leisured, full of outward reference and allusion. In the first fragment Hildegyth urges Waldere on to further deeds of courage. This Hildegyth has little in common with the shrinking, tearful girl of the Latin *Waltharius*; she resembles instead those women whom Tacitus described accompanying the Germanic warriors into battle, baring their breasts to remind their menfolk of the probable consequences of defeat and captivity.[15] Hildegyth encourages the hero on four counts: his fine weapons – associated with the legendary name of Weland himself – his lineage, past deeds and present good cause:

> ...   hyrde hyne georne:
> 'Huru Welandes   worc ne geswiceð
> monna ænigum   ðara ðe Mimming can
> heardne gehealdan;   oft æt hilde gedreas
> swatfag ond sweordwund   secg æfter oðrum.
> Ætlan ordwyga,   ne læt ðin ellen nu gyt
> gedreosan to dæge,   dryhtscipe ...
> ...   Nu is se dæg cumen
> þæt ðu scealt aninga   oðer twega:
> lif forleosan,   oððe langne dom
> agan mid eldum,   Ælfheres sunu'.   (ll. 1–11)
> ......
> 'Ne murn ðu for ði mece:   ðe wearð maðma cyst
> gifeðe to geoce unc;   ðy ðu Guðhere scealt
> beot forbigan,   ðæs ðe he ðas beaduwe ongan
> mid unryhte   ærest secan'.   (ll. 24–27)

[... eagerly she encouraged him: 'For sure the work of Weland won't fail any man who can grip tough Mimming; often in battle one warrior after another has fallen, bloodstained and wounded by this sword. You who fought in the vanguard of Attila, don't let your courage or leadership fail now. The day has now come, son of Ælfhere, when you must do one of two things – lose your life or achieve lasting fame among men. ... Don't worry about your blade: it was given you, the choicest of treasures, to help us both; with it you will humiliate Guthhere's boasting – since he started it unjustly, looking for trouble'.]

The second leaf contains two further fragments of dialogue: the conclusion of one speech and the opening of another. Further mention of famous swords by either Hagena or Guthhere, leads naturally to the remembrance of those ancient heroes who wielded them, serving traditionally[16] to kindle the fighter's resolve:

'. . . swilce bæteran
buton ðam anum,    ðe ic eac hafa
on stanfate    stille gehided.
Ic wat þæt hit ðohte    Ðeodric Widian
selfum onsendon,    ond eac sinc micel
maðma mid ði mece,    monig oðres mid him
golde gegirwan;    iulean genam,
þæs ðe hine of nearwum    Niðhades mæg,
Welandes bearn,    Widia ut forlet;
ðurh fifela geweald    forð onette'.    (ii. ll. 1–10)

['. . . a better one, apart from another one I have quietly hidden away in a
stone coffer. I know that it was Theodoric's idea to send it to Widia himself,
and also a great wealth of jewels along with the sword to clothe with gold
many others together with him; Nithad's kinsman, Widia, son of Weland,
received this reward for past deeds, releasing him from a difficult position; he
escaped thus from the power of monsters'.]

In reply Waldere both taunts and challenges Guthhere (here, as in
*Widsith,* identified not as a Frankish but a Burgundian leader – the
historical Gundaharius, finally slain by the Huns in 435),[17] extolling the
virtue of his father's armour, which he now wears as an heirloom:

'Hwæt, ðu huru wendest,    wine Burgenda,
þæt me Hagenan hand    hilde gefremede,
ond getwæmde feðewigges.    Feta, gyf ðu dyrre,
æt ðus heaðuwerigan    hare byrnan!
Standað me her on eaxelum    Ælfheres laf,
god ond geapneb,    golde geweorðod, . . .
. . . Ne bið fah wið me,
þonne wifle unmægas    eft ongynnað,
mecgum gemetað,    swa ge me dydon'.    (ii. ll. 14–19, 22–24)

['Well, you friend of the Burgundians, you clearly thought that Hagena's
hand would have done battle against me and eliminated me from the stand-
to fight. Come, if you dare, and take the grey mail-coat from one who is
exhausted with battle. Here on my shoulders lies Ælfhere's legacy, good and
broadly woven, adorned with gold. . . . It will not betray me when false
friends make a new onset with javelins, meeting me with swords, as you
did'.]

No less dramatic is the forty-eight-line heroic fragment known as *The
Fight at Finnsburh.* This comes closer to home, dealing not with events and
personalities from remote eastern Europe, but with an incident on the
Anglo-Frisian littoral of north-western Europe, and people directly related to the early Anglo-Saxon immigrants. Several of the protagonists are

mentioned in the *Widsith* catalogue. The *Finnsburh* fragment may well form part of a lost cycle dealing with events in the life of Hengest, mercenary war-leader and founder of the fifth-century kingdom of Kent (see above, pp. 1–2). The overall plot is problematic in many respects, but seems to incorporate a familiar heroic paradigm: the tragic consequences of conflicting loyalties in the self-consuming ethos of warfare society.

We can learn something of the background to the story from its incorporation as a digression in the full-length epic *Beowulf* (see below, p. 49f), although reference there is brief enough, allusive and with different emphasis since it is intended to serve a particular function within the context of the larger poem (ll. 1063–1159). But stripped of the feverish dialogue and physical immediacy of the fragment, the larger picture is allowed to emerge, a more synoptic view allowing the incident to be seen in fuller perspective.

The Finnsburh allusion is employed by the *Beowulf*-poet thus. The great Danish hall, Heorot, has been saved from destruction by a visiting Geatish hero, Beowulf. As part of the celebrations the resident minstrel sings a lay extolling an earlier Danish victory, involving *inter alia* the failure of a diplomatic marriage-alliance and the ultimate destruction of a hall by fire. Within the poet's overall structure, this ironically anticipates the final fate of Heorot, so recently saved, but doomed eventually to be destroyed – despite a peace-seeking marriage-alliance – during the course of the Heathobardan feud referred to in *Widsith* (see above, pp. 35–36). The outline of the minstrel's tale is as follows. Finn, king of the Frisians, has married the Danish princess Hildeburh. Her brother Hnæf together with his comitatus, which includes among other notables the Secgan prince Sigeferth and the possibly Jutish Hengest, have come to visit Finn's stronghold, Finnsburh, and are quartered in a separate guest-hall. Perhaps as a result of an old feud, only temporarily papered-over by the marriage-alliance, fighting breaks out between the followers of Finn and Hnæf, the former attacking the latter as they sleep in their hall at night. Hnæf's comitatus successfully resist. (This is the defence of the hall described in the Fragment.) There are heavy losses on both sides. Hnæf is slain and Hengest assumes leadership of the Danish group. Hildeburh, the emotional locus of conflicting passions, finds herself in the tragic position of committing to the one funeral pyre both a brother and a son, kinsmen killed fighting on opposite sides – a common heroic dilemma but particularly poignant in this case in view of the especially close relationship known to have existed between uncle and nephew in Germanic society.[18] With both sides heavily depleted, stalemate is reached. The remnants of Hnæf's comitatus decide to join Finn upon promises of honourable treatment. It is inevitable, however, that strife should recur. The heroic imperative remains; the revenge ethic festers. Hengest, Hildeburh, Finn – all participants – are enmeshed in a web of betrayal and irreconcilable demands. Eventually old scores will be settled. Hengest leads the attack: Finn is slain and Finnsburh destroyed, the plunder together with Hildeburh carried back to Denmark. The situation is emotionally highly charged; the unsatisfactory nature of compromise, albeit expedient, is clearly revealed. The obligation to acknowledge the suzerainty of one who has been responsible for the death of one's own leader, laid intolerable stress on the early Germanic warrior for whom it was unthinkable to leave the field under such conditions.[19] That this was no mere fictional convention for the Anglo-Saxons is clear from the killing-ground at Merton in 784 where kinsmen readily fought and died on opposing sides rather than flout the heroic ideal and desert their leader, alive or dead (see above, p. 8).

The Finnsburh-Heorot paradigm recurs in part of the Eormenric cycle preserved in the Old Norse *Atlakvitha* (Lay of Attila) or the Old High German *Nibelungenlied* (Song of the Nibelungs).[20] Attila (Etzel) has contracted a marriage-alliance with the Burgundian Princess Kriemenhild. She is visited at Etzelburg by her brother Gunther and his comitatus which includes Hagen and other notable warriors, who are, as customarily, lodged in a guest-hall for the duration of their visit; there at night they are attacked by the Hunnish forces. The Old High German account presents similarities not only in overall plot but in dramatic details. The attackers are detected by light glinting on their armour – it is just before dawn; the doorway is heroically defended. After a protracted resistance, the hall is burned down and the Burgundian heroes eventually defeated and slain. The literary formula, however insistent, must accommodate a different outcome – the actual historical defeat of the Burgundians by the Huns in 435.

Like *Waldere*, the *Finnsburh* fragment is substantially made up from direct speech – journalistic statements piling up one on another without subordinate clauses, giving a strong sense of drama and immediacy, direct challenge and reply. The fragment opens conveniently with the 'call-to-arms' motif well known in heroic literature. After an initial reference alerting us, and the defenders, to the vulnerability of their position to attack by fire, the 'war-young' Hnæf speaks:

> 'Ne ðis ne dagað eastan;    ne her draca ne fleogeð;
> ne her ðisse healle    hornas ne byrnað.
> Ac her forþ berað . . .'    (ll. 3–5)

[‘This is not the dawn in the east; nor is it a dragon flying here; nor are the gables of this hall burning here. But here they are bearing . . .’]

urgently breaking off in aposiopesis – leaving the verb without an object in dramatic anticipation, and picking up in a sudden change of tense which recognizes the imminence of onslaught, the carrion animals lurking in anticipation:

'. . .        Fugelas singað;
gylleð græg-hama.   Guð-wudu hlynneð,
scyld scefte oncwyð.   Nu scyneð þes mona
waðol under wolcnum.   Nu arisað wea-dæda
ðe ðisne folces nið   fremman willað.
Ac onwacnigeað nu,   wigend mine;
habbað eowre linda;   hicgeaþ on ellen;
windað on orde;   wesað onmode'.   (ll. 5–12).

['The birds will screech; the grey-coated wolf will bay. The war-wood will
resound, shield answering shaft. Now gleams the moon, drifting beneath
clouds. Now evil deeds are afoot which will perpetuate that people's malice.
But now awake my warriors; take up your linden shields; set your minds on
courage; advance to the vanguard; be resolute'.]

The emotional significance of the defended-hall *topos* is clear: the
comforting symbol of security dramatically changed to one of claus-
trophobic horror – guests treacherously attacked by a trusted host. The
defence of the doorway itself is no less important – both a practical
reality, since it might be held indefinitely by one or two determined
warriors, and thematically significant. The defending hero stands, both
literally and emotionally, on the threshold of dangerous possibilities – at
his back what is secure and known, in front of him only an uncertain and
violent world.[21] Named warriors advance to hold the entrance. Reference
to named individuals on both sides and the reporting of direct exchanges
between them serves to locate the fight as a specific event. Shifts in the
action are rapid: a sequence of brief but highly charged incidents, the
focus changing from defence to attack with little more than an end-stop to
the line. Although the encounter is said to have been protracted over five
days (ll. 41–42),[22] depicted in close-up the action is swift, moving with the
urgent pressures of real warfare, excitement mounting through relatively
brief verbal exchanges as opposing warriors confront each other before
being cut down.

Ða wæs on healle   wæl-slihta gehlyn.
Sceolde celæs bord   cenum on handa
banhelm berstan.   Buruh-ðelu dynede,
oð æt ðære guðe   Garulf gecrang,
ealra ærest   eorð-buendra,
Guðlafes sunu;   ymbe hyne godra fæla,
hwearflicra, hwær   hræfen wandrode
sweart and sealo-brun.   Swurd-leoma stod
swylce eal Finnsburuh   fyrenu wære.   (ll. 28–36)

[There was then in the hall the din of murderous blows. The bossed shield in the hands of bold men would shatter the skull's defence. The floor of the stronghold resounded, until Garulf, Guthlaf's son, fell in the fight, first among those dwellers on earth; around him many a good man perished, where the raven circled, sombre and darkly gleaming. The light flashed from swords as if all Finnsburh were in flames.]

As our tantalizingly brief glimpse of the action breaks off, another of the front-line fighters is badly wounded, while one or other of the commanders expresses concern for his men:

> Ða gewat him wund hæleð    on wæg gangan;
> sæde þæt his byrne    abrocen wære,
> here-sceorpum hror,    and eac wæs his helm ðyrl.
> Ða hine sona frægn    folces hyrde
> hu ða wigend hyra    wunda genæson,
> oððe hwæþer ðæra hyssa. . . .    (ll. 43–end)

[Then a hero came walking away wounded; he said, strong in his war-gear, that his mail-coat was hacked about, and his helmet was pierced as well. At once the people's guardian asked how the fighters were bearing their wounds, or which of the young men . . .]

Like the tales of Waldere and Finn, the story material utilized by the poet of *Beowulf*, the social picture it depicts and its material background, must have seemed decidedly antique from the point of view of the settled Anglo-Saxon world. Some of the *Beowulf*-poet's references are clearly intended to be historical, even in the context of the poem, like one to the fourth-century Ostrogothic Eormenric himself. The latest externally corroborated historical reference in the poem is to the death of Hygelac, Beowulf's own lord and uncle, whom we know to have been killed during a raid on Frisian territory in about AD 521. It is possible to erect a chronology on the known date of this raid. The visit of Beowulf to Hrothgar in Heorot must have taken place during the last decades of the fifth century. Then after Hygelac's death some time elapsed before Beowulf could be persuaded to take the Geatish throne – possibly as a puppet of the Swedish king Onela; and then we are told he had a long and successful reign before finally meeting his end confronting a dragon. If Beowulf can be said to have lived at all, then he must be reckoned to have died shortly after the middle of the sixth century, say between AD 550 and 570.

Of all the major characters mentioned in the poem, the hero is the only one for whom we do not have some external corroboration. Even if Beowulf actually had any real existence as king of the Geats, the last historical act ascribed to him by the poet is his raising of Eadgils to the Swedish throne in about 530 – an event which all other sources attribute to a Danish force sent by Hrothulf. However, the remainder of Beowulf's long and reputedly glorious reign rests quite without historical substance. The fact that he is described fighting fabulous monsters does not of itself discredit his historicity. (By the same yardstick, the feats popularly attributed to Richard Cœur de Lion would result in him being dismissed as a mere myth.) It is possible that all the major figures mentioned by the poet had some basis in actuality. But the question of Beowulf's historicity, like Arthur's, is unimportant. The effect of the poet's anti-quarian perspective is much like that Dickens achieved with *Pickwick Papers*. The author chose to set his theme in a time sufficiently close for its concerns to be clearly recognizable by the audience as relevant to their own age, and yet sufficiently far in the past for it to have entered that twilight period when heroes of gigantic stature could be believed to have lived in the earth – not occupying a never-never land, but stalking a real world with which we can still to some degree feel ourselves familiar.

Given the foregoing chronology, we may presume that the bulk of the story material – the semi-historical or mythical lays out of which the author composed his poem – came to England from across the North Sea some time during the second half of the sixth century, that is, by the end of the Migration Age proper, after which no very strong cultural links were maintained with Scandinavia; from the seventh century onwards Anglo-Saxon England looked to the Frankish Rhine rather than northern Europe.

No one could pretend that we read *Beowulf* for a racy story-line. The poet's style is by no means turgid in itself, but continual comment, allusion, and digression detract from what plot there is. In any case, if the poet's primary concern had been heroic narrative, there are curious omissions to account for. There is hardly any reference to normal battle events, and such as there is, is minimized. Beowulf has the reputation of heroic activity carefully built up around him, but the only direct des-criptions of his prowess we are given are when he encounters three supernatural beings. Old Norse analogues suggest that what was in origin a simple threefold repetition – three encounters with monsters that are essentially the same[23] – has been been turned into something not only more artistically contrived but more momentous in its significance. The *Beowulf*-poet separates out the trolls who maraud Heorot from the quite distinct dragon who guards the hoard – and presents the two parts as diagnostic stages in the hero's career: his rise to prominence, and his eventual fall. However, *Beowulf* is not obviously a narrative poem in anything like the usual sense of that term. Neither is it a continuous setting forth of the life and manners of its hero. The poem now goes by the name of its protagonist, and not without some reason; but it is not necessarily 'about' Beowulf in the way that we normally consider *Hamlet* to be about Hamlet. Nevertheless, the author's object is apparently to be achieved by our contemplation of Beowulf's glorious youth, and later of the same hero's inevitable doom and death in old age.

It is the means of setting out these two contrasted stages in Beowulf's life that makes for the major bipartite division of the poem – and which has caused problems for those twentieth-century critics who reckon it falls apart in the middle. But the the two halves are as integral to the whole as are the two parts of the Old English verse line.[24] The structure of the poem, being thematic rather than narrative, is just as rhythmic and just as complete in itself as the rise and fall of the individual verse line. And like its unstressed but cumulatively significant metrical elements, there occur a wide variety of narrative digressions. These are often disturbing to the classically educated reader, but of course the structure of *Beowulf* cannot be judged by classical criteria any more than we can analyse the Old English line in terms of classical syllabic metrics. Just as Old English verse allows for functional hypermetric elements, each allusion can be shown to be tightly tied in to the whole, and properly subordinate to the central theme, serving to illustrate, explain, or emphasize. Although it is now sometimes difficult to reconstruct all of the various stories to which the poet alludes, it is clear that the so-called 'digressions' of *Beowulf* are legitimate parts of a deliberately constructed artistic whole.

The reader encounters one such episode at the very beginning of the poem – that dealing with the death and burial of Scyld Scefing (ll. 1–52), the description of whose funeral bears such a striking resemblance to the discoveries at Sutton Hoo (see above p. 4). These lines have no obvious connection with the main narrative. But pursuing the metrical analogy, this sequence can be shown to be viable as a kind of structural *anacrusis*, (see below, p. 292), functionally comparable with the extrametrical introductory *Hwæt* at the beginning of the first line. In fact the Scyld Scefing episode provides the leitmotif to the whole poem, evoking the noble, heroic, glorious, and tragic atmosphere of the courts of Migration Age Europe. It reminds an informed audience with aristocratic and antiquarian interests of the noble origins of those whose exploits the poet is about to relate. Scyld Scefing had come to the Danish people in their hour of need, and had established the glory of their kingdom: 'That', says the poet, 'was a great king'. It is important for the poet to establish the heroic might of the Danish kingdom in order to heighten the contrast of the monster Grendel's onslaught, bringing chaos to the land of Scyld, threatening to destroy all that he had built, and to bring to an end the reign of his grandson and heir, Hrothgar. Had we plunged straight into the account of Grendel's attacks, the Danes would have given the impression of mere weakness, and Beowulf's subsequent achievements would have seemed the less heroic. It is not only the terrible nature of the monsters, but the imperium of their victims that enhance the hero. Just as

Scyld Scefing came to the Danes alone over the waves at a former time of national distress, so now another young hero comes to them from over the waves, another stranger who will also cleanse their land and re-establish the glory of their kingdom – but again only for a time, for in this life all is corruptible, every glory transient. This young man will also one day prove a great king, and the remembrance of Scyld offers a sad anticipation of the eventual fate of Beowulf himself, in the sure knowledge that, however laden with treasures and renown, death (and perhaps before death, failure) comes to all men. No man, counsellor or hero, was so wise as to know Scyld's ultimate destination. 'Sad was their mind', says the poet, 'mourning their mood' (ll. 49–50) – and ours also, because this is the burden of the poem: the overriding fact of mutability in the world.

This symbolic arrival and departure of a national folk hero by boat is by no means without parallel in heroic literature; it represents a framing mechanism commonly employed to distance an event and set it in a more universal perspective. The prelude to *Beowulf* deals with the beginnings and the end of the greatest of the kings of Denmark, thus foreshadowing the substance of the entire poem, which deals with the rise and fall of the greatest of Geatish kings – the establishment of his reputation with the troll-fights at Heorot and finally his death, facing the dragon at Eagles' Crag. The events of Beowulf's long and prosperous reign, half a century full of incident no doubt, are all passed over without comment, and it is perhaps surprising that we should be given no account of his successful kingship. Instead we are brought rapidly to his final battle with the dragon, his death, and the subsequent destruction of his kingdom. This structural telescoping of the narrative so as to bring the hero's downfall into deliberate juxtaposition with the struggle involved in his rise to prominence suggests that the two parts are intended to be compared in some way. The contrast is significant. *Beowulf* is a poem of beginnings and ends. It begins with the rise of the Danes under the leadership of Scyld Scefing; it ends with the very certain destruction of the Geats after the death of their leader, Beowulf. The opening fifty lines of the poem thus provide a totally apposite exordium, evoking the atmosphere of mystery, transitoriness, and inscrutable destiny, both of individuals and of entire nations. Just as no man knew what became of Scyld Scefing, neither did they know – nor do we know – what became of Beowulf's Geats; they both drift out of history.

The allusions intercalated with the first part of the poem, dealing with such figures as Scyld Scefing, Sigemund the dragon-slayer, Hama who stole the necklace of the Brosings, the avaricious Heremod, and others, are legendary. Those of the second part deal with more definitely historical events, referring to what was known of the history of the Danes under the Scylding dynasty, and the causes of their downfall, and of the history of the Geatish Wars until the final destruction of the Geats following the joint invasion of Franks and Swedes. This division is quite appropriate. The first part deals with the legendary rise of the hero, and appropriately links him with other great heroes of the past; such stories encrust a rich surface like jewels; they do not motivate the action of the plot, but add immeasurable resonances to an already dense structure. The second part concerns Beowulf's actual effect upon the people, the historical references being immediate and concrete, to events occurring within the hero's own lifetime, and touching himself or his people closely. Dramatic and vital, these motivate the progress of Beowulf's life and trick out his inevitable doom. They deal with the decline and fall of the Danish and Geatish kingdoms, both of which it had been Beowulf's life-work to maintain. The whole elaborately investigated matter of the Geat-Swedish Wars is structurally significant as part of a moving framework within which the tragedy of the hero can be enacted, imparting a universal quality.

The resonant nature of the slightest digression is usefully illustrated by an allusion to the ultimate fate of Heorot in the very midst of its present glories (ll. 82–85). The destruction of Heorot as a result of the Danish – Heathobard feud, like Hrothulf's ousting of Hrothgar's sons, touch upon events that were well known to the contemporary audience – both gaining their dramatic effect from being uttered at the very moment of secure and prosperous triumph. They are used to provoke an overwhelming atmosphere of foreboding. The lofty gold-adorned palace of Heorot, the glory of the kingdom of Denmark, is newly completed – it awaits only the furious surges of hateful flame, which are destined to reduce it to ashes. Just so, the ruling kinsmen, the noble Hrothgar and the heroic Hrothulf, sit together at the banquet, in high spirits and in friendship – for the time being. Queen Wealhtheow is confident that Hrothulf will act nobly towards her sons. But the audience already knew that Hrothulf would need to slay the young princes before taking the throne. Such examples of ironic anticipation are used throughout the poem to reinforce the note of impending doom struck at the very beginning.

Similar in its effect is the reference to Sigemund Wælsing (ll. 874f). This is introduced easily enough with the author's usual fluidity in transition between one narrative element and another. Beowulf has defeated Grendel – his renown is proclaimed, and the nobles of Hrothgar's court amuse themselves by letting their horses run on the sands, and by telling each other stories of great monster-killings of the past. A minstrel is said first to compose a lay about the achievement of Beowulf himself and then to devise an apt parallel. The parallel he chooses is that of Sigemund the dragon-slayer. This Sigemund, as the audience would know,[25] slew a dragon and seized its treasure; but the treasure had a curse laid upon it which ultimately brought about the death of the hero. Only the slaying of

the dragon and the taking of the treasure are mentioned in *Beowulf*, but it is certain that the audience would be familiar with the entire story. The point of the Sigemund digression is to suggest parallels between Sigemund's career and that of Beowulf. The minstrel pays a proper compliment in choosing to compare Beowulf with the greatest of monster-slayers known to the Germanic world. It is left to the audience of the poem to recall the tragic consequence of Sigemund's action, and to think of what will happen to Beowulf in later life when he is fated to face the same situation, and the same doom. Such digressions have their virtue not in the stories themselves, which were already well known and needed only to be partially related, but in the way they are employed to achieve a cumulative end. Unlike its Old Norse analogues, *Beowulf* presents not a straightforward narrative, but a series of vivid pictorial splashes against an unstable moving background, the allusions adding both colour and depth to the structure while never breaking its overall organic unity. The poem's structure, like its verbal style, progresses by a series of deliberative parallels and variations towards a unified whole. The net effect is monumental. A narrative poem does not necessarily lose anything by our being already familiar with the plot. It gains enormously in that kind of ironic anticipation peculiar to earlier Germanic literature. The poet is not concerned with suspense; he is, after all, writing not a detective story but a stately exposition of a particular theme.

The poet's theme is the nature of the heroic life – more specifically, the function and character of leadership in heroic society. The didactic content of the poem is high. Even where the poet is not directly moralizing, it is easy enough to see the poem advancing through a series of sententiae culminating in Hrothgar's so-called 'sermon' or 'homily' (ll.1687f). In the beginning we are presented with an image of strong Germanic kingship in the person of Scyld Scefing, the founder of his nation's prosperity; in the face of hostile armies, he struck terror into his neighbours, forcing them to pay tribute in submission. This is greeted in terms of unqualified praise: 'That was a great king!' It is the worst possible fate, insists the poet, for a nation to be without a strong king. Subsequently, we are shown a son born to Scyld, who by goodness and generosity won the support and loyalty of his people. Among all nations, says the poet, it is only through those actions which merit praise that a man may prosper. This is the key to the heroic ethic: action which leads to glory and praise, *lof* and *dom*, to the attainment of which all men should direct themselves. Life is fleeting: we shall all die; let us therefore so act as to merit the praise and remembrance of men. Scyld's great-grandson, Hrothgar, had been a fine example of the heroic king in his youth. Such success in arms and so great a fame attended him, we are told, that kinsmen were eager to serve him, and his comitatus increased in size to a formidable army. Princes from distant lands flocked to a court which seems to have been a northern equivalent of that of Arthur in the sub-Roman West.

It is against this background that we see the introduction of the hall Heorot, the major symbol of the first half of the poem – the integrity of which it is Beowulf's object to preserve. The power of the hall as a poetic image is clear: the practical and emotional centre of heroic society, all that a man could wish; and its destruction therefore the negation of all that society stood for. The home of Hrothgar's people, their source of joy and national harmony, Heorot is shown to be less the palace of a king than the symbol of Denmark as a nation state. It was given a princely name, and would be known to occupy a site of extreme sacred antiquity in the Germanic North. At its inauguration there is feasting and music, the universal symbols of order and harmony; the minstrel sings a hymn of creation. (ll.89–98). And yet at the very moment of its erection we are forewarned of its eventual destruction. The audience in any case knew very well what the end would be – and Beowulf has not yet entered into his business of saving it from the monsters. The implication is not that his actions are so much futile, as transient. All the glories of mankind are temporary; it is necessary to recognize the reality of this before we can begin to understand the nature of the heroic life.

Thus in his youth, Hrothgar had been the type of the ideal Germanic leader, possessed of both wisdom and courage, the mental and physical strength that such a position demands. But while old and full of years, and still the archetypal wise king, Hrothgar now no longer possesses the physical strength he once had. So it is that he has need of Beowulf's services. He is not a feeble king: he has had a great career behind him; and it would not be a worthily heroic picture if he were seen to be in any way weak or cowardly, a lame dog to be helped over a stile. He allows himself to accept Beowulf's offer of assistance, since it merely represents just repayment of help the young Hrothgar had once been able to afford the hero's father in an hour of need. At a time when Hrothgar's physical strength is failing with age, his court apparently falls prey to an external force of disruption. This takes the form of depredation by the monster Grendel, a wretched and unnatural outcast, creature of chaos and outer darkness.

Anglo-Saxon society felt itself closely surrounded by the whole para-phernalia of common pagan fear: hobgoblins, trolls, elves, things that go bump in the night, which dwelt in the wastelands, swamps, and deep forests, approaching human awareness only at night in darkness – and against which the warmth of the hall and its society offered the only security. Early medieval Europe had no alternative but to externalize its personal and institutional neuroses, and the monster provided a con-venient mechanism for fear, then as now. Whatever their origins, physical or mental, it is clear that such monsters represent an evil that could, and should, be encountered and opposed. Not that monsters like Grendel can be defeated once and for all; for as the perpetuation of the feud by Grendel's mother demonstrates, the price of freedom is eternal vigilance. The main outline of Grendel's function within the poem is plain: a creature of darkness and night, outcast by God from the society of men, together with hobgoblins and all other monstrous progenies hostile to human happiness. Associated by the poet with Cain, primordial kin-slayer and therefore symbol of elemental social disunity (ll.105–14), he stalks abroad, ravaging only by night when the sun, *Godes candel*, is far from the sky. He has made his home with all that is antithetical to Heorot, inhabiting an unvisited land, solitary paths, perilous swamps, and the misty wastelands. His lair is a place very like hell, a dreadful region shunned by all that is good in nature like the noble hart, *heorot*, a major Germanic symbol of both regality and purity (ll.1357–72). Banished from the society of men, obliged to take the paths of an outcast, he treads the wilderness as an exile, a solitary figure. Such loneliness has none of the romantic aura that a later age might ascribe to it. For heroic society, the solitary figure is invariably suspect and probably vicious, an object of fear and distrust. Although this monster has been proscribed by God, Danish society seems still to be subject to his depredation. He is not effectively banished for ever. Haunting the borders of human society, he is always present, neither in nor fully out of it, the corporeal substance of fear, always ready to intrude given opportunity enough. Well known to both the people and the counsellors of the king, Grendel and his dam tread the wastelands in the likeness of men, but misshapen, a mockery of the form of human society, and a public enemy. In this shape, then, some sort of evildoer is found among the Danes, a hidden enemy inflicting unheard-of injury, havoc, and disgrace. It is not the physical splendour of Heorot which so angers Grendel, but the order and peace he discerns there. Above all, it is the sweet sound of the harp, archetypal symbol of harmony, that the creature of chaos is unable to bear (ll.86–90). Thus it was that the outcast Satan beheld the newly created Eden according to the Cædmonian *Genesis* (see below, pp. 77f). Grendel has centred his destructive spite on the heroic society that inhabited the hall Heorot, and apparently without encountering any effective opposition.

The ancient order seems to have proved ultimately inadequate to oppose such an enemy. Heorot's king, although once a renowned war-leader and still both valiant and wise, is now incapable in his own person of bearing the brunt of the attacks. Those to whom he might have looked for support in such a situation, the counsellors of his people or his own comitatus, both fail him. Asleep in Heorot, grown fat with feasting, they prove all too easy a prey; and the monster has become accustomed to wreak havoc among them, taking up thirty thegns at a time. Despite boasting in their cups, the hollowness of heroic Scylding society based on a free *beot* is soon apparent, and the comitatus dwindles partly through sheer inactivity and partly through simple lack of courage. The onslaught is so forceful and persistent that the old pattern of free loyalties as represented by the company in Heorot breaks up, and the hall is abandoned.

It is plain that external vulnerability is merely symptomatic of internal debility, however; and as Beowulf himself is later to point out, Grendel could not have wrought such havoc unless the seeds of spiritless discord were already present in the state of Denmark (ll.590f). This disease is epitomized for us in the person of Unferth, the court orator who seats himself at Hrothgar's feet and in whom the king is said to place implicit trust. The name, literally, 'Discordia', or perhaps simply 'Lacking spirit', sounds fictional and possibly the figure was an invention of the author. The conventional 'wicked counsellor' is a common literary device employed to account for errors made by otherwise good rulers without compromising their greatness. It was at the instance of such personae that an otherwise good king might be prompted to embark on some disastrous course of action, to court defeat in war or to slay his own offspring.

The old pattern of loyalties proving unable to contain these new conditions, a new 'kind' of hero is required. The introduction of this hero into the decayed Danish kingdom is like the advent of a saviour – a breath of new and vigorous life. He is a stranger to the land, but is immediately recognizable for his plain virtues. Through the eyes of Hrothgar's coast-warden, the hero is seen as an essentially active agent, clothed in the fine, bright armour of his business. He is in every way remarkable, singled out from other men as a strong-willed leader. He is a man with a personal sense of mission. His fine war-gear is not merely the affection of pride, but the outward promise of strong action, equipment deserving respect. Arms and armour form a persistent and powerful symbol of heroic activity throughout the poem. And in contrast to the current Danish malaise, this is a man of decisive, strong, and vital action who can distinguish between words and deeds (ll.288–89). To such a one, the coast-warden recognizes, it will be given successfully to survive the hostile encounter. Nevertheless, as Beowulf himself admits, *Gæð a wyrd swa hio scel*. ['Fate will always go as it must'] (l.455). Returning victorious from his second fight against the underwater monsters, the hero concedes that this time his sole strength would have been insufficient without the intervention of Providence, the ruler of victories. He brings with him as proof of his exploit not only Grendel's head, but the hilt of the sword with which the deed was accomplished – and which significantly bears a pictorial allusion to the giants who had warred against God and were thus destroyed in the Flood. Hrothgar closely examines the hilt, so eloquent of the ever-present possibility of sudden change in fortune; and it is this he uses as the starting-point for his so-called sermon, which forms both the structural and thematic hinge of the poem (ll. 1687–1768). He contrasts Beowulf's virtues with the miserable savagery of the treacherous king Heremod, prophesying the hero's likely accession to power. Beowulf has both the strength and wisdom necessary for high office, but must be warned of the cardinal heroic sin of arrogance. Worldly success will often lull the conscience to sleep, and then a hero proves particularly vulnerable to the attacks of evil – for then suddenly, in a variety of ways, death may come upon him, either violently through sword or arrow, or simply through the inevitable decay of old age. Beowulf is therefore urged to take the better part, which is eternal gain, avoiding pride. Only a little while will he be at the height of his powers before old age, disease, or the edge of the sword will plunder his strength: its transience is inevitable.

The second half of the poem might be expected to assess how far the hero lives up to Hrothgar's prophecy of him in face of the inevitable facts of reality. But in fact we are shown very little of his subsequent career, although various allusions hint at such matters as his presence at the death of Hygelac and his role in the Swedish Wars. If, as some have supposed, *Beowulf* was intended as a 'mirror for princes', in which young men might enounter in imagination a variety of ennobling situations and thus learn the attitudes appropriate to their place in heroic society, we might have expected the poet to have given full rein to a taste for battle scenes, showing the hero engaged in noble exploits. But there are only oblique allusions to actual physical battles, and the poet seems deliberately to have minimized any battle scene in which the hero might possibly have taken part. Although he has a whole aura of courageous action built round him, the only enemies we see our hero confront are not even human, but incredible monsters and supernatural beings. This then is a curious kind of heroism in some ways. We are soon aware that Beowulf's struggles have broader implications than their outward appearance, involving not merely physical but moral courage. And if there is any moral content, then the conflict with monsters provides a more suitable vehicle than any human battle, however well described, could ever be, simply because the forces of evil are better seen in monstrous shapes. The age had not yet arrived when any human enemy could be considered entirely vicious. The open society of Migration Age Europe recognized no such concept as *lèse-majesté*, so that Hrothulf's displacement of Hrothgar's sons would be regarded as natural; and his subsequent reign was long remembered as a golden age in Scandinavian tradition. The greatness of an Ohthere or Ongentheow could be readily acknowledged because, though avowed enemies of Beowulf's people, they conform to the heroic ethic. Mere hostility is understandable, whereas greed and the swearing of false oaths are abhorrent because they corrode the fabric of heroic society. It is significant that in the event Beowulf is not destroyed by any human foe but by a dragon.

The monsters of the first part and the dragon of the second are similar in some respects. Both are elemental, primeval enemies; and both are public scourges, intent upon the humiliation of men, destroying their dwellings and ultimately the courts of their kings. Both are creatures of the night, unwilling to engage in their depredations by the light of day. However, whereas Grendel's enmity was self-motivated and aroused instinctively not by the material wealth and prosperity of Heorot but by its harmonious and joyful order, the dragon remains happily inactive until its anger is provoked by the theft of a jewelled goblet which the dragon believes to belong to itself alone. The man who rifles the dragon's hoard is not described by the poet as any kind of hero, but as an outlaw and a sin-troubled soul (1.2226). That dragons, like trolls, have some ulterior significance is obvious; as the tenth-century scientific writer Byrhtferth of Ramsey would say: 'What are dragons, but people who are evil and contentious and enemies of God, and the ruin of their own souls'. [26] Those well read in the Bible could find confirmation for the Satanic associations of dragons. But dragons had a long-established mythological history in the North, and any contemporary audience would readily have identified the beast of popular tradition. Their origins could be traced to those 'gold-guarding griffins' which Herodotus thought occupied the extreme north of Europe. [27] This function is well defined by the Old English verse maxim: 'The dragon dwells in a barrow, ancient and proud in treasures'. [28] Their maiden-devouring propensities were a later romantic innovation. Conventionally in early Germanic literature dragons act as the miserly hoarders of material wealth, concerned not to use it but simply to allow it to moulder while they sleep, coiled round both it and the barrows, the graves of dead men that traditionally contain it. This image of elemental parsimony, (the sin of Heremod which Beowulf had been adjured to shun), closely overlaps with the potent symbols of arms rusting through inaction, and the derelict hall. The so-called 'lay of the lone survivor' (ll.2247–66) lists those features of the orderly and active life which are now lacking. Those who formerly delighted in the dragon's treasure, as in every pleasure of hall, are now all passed away; there is none to wield the sword, nor to polish the cup. The arms and armour moulder and decay, like the warriors who had worn them. There is neither music of the harp, nor any stamping of swift steeds in the courtyard; no hawk swoops through this empty and desolate hall. All active agents are now dead, and the treasure is buried with the dead, useless. This is where the dragon finds it and covets it. It is simple, profitless greed that the dragon here represents, a slumbering in pos-session, which, as Hrothgar's sermon had insisted, is fatal to men.

The end comes about suddenly, almost accidentally. As Hrothgar had warned, one can never tell what change of fortune may occur. It is significant that when this trouble comes to Beowulf – the destruction of his own, like Hrothgar's court – he is in much the same position the Danish king had been in when, as a young man, the hero had lent the old king his strong aid. Beowulf has ruled his kingdom well and strongly for fifty years – just the length of time that Hrothgar had reigned – but now he too is old and subject to the weakness of age. But although old, Beowulf is still personally courageous. His weakness is of a different order from Hrothgar's inactivity. But the foe that now oppresses his kingdom is of a different order also. Contrary to his usual spirit, Beowulf falls prey to dismal thoughts. Although no coward, the hero is no longer resolute and self-confident, now despairing of God's strength to support his arm. Uneasy and restless, he gloomily anticipates his doom. The armour in which Beowulf trusts will prove no greater protection than the walls of the barrow in which the dragon puts its faith.

If the great king finally fails, however, there is another who does not. There comes to him *in extremis*, just as he himself once came to the aid of the elderly Hrothgar, a strong prince and heir to his spirit, Wiglaf. His action in joining battle is both an appeal to the heroic code and a recognition of the old king's personal stature. He is certain that, for as long as Beowulf had ruled the kingdom, he had been the most honoured hero in the world. And when at last Wiglaf ignores the express wishes of his leader in coming to his aid, it was because the old hero did not now deserve to die alone – if only for the sake of all his past deeds.

But Beowulf's death is merely the climax of the poem. The tragic denouement is to follow. Now, of course, as Wiglaf knows, the giving of swords and all the joys of native land must end, with the dispersal of Beowulf's people into enforced and despised exile (ll. 2884–90). Whether the entire Geatish nation was actually annihilated at this point as some historians suppose, is immaterial; for the purpose of the narrative the issue is clear. The messenger who announces the death of the king to his people serves to confirm both Beowulf's great *dom* and the dangerous vulnerability of the nation consequent upon the passing of so strong a ruler. The destruction of the kingdom is inevitable, the messenger gloomily prophesying a simultaneous invasion from both north and south (2910–23). Nevertheless, whatever may result, no one can deny that Beowulf had been a great king. As he had wished, his people erect for him a great barrow high up on Whale's Cape to be recognized from afar as both a memorial and a landmark for all those who in future will urge their ships over the darkness of the seas. The gold, which the hero had died to win, they again commit to the earth 'as useless to men as it was before'. But the final words of the poem belong to Beowulf's comitatus. They declare him to have been the greatest of heroes, of all kings in the world the gentlest and most gracious, kindest to his people and most desirous of renown – one who had truly achieved that *lof* and *dom* for which, as we learned in the beginning, all men should strive.

Death in some fashion or another must come at last to even the greatest of heroes. Given the ultimate fact of mutability, the Germanic hero is invariably a tragic hero; his virtues are characteristically seen in defence – and often in defeat. But his tragedy has far greater consequences than the merely personal tragedy we associate with the classical or Shakespearian tragic hero. Hamlet, for example, moves in a neurotic world of inner conflict and self-doubt; between his values and those of society at large there exists a wide gulf. Beowulf, on the other hand, does not feel Hamlet's need constantly to question his motives; he and his people share a community of interests. Although his personal stature is so great, and although in the end he goes out alone to face his fate, he nevertheless has the strongest ties with his people. He is the one hope of their culture – the culmination of a tradition, identifying and embodying the fundamental values and aspirations of his nation. Hamlet's disaster is individual to himself. At his fall Denmark is not destroyed; if anything, the kingdom is cleansed by Hamlet's death. Beowulf's death has epic implications: it marks the end of a way of life, the destruction of a civilization. The death of Hector resulted in the fall of Troy. Arthur's death meant the end of the Round Table. Beowulf's death will bring with it the demise of the kingdom of the Geats. The poet puts into the mouth of the messenger a full awareness of the fate Beowulf had gone so willingly to meet, and which as a result his people must also meet. In classical tragedy the hero struggles against the fate which some personal tragic flaw has brought about. In this kind of epic literature, however, evil is usually confined to agents external to the hero. The epic hero knows his opponent as well as the source of his own strength, though in the end this knowledge is of no use to him. The epic hero goes willingly to his fate, even though the awful consequences of his choice must be as clear to himself as anyone else. Beowulf dismisses his comitatus, but continues to act in the light of the ethical requirements of that group. He believes for an instant – the instant of *beot* – that he *may* overcome the dragon, that he *may* preserve the way of life they all know. The hero defies his fate, but in a spirit of resignation: fate will go always as it must; a man can achieve so much, and no more; he cannot, after all, live for ever. His decision may seem to be brought about by pride but, unlike the classical hubris, it is external and clear, not what he but society expects. And whether victorious or defeated, therefore, the end will be the glory, *lof* and *dom*, for which Beowulf, of all men, was the most eager.

In one sense therefore, heroic verse is concerned with the fate of the individual rather than that of his nation, although the two are often linked. While their lives are often played out against a background of significant events, the exploits recorded are not, in themselves, such as to affect the fate of nations. The protracted and savage wars between the Goths and Huns are reduced to a personal quarrel. The great struggle in which the Huns destroyed Gundahari's Burgundians is represented as merely a family dispute, as though it had no greater historical moment than the mutual decimation of a little-known group of Frisians and Danes at Finnsburh. Significant events are disregarded or reduced to the scene of an individual prince's hall. Although in fact armies of many thousands took the field, the heroic unit of reference is the comitatus. The reduction in scale serves to enhance the heroic integrity because the critical issues are unobscured by larger external affairs.

While the names of the heroes, like the stories attached to them, undergo strange mutations when recorded in different countries at different times, there is no reason to doubt that the persons described, if not all the exploits attributed to them, have some historical substance. Of course the poet shaped his material to meet artistic and other ends. Historical events and personalities are conflated, transferred, simplified. Relative chronologies, even simple relationships, are unimportant. Widsith's claims to have visited the courts of heroes who lived centuries apart simply underlines the point. The dynastic relationships suggested in *Beowulf* are incompatible with later Scandinavian tradition, and any effort to piece together a coherent history of the Germanic North based on this material is naturally frustrated. Historians who suppose incidental confusion rather than fundamental irrelevance, misunderstand the poet's premise. It is truly irrelevant whether Beowulf returned to eventually become king in Geatland, or remained at Heorot to live and die a favoured *berserkr* of Hrothgar's successor, Hrothulf.

The verse of the Heroic Age is clearly interpretative, the literary persona diverging from the historic one at a relatively early stage in its existence. The inventive element in the poem is important; heroes are often attached to, even identified with, a tribal myth of much greater antiquity. The respective stages are recognizable in *Beowulf*. The poet's primary function is seen in the praise of the brave defence of Heorot, enhancing the hero in question by comparison with a hero of former times whose exploits have already become legendary. The plot of *Beowulf* as a whole represents a developed stage in the simple encomium, in which the hero is identified with larger national myths: the troll-slaying *berserkr* and dragon-slaying king. (It was at an equivalent stage and similar date that Arthur became the subject of those aetiological myths of South Wales and the West Country which Nennius appends to his *Historia*.[29]) But in its final form *Beowulf* marks yet a third stage; writing at the very close of the European Heroic Age, the author has left a measured and highly sophisticated critique of heroic society as a whole and the role of leadership within it.

As in the *Finnsburh* or *Waldere* fragments, the persons depicted are

primarily types, defined by their actions rather than by close characterization, either of appearance or psychology. Even at so late a stage,
however, the world of romance is far away. The protagonist of heroic
literature stalks across a real world which the poet is at some pains to
delineate. Physical details are introduced not for the sake of decoration
but for the verisimilitude they impart. The scene is no never-never land of
fairy-tale wonder, but a material world which can be recognized by the
audience as its own. 'Once upon a time' is a formula for irrelevance.
There is no point in praising a hero who could never have lived. Our
native belief that giants once lived in the world derives not from imagination but from experience. With the passage of time the hero acquires a
more gigantic stature, magnified, distorted even, by the twilight through
which he moves. But he never appears supernatural rather than merely
superhuman. The hero may possess remarkable attributes, but they are
not magical. Beowulf's *berserkr* tendencies are well illustrated in the
perfectly credible, if heroic, account of his crushing to death the Frankish
champion, Dæghrefn, before escaping across the Rhine bearing a large
quantity of looted war-gear. It is merely an extension of this which sets
him to fight the hideous underwater trolls – and it may have seemed
appropriate that such a man should have ended his life facing a dragon
rather than a human foe. But although outmatching ordinary mortals,
the poet avoids any temptation to endow his hero with supernatural
properties. There is no mention of the shape-shifting stories which so
easily attach themselves to such men at other times or in other societies.
Fictional mechanisms such as disguises, dreams, speaking animals, all
await the development of romance. Neither God nor the gods motivate
the action. The underlying assumption is that man himself has sufficient
claim to our interest without recourse to supernatural powers on his
behalf. Heroic poetry is concerned with the possibilities open to the
human spirit, even if the standards set should seem too impossibly high to
emulate. It is avowedly unimaginative because of its claims to be true.

The circumstances of the hero's death are subject to particular
scrutiny, since this represents the culmination of his heroic career. It is
interesting because of its very inevitability. And because common to all
men, the fact of death is one element with which the audience may readily
identify. The manner of his death raises in most piquant and critical
terms the motives and standards of conduct which underly his
achievement. Here more than anywhere it is the poet's function to
transform the commonplace realities of misconduct and failure. The
heroic ethos will allow neither Eormenric's despair and consequent
suicide at the approach of the Huns, nor the more lurid haemorrhage of
Attila's wedding-night. These might be recorded accurately by the cold
eye of the classical historian, but the heroic poet brought both events into
alignment with the favoured Finnsburh model: death through vengeance

arising from the dilemma of divided loyalties. Nor are heroes slain in the random slaughter we know to have been the reality of a medieval battlefield. The death of a hero was best undergone confronting an opponent worthy of him; any less would detract from his stature. The greatness and heroic virtue of one's enemy is readily acknowledged. Political cause and effect are ignored; blame or praise for any issue are apportioned not in relation to external factors but in proportion to the individual's response to the situation which arises. It was Augustine or Jerome from a safe distance who would denounce Attila, *flagellum dei*, not those who encountered him face to face. No human enemy will yet be identified with Antichrist; the assumption of his brutality or inferiority belongs to a later age. It is this necessity which lies behind the many tales of single combat, real or supposed, of which we hear. And this too may account for the custom of ascribing one's own heroic deeds to the leader. Hygelac is fortunate that Beowulf should prove so unusually loyal to his leader's dynasty – at once the ideal and the natural development of the comitatus ethic, the only possible resolution of its inherently centrifugal tendencies. The existence of too close a contender for public estimation underlines the tensions always present in heroic society.

Heroic poetry celebrates mere episodes in the lives of men caught up in a constant process of disintegration and dissolution. The sudden reversal of fortune which is an ever-present theme of heroic literature had its model in reality, in the total eclipse not merely of an individual comitatus but of the greatest European powers: the destruction of the Hunnish Empire after the death of Attila, of the Vandals after Genseric, or the Ostrogoths after Theodoric. The early Germanic kingdoms, spawned from the disintegration of the Roman Empire in the West, proved short-lived themselves. Renown, as Tacitus remarked, is easier won among perils,[30] and the greatest heroes emerge not in the heyday of a culture but at its end. Beowulf and Arthur, close contemporaries, emerge in the twilight of their nations, the sole rallying-point, the only hope of a people in the throes of its historical destruction. According to Cassiodorus, the Ostrogothic hero Gensimundus, who reigned in the ruins after Eormenric's empire had been destroyed by the Huns, was widely celebrated in poetry, but has left only his name to history.[31] These heroes strut out their brief lives in a misty age which endows them with both magnitude and poignancy, theirs being a heroic task because hopeless, defying an apparently inevitable consequence.

It is the facts of reality which impart the elegiac tone that pervades all heroic verse. When Gelimer, last king of the Vandals, was facing final defeat by Herulian mercenaries in Byzantine pay, he asked their leader to send him a lyre with which to accompany a song he had composed on his own misfortune. We are not told the content of Gelimer's dirge, but he could not have failed to recall that less than 100 years earlier his predecessors dominated Europe, sacked Rome itself, and founded the singularly wealthy kingdom of Carthage. Led captive with his comitatus through the streets of Byzantium, he is described repeating to himself: 'Vanity of vanities, all is vanity'.[32] Mutability, national and personal, is the *Beowulf*-poet's constant theme. Either violence or, much more dreadful, the decay of old age will sooner or later frustrate the heroic impetus. The elderly Hrothgar wept when he remembered the exploits of his youth, just as the minstrels who told of Attila's deeds roused some in spirit, but caused older men to weep since, enfeebled by age, their courageous spirit must perforce remain unsatisfied.[33]

There is no doubt but that one of the functions of such poems was to inspire emulation; the audience is constantly exhorted: 'Learn from this . . . thus ought a man to do. . . '. The early Germani chanted the praises of heroes as they advanced into battle, and the songs Aneirin describes the British warriors of Gododdin singing as they rode into defeat against the Saxons at Catraeth[34] were probably of the same order. The only specific information we have as to the likely nature of such battle-songs comes from the eleventh century: before Hastings the *Song of Roland* and before Stikelstad the *Bjarkamál* (concerning the disastrous attack on Lejre/Heorot in which Hrólfr Kraki and his comitatus, including Bjarki/Beowulf, all die).[35] It was apparently not the glorious victory but the glories of defeat that best suited the heroic temper. The songs thought appropriate during the celebrations following Grendel's defeat were said to be 'true and sad' (l. 2109).

*Roland* and *Bjarkamál* are songs of defeat, but not defeatism. Indeed, the heroic posture depends upon the possibility of defeat, which is at once acknowledged and defied. An awareness of the universality of mutability should not be mistaken for mere pessimism or a sense of futility, although in a closed rather than open society it might engender fatalism, degrading the activity of the individual will. The fundamental assumption is that man's will, because free, may prove superior to the fate which sooner or later must destroy him – a dynamic ethic of active courage, asserting human capacity for achievement unaided by supernatural means, whether divine or merely magical. The hero's role is to develop his potential to the greatest his *wyrd* will allow, living each day as if it were his last. At any time a reversal of fortune might occur: 'Fate always goes as it must'. The hero inhabits a world of risks and decisions, and our admiration is aroused by the unflinching spirit with which he confronts the realities of that world, attempting tasks beyond the imagination, or at least the abilities, of the rank and file. The dangerous environment does not of itself engender heroism. Unlike the Roman, the 'barbarian' was not necessarily prepared to participate in violence for its own sake; Saxon captives would commit mutual suicide rather than engage in the gratuitous violence of gladiatorial contests.[36] Heroism in the technical sense is not to be confused with bravery, nor yet recklessness. Tacitus said of the Germanic *comites* that they would debate at a time that cuts out pretence but decide at a time that precludes mistake.[37] When the *beot* coincides with action, heroism is the result: the boast achieved. The hero's *beot* is a defiant exercise of will in face of what will sooner or later prove his downfall, the *wyrd* he is incapable of postponing.

*Wyrd* is a sophisticated concept, corresponding exactly to neither 'fate' nor 'fortune', but meaning rather 'course of events, that which will come about'. Whether or not this is pre-ordained in some way is strictly irrelevant to the moral issue. The hero must strive for *lof* and *dom* in the face of whatever odds he happens to encounter. Eventually the odds must prove too great; in the meantime the fact that *lif is læne* was no excuse for the hesitancy or despair which, as Beowulf asserts in at least his early life and in the advice he gives, is the enemy of heroism. This anti-defeatist assertion of heroic free will found its moral counterpart in the Christian world in Pelagius's insistence that man ought properly to be considered master of his own fate, defying secular and ecclesiastical bureaucracies in striving after perfection – the unrealizability of which should not be admitted, although witnessed on all sides. The heroic act, religious or secular, consists in the progression: *posse, velle, esse.* In so far as God will intervene, it is to help those who help themselves: *yðelice, syþðan he eft astod (Beowulf,* l.1556).

Beowulf's three great fights mark a progression in our understanding of the source of the hero's power: from total self-reliance, through closer questioning of the adequacy of his sole strength and recognition that God provides the necessary resources to the right man; and finally in old age falling into despair thinking that he must have offended God in some way. The figure of Beowulf himself contains the dilemma of heroic society – the need for a strong man, and yet uncertainty as to the source of his authority. The poem is full of ambiguity and unease at the condition of heroic society, and already anticipates the clerical response of Alcuin – the notion that man's power is greatest when acknowledging that he is merely the channel through which God's power flows into the world, with the consequent feudal ideology of *auctoritas dei gratia* (see above, p. 11). The hero's self-awareness, his recognition of the nature of the world and his own part in it, is easily mistaken by lesser men for lack of due humility. 'It is no man's measure but mine alone to display heroism', says Beowulf before dying. He believes for an instant – the moment of *beot* – that he may still overcome. It is an excess of heroism which denies the essentially reciprocal nature of comitatus society. The active ideal of self-reliance is an élitist and isolative one, and ultimately alien to the open society which engenders it. In practice the discord that Grendel and his kind represent is always ready to intrude. The 'adventurous act' leaves its record in a genuinely ethical literature which, albeit fragmentary and mutilated, may still arouse our admiration and awe. The conflagration kindled by the barbarian incendiaries of a devastated world could make a slum look like Valhalla.[38]

## Notes

1. Compare *Cornelii Taciti, Opera Minora*, edited by M. Winterbottom and R. M. Ogilvie, (Oxford, 1975), p. 38; *The Annals of Tacitus*, edited by F. R. D. Goodyear (Cambridge, 1972, in progress), II, p. 60; Jordanes, *Getica*, edited by T. Mommsen, *Monumenta Germaniae Historica, Auctorum Antiquissimorum*, v (1) (Berlin, 1882), p. 65; etc.

2. Jordanes, *Getica*, edited by Mommsen, p. 138.

3. *The Genealogical Preface to the 'Anglo-Saxon Chronicle'*, edited by B. Dickins (Cambridge, 1952).

4. Bede refers to a Continental volume of 'cosmographies' which Ceolfrith, Abbot of Monkwearmouth-Jarrow from 690 to 716, gave to the scholarly King Aldfrith of Northumbria in exchange for some land; *Opera Historica*, edited by C. Plummer (Oxford, 1896), I, p. 380; compare J. D. A. Ogilvy, *Books Known to the English, 597–1066* (Cambridge, Massachusetts, 1967), pp. 123–24.

5. Compare *Nornagests þáttr*, edited by G. Jónsson and B. Vilhjálmsson, *Fornaldarsögur Norðurlanda*, (Reykjavik, 1943–44), I, pp. 305–35.

6. *Sources and Analogues of Old English Poetry*, edited by D. G. Calder (Cambridge, 1983), II, p. 104.

7. *Monumenta Germaniae Historica, Scriptores Rerum Langobardicarum et Italicarum, Saec. VI–IX*, edited by G. Waitz (Hanover, 1878), p. 600.

8. G. B. Brown, *The Arts in Early England*, second edition (London, 1926–37), VI (1), p. 29, pl. vii.

9. *Edda: Die Lieder des Codex Regius nebst verwandten Denkmälern*, edited by G. Neckel, third edition, revised by H. Kuhn (Heidelberg, 1962), pp. 116–23.

10. Ibid., p. 122, para. 31.

11. Compare the Old High German *Nibelungenlied*, edited by K. Bartsch, second edition, revised by H. de Boor (Wiesbaden, 1979), and the Old Norse *Þiðriks Saga af Bern*, edited by H. Bertelsen (Copenhagen, 1905–11).

12. Compare the Old High German Horant, in *Kudrun*, edited by B. Symons, fourth edition, revised by B. Boesch (Tubingen, 1964), *passim*, or the Old Norse Hjarrandi, in *Die Bosa-saga*, edited by O. L. Jiriczek (Strasbourg, 1893), p. 46; see

also W. K. Grimm, *Die Deutsche Heldensage*, third edition, revised by R. Steig (Gütersloh, 1889), p. 377.

13. It seems to have been common practice for patrons to give their court minstrels nicknames; see F. Jónsson, *Den Oldnorske og Oldislanske Litteraturs Historie*, second edition (Copenhagen, 1920–24), I, p. 328ff.

14. *Monumenta Germaniae Historica, Poetae Latini*, VI, edited by K. Strecker (Weimar, 1951), pp. 1–85.

15. *Cornelii Taciti, Opera Minora*, edited by Winterbottom and Ogilvie, p. 41.

16. Ibid., p. 38.

17. See E. A. Thompson, *A History of Attila and the Huns* (Oxford, 1948), pp. 65–66; the later ascription is presumably geographical rather than racial, since at this time the Burgundian kingdom lay on the Meuse, later Frankish heartland territory.

18. *Cornelii Taciti, Opera Minora*, edited by Winterbottom and Ogilvie, pp. 47–48.

19. Ibid., p. 44.

20. *Edda*, edited by Neckel, third edition, pp. 240–47; *Nibelungenlied*, edited by Bartsch, second edition.

21. For the *locus classicus* of the hall image, see Introduction, p. 9.

22. Such lengthy encounters are attested from historical sources; see for example, the three-day battle during which the Goths were defeated by Narses, Procopius Caesariensis, *Opera Omnia*, edited by J. Haury, revised by G. Wirth (Leipzig, 1963), II, p. 673.

23. See G. V. Smithers, *The Making of 'Beowulf'* (Durham, 1962).

24. An observation deriving, like the title of this chapter, from J. R. R. Tolkien's seminal lecture, '*Beowulf*: the Monsters and the Critics', *Proceedings of the British Academy*, 22 (1936), 245–95 (pp. 273–74, 278).

25. Compare *Vǫlsunga Saga: The Saga of the Volsungs*, edited by R. G. Finch (London, 1965).

26. *Byrhtferth's Manual*, edited by S. J. Crawford, Early English Text Society, Original Series, 177 (London, 1929), pp. 140–41.

27. *Heroditi, Historiarum Libri IX*, edited by H. R. Dietsch, second edition, revised by H. Kallenberg (Leipzig, 1894), p. 326.

28. *Maxims II*, ll. 26–27, in *The Anglo-Saxon Minor Poems*, edited by G. P. Krapp and E. v. K. Dobbie, The Anglo-Saxon Poetic Records (London, 1931–53), VI, p. 56.

29. *Monumenta Germaniae Historica, Auctorum Antiquissimorum*, XIII, edited by T. Mommsen (Berlin, 1898), p. 199ff.

30. *Cornelii Taciti, Opera Minora*, edited by Winterbottom and Ogilvie, p. 44.

31. *Cassiodori Senatoris Variae*, edited by T. Mommsen, *Monumenta Germaniae Historica, Auctorum Antiquissimorum*, xii (Berlin, 1894), p. 239.

32. Procopius Caesariensis, *Opera Omnia*, edited by Haury, i, pp. 447, 457.

33. Priscus, *Opera*, in *Historici Graeci Minores*, edited by L. Dindorf (Leipzig, 1870), i, p. 317.

34. *Canu Aneirin*, edited by I. Williams, second edition (Cardiff, 1961), pp. 4, 7, etc.

35. Wace, *Le Roman de Rou*, edited by A. J. Holden (Paris, 1970–73), ii, p. 183; Snorri Sturlasson, *Óláfs Saga Helga*, in *Konunga Sögur*, edited by G. Jónsson (Reykjavik, 1967) i, pp. 349–50.

36. Symmachus, *Opera*, in *Monumenta Germaniae Historica, Auctorum Antiquissimorum*, vi (1) edited by O. Seeck (Berlin, 1883) p. 57.

37. *Cornelii Taciti, Opera Minora*, edited by Winterbottom and Ogilvie, p. 49.

38. An image borrowed from A. J. Toynbee's monumental *A Study of History* (London, 1934–59), viii, p. 79.

# Chapter 3
# Verbum de Verbo

*Cædmon's Creation-Hymn, Genesis A,*
*Exodus, and The Dream of the Rood.*

The circumstances surrounding the development of Christian literature in
Old English are fortuitously recorded by Bede – monk, scholar, and
historian of Jarrow, Co. Durham (*fl.* 695–735) in a remarkable piece of
descriptive literary history included in his *Historia Ecclesiastica*.[1] Some time
during the period in which his friend Abbess Hild presided over the mixed
monastery of monks and nuns at Whitby in East Yorkshire (658–80), local
people brought to the community there a farm-labourer called Cædmon
who had been the subject of a strange experience which they considered
miraculous and concerning which they sought an authoritative opinion. It
seems that because of some physiological or psychological disability
Cædmon had never been able to join in the customary exchange of
convivial songs which formed such an important part of evening entertainment in the hall. Embarrassed at the approach of the lyre, he would
get up from the table and leave, even in the middle of a meal. On the
occasion in question he had the perfect excuse since it was his turn to tend
the animals that night. So leaving the hall, he lay down to sleep in the
cowshed. There, in a dream, there came to him 'a certain person',[2] who
insists, despite Cædmon's protested lack of ability, that the man should
recite something – and gives him a theme: the Creation. At this Cædmon
immediately began to sing verses he had never before heard in praise of
God the Creator. Bede provides only a Latin paraphrase of Cædmon's
*Creation-Hymn*, but an early Northumbrian hand had added the English
text in the margins of two near-contemporary local manuscripts:

> Nu scylun hergan    hefaenricaes uard,
> metudæs maecti    end his modgidanc,
> uerc uuldurfadur    sue he uundra gihuaes,
> eci dryctin,    or astelidæ.
> He aerist scop    aelda barnum
> heben til hrofe,    haleg scepen;
> tha middungeard    moncynnæs uard,
> eci dryctin    æfter tiadæ
> firum foldu,    frea allmectig.

[Now let us praise the Keeper of the kingdom of heaven, the might of God
and the wisdom of his spirit, the work of the Father of glory, in that he, the
eternal Lord, ordained the beginning of everything that is wonderful. He, the
holy Creator, first created heaven as a roof for the children of men;
afterwards the Keeper of mankind, the eternal Lord, almighty Governor,
fashioned the world, the middle-earth, for mortals.]

In the morning Cædmon found not only that he could remember the
song but was able to add supplementary verses in the same style. Upon
revealing his experience to the steward of the estate on which he worked,
he was taken to be examined by the teaching staff at Whitby. They
choose to test his new-found powers of extempore composition by requiring him to render into poetic paraphrase overnight certain passages
of Scripture read out to him – which after a reflective interval he does.
While latter-day critics may, quite properly, require some alternative
explanation for the phenomenon, it is clear that Cædmon's contemporaries, the scholars at Whitby, and Bede himself, were convinced
that this transformed condition was nothing less than miraculous.

Of course the story of the divine gift of song received in one's sleep is a
familiar one in the early medieval world.[3] It is merely, after all, the
Christian counterpart of the divine frenzy attributed to classical poets – a
specifically pious muse. The pages of Bede contain frequent reference to
visionaries – often living in humble circumstances – whose souls are
abstracted, or conducted elsewhere by heavenly visitants while in a
trance or sleeping, which experience inspires at least greater devotion and
sometimes a transformation of life. This mystic phenomenon seems
especially characteristic of the insular Church and it may not be insignificant in this respect that Cædmon bears a Celtic rather than
Germanic name. Of course all human talents would be conventionally
ascribed to the gift of God,[4] but none more specifically so than that of
poetry. The probably ninth-century Christian poet Cynewulf in an
avowedly autobiographical passage would speak in specifically physical
terms of the act of God in 'unlocking the art of poetry his breast contained'.[5] The composition of religious literature would be considered a
form of inspired revelation for Old English authors no less than for
Moses, reputed author of the Book of Genesis, or for David, author of the
Psalms. Aldhelm relates poetic utterance directly to the doctrine of the
Logos, the poet's word inspired by the Word, *verbum de Verbo*.[6] For Bede
then, who would associate the composition of religious verse with the gift
of Pentecostal tongues,[7] Cædmon's simple nine-line hymn, unpre-
tentious, trivial even, by later standards, was necessarily imbued with a
sacred quality by reason of its numinous inspiration – a manifest instance
of divine intervention in the world of men, and as such intended to stir
men to devotion. Bede feels it necessary to apologize for the inadequacy of
his Latin paraphrase in what is the *locus classicus* of the translator's plea:

'for verse, however finely composed, cannot be translated without loss of grace and dignity'. He may well have been in awe of a venerated text, the prestige of which served to maintain its literal integrity despite extensive circulation and complex transmission. Whereas most Old English poems survive in at most one or two copies, Cædmon's *Creation-Hymn* is found in a considerable number of manuscripts with remarkably little textual variation. The 'letter' is now apparently endued with an authority inconceivable in oral tradition.

Although this order of poetry was evidently not the product of any normal literary impulse, and a purely aesthetic assessment might represent an incomplete response to its religious content, the admiration Bede evinced for Cædmon's work suggests that its perceived virtue was not dependent alone on the visionary circumstances of its origin. It is not unnatural, given Cædmon's mental preoccupation as we may assume it from his subsequent career, that his mind should first have turned to a hymn in praise of God the Creator; this places him firmly within a tradition of Christian–Latin poetry from the third century onwards. The description of Cædmon's mode of composition as a mature poet suggests a reminiscent and reflective mode of composition, listening and remembering all that he was told, turning it over in his mind 'like an animal chewing the cud', then reproducing it in the form of the most delightful verse. His mind must have been filled with all the traditional formulas, phrases, and plot- and *topos*-sequences he had heard resounding in the hall over the years. The product of Cædmon's experience was not a merely private revelation peculiar to himself alone. Active rather than contemplative, it assumes public form: the complex rhetorical medium of traditional heroic verse form intended for performance, the materials of which must have been so familiar, even if some impediment prevented his personal participation hitherto. Cædmon's language is totally traditional, consisting of a received network of oral formulas conventionally employed in the poetic eulogy of a Germanic prince, adapting his inherited phraseology just enough to make it suit his purpose. Thus for example the term *rices weard* [keeper of the kingdom], traditional epithet for a king (cf. *Beowulf*, l.1390) becomes *heofenrices weard* [keeper of the kingdom of heaven], and thus applicable to God. Cædmon's innovative genius consists in the transference of a whole range of vocabulary from one sphere to another, investing traditional formulas with a wholly new register of religious reference. Although seemingly trite enough to a later age, such coinages must originally have possessed a freshness and originality before in course of time they entered the common poetic stock.

Although Cædmon's documented deployment of heroic terminology to express religious concepts represents the diagnostic *locus* of this *Germanisierung des Christentums*, it is not impossible that such concepts should have been expressed thus in a prosaic, casual manner for some time, albeit previously unrecorded. The Christian mission of Augustine had been charged with a policy of deliberate social gradualism, adopting and modifying vernacular customs,[8] and there were distinct linguistic implications in this conciliatory spirit of prudent adaptability. By employing terminology normally associated with the comitatus, and thus gaining for its own ends some of the moral fervour it derived from this sphere of personal relationships, the Church inevitably disturbed the semantic fields to which they applied. This was not necessarily in itself part of any deliberate process; these were simply the most convenient terms the language offered. But of course the net effect is the same. Cædmon's *Creation-Hymn* three times employs the term *dryhten* to describe the Christian God, a word which seems originally to have expressed a distinctively military function. Now it was available in the dual sense of either secular leader or spiritual Lord. But the ambiguity which would allow a later poet to play on such terms for special effect (see below, p. 117), all too readily transferred to the secular arena. Soon enough there would arise earthly lords keen to claim a God-like authority.

Interestingly Bede's claims for Cædmon's primacy in the development of vernacular Christian verse quite ignores the Northumbrian poet's southern contemporary the erudite Aldhelm (see above, p. 24), whose Latin work Bede certainly admired[9] and whose learned style we might have imagined would be more to his scholarly taste. No less an authority than King Alfred himself is said to have been of the opinion that Aldhelm was unequalled in his ability to compose verse in his native language.[10] Although no surviving English poem can with any certainty be attributed to Aldhelm,[11] he may well have shared Cædmon's concern to accommodate traditional vocabulary to Christian concepts. In his Latin writings certainly he would enthusiastically Christianize the pagan epithets of classical verse: depicting God as the Ruler of Mount Olympus as readily as of Mount Sion, while Tartarus is an apt equivalent for hell.[12]

Learned appreciation of Cædmon's *Creation-Hymn* would be informed by a method of reading which sought in all things to acknowledge God's revealed truth – biblical exegesis providing a model for approaching all religious literature, seeking to identify underlying structures and significance, distinguishing core from cortex. Cædmon's referential source must of course lie in the earliest verses of the Book of Genesis which was itself considered to have been inspired in Moses by divine revelation.[13] But his opening exhortation, *Nu scylun* [Now let us . . .] suggests that the hymn may have been liturgically inspired, and certainly we may recognize a sequence of thought organized along lines reminiscent of the preface to the canon of the mass, with which as a conscientious Christian he would have been familiar by repetition. Such a structure might be no less the result of ruminative gestation than the verbal formulas with which the poet gave that structure utterance. But irrespective of so authoritative a precedent, the connection of ideas is a natural one, since the sole purpose of Creation is to praise its Creator, and the avowed function of Cædmon's *Creation-Hymn* is to promote that praise. In doing so Cædmon refers not merely to the Creator of Genesis, but the Trinitarian aspects of the Creator expounded by contemporary exegesis, in the three parallel epithets: *metudæs maecti* [the might of God] (the Father), his *modgepanc* [his thought/wisdom] (the Son), and *uerc uuldurfadur* [the work of the glorious father] (the Holy Spirit) (ll. 2–3). And then, systematically narrowing its focus, the *Creation-Hymn* moves from the eternal to the physical aspects of creation referring in turn to sky, earth, and the sons of men, for God is no less the guardian of mankind as of heaven: *hefaenricaes uard . . . moncynnæs uard* (ll. 1, 7).

Bede outlines something of Cædmon's subsequent career which, except for a prophetic intuition of his own approaching death, is straightforward enough. Recognizing the man's remarkable talent, Hild accepted him into the Whitby community, and set him to work where his abilities might be best employed. In what was still very much a mission field – little more than a generation after Paulinus's journey to the North – the Church might be well served by the provision of basic texts in a popular vernacular style. Of course formal translations would soon be necessary; Bede himself was said to be completing an English version of St John's Gospel when he died.[14] But in the meantime Cædmon, like Aldhelm, would ensure that the devil should not have a monopoly of the best tunes. Following the pattern of his initial test piece, Cædmon was set to compose an epic, or series of epics, apparently picking up where his dream poem left off and going on to cover everything from the beginning to the end of the world in a biblical scheme. Bede's perhaps over-systematic catalogue lists poems on: the creation of the world, the origins of the human race, and the whole Genesis story; on the Exodus of the Israelites from Egypt and their entry into the Promised Land; and 'very many other biblical narratives' including poems on the Incarnation of Christ, his Passion, Resurrection, and Ascension into heaven, the coming of the Holy Spirit, and the teaching of the Apostles. He also composed many poems about the Last Judgement: the horror of infernal punishment, and the sweetness of the kingdom of heaven. 'In all of this', adds Bede, recognizing a clear didactic intent, 'he sought to turn his hearers from delight in wickedness and to inspire them to love and do good'. What Bede gives us is not necessarily a bibliographical list of titles, but merely a range of topics – traditional to the early medieval Church as a whole – on which Cædmon composed. In fact there is no reason to believe that vernacular poems were ever given titles; in the oral tradition the demand made of the minstrel is not 'Recite X' but 'Tell me *about* X'. We should expect not translation or paraphrase *per se*, but rather independent works based on the biblical narrative as it was understood by the contemporary Church.

Christianity is pre-eminently a literary religion, its primary source of authority a sacred text which presented truths the validity of which was independent of chronological or geographical location. The text is sufficiently complex to require scholarly, i.e. literary, exposition, while as an instrument of liturgical ceremony it was often at this date sumptuously written and decorated. At once theurgic and self-authenticating, it claimed the authority not only of divine inspiration but also of ultimate antiquity, being supposedly the very first literature ever written by men. The Bible offered not merely a new faith – the promise of salvation – but an entire schematic context for the human condition, a ready-made universal history extending far beyond the limits of oral tradition. Before long, Anglo-Saxon kings would trace their lineage through Sceaf (who figured in the poem *Beowulf* but 'was born to Noah in the Ark'), and thus via Lamech, Enoch, Seth, and others, to 'Adam the first man, and our father who is Christ'.[15] It could accommodate not only the Germanic history of their own times but, as presented by ecclesiastical scholars, proffered a schematic understanding of history past and present and future. Since at this stage the Church exercised a monopoly of education, the Bible provided both the framework and sourcebook for all formal studies. But although, and perhaps *because*, inspired, the Bible was not a simple book to understand. Some passages simply made no sense at first sight; others like the commonplace reference to concubinage or incest, blessed by God, proved embarrassing to Church morality and might lead the reader into error if taken literally.

The Church therefore promoted a symbolic interpretative mode, deducing cryptic significance beyond the merely literal, adopting and developing a method of exegesis employed by various Greek philosophers to deal with the mythologies of Homer and Hesiod. If textual conservatism, enhanced by the authority of Jerome's Vulgate, insisted on the stability of the text, unlike the shifting oral transmission, exegetical interpretation opened new avenues for intellectual appreciation. Since there may evidently often be discerned levels of 'significance' beyond the literal meaning, an adequate appreciation of religious literature apparently requires a plurality of response. This approach is not entirely foisted on to the text by theological scholars; it is a mode of reading fundamental to the parables of Jesus (cf. Matthew 13. 10–13), and extended backwards by the proto-exegete Paul to explain otherwise puzzling details of the Old Testament, 'which things are an allegory' (Galatians 4. 21–31). Paul distinguished three distinct levels of significance lying behind the primary surface or cortex: i.e. that indicating its implication for the Church (the allegorical), that referring to the individual believer (the tropological), and that referring to the afterlife (the anagogical). A wholly intellectual response, this fourfold method of analysis was taken up with enthusiasm by the early Church, seeking in particular a whole series of detailed and often bizarre typological correspondences between Old and New Testaments.

The narrative text did not now stand alone, but was supplemented by a whole range of explanatory commentary, both literal and figurative, to assist in the identification of significance rather than sense. Appreciation was necessarily slow and attentive, intent on rewards hidden beneath the skin of literal sense, 'for often the simple man of studious inclinations will enjoy what the careless man of talent misses'.[16] Since scriptural exegesis was by no means a closed continuous or consistent scheme, systematic analysis might reveal a whole range of levels of meaning, or rather *possibilities*. Inasmuch as one figure might provoke any number of possible associations, the reader might choose one of a series of referents depending on variable contextual factors. The likelihood, even inevitability, of plural response to public literature of this kind is clear. Since all figures are intended to lead the reader to a fuller understanding of truths that are intentionally cryptic, the reader is free to apply to the text whatever method will yield the most interesting result.[17] The opportunities for ambiguity (a positive rather than negative quality in this sense) are obvious. Literature which anticipates multiple response is rational rather than dramatic or sensual in its direction: at its best powerfully symbolic, at its worst wilfully esoteric. But initial obscurity need not be totally lacking in literary virtue. As Augustine was aware,[18] there is a recognizable pleasure that attends postponed revelation, requiring clues to be recognized, riddles solved, codes cracked, even if such recondite delights often seem more akin to those one might normally associate with crossword puzzles, rather than with literature.

Such scholarly determinants could scarcely have been natural to the rustic Cædmon. There is no reason to suppose that he ever learned to read or write. At the time of his formative experience, Cædmon was said to be already advanced in years. But whether or not too old to benefit from a regular monastic education, Cædmon undoubtedly worked in a literate, even learned, context. Even if technically illiterate, he could be provided with access to written sources through professional readers, while his own finished work was dictated to an amanuensis. He already was or would become – with the necessarily capacious and detailed memory of the talented oral poet – familiar with those parts of the Bible narrative used in the services of the Church, and with the liturgy. Whatever he lacked in scholastic theology which interpretative scriptural verse might require, could be made up no less readily than the narrative line by his oral informants. It is not without significance that Bede describes the scholars at Whitby not merely reciting but 'expounding' (*exponebant*) to him passages of both sacred history and doctrine.

Among all works listed as Cædmon's, only the dream-hymn can be identified with any certainty, although some other biblical narrative poems are clearly 'Cædmonian' in spirit. Material contained in the first book of the Bible, Genesis, would speak powerfully to the early Anglo-Saxon religious sentiment, offering a substantial mythic *cosmopoesis* of the human condition. Quite apart from direct access to the text, its substance would be familiar from the continuous public readings of the early Anglo-Saxon lectionary which, following the Antiochene tradition, pursued the story of Genesis from Lent until Easter, beginning with the first verse and ending with the story of Abraham and Isaac. Yet what the poet offers is no mere paraphrase. Each major narrative incident: the Fall of Adam and Eve, the slaying of Abel by Cain, Noah's Flood, and Abraham's sacrifice of Isaac, was informed by supplementary exegetical tradition in which all was understood to prefigure the act of Redemption at Easter. Either implicitly or explicitly such interpretative assumptions are woven into the narrative text, making accessible a whole range of learned referents beyond the literal. The authority of the poet's various sources repeatedly signalled: *þæs þe us secgað bec . . . swa us gewritu secgeað* [which books tell us . . . as writings say . . .] (ll.227, 969, 1121, 1239, 1630, 1723, 2565, 2612–13). Whether the poet presents the sacred text itself, or merely a dilative reflection upon it as revealed by a Christian muse, he necessarily disclaims originality. The stories of the biblical heroes could lay claim to truth beyond that of the pagan protagonists of secular tales. Like Milton, the Old English *Genesis*-poet seems set to justify the ways of God to men.

The main body of his poem is determined by the linear narrative structure of his source. But he opens with a strictly non-biblical prelude (ll.1–111), organized around a body of ideas parallel to those voiced in Cædmon's *Creation-Hymn*, emphasizing the duty of men to praise God in tune with the angels in heaven, since the sole purpose of Creation was to praise its begetter – an exhortation summarized in the opening statement:

> Us is riht micel    ðæt we rodera weard,
> wereda wuldorcining,    wordum herigen.    (ll.1–2)

> [It is our great duty to praise with words the Guardian of the heavens, the glorious King of hosts.]

The poet moves directly and naturally to speak of the fall and exile of Lucifer, since that supplied the logical and dramatic rationale for the creation of man – to fill the place in heaven left empty by the fallen angels. The war in heaven is conceived in physical, human terms, Lucifer and his followers thinking to share power with God and seeking their own palace in another part of heaven (ll.32–34). But with the boasting, treacherous throng thrust into ignominious exile, 'the glorious homeland now lacked inhabitants' (ll.83–89). The fall of the angels thus directly motivates the creation of man – his role being to praise God, and his destiny a place in heaven if through obedience he should prove worthy. The preface having accounted for the creation of the empyrean or spiritual heaven, the poet is free to embark on a regular biblical paraphrase controlled by the given text, beginning with Chapter 1, verse 1:

Her ærest gesceop    ece drihten,
helm eallwihta,    heofon and eorðan.    (ll. 112–13)

[In the beginning the eternal Lord, defence of all created things, made heaven and earth.]

The sheer potentiality of physical creation is suggested in negative terms, either text-derived: *garsecg þeahte sweart synnihte side and wide, wonne wægas* [dark unending night muffled the ocean and its gloomy waves] (ll. 117–19), or imaginatively independent: the earth *græsungrene* [grass-ungreen] (l. 117), anticipating the subsequent luxuriance and fruitfulness of an *eorðan ælgrene* [totally verdant earth] (l. 197 *et passim*).

The poet does not set out to offer a complete programmatic rendition of his biblical source but to transform its material into a fresh narrative by dint of magnifying the interest of certain parts and transforming others in context and ethical significance. Indeed, he includes material from only the first third of the biblical text, significantly breaking off dramatically in Chapter xxii with the events surrounding Abraham's sacrifice of his only son Isaac – an episode which was understood to prefigure the Crucifixion of Christ; thus in itself the poem presents a fully completed programme from Fall to Redemption. Bede's commentary on Genesis stops short of the sacrifice itself, concluding with the academically correct details of Isaac's confirmation as heir to the kingdom.[19] The poet chooses instead to end with the more dramatic and heroic moment, as the ram's blood spreads across the reeking altar, and Abraham, brandishing his sword, gives praise to God (ll. 2932–36). In any case, the point on which the poet concludes is not theologically inadequate since for Bede, as for all commentators, this represents the major Old Testament symbol of the sacrifice of the Son in the Redemption.[20] Explicit signals at this late stage in the poem are quite unnecessary. That the whole scheme is understood to anticipate the figure of Christ is clear from the very beginning of the poem where, among a whole host of epithets for God, we find that it is already 'our Saviour' (*ure Nergend*) who divides night from day (l. 140), who walks for pleasure in the gardens of paradise (l. 855), who banishes the serpent (903) or blesses Noah's Ark (ll. 1285f). Although quite illogical, in any narrative sense, prior to the Fall, the epithet is clearly employed without any sense of theological impropriety. The same Trinitarian sensibility is at work in the illustration of the unique, if late, manuscript of the poem, which depicts a small cross, the symbol of atonement, concealed in the uppermost branches of the tree of life in the Garden of Eden – the salvation of fallen man prefigured from the very moment of his creation – and which shows the figure of Jesus blessing those who enter the Ark.[21]

The poet's reworking of his material would naturally tend to eliminate the narrative deficiencies, especially any confusion or duplication, found in the original source, judicious omission and transposition presenting a tighter, more consistent and immediately accessible story-line. For example, the biblical account suggests a double creation of Eve – the first rationally in the same breath as the creation of Adam (Genesis 1. 27), then later in the parthenogenic myth which creates a companion for the lonely Adam out of a rib taken from his side (Genesis 2. 20–25). But since two creations of Eve are unnecessary and unedifying, the poet sensibly and dramatically brings the graphic and dramatic material of the myth forward as part of the original creation, rather than an awkward afterthought, thus making both a more coherent and a domestic scene in which Adam and Eve together are given charge of Paradise – and the injunction not to eat of the tree of knowledge is given to them both. But while this makes for a clearer narrative, it necessarily forfeits the typological parallel, since Eve would not now be created on the sixth day – corresponding to the sixth age of the world in which the second Adam, Christ, would create his bride, the Church. Perhaps the allegorical suggestion that Eve, who comes to represent the avenue of evil, should equally equate with the body of the Church,[22] was considered too paradoxical to be readily signalled. Nevertheless the incident is exegetically enlarged by the information that Adam felt no pain in the operation (ll. 178–81).

A similarly effective rearrangement is made by intercalating the first verse of Genesis 11, 'and the whole earth was yet of one tongue', between Genesis 10. 10 and 20, which serves implicitly to identify Babel with Babylon and its ruler Nimrod, omitting any reference to him as 'a mighty hunter before the Lord', so as to underline his role as the first tyrant and figuratively the devil:[23]

> yrfestole weold,
> widmære wer,    swa us gewritu secgeað,
> þæt he moncynnes    mæste hæfde
> on þam mældagum    mægen and strengo.    (ll. 1629–32)

[he ruled an inherited throne, a famous man, as writings tell us, in that he had the greatest might and strength of all men in those far-off days.]

These terms were perhaps foisted on to the text from their association with giants in the Septuagint. Such extra-biblical dilation is frequent. For example, the identification of Cain's slayer (not named in the Bible, Genesis 4. 23) with the blind bowman Lamech (ll.1090–1103), or the irreverent detail of the mocking laughter of Ham at his father Noah's nakedness (1582), both follow Talmudic traditions adopted by Bede.[24] The pillar of salt which was Lot's wife, still survives, 'say the books', as one of the wonders of the world (ll.2565–75).[25] The raven that fails to return to Noah's Ark, unexplained in the Bible, is visualized graphically as a hostile agent, *se feond*, perched not on dry land but on some dead body floating in the water (l.1447) – the swarthy raven, in contrast with the holy dove, representing the enemy of God or the devil himself preying on the damned.[26]

There is the occasional expansion apparently quite unprompted by the text, like the gloss added to Cain's murder of Abel, familiar as a type of Christ the innocent Shepherd.[27] First we are given a graphic picture of the earth swallowing up Abel's blood – just as the Church mystically receives Christ's blood. Then employing a horticultural image wholly appropriate to Cain the cultivator, the poet speaks of the consequences of Cain's action as a cutting from the tree of sin which will burgeon into luxuriant atrocities:

> Of ðam twige siððan
> ludon laðwende    leng swa swiðor,
> reðe wæstme.    Ræhton wide
> geond werþeoda    wrohtes telgan;
> hrinon hearmtanas    hearde and sare
> drihta bearnum:    doð gieta swa.
> Of þam brad blado    bealwa gehwilces
> sprytan ongunnon.    We þæt spell magon,
> wælgrimme wyrd,    wope cwiðan,
> nales holunge;    ac us hearde sceod
> freolecu fæmne.    (ll.988–98)

[From that twig there subsequently grew – more vigorously as time went on – malignant, violent fruit. The tendrils of that enmity reached far and wide through the nations; its harmful branches lashed the children of men hard and grievously – just as they still do. From them plentiful fruits of all sorts of atrocities began to burgeon. We do not lament that story, weep over that deadly grim event, without cause; for the lovely woman injured us severely.]

The image is doubly appropriate since the roots of Cain's sin lie figuratively in Eve's.

Some of the poet's omissions may be accounted for by the control of a mnemonic rather than literary sensibility. For example he omits to render the significance of Eve's name: the mother of all living (Genesis 3. 20); and yet if this was in order to concentrate on Adam's punishment, it is curious that he should also have omitted the immediately preceding verse, which gives the conclusion of God's curse, and the substantial definition of man's mortality: 'dust thou art and to dust thou shalt return' (Genesis 3. 19). Of course, the poet's reshaping of a given source and informing it with supplementary materials is very much in the oral tradition (see above, p. 53), and quite in accordance with Bede's account of Cædmon's own method of composition.

Despite the range of learned apparatus to which the *Genesis*-poet apparently had access, his work is firmly embedded in a traditional oral matrix. This becomes more obviously so when his source moved on to topics with which he could more readily sympathize, and which his traditional formulas could better accommodate. Leaving the exegetically dense mythical matter of the earlier part of the book, the poet found himself on more familiar ground; the warfare and wanderings of the Migration Age tribal leader Abraham found immediate echoes in traditional heroic themes, scenes and verbal formulas: one set of warring protagonists was simply exchanged for another. The earlier conventional reference to textual authority: *swa boceras secgeð*, is now replaced by the formula: *þa ic gefrægn,* (ll.1960, 2060, 2244, 2484, 2542), signalling more expansive narrative treatment in the traditional oral manner. The poet's free treatment of Abraham's war against the kings of the North, begins with an epic formula reminiscent of the opening of *Beowulf*:

> Ða ic aldor gefrægn   Elamitarna
> fromne folctogan,   fyrd gebeodan,
> Orlahomar.   (ll.1960–62)

[Then I heard that the prince, the fierce national leader of the Elamites, Chedorlaomer, summoned an army.]

and extends for some twelve dozen lines, allowing full rein to a taste for traditional battle-poetry. The outcome of the victory of the five northern kings over the southern kings of Sodom and Gomorrah is anticipated in terms not disimilar to those fortelling the defeat of Beowulf's Geats (see above, p. 60).

> Þa wæs guðhergum   be Iordane
> wera eðelland   wide geondsended,
> folde feondum.   Sceolde forht monig
> blachleor ides   bifiende gan
> on fremdes fæðm;   feollon wergend
> bryda and beaga,   bennum seoce.   (ll.1967–72)

[Then an invading army spread over the homeland of men beside Jordan; there were enemies in the land. Many a frightened woman, white-faced, had to go trembling into the embrace of a foreigner; the defenders of brides and rings fell, sick with wounds.]

After twelve years of subjection the conquered tribes rebel: 'the dark bird sang, dewy-feathered under javelin-shafts, in anticipation of corpse-meat' (ll.1983–85), but again the northern kings 'hold the place of slaughter' (l.2005), the dire consequences of defeat once more marked by the plight of the women, 'girls and widows, their menfolk slain, leaving the shelter of their homes' (ll.2009–11). Abraham's nephew Lot is among those taken captive – a particular cause for distress in view of the favoured nature of this relationship in Germanic society, and marked by a striking intrusion of the minstrel voice, drawing attention both to the significance of the event, and to his own presence[28]:

> We þæt soð magon
> secgan furður,    hwelc siððan wearð
> æfter þæm gehnæste    herewulfa sið,
> þara þe læddon Loth    and leoda god,
> suðmonna sinc,    sigore gulpon.    (ll.2013–17)

[We can tell the further truth of what came about following the conflict, the war-wolves' expedition: those who led into captivity Lot and the people's property, the treasure of the men of the South, boasted of victory.]

A survivor escapes, bringing news of the disaster to Abraham who promptly gathers a small war-band no more than 318 strong to confront the hosts of the North, comforted by his faith that 'the eternal Lord can easily grant good speed to the spear-strife' (ll.2058–59). As battle is engaged the poet again employs the introductory epic formula: þa ic neðan gefrægn under nihtscuwan hæleð to hilde [Then I heard how under cover of night the hero ventured forth to battle] (ll.2060–61). Audacity in attack is rewarded, 'Abraham gave not twisted gold but war as a ransom for his nephew' (ll.2069–71); Lot is set free, both women and treasure recovered, the bodies of the enemy, 'sword-slaughtered, ripped by carrion birds' (ll.2088–89). The section concludes by exclaiming how remarkable it was to have conquered so great a force with so small a troop of men (ll.2092–95), a natural enough comment, although employing very much the same formula as Bede's commentary.[29] Of course, if any chose to see further significance in all of this, then exegetes like Bede could provide it, drawing for example on Greek number-symbolism to reveal how the specific number of men in Abraham's war-band was indicative of the Redemption through which the Christian warrior would triumph in his struggle against the forces of evil. But such an interpretation is quite unsignalled in the text, and it seems clear that at this point the straightforward literal exposition is sufficient, the poet finding merely traditional pleasure in describing a heroic feat of courage against overwhelming odds.

The 'Cædmonian' manner is a natural response to the age-old necessity to recast old stories in a contemporary vein – now a sympathetic 'Germanization'. This mode permeates not merely the account of Abraham's warlike adventures, but the whole of the Genesis story from the very beginning. The potentially tedious genealogical listings of the generations of Noah employ much the same epic formulas found in *Widsith*, enlivened with appropriate heroic dilation. Japheth, for example, merely a name in the biblical list (Genesis 10. 2), is described in comitatus terms as 'the head of a happy hearth-troop', until at his death his son Gomer inherits the hall-floor, sharing his father's treasure among friends and kinsmen (ll. 1604–12). The same heroic frame of reference is employed where even less appropriate, in resolving the same difficulties as confronted the original biblical authors in attempting to accommodate metaphysical concepts to the body of mundane experience. Thus, God's relationship with the empyrean angels is conceived in terms of the comitatus, employing phrases with a known cultural resonance to establish the ethical base of an otherwise indescribable situation. If God is leader and king, *weard, frea, drihten* (ll. 1, 5, 7), the angels are naturally his troops, *wered, þreat* (ll. 2, 13), the thegns of his tried band, *þegnas, duguþ* (ll. 15– 17), pledged to fundamental principles of love and loyalty in return for all the benefits of heaven which are described in terms of the pleasures afforded by the mead-hall: *gleam, dream*, and *blæd micel* (ll. 12–14), until tragically forfeited by rebellion. The traditional poetic vocabulary would serve as a selective screen, admitting only those features for which meaningful referents were available and could therefore be satisfactorily rendered. Even 'the beautiful woman' Eve uses military language of her error, as though it were a battle: 'an enemy attack', *feondræs*, 'a hostile act', *fæhð*, in 'plundering' the tree of its fruit (ll. 900–01). The necessity for faithfulness and loyalty, and the dire consequences of rebellion against the accepted societal values are recurrent Old Testament themes with which the Anglo-Saxon would recognize an immediate affinity. The Old English poet could as readily accommodate the biblical ethos to his own system of values, as equip the patriarchs with his own heroic accoutrements, and place them within his own intellectual and emotional landscape. The force of the term *wærloga* [faith-breaker] is to mark the breakdown of society, whether that of angels or the sons of men (l. 36 *et passim*). The pain and pity of exile, *wræc*, is the same, whether it refers to the expulsion of the rebellious angels from heaven, or Adam from Eden. In speaking of Cain's exile in the land of Nod, the poet enlarges the simple biblical phrase 'a fugitive and a vagabond' (Genesis 4. 12, 14) into a passage some forty lines long deploying all the traditional exilic motifs to create a desolate and almost compassionate picture of a man condemned 'to tread remote paths, abhorrent to your kinsmen' (l. 1021) (see below, p. 106).

At the end of the poem the author chooses to omit the lengthy description of the circumstances surrounding the proposed sacrifice of Isaac by his father – not because of any complex allegorical implication, but probably because the early Germanic audience would not have found the pathetic elements of the situation (which so much appealed to later medieval sentiment), quite so heart-rending; sons were as a matter of course sacrificed one way or another in the real world of warfare society. Instead emphasis is laid on Abraham's prompt and heroic obedience to his Lord:

> Ne forsæt he þy siðe,    ac sona ongann
> fysan to fore.   Him wæs frea engla
> word ondrysne    and his waldende leof.   (ll. 2860–62)

[He did not put off the journey, but promptly set out on the expedition. The word of the Lord of angels inspired him with awe, and he was dear to God.]

He forsakes his night's rest, unwilling in any way to obstruct the Saviour's command (2864–65), an expression of both urgency and res- olution. The redemptive deed, a test of loyalty, is undertaken with determination; Abraham hastens, seizes the sword quickly, single-minded – the epitome of faith and obedience treated in heroic terms. The poem ends, as it began, on a note of thanks and praise to God.

In the Book of Exodus the Anglo-Saxons would find an even more sympathetic theme – a potentially heroic story of the migration of a warlike tribe, under stress, seeking a new homeland. The general approach to biblical material in the Old English *Exodus* is similar to *Genesis*, but theologically more sophisticated, thematically tighter, and exegetically more controlled. Less than a quarter the length of the former poem, *Exodus* relates only a small part of the biblical story. It tells of the journey of the Israelites out of Egypt led by a mysterious pillar of cloud and fire and their crossing of the Red Sea just ahead of the pursuing Egyptian army – who are destroyed in the waters – events which occur in just one and a half chapters (Exodus 13. 17 – 14. 31). While the poet has certainly made use, in one way or another, of much of the biblical phraseology, the poem is much less of a paraphrase than *Genesis*. The *Exodus*-poet by no means presents a straightforward story strictly contro- lled by his narrative source, but a clearly independent structure, so that the reader does not remark any awkwardness in non-biblical intrusion of any kind, whether in detail of phraseology or image or any larger addition.

The poet adopts the expansive style of the later part of *Genesis*, but in a flamboyant exegetical manner. His stance is established with the opening lines:

Hwæt, we feor ond neah    gefrigen habbað
ofer middangeard    Moyses domas,
wræclico wordriht,    wera cneorissum –
in uprodor    eadigra gehwam
æfter bealusiðe    bote lifes,
lifigendra gehwam    langsumne ræd –
hæleðum secgan.    Gehyre se þe wille!    (1–7)

[Look, far and near throughout the world we have heard men tell of the
decrees of Moses, wondrous laws for the generations of men – of the reward
in heaven for each of the blessed after the terrible journey, everlasting benefit
for all living. Let him who will, take heed!]

Although the poet begins with the traditional narrative formula, it is
immediately apparent that what is to follow is far from the direct story-
line we might have expected. How could the Laws given Moses on Mount
Sinai relate to the crossing of the Red Sea unless on a level other than that
of simple narrative? In point of fact, both are brought together as
Ascension Day readings in the Antiochene tradition inherited by the
Anglo-Saxon Church. The poet goes on to make it quite clear that what
he has to say relates not merely to the historical Israelites but has obvious
moral implications for a Christian audience, in the light of which his
concluding words: *Gehyre se þe wile*, bear in addition to the age-old
minstrel's plea, the admonition of the parable: 'He that hath ears to hear,
let him hear' (Mark 4. 9).

But despite its overt typological underpinning, the dramatic line of
*Exodus* is sufficiently strong to entertain at a purely literal level. Exciting
and colourful, it presents a familiar biblical story in dramatic and original
terms. The author draws on a variety of sources to supplement his
material in an evidently confident academic manner. If the 'Cædmonian'
*Genesis* represents a mnemonic sensibility at work, then *Exodus* is more
clearly literary – almost Aldhelmian – in its manner of presentation. Most
importantly the poet incorporates a wide range of material from
elsewhere in the Bible, either explicitly or in covert allusion. In particular, details from the Books of Numbers, Deuteronomy, and Genesis
significantly broaden the scope of narrative events, for reasons that may
be either doctrinal or dramatic, or both. For example, whereas the
received biblical image is of the Israelites fleeing Egypt as a band of
refugees, the Old English poet makes it clear that they come to the Red
Sea as an army. Possibly the projective hint, *armati* (Exodus 13. 18), may
have been sufficient, but in any case it would probably have been inconceivable to an early Anglo-Saxon audience that a nation on the march
was not also a nation in arms. In the Bible the Israelites are not spoken of
as an army until the Book of Numbers, when the army is formed in
Numbers 1. 17–46, and their marching order described in Numbers 10.

14–28. In the poem, however, this material is brought forward so that the Hebrew army is appropriately and heroically formed on the shore of the Red Sea (ll.224–48), and the marching-order given as they enter the Sea itself (ll.310–61). In both cases the biblical source is heroically embellished. In place of the bare statement that the army was composed of 'every male of 20 years and upward', we are given a graphic account of the formation of a comitatus of battle-hardened warriors:

> Wace ne gretton
> in þæt rincgetæl    ræswan herges,
> þa þe for geoguðe    gyt ne mihton
> under bordhreoðan    breostnet wera
> wið flane feond    folmum werigean,
> ne him bealubenne    gebiden hæfdon
> ofer linde lærig,    licwunde spor,
> gylpplegan gares.    Gamele ne moston,
> hare heaðorincas,    hilde onþeon
> gif him modheapum    mægen swiðrade,
> ac hie be wæstmum    wigheap curon,
> hu in leodscipe    læstan wold
> mod mid aran,    eac þan mægnes cræft
> garbeames feng    gretan mihte.   (ll.233–46)

[The leaders of the army did not accept weaklings into that company of warriors, those who because of their youth could not defend with their fists behind a shield's protection the mail-coat of a man against the treacherous enemy, or who had not experienced grievous injury over the shield-rim, the mark of some body-wound, the boastful play of a javelin. Aged and white-haired warriors could be of no service in battle if, in the bold troop, their physical strength failed them; rather they picked the war-band for stature, and the way courage and honour, plus the power of physical strength, the grip on the spear-shaft, might perform on behalf of the nation.]

At a primary narrative level, the poem has all the air of a traditional heroic epic. Moses is represented as the archetypal Germanic war-leader, the Israelites a loyal and courageous army who bear all the heroic virtues – although it may have puzzled the Anglo-Saxon audience that an army said to number 600,000 (ll.224–32; Exodus 12. 37) should have found it necessary to retreat. As the Egyptian army draws dangerously near, a dreadful foreboding of the likely outcome is evoked by reference to the beasts of battle:

> Onhwæl þa on heofonum    hyrnednebba
> (hreopon herefugolas    hilde grædige,
> deawigfeðere)    ofer drihtneum,
> wonn wælceasega.    Wulfas sungon
> atol æfenleoð    ætes on wenan.   (ll.161–65)

[In the skies the bird of prey cried out expectantly, (dewy-feathered, dark carrion-birds greedy for battle screeched), in anticipation of dead armies, a sombre chooser of the slain. Wolves sang a terrible evensong in hope of feasting.]

But despite the Israelites' frank terror, it is not they who will provide the carrion in the event. However, by crossing the Red Sea they were freed from the oppression of the Egyptians only to find themselves starving in the Wilderness. Nevertheless the later prophets nostalgically referred to this as a period when their people were significantly closer to God than in later degenerate days; the crossing of the Red Sea was understood typologically by the early Church to signify the attainment of the kingdom of God in a spiritual if not yet a physical sense.[30] The poet makes this identification quite clear in bringing forward the valedictory speeches of Moses to the Israelites before their entering the Promised Land (Deuteronomy, *passim*), to a point immediately following their passage of the Red Sea (ll. 516ff. The effect of this juxtaposition is to identify the passage of the Red Sea with the crossing of the Jordan and entry into the Promised Land, corresponding with the journey of the Christian soul through life towards its true and promised home, which is heaven.

From earliest times the Exodus story is one that was loaded with extraliteral 'significance' – of which the poet shows himself fully aware. Making full and confident use of exegetical traditions, he employs his narrative as a vehicle to carry a series of Christian themes, the summation of which, for the poet as for the expositors, is Salvation.

*Exodus* is composed in such a way that it does not have one simple meaning, but rather the power to generate diverse meanings. The tradition of scriptural exegesis not only allows but encourages a considerable degree of ambiguity, so that a single narrative sequence might carry several thematic threads. The poet cultivates an allegorical mode in order to generate a carefully controlled pattern of meaning. His narrative framework carries a network of theological elements, strands that run throughout the length of his text, systematically interlocking, often hidden, but emerging to reveal the existence of a considerable body of Christian doctrine supporting the body of the poem. Conceptually it compares with that interlaced style of decoration which was introduced to the Anglo-Saxon world from the Mediterranean at the same time and through the same avenues as the exegetical mode itself, and formed such a definitive decorative motif for the early Anglo-Saxon Church, characteristically applied to their central texts,[31] and pre-eminently the sumptuous gospel books, in a complex series of plaited and intertwined threads, each present but only sporadically visible, often gathered in such a way that the shape of the cross, symbol of salvation, is apparent to the informed eye.

We may identify in the poem three major threads of meaning, systematic to the Christian doctrine of salvation: initiation into the faith (baptism), the good life (covenant and obedience), and its reward (judgement and salvation). Without being baptized no man can be saved, for he is marked with the stain of original sin as a result of the Fall. The poet anticipates this theme in speaking briefly of the Passover – which offered a striking, if unspoken, correspondence with the deliverance at the Red Sea, since in both cases the Israelites are protected and the Egyptians defeated by the hand of God. The poet here ignores the dominant eucharistic significance of the Passover in favour of the baptismal, alluding only to the action of the destroying angel in sparing the first-born of the Israelites, their doorposts being significantly marked with the blood of the lamb.[32] The crossing of the Red Sea itself, taken as a symbol of baptism by Paul (I Corinthians 10. 1–2), was elaborately developed by the early Church. Like the Israelites, the baptized soul is saved from its enemies (i.e. sin and the devil), and by passing through the waters of life eventually reaches its true home, which is with God. As the Israelites were guided and protected by Moses and the pillar of cloud and fire, the Christian is led by Christ and the cross. The pillar of fire, the 'candle of heaven' (l.115) which led the Israelites is ceremonially echoed in the candle symbolizing the Deity which conventionally led the catechumen in the baptismal procession.[33] The poet's non-biblical emphasis on the military aspect of the Israelites encamped on the shores of the Red Sea also has some typological significance. In literal terms this picture of the Israelites preparing for battle before what is, after all, a physical defeat, albeit turned Dunkirk-like into a moral victory, seems incongruous; but it corresponds readily with the tradition in which the catechumen was visualized going to the font as a soldier to battle[34] – incipiently an image of the *miles Christi* which was later to be so influential (see p. 142f). The effect of the Germanization at this point is thus twofold: both elaborating the main line of the narrative by adding excitement and sympathetic interest on a purely literal level, and also enlarging one of the underlying strands of meaning which make up the doctrinal substance of the poem.

The second necessary stage on the road to salvation is leading the good life, the most important elements of which are obedience to God and keeping faith with his covenant, for without the promise of his grace the Christian cannot attain salvation. The importance of keeping faith with God is stressed throughout the Bible, but definitively in Exodus 19. 5, where in the wilderness beyond the Red Sea a special relationship is established between God and the children of Israel. The Old English poem naturally stresses not only the covenant between God and man but also that between man and man, and the punishment for those who break faith, an act naturally abhorrent to early Anglo-Saxon society, for whom loyalty, personal and national, formed the sole basis of social security. At the literal level the Egyptians are roundly condemned for breaking their agreement to allow the Israelites to live in the land of Goshen, their betrayal of this pledge being listed among their worst crimes (ll. 140–47). The idea of covenant between man and God is more complex, involving complete obedience in return for comfort and protection. The notion of total obedience to God runs through the poem parallel to that of covenant, and the two are often indissolubly linked. In order to attain salvation the Christian must live a life of obedience as the Israelites do. The Israelites are obedient to God and are consequently rewarded by being consistently saved from the forces of evil, as represented by the Egyptians.

The final step in the journey of the Christian soul to salvation is that of judgement. This theme is already clearly present in the poem from the brief, if graphic, allusion to the coming of the destroying angel at the Passover, who kills the first-born of the sinful Egyptians while allowing the faithful Israelites to live, and then redoubled at the Red Sea when the Israelite host is once again allowed to live while the Egyptians are terribly drowned. The typological interpretation of the Red Sea crossing as the predictive representation of a great moral judgement, already heavily drawn upon by the Old Testament prophets (cf. Ezekiel 20. 36–38; Isaiah 51. 10–11), was enthusiastically taken up by the early Church as a major prefiguration of the Last Judgement itself. Within the Old English poem, this central act of judgement (the horrific scene in which the Egyptian army is horribly drowned as it attempts to pursue the Israelites across the Red Sea) is at one level a dramatic and vivid description of a literal judgement on evil and treacherous foes who are explicitly condemned. A graphic picture, employing highly charged poetic imagery: (e.g. 'the discoloured air mingled with blood', l. 477), it contains within it a network of references clear enough to those familiar with exegetical modes of thought.[35] The poet systematically incorporates a whole range of eschatological signs revealing a thoroughgoing knowledge of the whole Bible. From line 447 to 515 allegorical significance is allowed to break through the literal level for more than a line or two at a time, laying realism aside so that the literal meaning of the drowning first merges and then is replaced by the symbolic vision of Judgement Day. It is, of course, a 'sudden disaster' (l. 453); it is natural that the sea should flood the land in the circumstances, and that those seas should rage (ll. 458–60, 469, 490), but these are also well-known signs of Judgement Day (I Thessalonians 5. 3; Matthew 24. 39; Luke 21. 25). There is naturally terror among the people and lamentation (ll. 447, 461–63, 490–91), but also darkness in the sky (l. 462). cf. Luke 21. 25–26; Matthew 22. 13; Amos 5. 18. In a single forceful half-line reinforced by continuous rhyme, the sea is said to turn to blood: *Flod blod gewod* (l. 463), appropriate enough for a battle scene at first sight (although drowning is scarcely a bloody business), but also one of the graphic signs of Judgement Day referred to twice in the Book of Revelation, where those who are in the sea, having shed the blood of the saints, all die (Revelation 8. 7–8; 16. 3).

Folc wæs afæred;   flodegsa becwom
gastas geomre;   geofon deaðe hweop.
Wæron beorhhliðu   blode bestemed,
holm heolfre spaw,   hream wæs on yðum,
wæter wæpna ful;   wælmist astah.
Wæron Egypte   eft oncyrde,
flugon forhtigende;   fær ongeton,
woldon herebleaðe   hamas findan –
gylp wearð gnornra.   Him ongen genap
atol yða gewealc,   ne ðær ænig becwom
herges to hame,   ac behindan beleac
wyrd mid wæge.   Þær ær wegas lagon
mere modgode   (mægen wæs adrenced),
streamas stodon.   Storm up gewat
heah to heofonum,   herewopa mæst;
laðe cyrmdon   (lyft up geswearc)
fægum stæfnum.   Flod blod gewod.   (ll. 447–63)

[The people were panic-striken; terror of the flood overcame their sorrowful spirits; the sea threatened death. The mountainous waters were bedabbled with blood, the ocean spewed forth gore, there was uproar amid the waves, the water full of weapons; the reek of carnage arose. The Egyptians were turned back, fled in terror; they had experienced sudden disaster, the cowards wanted to go home – their boasting became less optimistic. The dreadful turmoil of the waves engulfed them in darkness, and none of the army there came home, for fate blocked their rear with the flood. Where previously paths had lain, the ocean raged and tides appeared; the army was drowned. A tumult arose high into the skies, a mighty cry of despair from the army; the enemy screamed with doomed voices – the air above grew dark. The flood was pervaded with blood.]

The strong sense of panic and confusion present is reflected in the staccato movement of the passage, broken into a jumble of half-line units. The warriors' arms and armour, described in such impressive military terms as the Egyptians advanced (ll. 154ff), become suddenly tiny and helpless, tossed about admidst towering seas: *randbyrig wæron rofene, rodor swipode meredeaða mæst . . . wigbord scinon; heah ofer hæleðum holmweall astah,* [the ramparts were rent, the greatest of sea-deaths lashed the sky . . . war-shields gleamed; high above the warriors, the wall of ocean rose up] (ll. 464–68). God the all-powerful is identified with the storm (ll. 480, 489); at the end of this terrible scene, comes the forceful, explicit statement: *Hie wið God wunnon* [They strove against God] (l. 515); there can be no mistaking that the dreadful fate of the Egyptians was an act of divine judgement.[36]

There follows a short statement, not dissimilar to that in II Corinthians
3. 6, on the importance of an exegetical approach to biblical materials,
and by implication to the substance of this poem – without which it must
appear merely a disjointed and at times rather bizarre, if flamboyant,
retelling of the story. At the same time the poet makes explicit the
Doomsday references his work contains:

> Gif onlucan wile    lifes wealhstod,
> beorht in breostum,    banhuses weard,
> ginfæsten god    Gastes cægon,
> run bið gerecenod,    ræd forð gæð; . . .
> nu us boceras    beteran secgað,
> lengran lyftwynna.    Þis is læne dream
> wommum awyrged,    wreccum alyfed,
> earmra anbid.            . . .
>             . . .    Eftwyrd cymeð,
> mægenþrymma mæst,    ofer middangeard,
> dæg dædum fah.    Drihten sylfa
> on þam meðelstede    manegum demeð,
> þonne He soðfæstra    sawla lædeð,
> eadige gastas,    on uprodor,
> þær bið leoht ond lif,    eac þon lissa blæd.

(ll. 523–26, 531–34, 540–45)

[If that which interprets the meaning of life, the body's guardian, radiant
within the breast, has the will to unlock the great benefits with the keys of the
Spirit, the secret will be explained and understanding result. . . . Now
scholars tell us of the better, more lasting joys of heaven. This is an
ephemeral pleasure, spoiled by sins, which is afforded us exiles, the
expectation of wretches. . . . The Last Judgement is approaching, the
greatest of majesties upon earth, the day which punishes deeds. The Lord
himself will judge the multitudes in the meeting-place, then he will lead the
souls of the righteous, blessed spirits, into heaven on high, where there is
light and life and also bliss in abundance.]

The poet returns to the literal level to conclude with a description of the
rejoicing of the Israelites on the further shores of the Red Sea, praising
the Lord for their salvation and dividing the spoils of the drowned
Egyptians among themselves. The audience needs now no explicit signal
to identify these spoils with the treasures of heaven. We are obviously
invited to compare the contrasting fates of the two parties at Doomsday,
the damned and the saved.

Within what is clearly a highly considered, well-wrought doctrinal
frame-work, an apparently clumsy Noah-Abraham digression makes
perfect sense; incongruous perhaps at a narrative level but perfectly
consonant with the pattern of thought of the poem as a whole. The Flood

story is introduced, rather suddenly in narrative terms but with typologically strategic timing, at the climactic point where the Israelites proceed across the sea-bed in systematic genealogical order (ll.362f). Arguably this might form a reminiscent digression similar to those employed by the *Beowulf*-poet, since backward references to Noah and Abraham, both victorious predecessors successful through faith in the protecting hand of God, are such as might well occur naturally to the war-leader Moses. The genealogical stimulus (ll.359–61) is perhaps sufficient to recall both Abraham and Noah, direct forebears of all the tribes of Israel. But if the narrative link seems weak, the thematic bond is strong, substantially informing the exegetical structure of the poem. Both the Flood story and the sacrifice of Isaac share strong typological affinities with the Red Sea story. All embody the doctrinal theme of the poem: all are acts of salvation in which obedient and God-fearing men are saved from impossible circumstances. The Flood in particular is a major Old Testament symbol of judgement (Matthew 24. 37–39; II Peter 2. 5), and of baptism, the waters destroying all that is evil (I Peter 3. 18–21). There is an additional literal appropriateness in the story of Noah, inasmuch as in both the Flood and the Red Sea crossing the children of God were saved from inundating waters; and the subsequent covenant established between God and Noah forges a direct link with the central events of the Exodus story, for after the Flood God had made a specific promise never to destroy the descendants of Noah by drowning (Genesis 9. 11).

In the story of the Flood the obedient and God-fearing are saved, while the rest of sinful humanity drown. Typologically as Noah was saved by the Ark, so by the Church we also may be saved. Thus the Ark becomes a figure of the Ship of the Church in which the faithful are carried to salvation.[37] But for those who would earlier have recognized the verbal signals, this image was already implicitly present in the poem. In contrast to the Egyptians, who are described as 'landsmen' (l.179), the Israelites are repeatedly spoken of as seamen, *flotan, sæwicingas*, a nicely ironic metaphor in view of their actual circumstances, since they will not sail but march dryshod across the bed of the sea (ll.133, 223, 331, 333). At a further level this clearly refers to those embarked in the familiar vessel which carries the Christian soul across the troubled sea of life to its heavenly home, its mast the cross of Christ, its sails filled with the breath of the Holy Spirit. In fact this image of the ship was explicitly present long before the Red Sea was in sight. The pillar of cloud with which God has protected his people in the scorching desert was spoken of metaphorically thus:

> hæfde witig God
> sunnan siðfæt    segle ofertolden,
> swa þa mæstrapas    men ne cuðon,
> ne ða seglrode    geseon meahton
> eorðbuende    ealle cræfte,
> hu afæstnod wæs    feldhusa mæst.    (ll. 80–85)

[wise God had screened the sun's course with a sail, although men dwelling on earth, for all their skill, could not understand the rigging, nor see the sailyard, nor how this greatest of tents was made fast.]

This striking and dramatic image is pursued, albeit illogically in any normal sense. It is no longer the desert, but an ocean to be traversed:

> Forð gesawon
> lifes latþeow    lifweg metan;
> segl siðe weold,    sæmen æfter
> foron flodwege.    (ll. 103–06)

[Ahead they saw their life's guide measure out the way of life; the sail directed their journey; behind it the voyagers travelled the ocean-path.]

This beacon which guides and protects the Israelites lest 'the grey terror of the desert', *westengryre, har hæþbroga*, should put an end to their life by their being suddenly overwhelmed by ocean storms, *holmegum wederum* (ll. 115–19), is described reasonably enough as a 'beam', i.e. ray of light (ll. 94, 111, 121, 249), and is finally revealed towards the very end of the poem as Christ's cross itself, employing a well-recognized epithet, *wuldres beam* [the beam (i.e. wood) of glory]:[38]

> Folc wæs on lande;
> hæfde wuldres beam    werud gelæded,
> halige heapas,    on hild Godes.    (ll. 567–69)

[The nation had come to land; the glorious beacon had led the host, the holy band, under God's protection.]

There can be no doubt by now that the poet intended his audience to interpret the journey of the Israelites at a further level as the journey undertaken by the Christian soul, guided by the cross, to salvation.

While it could accommodate splendidly the acknowledged historical matter of Old Testament folk-wanderings and warring kings, the traditional heroic medium might seem at first sight less suited to deal with the gentler substance of New Testament theology. Christ's teaching and example of forgiveness and humility were not directly consonant with heroic values. But in applying the vocabulary of early Anglo-Saxon society to the major Christian story of the Crucifixion, the short poem known as *The Dream of the Rood* represents a wholly remarkable achievement in poetic, intellectual, and inconographic terms. A dramatic and original composition, it is quite without parallel; no model is to be found among any of the large number of contemporary Latin cross-poems. Although engaging with its subject at the most sophisticated theological level, it cannot be shown to derive from either the liturgy, like Cædmon's *Creation-Hymn*, or patristic theology, like *Genesis* or *Exodus*. We are obliged to consider the poem entirely in its own terms as a vigorous but natural development out of the religious concerns of its day. Unlike the later Gothic sensibility which stressed the explicitly pathetic details of the Crucifixion narrative, the early Church was less concerned with literal description than with analysing its significance as the pivotal event of Christian history – although in meditative terms *The Dream of the Rood* is unambiguously exhortatory in its attempt to persuade to action. The poet appeals directly to his audience with his opening words:

> Hwæt, ic swefna cyst    secgan wylle,
> hwæt me gemætte    to midre niht,
> syðþan reordberend    reste wunedon.    (ll. 1–3)

[Look, I want to tell of the most remarkable of visions, that I dreamed in the middle of the night when chattering men lay at rest.]

Whether or not an actual dream occasioned the poet's work is irrelevant. Not only was the Church of Bede thoroughly acquainted with the dream or vision as a vehicle of prophecy or universal truths, often vouchsafed through the medium of a heavenly messenger or guide, such visions may well have been considered appropriate to the religious poet at this time. The dream which occasioned Cædmon's *Creation-Hymn* (see above, p. 70) affords a convenient parallel. Both require the poet to celebrate a particular theme – Cædmon the Creation and the *Dream*-poet the Redemption. The dream convention may in any case have been recognized as particularly appropriate to a cross-cult poem. After all, tradition attributed the very origins of the cult to such a dream, for the Emperor Constantine's conversion to Christianity on the eve of his victory over Maxentius in 312 had been directly related to his dream or vision of the 'heavenly sign' of a cross, which he believed to be the divine pledge of his triumph.[39]

This 'choicest of dreams' takes the form of the vision of a strange tree, the brightest of wood, towering into the heavens, wound round with light (ll. 4–6), contriving to reflect the Constantinian vision while postponing any explicit identification with the cross of Christ.

Instead of an immediate recognition of the vision's significance, a gradual revelation is brought about. A complex series of oblique statements erects a sophisticated structural conception of the meaning of the cross in a way not open to straightforward prose; the theme is one of paradoxical complexity which even theologians found difficult. The vision is of no simple forest tree merely; it is at the same time a symbol or standard, *beacen* [vexillum], appropriately covered with gold and jewels like Constantine's *labarum* (ll.6–9). The verb *begeotan* [to sprinkle, drench], normally associated with water or blood, is unexpected in the phrase *begoten mid golde* (l.7). The application of such an unusual, and perhaps original, word as *eaxlegespann* [shoulder-span] (l.9), to the part which bears jewels, similarly requires explanation. The use of the term *sigebeam* [victorious gleam] or [victorious wood] (l.13) is puzzling. And why should it be denied that this was a criminal's gallows? Statements follow one after another, arousing a series of expectations in the mind of the reader which the poet must subsequently satisfy in the body of his work.

The abstract import of the vision is already implicit, however. This mysterious jewelled ensign stretches across the entire world, quartering the universe, where it is the subject of adoration by hosts of angels as well as men upon earth and the whole of creation (ll.7–12). Now in a unique fusion of realism and symbol, abstract and physical aspects of the tree are brought into direct juxtaposition as the poet introduces personal, spiritual qualities to the material object:

> . . .    ic þurh þæt gold    ongytan meahte
> earmra ærgewin,    þæt hit ærest ongan
> swætan on þa swiðran healfe.    (ll.18–20)

[ . . . through that gold I could perceive the former aggression of wretched men, in that it first began to bleed on the right side.]

The bleeding tree was not without significance. Trees were believed to have bled at the Crucifixion in recognition of Christ's divinity,[40] and a similar sign would herald the approach of Judgement Day.[41] The image here therefore tightens the structure of the poem, anticipating not only its climax in the Crucifixion but also its final apocalyptic vision. The use of the verb *swætan* to describe the bleeding similarly looks forward to the identification of the tree with the physical person of Christ, as does the fact that the tree is specifically said to bleed on the right-hand side.

The mutable focus appropriate to the dream convention serves also to define further the mystery of the symbol while still only partially revealing its identity. The poet thus obliquely contrives to introduce the dual role which, deriving from Christ's own, forms the visual representation of the cross. It is at once both the shameful instrument of pain and death and the means of triumphal victory and life eternal. At times, therefore, it seems the simple rough wood of the gallows, squalid, stained with blood; at other times it reverts to a bejewelled treasure:

> Geseah ic þæt fuse beacen
> wendan wædum ond bleom;   hwilum hit wæs mid wætan
> bestemed,
> beswyled mid swates gange,   hwilum mid since gegyrwed.
> (ll. 21–23)

[I saw that shifting symbol change its clothing and colouring; at times it was soaked with wet, drenched with a flow of blood, at times adorned with treasure.]

Only now with so many aspects of the vision explored, is it clearly recognized to be the symbol of the Saviour's universal dominion, *Hælendes treow* (l. 25). Still, however, until the actual moment of crucifixion the poet hesitates to employ the bluntly explicit word *rod* (l. 44).

The position has been rapidly built up in a series of swift economical movements: rapid compound sequences of short half-line syntactic units in a staccato rhythm with no elaborate repetition or loose variation to impede progress. Now a different tone is introduced with the words of the cross, no less flowing, but with a broader more dignified movement brought about by an extraordinary use of hypermetric verse (see below, p. 292).

That the gallows speaks is in no sense grotesque. The early Church believed that the cross possessed life and an individual personality and power. And as a literary device the speaking cross was not unknown to early religious writings.[42] But in any case the attribution of personality to inanimate objects was an Anglo-Saxon commonplace. Valued objects such as swords or jewels sometimes bore inscriptions in the form of a personalized statement of identity or origin, and a later Anglo-Saxon cross-reliquary inscription which begins + *Rod is min nama*,[43] is simply one of the last of a long tradition.

A more literary precedent for the mode existed in the popular type of Anglo-Saxon riddle in which an enigmatic object is made to describe itself in oblique terms, sometimes telling its history.[44] Whether or not the author of the *Dream* consciously imitated such riddle forms in this part of the poem, his employment of an articulate persona for the cross brilliantly contrives to propound the theological subtleties of his theme while simply sidestepping the many difficulties. The attribution of personality, and therefore volition, allows a moral as well as physical parallel to be established between Christ and the cross. Thus it is that the words of the cross can bring us dramatically close to the events of the

Crucifixion, enabling the reader to share in a unique imaginative recon-
struction of Christ's suffering, but at the same time evading the bewildering problem as to the nature of Christ's consciousness, and without
the assumptive blasphemy that might have been involved.

However, in coalescing the persona of the cross with that of Christ
himself the poet draws upon a concept implicit within the traditional
liturgical use of the cross and explicitly propounded in the Paulician
doctrine that the real cross was not the gallows but the body of Christ
himself. This complex theological analogue between Christ and the cross
for which we have been prepared since the opening vision of the poem is
elaborated in the subsequent narrative. The cross had been chosen from
all the trees of the forest simply because it stood convenient at the edge of
the wood (l.29), as arbitrarily singled out as Mary from among all women
(ll.90–94);[45] it has a mysteriously mixed nature, at once mundane and
precious; abstract qualities like 'victory' are attributed to its physical
substance; it is made a spectacle, mocked, and suffers pain and indignity
which it had the power to avoid; it is buried, rediscovered, and achieves a
final state of glory in heaven, honoured by men and a power in their lives,
and looked to for a second coming. Physical contact between Christ and
the cross is provided in the nails which, driven through the hands and feet
of the one into the other, link the two. That the cross itself thus suffers,
allows the agony of the Saviour to be succinctly and dramatically represented without putting unwarranted words into the mouth of Christ
himself. The device thus allows the poet to maintain a fine balance,
offending neither those who maintained that the incarnate *Logos* could
experience no suffering nor those who insisted upon his real human
frailty.

The particular function of the cross in the act of Redemption is explained in terms of its own natural history. Its origin in the forest tree not
only draws naturally on contemporary representations in which the cross
is seen as the burgeoning stem of the Tree of Life, putting forth leaves,
fragrant with flowers, but derives thematic significance from its apparent
simplicity. There is no confusion as to the different types of wood of which
the cross could have been composed; neither is there any unnecessary
reference to the tree's Old Testament antecedents, both of which so
engaged contemporary exegetes. The use of the simple, natural tree,
while concealing within its metaphor this body of traditional theology,
remains a convenient and convincing symbol of the beauty in creation
perverted by the evil in men for their own ends. Its personal voice
provokes immediate sympathy; the tree recalls its fate with pained outrage: hacked down, torn from its root, seized, and turned into an unnatural, shameful spectacle by powerful and wicked men. The evil in men
is represented not only by the *wergas* he is ordered to lift up; those who
oblige him to do so are also *feondas* (ll.30–33). It is not simply individual

men or even mankind that is involved in the Crucifixion, however, but the whole of creation represented in the archetypal world-tree – now the cosmic symbol stretching to the four quarters of the universe. With an almost eastern abstract simplicity the poet contrives to embrace within the one concept so much extranea which a later age might have allowed to detract from the philosophic content of the event. There are no explicit bystanders, soldiers, or Jews; the *feondas* are forgotten – no weeping women; all are subsumed within the one representative, the sympathetic and yet unwilling instrument of death. The Creator is destroyed by his Creation. This is a poetically dense concept, involving here also the tragic heroic dilemma of the follower not only refused permission to avenge the death of his Lord, but himself the *bana* (l.66) obliged to play a major part in it. The poet has avoided the obvious temptation to utilize the heroic implications of the disciples' wavering loyalties and ultimate desertion of their Lord. Instead the conflict between heroic ideal and Christian obedience is utilized powerfully to augment the personal perplexity of the cross, reinforced by a repetition of the words *ne dorste ic* [I dare not] four times within a short space (ll.35–47).

The actual Crucifixion is presented in simple, starkly dramatic terms. The poet seems less concerned with specific details of the biblical narrative than to provide an economic representation of what were considered the theological essentials of the event. The imaginative construction that the poet erects so as to tread so careful a path between doctrinal niceties results in a singularly memorable visual effect. Natural pathos is absent. No flogged, suffering, stumbling Christ drags the cross to Calvary; it stands already, a stark symbol set up on a hill. We have been led to infer that the cross has already been used to execute felons (ll.31, 87–88) so that a gallows image is already established, contrasting implicitly with the innocence of Christ, which need not therefore be mentioned to detract from the heroic status of the warrior-Lord. Christ indeed is not led there by a jeering mob; he is stripped by no mocking soldiers. Instead, as in contemporary iconography or as seen by Ambrose or Cynewulf, he is a young and confident champion striding from afar:[46] *efstan elne mycle þæt he me wolde on gestigan* (l.34). Vigorous and single-minded, he strips himself for battle and a kingly victory. The action is entirely his, an eager sacrifice; there is no question at this point of his being nailed to the cross. Instead he climbs to embrace it (ll.40–42). It is pre-eminently an act of dominant free will by a prince confident of victory. With the agony transferred to the cross, Christ can sensibly be seen to rule from the gallows.[47]

It is at this point rather than several hours later that the earth's surface shakes (ll.36–37), thus tightening the structure of the narrative, and allowing for a contrast between trembling earth and steadfast cross, firm at the command of Christ. It is at the climax of the event that darkness covers the earth, shadows serving at once to heighten and subdue the radiance of the Lord's body (52–55), thus utilizing a biblical incidental to involve the whole of nature in the recognition of Christ on the cross. If there are no weeping women, as might have been used by later writers to emphasize the pathos of the scene, the whole of creation weeps, laments the fall of the King, the poet returning now to stark, simple half-line syntactic units: *Crist wæs on rode* (ll.55–56). In human terms, misery is absent; the lament of all creation is on far larger a scale.

Suffering is implied, but nowhere described so as to distract from the broad significance of the action. The emotional intensity of Christ's agony is conveyed by a device that evades the awkward issue of his susceptibility to pain. Christ's humanity is transferred to the person of the cross, which insists that the nails were driven into *himself*, on *him* the malicious wounds are to be seen; it is *he* who is stricken with arrows, covered with blood (ll.46–48, 62), the culmination of all the cruel deeds he had endured (ll.50–51). The parallel is maintained; the cross takes on aspects of Christ's dual will and operation. Its whole inclination is to bow before its creator, to shrink from the task set before it, but against the will of God it dare not bend or break; like Christ himself it might so easily have slain all its enemies, but it stands firm at the Lord's command (ll.35–43).

The Crucifixion story is completed and the Invention tradition, found *in extenso* in *Elene*,[48] briefly introduced within a few allusive lines. The treatment is still rapid and compact, conflating the narrative in simple but concretely dramatic terms. Unnamed men eager to serve their Lord, but doomed in his departure, come to take down their exhausted God – their impersonality allowing no impediment to the doctrinal outline. They bury him not in a distant cave but in an Anglo-Saxon coffin carved at the foot of the cross – i.e. in the sight of his slayer. Even as the corpse grows cold the cross is cut down and hidden in a deep pit. The rediscovery of the cross, we are led to infer, is made, not centuries later by different people, but promptly by Christ's own disciples, the Lord's thegns. This leads to its decoration with the gold and silver of the reliquaries, an echo of the opening vision of the poem. As before, the treatment is carefully restrained. The poet introduced no unnecessary detail which might diffuse his material and disperse its impact. Nothing is allowed to detract from the essential theological relevancies. There is in the poem an almost Byzantine insistence on the importance of ideas, to which the shallower matter of narrative and descriptive detail are wholly subordinate.

As throughout, these passages betray a fine artistic accommodation of style to sense. The sequences of expanded verse which end with the 'death' of Christ (*his gast onsended*, l.49) are replaced by the rapid movement of normal lines in the asides of the cross commenting on its fate, the response of nature and the shadow and weeping which build up to the climax: *Crist wæs on rode* (l.56). The sequence dealing with the deposition, however, reverts to broadly moving hypermetric lines, suitably underlining at once the grave dignity of the events and the bewildering theological proposition which underlies it. Hitherto the extent of Christ's physical condition had been carefully masked in favour of his victorious rule from the cross. Now close contact with physical reality is inevitable, and his essentially corporeal humanity – his nature not only as God but also as frail man – is expressed through a literary use of the theological *communicatio idiomatum*. This device is found here some ten times within thirty lines, providing all the shock and astonishment of violent paradox in a deliberate distancing of verb and subject: *Genamon hie þær ælmihtigne God, . . . gestodon him æt his lices heafdum . . . heofenes Dryhten, . . . gesetton hie ðæron sigora Wealdend* (ll.60–67).

Once the Crucifixion has been acted out and the function of the cross as symbol of the act of Redemption made plain, the vision reverts to its opening character (recapitulating over lines 12 and 82). Now moving from the role of dramatic participant to spiritual mentor, it can explain to the dreamer in its evangelical capacity the motivating force behind the cult of the cross – how now in glory it is revered and feared by men upon earth for the healing power it possesses. Its doctrinal significance is underlined by rhetorical balance: although once the instrument of squalid death, it is now become the means of eternal life (ll.87–89). The word used of those to whom salvation is brought is *reordberend*, inevitably recalling the use of the word at the beginning of the poem. The significance of the opening scene in anticipating such an end is now clear. It had contained significant features of the conventional doomsday vision when the day of the Lord should come in darkness *æt midre niht*, suddenly surprising careless men wrapped in sleep and bringing misery to those unprepared, while the faithful are gathered in from the four corners of the earth. Here, however, there is yet time. Salvation is to be brought to those that sleep, careless of their suffering Lord, ignorant of the word of his messengers. It is to these that the dreamer is given his evangelical mission. Like the cross itself in the Gospel of Peter,[49] he is to preach to them that sleep. Now the Crucifixion is linked naturally with a view of Judgement Day. A fast compound sequence running over the antithetical balance – *Ne mæg þær ænig unforht wesan . . . Ne þearf ðær þonne ænig unforht wesan* (ll.110–17) – contrasts the terror then of the unjust with the calm of the righteous, reliant on the simple power of the cross to save.

The view then reverts to that of the original visionary. To have finished simply with the words of the cross would have been structurally and emotionally inadequate. The whole thrust of early Church literature leads one to expect a homiletic coda of some kind at this point, whether following the broad Augustinian model of *exhortatio* following *narratio*, a sermon to strengthen the audience's response to the story, or the more detailed pattern of contemporary rhetorical analysis: *exordium, narratio, partitio, confirmatio, reprehensio et conclusio.*[50]

If the style differs at this point then it is appropriate. The memorable static imagery of the opening vision is replaced by a swifter, simpler style. The conclusion to the poem may be more diffuse than its highly wrought opening, but it is no less organized structurally. The poet's theme is developed consistently and meaningfully. It is perhaps best seen as a formal progression in our view of the cross: from that of the dreamer persona for whom the cross represents a tropological symbol of practical faith – the exhortation to a religious life – through a central allegorical resolution in which the cross is shown as institutionalized doctrine on the persona and death of Christ, to its final anagogical development here in an apocalyptic consummation.

Catalysed by his vision, the poet's resolution forms the directly devotional basis of the poem's conclusion. The visionary no longer lies passive and silent. Now an independent personal identity, he declares his veneration for the cross powerfully, but within conventional machinery. As commonly with the religious persona (see below, p. 114), he is now old and friendless, his soul yearning to follow those who have already sought and won their heavenly home. The confession of world-weariness (*langung-hwila*, l. 126) is linked with a hope of heaven. But although made possible by the sacrificial death of Christ, it is to the deified cross, living symbol of the deed, that he looks to fetch him from his transient life to the joys of heaven.[51] The tension contained within the heroic conception of the cross is pursued; the dreamer now ironically finds his patron, *mundbyrd*, in the slayer, *bana*, of his lord (ll. 130–31).

## Notes

1. *Bede's Ecclesiastical History of the English People*, edited by B. Colgrave and R. A. B. Mynors (Oxford, 1969), pp. 414–19.

2. While Bede does not specify that this was an angelic visitation, as much seems to be implied.

3. For a general survey of analogies to the Cædmon story, see G. A. Lester, 'The Cædmon Story and its Analogues', *Neophilologus*, 58 (1974), 225–37. The best-known and most remarkable parallel is that of Muhammad's revelation near Mecca in the same century: 'He was asleep or in a trance when he heard a voice say, "Read!". He said, "I cannot read". The voice again said, "Read!". He said, "I cannot read". A third time the voice, more terrible, commanded, "Read!". He said, "What can I read?". The voice said, "Read: In the name of the Lord who createth

man from a clot". When he awoke the words remained "as if inscribed on his heart"', *The Meaning of the Glorious Koran: An Explanatory Translation*, edited by M. Pickford (London, 1930), p. 2.

4. See generally *The Gifts of Men*, especially ll. 49–50, in *The Exeter Book*, edited by G. P. Krapp and E. v. K. Dobbie, The Anglo-Saxon Poetic Records (London 1931–53), iii, pp. 137–40.

5. *Cynewulf's Elene*, edited by P. O. E. Gradon, second edition (Exeter, 1977), pp. 71–72, ll. 1242–51.

6. 'I do not seek the pastoral Muses for my verse . . . but rather I strive to move the Thunderer with my prayers, who grants to use the oracles of the peaceful word; I seek the word from The Word, whom the psalmist celebrated, born in the heart of the Father . . .', *Aldhelmi Opera*, edited by R. Ehwald, *Monumenta Germaniae Historica, Auctorum Antiquissimorum*, xv (Berlin, 1919), pp. 353–54.

7. In the preface to his verse *Life of St Cuthbert* (a claim interestingly ignored in Bede's parallel prose life of the saint), edited by J. -P. Migne, *Patrologia Latina*, (Paris, 1844–90), xciv, col. 577.

8. *Bede's Eccles. Hist.*, edited by Colgrave and Mynors, pp. 106–09.

9. Ibid., pp. 514–15.

10. In the lost *Handboc* consulted by William of Malmesbury, *De Gestis Pontificum Anglorum*, edited by N. E. S. A. Hamilton, Rolls Series, 52 (London, 1870), p. 336.

11. With the possible exception of a translation of his Latin 'breastplate riddle', *Three Northumbrian Poems*, edited by A. H. Smith, revised edition (Exeter, 1978).

12. *Aldhelmi Opera*, edited by Ehwald, pp. 133–34.

13. Pseudo-Bede, *In Pentateuchum Commentarii*, edited by J. -P. Migne, *Patrologia Latina*, (Paris, 1844–90), xci, col. 189f.

14. *Epistola Cuthberti de obitu Bedae*, in *Bede's Eccles. Hist.*, edited by Colgrave and Mynors, pp. 582–85.

15. *Two of the Saxon Chronicles Parallel*, edited by J. Earle and C. Plummer (Oxford, 1892–99), i, p. 67.

16. Pseudo-Bede, *In Matthaei Evangelium Expositio*, edited by J. -P. Migne, *Patrologia Latina*, (Paris, 1844–90), xcii, col. 66.

17. See generally, Bede, *De Schematibus et Tropis*, in *Rhetores Latini Minores*, edited by C. Halm (Leipzig, 1863), pp. 616ff.

18. Compare *De Doctrina Christiana*, edited by W. M. Green, *Corpus Scriptorum Ecclesiasticorum Latinorum*, lxxx, (Vienna, 1963), pp. 36, 141.

19. Bede, *In Genesim*, edited by C. W. Jones, *Corpus Christianorum, Series Latina*, cxviii(a), (Turnholt, 1967), p. x.

20. Ibid., p. 181.

21. *The Cædmon Manuscript of Anglo-Saxon Biblical Poetry, Junius XI in the Bodleian Library*, edited by I. Gollancz (Oxford, 1927), pp. xl, 7, 66. For the literary possibilities of this Trinitarian sophistication, see R. Frank, 'Some Uses of Paronomasia in Old English Scriptural Verse', *Speculum*, 47 (1972), 207–26 (pp. 212–15).

22. Bede, *In Genesim*, edited by Jones, p. 56.

23. Ibid., pp. 144–45.

24. Ibid., pp. 89–90, 137.

25. Ibid., p. 227.

26. Pseudo-Bede, *In Pentateuchum,* edited by Migne, *Patrologia Latina,* xci, cols 100–02, 223.

27. Bede, *In Genesim,* edited by Jones, p. 81.

28. A similar intrusion of the personal voice occurs earlier in begining a fresh section following the expulsion from Eden: *Hwæt, we nu gehyað hwær . . . hearmstafas* [Look, now we shall hear how bitter troubles . . .] (l.939).

29. *In Genesim,* edited by Jones, p. 187.

30. Compare Augustine, *Ennarationes in Psalmos,* edited by E. Dekkers and J. Fraipoint, *Corpus Christianorum, Series Latina,* xxxviii–xl, (Turnholt, 1956), p. 1091.

31. Compare J. G. G. Alexander, *Insular Manuscripts, 6th to the 9th Century* (London, 1978), *passim.*

32. Pseudo-Bede, *In Pentateuchum,* edited by Migne, *Patrologia Latina,* xci, col. 307; see D. G. Calder, 'Two Notes on the Typology of the OE *Exodus', Neuphilologische Mitteilungen,* 74 (1973), 85–89.

33. For an elaborate examination of this aspect, see J. W. Bright, 'The Relation of the Cædmonian *Exodus* to the Liturgy', *Modern Language Notes,* 27 (1912), 97–103.

34. See J. E. Cross and S. I. Tucker, 'Allegorical Tradition and the Old English *Exodus', Neophilologus,* 44 (1960), 122–27 (p. 125); and generally J. F. Vickrey, '*Exodus* and the Battle in the Sea', *Traditio,* 28 (1972), 119–40.

35. See further, R. M. Trask, 'Doomsday Imagery in the Old English *Exodus', Neophilologus,* 57 (1973), 295–97.

36. The same phrase is used elsewhere of the damned (*Christ,* l. 1526, in *The Exeter Book,* edited by Krapp and Dobbie, p. 45), and of the monsters destroyed in Noah's flood (*Beowulf,* l. 113).

37. Compare E. Peterson, 'Das Schiff als Symbol der Kirche', *Theologische Zeitschrift,* 6 (1950), 77–79; R. E. Kaske, 'A Poem of the Cross in The Exeter Book', *Traditio,* 23 (1969), 41–71 (pp. 54–55); P. J. Lucas, 'Old English Christian Poetry: The Cross in *Exodus',* in *Famulus Christi: Essays in Commemoration of the Thirteenth Centenary of the Birth of the Venerable Bede,* edited by G. Bonner (London, 1976), pp. 193–209.

38. Compare *The Dream of the Rood,* l. 97, edited by M. Swanton, second edition (Manchester, 1978), p. 95, and *Cynewulf's Elene,* l. 217, edited by Gradon, second edition, p. 35.

39. Eusebius represents this as an actual apparition seen in the sky, and Lactantius as a dream vision: *Patrologia Graeca,* edited by J. -P. Migne (Paris, 1859–1912), xx, cols 944–45, 948; *Patrologia Latina,* edited by J. -P. Migne (Paris, 1844–90), vii, cols 260–62. It was the second of these traditions that the Anglo-Saxons adopted, compare *Elene,* ll.69–98 (*Cynewulf's Elene,* edited by Gradon, second edition, pp. 29–30).

40. Compare *Christ,* ll. 1174–76, in *The Exeter Book,* edited by Krapp and Dobbie, p. 35. The concept presumably derives from the Apocrypha, ii Esdras 5. 5.

41. Compare Pseudo-Bede, *De Quindecim Signis,* edited by J. -P. Migne, *Patrologia Latina,* (Paris, 1844–90), xciv, col. 555, or the apocalyptic Vespasian homily, *Early English Homilies,* edited by R. D. N. Warner, Early English Text Society, Original Series 152 (London, 1917), p. 90.

42. Compare *Bruchstücke des Evangeliums und der Apokalypse des Petrus*, edited by A. Harnack (Leipzig, 1893), p. 11, and the dramatic passage in a pseudo-Augustinian sermon, *De Resurrectione Domini Nostri*, edited by J. -P. Migne, *Patrologia Latina*, (Paris 1844–90), xlvii, cols 1155–56.

43. H. Logeman, *L'Inscription Anglo-Saxonne du Reliquaire de la Vraie Croix au Trésor de l'Église des SS. Michel-et-Gudule à Bruxelles* (Ghent, 1891); and compare S. T. R. O. d'Ardenne, 'The Old English Inscription on the Brussels Cross', *English Studies*, 21 (1939), 145–64, 271–72.

44. There are Latin cross riddles by Hwætberht, Abbot of Monkwearmouth-Jarrow from 716, and Tatwine, Mercian Archbishop of Canterbury from 731 to 734 (*Collectiones Aenigmatum Merovingicae Aetatis*, edited by M. de Marco, *Corpus Christianorum, Series Latina*, cxxxiii (Turnholt, 1968), pp. 176, 227), and others in the Old English Exeter Book which might be resolved thus, e.g. nos. 30, 55, or 67, to which the power of speech is specifically attributed as one of several enigmatic features (*The Exeter Book*, edited by Krapp and Dobbie, pp. 195–96, 208, 231). Others from the Exeter Book collection, however, like no. 53, 'battering-ram', or no. 72, 'spear', afford a better structural analogy to the words of the cross here; they tell much the same history – how, living in the forest, they had been cut down and fashioned by men for a particular purpose (Ibid., pp. 207, 232–33).

45. Compare Ælfric, *The Homilies of the Anglo-Saxon Church*, edited by B. Thorpe (London, 1844–46), ii, p. 306.

46. Ambrose, *Expositio Evangelii Secundum Lucan*, edited by C. Schenkl, *Corpus Scriptorum Ecclesiasticorum Latinorum*, xxxii (4) (Leipzig, 1902), pp. 496–97; Cynewulf's *Christ*, ll. 744–46, or, presumably referring to the Song of Solomon 2. 8, ll. 715ff (*The Exeter Book*, edited by Krapp and Dobbie, p. 23). Conventional iconography, as on the eighth-century Northumbrian Genoels-Elderen diptych, represents Christ as a victorious warrior, often transfixing hostile beasts using his cross as a spear (J. Beckwith, *Ivory Carvings in Early Medieval England* (London, 1972), pp. 20, 118, fig. 14).

47. As in the line of Fortunatus's hymn 'Vexilla Regis', 'regnavit a ligno Deus' (*Opera Poetica*, edited by F. Leo, *Monumenta Germaniae Historica, Auctorum Antiquissimorum*, iv (1) (Berlin, 1881), p. 34 (l. 16); compare the *textus receptus* of Psalm 95. 10, 'dominus regnavit a ligno'.

48. *Cynewulf's Elene*, edited by Gradon, second edition.

49. *Bruchstücke des Evangeliums*, edited by Harnack, p. 11.

50. Compare Augustine, *De Catechizandis Rudibus*, edited by J. -P. Migne, *Patrologia Latina*, (Paris, 1844–90), xl, cols 317f; Alcuin, *Disputatio de Rhetorica et de Virtutibus*, in *Rhetores Latini Minores*, edited by Halm, pp. 525–50, *passim*.

51. The cross traditionally conveys the soul to heaven; compare W. Bousset, 'Platons Weltseele und das Kreuz Christi', *Zeitschrift für die neutestamentliche Wissenschaft und die Kunde des Urchristentums*, 14 (1913), 283.

# Chapter 4
# The Ruin of Time

## The Wanderer, The Seafarer, The Ruin, and The Phoenix

The introduction of Christianity did not so much replace the native mode of thought respecting man's view of himself and his place in the order of things, as present an authoritative and systematic framework for his moral stance. The sentiments so graphically voiced by Edwin's anonymous adviser (see above, p. 9), are taken up by the author of an untitled but probably eighth-century poem we call *The Wanderer*. Cast in the form of a dramatic monologue, it explores the topic of man's search for some kind of comfort in distress.

The speaker is progressively redefined, first as *anhaga* (l. 1), the sense of which encompasses both 'a solitary' and 'one who thinks deeply', through *eardstapa*, 'a wanderer' (l. 6), before finally moving to the state of *snottor on mode* [the wise in heart] (l. 111), a mimetic maturation, moving from the personal, individual voice to the general view. Although the conditions of oral performance may well have encouraged the audience to envisage separable *dramatis personae*, the introduction of a second voice does not necessarily indicate the presence of a second speaker rather than different aspects of a single complex persona. The picture presented is active rather than static, the separable elements of personal experience and philosophic reflection reconciled, offering a profoundly moving view of the human condition.

The poem opens with a dramatic statement encapsulating the subsequent movement contained within the body of the poem:

> Oft him anhaga     are gebideð,
> Metudes miltse,     þeahþe he modcearig
> geond lagulade     longe sceolde
> hreran mid hondum     hrimcealde sæ,
> wadan wræclastas.     Wyrd bið ful aræd.     (ll. 1–5)

[Often the solitary man will experience grace, the mercy of God, even though for a long time, anxious in spirit, he must stir with his hands the ice-cold sea, travel the paths of exile over the watery way. Fate is utterly fixed.]

The gnomic mode is established by the characteristic use of *oft*, the third person singular and the present tense,[1] concluding with a solemn and foreboding half-line exclaiming on the inexorability of fate: *Wyrd bið ful aræd*, a familiar stoical statement reflecting the view of one whose primary experience of the world is that life is often disappointing, always uncertain. His anxiety is repeatedly stressed: *modcearig, earmcearig, wintercearig* (ll.2, 20, 24). The definitive condition expressed is that of an exile, the sorrows and hardships borne by one deprived of the security of the hall and the companionship of his fellow men. At once literal and figurative, the uncertainties of life outside the *locus comitatus* – the unknown but undoubtedly harsh region from which the sparrow came and to which he will come again – supplies a ready correlative for that which is beyond worldly experience. The figure of the exile haunts the Anglo-Saxon imagination as a constant nagging fear of the possibility, even likelihood, of the dispersal of the comitatus consequent on internal dissension or external attack. Since one's place in the hall is what gives one's life significance and meaning, to be deprived, for whatever reason, of a place in that society, is the ultimate catastrophe that might befall an individual. Outside those known bonds lay an alien and hostile world in which even the best of men might well be incapable of establishing new relationships. The lonely man was not yet imbued with the romantic aura that a later age might ascribe to him. The solitary outsider was not just to be pitied, but distrusted: the wolf's-head of the outlaw especially shunned. There were all sorts of reasons for being in the state of exile – not all of them the result of innocent misfortune. In real life a man might be exiled from society for all sorts of wickedness, like the West Saxon king and war-leader Sigeberht, ultimately driven out into the Wealden forests to die violently and alone in the miserable events leading up to the *coup d'état* at Merton (see above, p. 8). In literature the list of wicked exiles is headed by Cain, his brother's slayer, condemned by God himself to be shunned (see above, p. 83), and from whom were descended a whole brood of outcast monsters, hobgoblins, and trolls, most notably Beowulf's opponent Grendel himself 'who bore God's anger' (see above, p. 56).

But the role of exile was not unfamiliar to the heroes of contemporary literature – a Waldere or Hengest – who either find themselves exiled at some stage in their personal history, or act out their adventures far from home. The persona adopted by the poet-figure himself – Widsith by definition and Deor by history – is characteristically that of the lone wanderer. This was not peculiar to the Germanic consciousness alone, but arises naturally from the prevailing conditions of warfare society in north-western Europe; in contemporary Latin and Celtic elegies the voice is frequently that of an exile who contrasts his former happiness with his present miserable condition.[2] The persona is one with whose concerns the audience might readily identify: forceful not only by reason of correlating so nearly to the fears of actual experience but in fulfilling a fundamental mimetic role, since the traveller, whether exile or pilgrim, is removed from his context and, deprived of his defensive network of reliance, is rendered at once vulnerable and open. The individual is more amenable to suggestion, more prepared to admit the truth of his condition, when lacking the comfortable, or compromising, support of familiar circumstances.

Now the *anhaga*, if not literally identified with, is an emphatic referent for the *eardstapa* whose voice makes up the body of the poem. But whereas the voice of Deor or Widsith speaks from a known historical and geographical setting, precise and recognizable, albeit fictive, the ethopoetic wanderer persona is located in no particular time or place. The narrative voice which speaks forcibly, movingly – and credibly – about its individual experience, remains nevertheless 'representative', its faceless quality enduing it with strength and application. Requiring no one physical image, the face he adopts may be that of the individual reader, or of mankind. However, it is soon clear that the particular circumstance leading to the speaker's condition was the violent dispersal of a comitatus with the death of its leader:

> Swa cwæð eardstapa    earfeþa gemyndig,
> wraþra wælsleahta,    winemæga hryre.    (ll.6–7)

[Thus spoke the wanderer, remembering hardships, the slaughterous attacks of enemies, the fall of loving kinsmen.]

The Wanderer-figure proceeds to expatiate on his own personal experience of loneliness in a reflective and expansive manner – the introduction of the first person claiming immediacy, authenticity, and additional sympathy in so far as the depth of his misery and hardship is exacerbated by the fact that the audience receives this account of his condition in what are likely to be relatively comfortable and secure circumstances.

> 'Oft ic sceolde ana    uhtna gehwylce
> mine ceare cwiþan;    nis nu cwicra nan
> þe ic him modsefan    minne durre
> sweotule asecgan'.    (ll.8–11)

['I have often had to bewail my sorrow alone at each dawn; there is now no one living to whom I dare openly speak my heart'.]

What makes the speaker's suffering intolerable is not mere hardship – in an age when material want, hunger even, must have been commonplace – but desperate loneliness. It is the fact that, friendless and leaderless, there is now no one in whom he can confide, which is the occasion of his speech – and our poem. His grief is such as to demand utterance (indeed paradoxically we cannot know of it otherwise). Yet ironically he is well aware of the classical virtue of reticence in face of adversity:

'Ic to soþe wat
þæt biþ in eorle    indryhten þeaw
þæt he his ferðlocan    fæste binde,
healde his hordcofan,    hycge swa he wille'.    (ll. 11–14)

['I know, of course, that it is a noble virtue in a man to bind fast his breast, keep his heart in check, whatever he may feel'.]

But mere stoicism proves inadequate, as the very existence of the poem betrays. So desperate is he to have someone to share his life that he will personify even sorrow itself as a companion – cruel company – the gnomic formula again inviting sympathetic assent: *Wat se þe cunnað hu sliþen bið sorg to geferan* [He who tries knows how cruel is grief as a companion] (ll. 29–30). Underscoring the actuality of individual experience, the effect of gnomic generalization, no less forceful for all its universal application, in no way dissipates the personal intensity of the statement, but rather achieves simultaneous immediacy and general validity, at once emotional and intellectual, with a greater claim to authority than the speaker's experience alone. There develops a singularly convincing portrayal of suffering mankind, invested with a wealth of realistic imagery. The Wanderer's condition is realized by way of concrete details; his decidedly bleak landscape – windswept headlands, frozen seas, and harsh weather – is not merely the experiential matrix of human hardship but the appropriate metaphorical expression of spiritual desolation: his spirit being no less frozen than his surroundings, heart and soul in the grip of winter, *wintercearig* (l. 24). The speaker feels himself to be – as at a literal level he is – all at sea – and a cruel sea it is. When eventually 'sorrow and sleep together bind the wretched man' (ll. 39–40), the expected relief of even temporary oblivion is disturbed by the dream that he is back once more with his beloved leader, engaged in the ceremonies of hall-life – the dreadful reality to which he awakens only made worse by the tantalizing nature of his dream:

Ðonne onwæcneð eft    wineleas guma,
gesihð him biforan    fealwe wegas,
baþian brimfuglas    brædan feþra,
hreosan hrim ond snaw    hagle gemenged.
Þonne beoð þy hefigran    heortan benne,
sare æfter swæsne.    Sorg bið geniwad.    (ll. 45–50)

[Then the friendless man wakes up once more, sees before him fallow waves, sea-birds bathing, spreading their feathers, frost and snow falling mingled with hail. Then the heart's wounds are the harder to bear, sore in the wake of loved ones. Sorrow is renewed.]

Finally, in a fine touch of psychological realism, the Wanderer's mind gives way to hallucination. The pain of deprivation is such that he is driven to re-create in his mind the joys of his past life – not the indulgent nostalgia of comfortable retirement, but torturing remembrance, a poignant fantasy. The Wanderer eagerly greets the old friends that he thinks are before his eyes – only to find their images fade on the drifting waters: 'The company of fleeting figures brings no familiar songs, and anxiety is renewed' (ll.54–55). However the mind may twist and turn, inescapable reality is reiterated by an echo over lines 50–55: *Sorg/Cearo bið geniwad*. This leads immediately to a reflective summary on the transitoriness of human life and a direct parallel with the state of the world itself which, like man, seems to be falling into the sere – the significance of which is signalled by the opening conjunction, *Forþon*:

'Forþon ic geþencan ne mæg    geond þas woruld
for hwan modsefa    min ne gesweorce
þonne ic eorla lif    eal geondþence,
hu hi færlice    flet ofgeafon,
modge maguþegnas.    Swa þes middangeard
ealra dogra gehwam    dreoseð ond fealleþ'.    (ll.58–63)

['Therefore I cannot think why in the world my heart should not grow dark, when I really think about the life of men, how suddenly they relinquished the floor of the hall, brave warrior-thegns. Just so this middle-earth day by day declines and decays'.]

Here the poet draws on more than merely the pathetic fallacy. It was a commonplace to contemporary thought that the world as it neared the millennium would show clear signs of decline if not of actual decay. Quite evidently things were not what once they were. All over western Europe lay the tangible ruins of a once-great civilization: towns, villas, and public buildings lying desolate and empty. The persistent human instinct that a golden age lay somewhere in the past, here corroborated by the witness of their eyes, was underlined by elaborate academic analysis. Of the seven ages of man since the time of Creation, five, up to the appearance of Christ on earth, had passed and man was now living in the sixth which itself was hastening on to its end when, with all the terrors of eschatology, the last trump would sound and Judgement Day, the end of the world, would arrive. The physical substance of the world, no less than man, was involved in a process of real and inevitable decay prior to destruction. Man was bound to undergo this process of decay primarily because of his first fall from grace and his expulsion from Eden. Since this expulsion, man as an exile on earth, bound to labour and go in sorrow, was forced to wander through this transitory vale of tears until one day he would be able to re-enter his true, heavenly home.[3]

A further *Forþon* sequence marks a decisive shift from narrative to didactic tone. The intensely personal lament of the solitary is finally resolved by a degree of philosophic detachment from his individual circumstances, remarking how men do not recognize the true significance of ever-present decay until the reflection of the years makes it a personal rather than rational experience – acknowledged *pathei mathos* – the proverbial truism that wisdom comes only with suffering:[4]

> Forþon ne mæg wearþan wis  wer ær he age
> wintra dæl in woruldrice.   (ll. 64–65)

> [A man cannot become wise, therefore, until he has had his share of winters in the kingdom of the world.]

The poet goes on to list solid pragmatic *sententiae* – the classic stoical responses to the human situation, the need to display fortitude and moderation in life – in an anaphoric sequence of the type: 'not too X, not too Y', spreading over lines 66–69. Expressing the experiential wisdom of maturity rather than the trimmer's self-apology, this philosophic stance is linked with the eventual fate of the whole world; for the prudent man, we are told, will recognize an ultimate pattern in his experience, anticipating the appalling scene of a total Doomsday wasteland. The world is hastening to its ruin, just as now at random, individual ruined halls mark the transience of human glory: the fall not only of individual fortunes, but the ruin of society intimately associated with the desolation of its physical context:

> Ongietan sceal gleaw hæle  hu gæstlic bið
> þonne eall þisse worulde wela  weste stondeð,
> swa nu missenlice  geond þisne middangeard
> winde biwaune  weallas stondaþ,
> hrime bihrorene,  hryðge þa ederas.
> Woriað þa winsalo,  waldend licgað
> dreame bidrorene;  duguþ eal gecrong
> wlonc bi wealle.   (ll. 73–80)

> [A clear-sighted man must realize how ghastly it will be when all the riches of this world stand waste – just as now variously throughout this middle-earth walls are standing, blown by the winds, hung with frost, precincts swept with snow. The wine-halls are crumbling, their rulers lying dead, bereft of pleasure; the whole proud comitatus has fallen by the wall.]

Just as the hall crumbles into ruins, so those who enjoyed it are physically dispersed – not just as a society but individually fragmented: taken off by war, or rent by the carrion beasts (ll.80–84). But whether or not this violence is understood to indicate the Wanderer's personal cause of distress, it is clear that this ruination is not a matter of individual bad luck, but part of the general nature of earthly things determined by God himself. Just as the wind and the frost destroy the walls of the hall, just as the sword and wolf have destroyed the bodies of the comitatus, it is the Creator who ordains the transient nature of his creation:

> Yþde swa þisne eardgeard   ælda Scyppend
> oþþæt burgwara   breahtma lease
> eald enta geweorc   idlu stodon.   (ll.85–87)

[Thus did the Creator of men lay waste this dwelling-place until the ancient work of giants stood desolate, lacking the noise of citizens' revelry.]

Having broadened his focus from the mead-hall to the deserted Roman cities – the work of past civilization and mute witness to the vanity of human wishes – the poet takes a further step in the universalization of the image. The lesson abstracted from reflection on the ruined hall is that the individual is helpless in face of the universal condition of earthly decay, both of the work of man's hands and of his affections. This prompts deep reflection on the impermanence of all earthly things, particular and general, for those who seriously think about 'this dark life' (ll.88–89). As previously, it is the reality of the objective correlative of earthly glory that speaks most forcibly; the emotional pitch rising with a cluster of questions posed by the hypothetical 'wise man' – a familiar rhetorical exclamation[5] in which a series of unanswerable questions are posed, or rather, questions the answer to which is only too obvious, and dreadful in its cumulative effect:

> 'Hwær cwom mearg?   Hwær cwom mago? Hwær cwom
>                                            maþþumgyfa?
> Hwær cwom symbla gesetu?   Hwær sindon seledreamas?
> Eala beorht bune!   Eala byrnwiga!
> Eala þeodnes þrym!   Hu seo þrag gewat,
> genap under nihthelm   swa heo no wære'.   (ll.92–96)

['What has become of the steed? What has become of the man? What has become of the treasure-giver? What has become of the place of feasting? Where are the pleasures of the hall? Alas for the bright goblet! Alas for the mailed warrior! Alas for the glory of the prince! How that time has passed away, grown dark under the shadow of night, as if it had never been'.]

The initial sequence itemizes particular things which men have held dear and which have passed away, things not important in themselves but for what they symbolize, graphically representing the lost age. Significantly the poet chooses to employ not the classical formula *Hwær biþ* . . . [Where are . . .] but *Hwær cwom* . . . [What have they come to?]. The unvoiced answer is, of course, they have all come to nothing, for everything passes – the less acceptable aspect of Deor's consolatory argument. The poet then passes on to lament the loss of delights in a similar progressive list, moving from tangibles to a greater intangibility; all is lost, not merely the cup but he who enjoyed it – and his glory. The final poignant summary serves to question the ultimate reality of things, recognizing the illusory nature of both man's works and man's affections, fading like the Wanderer's dream-companions. But if all the past has come to nothing, the dreadful reality of what does now come in its place is explicitly described:

> ond þas stanhleoþu    stormas cnyssað;
> hrið hreosende    hrusan bindeð,
> wintres woma;    þonne won cymeð
> nipeð nihtscua    norþan onsendeð
> hreo hæglfare    hæleþum on andan.    (ll. 101–05)

[Storms beat upon the ruin; falling snow, the terror of winter, fetters the earth; then comes darkness, the shadow of night spreads gloom, sends from the north fierce hailstorms to the distress of men.]

Picking up and developing several of the images of the first part of the poem, and thus universalizing the experience of the individual Wanderer, the final statement represents not one wallowing in self-pity but the quietude of dignified self-realization, aware of his place in the mutable flux of the world's being. Transcending the grim experience of his individual plight, the Wanderer moves from signs of physical dissolution to a metaphysical understanding concluding with an echo of the doom-laden line 74.

> Eall is earfoðlic    eorþan rice;
> onwendeð wyrda gesceaft    weoruld under heofonum.
> Her bið feoh læne,    her bið freond læne,
> her bið mon læne,    her bið mæg læne.
> Eal þis eorþan gesteal    idel weorþeð.    (ll. 106–10)

[Everything in the kingdom of the earth is full of hardship; the decree of fate makes mutable the world beneath the heavens. Here wealth is ephemeral, here friends are ephemeral, here man is ephemeral, here woman is ephemeral. The whole foundation of this earth will become desolate.]

The consolation exists in acknowledging the general condition. One way of coping with personal grief is to put it into perspective, to recognize, as Deor argues, that our lot is not unique but part of the natural order. And yet the effect of the consolation is the converse of Deor's propagandistic 'all things pass'. Both the Wanderer and the landscape of which he is part, are merely symptomatic of the present decline and latent but certain destruction of mankind and all his works. The burden of the poem is that wisdom begins only as man comes to realize his part in the transitory nature of things. Such wisdom may bring about acknowledgement, it may even bring about resolution; but it will not change the issue: all things pass. It is not until the Wanderer has run the gamut of hopelessness that he can properly learn the point of ruin – mutability and transience – the lesson that it is adversity which brings about wisdom, allowing him to transcend merely material, earthly values, and to resolve for himself the limitations of the human condition. Once we can face with resolution the transitoriness of everything around us, everything we most value, then we can acknowledge even the terrifying fact of ultimate mutability, the ruin of the world and the dissolution of Creation itself. It is the burden of the Wanderer's final eschatological vision, implicitly present in the body of the poem, that the eternal remains – that which stands beyond mutability.

And so at the end, the poet turns to God – his point of departure at the beginning of the poem – briefly, but in metrically expanded, longer and more dignified lines, to draw the poem to a conclusion. The final words of the poem revert to the two-line framework and offer not so much an alternative to patient suffering – which is itself a Christian virtue[6] – but the hope of additional spiritual security – an echo of the opening words of the poem, *are gebideð . . . are seceð*, emphasizing the movement from a formerly passive to a now active involvement:

> Wel bið þam þe him are seceð,
> frofre to Fæder on heofonum,    þær us eal seo
> fæstnung stondeð.  (ll. 114–15)

[It will be well for him who seeks grace, solace from the Father in heaven, where abides security for us all.]

A syntactic parallel over lines 112–14: *Til biþ se þe . . . Wel bið þam þe . . .*, underscores the virtue of the new faith while acknowledging the traditional heroic virtues of fortitude and resolution propounded by the *gleaw hæle*. The courageous man is called fortunate since he is armed against sorrow by fortitude, whereas the truly blessed has the added solace of security in heaven. The religious potential minimally stated in the opening and closing lines, remains quite undeveloped. The author is apparently not concerned to develop any distinctively Christian affirmation of faith; his conclusion is seemingly almost incidental. And the body of the poem is set firmly within the matrix of earthly desires.

However, the further implications of this two-line framework are extensively developed in *The Seafarer*, a poem that has much in common with *The Wanderer*, emerging from much the same cultural landscape. Similar in length, it employs the same ethopoetic device, exploring a moral theme through the expressed experience of an individual persona. An anonymous voice makes much the same complaint, depicted in similar circumstances – experiencing physical and mental distress. Alone in a harsh environment he seeks some kind of consolation. But there the similarity ends; the effect and resolution of his complaint are quite different. The Wanderer's authenticity is convincingly but implicitly developed literally and psychologically in the body of the poem. The voice of the Seafarer claims explicit personal veracity for his tale of suffering from the very beginning:

> Mæg ic be me sylfum     soðgied wrecan,
> siþas secgan,     hu ic geswincdagum
> earfoðhwile     oft þrowade,
> bitre breostceare     gebiden hæbbe,
> gecunnad in ceole     cearselda fela,
> atol yþa gewealc.     (ll. 1–6)

[I can tell a true tale of myself, speak of journeys, how I have often suffered times of hardship in days of toil, endured bitter anxiety at heart and experienced many an anxious lodging on board ship, the dreadful rolling of waves.]

The speaker goes on to portray a graphic picture of the harsh and hazardous conditions of the night-watch at the ship's prow tossing by the cliffs, outwardly his limbs fettered by frost, inwardly hot at the heart with surges of anxiety (ll. 7–11), for in addition to physical exhaustion a spiritual hunger for security tears the sea-weary spirit (ll. 11–12). Like the Wanderer, the Seafarer also treads the paths of exile, cut off from kinsmen (ll. 15–16). In both cases the drear and desolate environment is an appropriate objective correlative for the speaker's inner state. But the two speakers' attitudes to their suffering are different. The Wanderer-figure resents his material deprivation not so much for itself but for what it represents – the emptiness and desolation of life cut off from personal relationships. The Seafarer, on the other hand, seems to find significance in the fact of physical hardship of itself, which is merely made worse by lack of companionship. Describing his experience wholly in terms of physical wretchedness, the speaker lays considerable stress on the bodily discomfort of exposure to the storms of winter; he is nipped with frost on an ice-cold sea, hung around with icicles, pelted with hail (ll. 8–17).

Although naturally the company of men is absent in the circumstances he describes, we feel that this exacerbates the speaker's plight rather than represents its direct cause.

> Þær ic ne gehyrde    butan hlimman sæ,
> iscaldne wæg.    Hwilum ylfete song
> dyde ic me to gomene,    ganetes hleoþor
> ond huilpan sweg    fore hleahtor wera,
> mæw singende    fore medodrince.
> Stormas þær stanclifu beotan,    þær him stearn oncwæð
> isigfeþera;    ful oft þæt earn bigeal,
> urigfeþra;    nænig hleomæga
> feasceaftig ferð    frefran meahte.    (ll. 18–26)

[There I heard nothing but the roar of the sea, the ice-cold wave. At times I would take the song of the swan as my entertainment, the cry of the gannet and the call of the curlew in place of human laughter, the gull's singing in place of the drink of mead. There storms beat upon rocky cliffs where the tern, icy-feathered, answered them; very often the eagle screamed around, wet-feathered; no protective kinsman could comfort the wretched spirit.]

We seem clearly to be among those early Saxons whom the Gallo-Roman poet Sidonius describes as being 'inured to the hardship of the sea and shipwreck – for whom the dangers of the deep are not casual acquaintances but intimate friends'.[7] Whereas *The Wanderer's* controlling motivation is the contrast between present misery and past happiness, the decisive contrast for *The Seafarer* is that between the hardship of life at sea and the luxury of life on land. Twice it is emphasized that those living in comfort on land, proud and flushed with wine, *wlonc ond wingal*, can know nothing of the miseries endured by one who lives the life of the Seafarer (ll. 12–15, 27–29). Now with the scene set and our sympathy engaged, the narrator can afford to move into a paradoxical extension of his thesis, marked by a correlative *Forþon* sequence. It is apparently a direct consequence of the acknowledged suffering involved that the Seafarer feels led to embark on his journey:

> Forþon cynssað nu
> heortan geþohtas    þæt ic hean streamas,
> sealtyþa gelac    sylf cunnige –
> monað modes lust    mæla gehwylce
> ferð to feran,    þæt ic feor heonan
> elþeodigra    eard gesece.    (ll. 33–38)

[Now therefore, the thoughts of my heart are stirred to explore the high seas, the surging of salt waves, for myself – the yearning of the spirit time and again urging the soul to set out, so that I may seek out an alien land far away.]

Just as his body is tossed by the waves (*cnossian*, l.8) so his mind is now tossed by conflict (*cnyssan*, l.33). Curiously he seems deliberately to have abandoned the comfort and security of his homeland to seek out the uncertainties and hostility of an alien country. Whereas the Wanderer rails against his circumstances but comes to recognize suffering as a fact of life and achieves self-awareness on that account, for the Seafarer physical hardship – less grief than pain – is apparently worth exploration for its own sake. Although the Seafarer's tale has hitherto been expressed in the past tense (unlike the Wanderer's continuous present), it is a future journey he now anticipates, willingly submitting to hardship and pain for reasons that are not yet apparent. There is no stated rationale for the considerable physical risks involved – neither commerce, piracy, or pilgrimage – nor yet the tourist's delight in foreign travel for its own sake. Despite cold and hunger, the acknowledged hardship of life at sea, he has deliberately forsaken the laughter of men and the drink of mead in favour of these crying, wheeling sea-birds. And he adds to boot the corollary that those who remain on land can know nothing of such hardship – concluding, somewhat curiously at first sight: '*Therefore* my heart now urges me to make trial of the high seas, the tossing of the waves' (ll.33–35). He feels a *lust*, a *longung*, to go. Now this is very curious, unless the speaker is either a masochist or schizophrenic – neither of which would be acceptable in a literal appreciation. The *Forþon* sequence is simply inexplicable until we enter the affective perspective, when it becomes completely logical at a thematic level. The Wanderer's mere passive resignation is turned into an active contempt for the world. The Wanderer's statement of *pathei mathos*, 'wisdom through suffering', is taken one dreadful, yet logical step further – in the classical ascetic response to hedonism: 'If wisdom comes through suffering, then we should seek to suffer'. The Wanderer comes to acknowledge the illusory nature of material pleasures; the Seafarer will actively seek to shun the source of all worldly affections. Unlike the Wanderer, the Seafarer-persona undergoes a structural rather than psychological development.

A further *Forþon* sequence makes it clear that the journey involved in any case is not quite so straightforward as it might seem:

Forþon nis þæs modwlonc    mon ofer eorþan,
ne his gifena þæs god,    ne in geoguþe to þæs hwæt,
ne in his dædum to þæs deor,    ne him his dryhten to þæs hold,
þæt he a his sæfore    sorge næbbe,
to hwon hine Dryhten    gedon wille.    (ll.38–43)

[For there is no man on earth so bold in spirit, nor so generous with his gifts, nor so vigorous in his youth, nor so courageous in his deeds, nor with a lord so gracious to him, that he is never anxious in his seafaring, as to what the Lord will send him.]

It seems that more people than just the persona of the poem are engaged in this seafaring. Many, perhaps all, men are involved in the journey of which the voice speaks – men who have all the social attributes: generosity, daring, and enjoying gracious lords. Not all need be like the narrative persona, bereft of these things, although as an exemplum, his particular plight is the more instructive. The parallel over lines 41–43 employing the word *dryhten* in its two senses of earthly leader and heavenly Lord makes the point. What the Seafarer's voyage has come to represent is the straight and narrow way, full of physical and mental sacrifice, which leads to heaven. 'He will have no thought for the harp, or ring-giving, nor for the pleasure of a woman, nor worldly hope – not about anything else whatever, but only the surging waves' (ll. 44–47). Accepting the words of Christ which promised a hundredfold recompense to those of his adherents who relinquish the world: property, kinsmen, wife, to follow him (Matthew 19. 28–29), the insular Church, Celtic and Saxon alike, would recommend the virtues of a literal exile *pro amore deo*. Voluntary exile was a familiar ethic in secular life; the bond of personal loyalty might require a man to accompany even an unworthy earthly leader into exile during a low ebb in his fortunes,[8] so that to follow his heavenly Lord into exile – to be despised for his sake – was not quite so alien as it might seem. For many it would be sufficient to withdraw from the world into one or other of the burgeoning eremetic communities,[9] but others who must needs make their metaphors a reality would embark on a genuine penitential voyage.[10]

The preparation of one's soul for its final pilgrimage of death was best undergone by the endurance of hardships here on earth – and at its clearest of the hardships of exile willingly undergone for the love of God. The journey of exile itself could be regarded as a sort of 'pilgrim's progress' through which the lonely sufferer might approach the kingdom of heaven.[11] And in fact such *peregrini pro amore deo* were common enough figures of the contemporary scene. Of course many people did engage in pilgrimages of the conventional type for what they took to be the good of their souls, but the motivation was not of itself some experience at a distant shrine, but the inevitable hardships involved, voluntarily undergone for spiritual ends. Diagnostic is the case of three men washed up on the Cornish coast in 891 who claimed to have undertaken their journey in a small coracle, without any means of 'human steerage' because they longed, for the love of God, to be on a foreign journey – they cared not where.[12] This strong physical compulsion must have provided the motivating force for so many of the Anglo-Saxon and Celtic missions to the

Continent at this time. The *peregrinus* then, actual or figural, leaves his homeland to live for a period, or for the remainder of his life, in a strange country, as an alien in the land. And as an alien he links naturally with Adam, whose exile from Eden marked the beginning of earthly affliction for men, and with a whole host of scriptural figures who had undertaken journeys in faith which might be interpreted figuratively – like Noah's voyage though which he became an heir to righteousness, or Abraham's wanderings in the desert – and ultimately with all who 'confess that they are strangers and pilgrims on the earth, and declare that they seek a better country, that is a heavenly' (Hebrews 11. 7–16).

Now the narrative voice of *The Seafarer* may well have been visualized as that of an actual *peregrinus* figure,[13] but contemporary epistemology would treat fact and figure in a manner so close as to imply that one was no more than an aspect of the other. What appears to be a concrete referent, like the persona of the Seafarer here, may prove to be no more than the description of a mood. There existed the common platonic tendency to experience a stimulus simultaneously under its separable aspects, each discrete, independent, and self-authenticating, but at the same time forming part of some transcendent whole. Its literary exposition is neither realistic nor strictly allegorical, but the development of a vividly imagined situation to figure forth with immediate concrete force that abstract doctrine or experience which motivates the poem's structure. The development of interpretative biblical literature of the type of *Exodus* allowed that any serious poetry might be allusive, symbolic, enigmatic, in which the reader is led to seek out covert significance. So while there is no extant evidence for the interpretation of other than explicitly religious writings in this manner, some part of the audience, conditioned by this all-pervasive and infectious mode of visualizing the world, must always, as now, have been ready to discover in the lines a meaning *parti pris*. While no exclusive meaning can be allotted to a poem without explicit signal of any kind, in the case of *The Seafarer* this proves a reasonable critical stance to adopt in view of both the strong imagery involved, and the need to explicate an otherwise difficult structure. The sea-journey represents a forcible life-metaphor in itself; nothing more lonely – except it be a sparrow in the darkness – than a ship at night alone on the sea, where mist and snow serve merely to disrupt preconceptions of time and space. But through poems like *Exodus* a whole range of seafaring imagery – foreign to biblical thought but adopted from Hellenistic elements in the early Church – had been given specific religious associations (see above, pp. 92–93). At least part of the contemporary audience would readily identify the stormy sea of Matthew 8. 23–27 as a familiar symbol for this world, and the ship as an allegorical portrayal of the Church, or tropologically as the Christian faith, in which the faithful Christian was carried through the uncertainties of this world.[14]

Once this aspect of the Seafarer's role is identified, its subsequent elaboration, puzzling at a literal level, is more readily explicable. In returning to the theme of his voyage, the speaker emphasizes that his yearning is increased at the very moment the pleasures of the world are at their most desirable:

> Bearwas blostmum nimað,    byrig fægriað,
> wongas wlitigað;    woruld onetteð;
> ealle þa gemoniað    modes fusne
> sefan to siþe    þam þe swa þenceð
> on flodwegas    feor gewitan.   (ll. 48–52)

[The woodlands put forth blossom, adorning cities, making beautiful the plains; the world quickens; all of which urges the eager of mind and spirit to a journey, him who thus thinks to travel far upon the seaways.]

With the passing of winter, nature is no longer an affliction in itself, but apparently a cause of distress in its very allurement – puzzling to those accustomed to think of spring only as the harbinger of pleasant, sunny days. But if, at a literal level, the world quickens, reviving as the leaves and flowers spring forth, figuratively it also hastens towards its ultimate end; the eschatological implications of the season are commonplace in Doomsday literature,[15] the flower of the field a familiar symbol of both earthly decay and individual death (Job 14. 2; James, 1. 10–11; i Peter 1. 24). The disturbing paradox is redoubled as the note of the cuckoo sounds a sombre note of doom, a bird of lament anticipating only death and judgement:[16]

> Swylc geac monað    geomran reorde;
> singeð sumeres weard,    sorge beodeð
> bitter in breosthord.   (ll. 53–55)

[So also exhorts the cuckoo with its melancholy voice; summer's watchman sings, warns of sorrow, bitter to the heart.]

Any difficulty we might experience with this unexpected shocking alternative is explicitly anticipated by the poet:

>                   Þæt se beorn ne wat,
> sefteadig secg,    hwæt þa sume dreogað
> þe þa wræclastas    widost lecgað.   (ll. 55–57)

[That man, the fellow blessed with affluence, does not know what some of those endure who so widely follow the paths of exile.]

The first half of the poem concludes with an identification of the existence of men on land, as not merely transitory but dead in contrast with the life of men at sea – which, as in *Exodus*, is the way of the righteous: *Forþon me hatran sind Dryhtnes dreamas þonne þis deade lif, læne on londe* ['Thus the joys of the Lord give me more pleasure than this dead life, transitory on land'] (ll.64–66).

Thereafter through the second half of the poem there needs no further reference to the sea, since the metaphor has achieved its purpose in conveying the notion of movement in life, and the need for suffering to enter a state of grace. Nevertheless, the exhortations of the later, didactic half of the poem: the exhortation to fear God, be humble, and take thought of our ultimate destination, has its basis in the harsh experience dramatically enacted in the mimetic half: of being at the mercy of wind and weather, and feeling the insignificance and powerlessness of humanity when faced by the elemental forces of nature.

The poet goes on to adduce a direct moral from the acknowledged mutability of the world to which all things are subject, in age and eventual decay. Since nothing lasts and death comes to every man, we should seek to win a more certain glory than mere wealth. The sequence of thought is clearly adopted from the *sententiae* of contemporary secular verse intended to encourage a young man to deeds of courage by means of the assertive paradigm which runs: 'death is inevitable, therefore so act against foes as to win glory, the praise of men', seen for example in the closing words of *Beowulf* (above, pp. 60–61). The poet begins with a minimal feint towards the heroic posture (ll.72–74), but then develops a religious redaction with some loss of brevity, but no less force, thus: 'death is inevitable, therefore perform such deeds against the devil as to gain eternal glory, the praise of angels for ever' (ll.75–80). This is no less a heroic assertion than that with which the heroes of secular story faced a hostile world (see above, pp. 65–66, below, pp. 172–74). In the Cædmonian manner the poet employs vocabulary with known heroic resonance, identifying those who dwell in the halls of heaven as the comitatus of the Lord: *ecan lifes blæd, dream mid dugeþum* (ll.79–80). The Lord envisaged is apparently less the biblical Jesus than the war-leader of the *Dream*-poet (see above, p. 98).

There follows a natural reflection on the decline of the world, the decay of earthly things matching mankind's own age and debility, similar in some respects to that stated in *The Wanderer*, but a less personal, lengthier rationale of worldly degeneration:

> Dagas sind gewitene,
> ealle onmedlan    eorþan rices;
> nearon nu cyningas    ne caseras
> ne goldgiefan    swylce iu wæron,
> þonne hi mæst mid him    mærþa gefremedon
> ond on dryhtlicestum    dome lifdon.
> Gedroren is þeos duguð eal,    dreamas sind gewitene;
> wuniað þa wacran    ond þas woruld healdaþ,
> brucað þurh bisgo.    Blæd is gehnæged,
> eorþan indryhto    ealdað ond searað,
> swa nu monna gehwylc    geond middangeard.    (ll. 80–90)

[Times have changed, and all the pomp of the kingdom of the world; there are now neither kings nor emperors nor givers of gold like there used to be, when they performed the greatest deeds of glory among themselves and lived in most noble renown. This whole company has fallen, the pleasures have departed; the weaker remain and possess the world, occupy it by toil. The splendour is humbled, earth's majesty is growing old and withering, just as each man now does throughout the middle-earth.]

The parallel to what went before is emphasized by the redeployment of the key terms: *duguð*, *dream*, and *blæd* (ll. 79–80, 86–88). The Wanderer's anguish at individual loss, acceptable merely because universal, is now explicitly rationalized: it is a degenerating world, in which man and the world of which he is merely part are linked in a post-lapsarian state.

One's natural wish to honour the dead – 'to strew the grave with gold' in the Beowulfian manner (ll. 97–102) clearly is pointless in face of the awesomeness of God, when, as the Wanderer pointed out, gold and gold-giver, warrior and weapon, moulder together (see above, pp. 111–12). The Cædmonian Creator holds firm the fate not merely of individuals but earth and sky. In the face of universal mutability, only the very foolish will not be in awe of a God who holds stable even the earth's foundations and may give no less stability to the heart (*gestaþelade*, *gestaþelað*, ll. 104, 108). In extending the point, the poet shows that the seafaring metaphor is not quite forgotten: *Stieran mon sceal strongum mode, ond þæt on staþelum healdan* [A man must steer a wilful spirit and keep it fixed on stable points] (l. 109); and he concludes with the direct exhortation: 'Let us take thought where our home is, and how we may come there' (ll. 117–18). The final implication of the Seafarer's journey is of journey's end, whether envisaged as the haven of Christ and Paradise or merely death and the grave.[17] The concept of a journey of death is an archetypal Indo-European one, and certainly not unfamiliar to those early Anglo-Saxons who consigned their heroes to actual ships for what they took to be their final voyage from this world to the next (see above, pp. 4, 51).[18]

In both *Wanderer* and *Seafarer* the exilic theme is linked dramatically and philosophically, literally and symbolically with the explicit or implicit contemplation of a ruin: an appropriate stimulus to reflection since it represents the abnegation, enforced or voluntary, of all those features of life the hall-building symbolized, and thus leads directly to the journey, actual or figural, in search of an alternative. This archetypal image recurs *in extenso* in a poetic fragment found in the same manuscript as the former two poems, and known appropriately as *The Ruin*. It has much in common with the two poems previously considered, but is apparently quite distinct, (in the admittedly mutilated form in which it survives), inasmuch as it is presented not mimetically but objectively, dealing solely and protractedly with the one image, and in the impersonal voice. Instead of forming part of the psychological setting for the *snottor's* musings – like the bleak weather, part and parcel of the Wanderer-persona's interior landscape, or the sophisticated doctrinal rationale of the Seafarer – we are left to point the implications for ourselves: that all the works of men, and most graphically their material monuments, are subject to the same destructive imperative. But we are presented with neither the direct admonition of *The Seafarer* nor the immediate personal lament of *The Wanderer*. The narrative voice of *The Ruin* is never introspective; rather than speak of its own circumstances, it concentrates on the demise of past generations and the vanity of mankind's belief in its superiority to fate. This desolate theme does not impinge upon the condition of the narrative voice; we feel no real sense of regret or nostalgia for past glories.

Any critical evaluation of the poem is necessarily tentative in view of its incomplete state, although paradoxically it is this very incompleteness which lends a special attraction to those who might appreciate *The Ruin* as a poem of re-enactment, in which not merely the imagery but its broken syntactic structure endorses its theme and deepens its present significance. The ruined state of the poem, far from obstructing our appreciation of it, only corroborates the truth it imports. Here is an impressive, beautiful, and complex construction, carefully and cleverly put together – but itself in the very ruined state it seeks to expound. It is possible to enact the deconstruction of the building into its constituent elements, block by block, each image or syntactic unit supporting and holding together the construction – except that it is now dilapidated – and the manuscript a ruin of tumbled blocks of masonry and phrases – the poem falling into fragments of description and commentary. Conversely and paradoxically, however, there is as one moves through the poem a sense of building and growing, of the massiveness of the constructions before the mind's eye simultaneous with the tragedy of their fallen state. Most appropriately as the poem falls finally into incoherent lacunae, the last recognizable phrases are of approval:

. . . . . . . . þær þa baþu wæron
þonne is . . . . . . . .
. . . . . re;    þæt is cynelic þing,
hu se b. . .    . . . . . burg . . .    (ll. 46–49)

[. . . then, where the baths were . . . It is a splendid thing, how the . . .
city . . .]

The poet's theme is the recurrent one of the impermanence of both the
works of man, and man himself. The first sentence sets the tone, containing the conflict and concern of the body of the poem: the utterly
irresistible transience of even the greatest earthly glory:

Wrætlic is þes wealstan,    wyrde gebræcon;
burgstede burston;    brosnað enta geweorc.    (ll. 1–2)

[It's remarkable, this masonry, broken by fate; the precincts of the city have
crumbled; the work of giants is in decay.]

The significant juxtaposition is present in the opening line. The masonry
has been broken not just literally but figuratively – by fate (l. 1b). The
engineering which so amazed in its awesomeness, is at one and the same
time cause for wonder and dismay – substantial and tangible evidence for
declining standards – material corroboration of the unsatisfactoriness of
present times, beyond which we instinctively identify a golden age of
material and moral security. Our awareness of the awesome
sophistication of those who went before provokes an almost religious
sense of the inferiority of later generations, whose talents seem fewer,
whose achievements seem the lesser, whose very stature is the less
spectacular with the passage of time.[19] Giants no longer bestride the
world as they seem always to have done in former times. The early
Anglo-Saxons very clearly felt themselves living in a degenerate age,
when scattered around them lay the mute monuments to a once-great
civilization – roads, canals, cities, fortresses – which they might admire
and utilize, but which they could not emulate.

The fact that like the ruin which stimulated the Wanderer's reflection,
*eald enta geweorc* (l. 87), this ruin is said, conventionally enough,[20] to be the
work of giants, reflects more than mere reverence for the greatness of the
past. Any human response to such giants is necessarily ambiguous. We
are naturally in awe of their potential and evident power. Yet despite,
and perhaps because of their awful might, are they not unnatural? And
was it not giants who for so long warred against God, and whom he
destroyed in the Flood for their wickedness – part of that monstrous
progeny of Cain, the offspring of evil spirits coupling with mortal
women.[21] It was the sons of Cain whose pride would cause their cities –

Babel, Sodom, and Gomorrah – to be overturned by the hand of God and to remain desolate for generation after generation (Isaiah 13. 19–22). But as the Church Fathers pointed out, 'while Cain built a city, Abel was a pilgrim and built none – for the city of the saints is above'.[22] It may well be that the failure of these walls to withstand fate is to be regarded as an inevitable corollary of their origins.[23]

The poet goes on to enumerate features reminiscent of the great Roman cities referred to by Bede in his description of Britain, great towers and the firmest of locked gates:[24]

> Hrofas sind gehrorene,  hreorge torras,
> hrungeat berofen,  hrim on lime,
> scearde scurbeorge  scorene gedrorene.  (ll. 3–5)

[There are tumbled-down roofs, towers in ruins, gateways broken in, frost on the mortar, a gaping tile-cover, rent and collapsed.]

The cinematographic shift in perspective from large panorama to small details is significant, since it is the detail which focuses the sentiment of the whole, in a sensitive material awareness. In *The Wanderer's* bleak landscape it was merely appropriate to find 'frost on the walls' (ll. 76–77); here it is specifically said to be the famous Roman mortar that the frost seeks out, *hrim on lime* (l. 4) – the destructive agent attacking the cement of civilization itself, dentist-like, probing vulnerable fissures. Most obviously the lines contain a number of startling contradictions, listing building units that ironically fail to serve their purpose – a fundamentally disturbing reversal of function. The neo-Platonic Christian notion of reality as an absolute conception held permanently within the mind of God, could find little to admire in that which had forsaken the shape assigned to it. The palace was beautiful only as a palace; as a ruin it ceased to be so. Decay could only diminish its ideal form – not lead to a secondary stage of existence which might claim significance and beauty of itself. The concept of 'pleasing decay' would have been meaningless. Only a later age could come to appreciate a ruin on account of its intrinsic beauty, or as the venerable relic of some golden age, irrevocably lost, but for which the learned might feel a kind of academic nostalgia.

The image of the ruined hall was no mere literary device. Abandoned and ruined buildings overgrown by brambles were a common feature of the European landscape during these years. The incidental des-tructiveness of the *Völkerwanderungzeit* and the internecine warfare of heroic society will have meant that the face of Europe was littered with ruins, the present insecurity of the countryside vesting the stronghold with greater significance, and its loss the more poignant. But despite specific detail, the effect of *The Ruin* is unlike that of the early *excidio* tradition in which the poet laments the downfall of a particular patron's dynasty and the concomitant ruin of its seat, as when for example Venantius Fortunatus laments the fall of the house of the Thuringian princess Radegunde[25] or Llywarch Hen speaks of the fall of Urien's Rheged,[26] both of which, having respect to personal loss, have more in common with the lament of *The Wanderer*. *The Ruin* has still less in common with the later type of *encomium urbis* intended to enhance the prestige of a living town, like Alcuin's celebratory poem on his home city of York[27] or the vernacular poem on the site of Durham.[28] The picture depicted in this poem seems to reflect an intermediate phase in which former Roman cities and great villas, although appreciated by their Germanic successors, were falling into inevitable decay – not as the direct consequence of any one particular violent event, but simply as part of an inexorable process inherent in the nature of the world. With the seventh and eighth centuries the engineering skills necessary to maintain the admired technology were no longer available, 'those who might effect the repairs having fallen', *betend crungon* (l.28). It is clear that men would view the remains of Roman Britain: fine public buildings, hot baths, statuary, mosaics, and frescoed walls, with interest; the inhabitants of Carlisle proudly showed visitors the massive Roman foundations of their city walls.[29] As late as the twelfth century antiquarians like Gerald of Wales could point to substantial remains of a legionary fortress like that at Caerleon-on-Usk, readily identifying the sites of temples, baths, and theatres.[30]

But whether the ruin described by the poet is a composite or general picture, or recalls the particular details of some known site like Roman Bath, specific identification is merely adjacent to our appreciation of the poem it provoked. Although without the claim to that inner veracity of which the Seafarer's *soðgied* speaks, it proffers, like *The Wanderer*, an apparent location and relationship to external facts sufficient to its purpose. But although dispassionately observed, with a degree of impersonal objectivity, the poet's theme has recognizable moral implications which could scarcely have been lost on a contemporary audience: the collapsed walls intimately linked with the collapse of a whole social structure. The fabric of society, like that of the building, is best understood in dissolution, just as the nature of men is best revealed in conditions of stress. As with *The Wanderer*, the parallel between the fate of the city and those who built it is explicit: both are brought low by time, the great leveller:

> Eorðgrap hafað
> waldendwyrhtan,   forweorone geleorene,
> heard gripe hrusan.   (ll.6–8)

[An earthy grasp, the cruel grip of the ground, has hold of the noble builders, perished and gone.]

the linkage of rhyme emphasizing the point that both buildings and their builders are subject to the same process of decay: *gehrorene . . . scorene gedrorene . . . forweorone geleorene* (ll.3, 5, 7).

However, if personal loss gave cause for personal lament, the detached observer might find such calamity a genuine, if somewhat curious, cause for consolation. Ambrose, for example, finds himself innured to the thought of his own puny mortality when contemplating 'the corpses of so many towns'.[31] But Christian thinkers would recognize in this part of a larger deterministic pattern. Just as in biblical times God had destroyed Babylon and the cities of the plain for their moral degeneracy, it is the burden of Gildas's *Liber de Excidio et Conquestu Britanniae* that the destruction of the cities of Roman Britain – first by pestilence and then by the 'valiant Saxons' – came about as a direct consequence of their inhabitants' depravity, their ruins remaining as witness to God's vengeance.[32] In the view of Augustine, God had allowed the Goths to sack Rome – his 'city of the world', founded as it was in fratricide, as distinct from the 'city of God' – in order first to chastise his people before consoling them.[33] But further, the fall of Rome and Roman civilization was part of a wholesale systematic explanation for the rise and fall of cities and empires which offered an academic explanation for worldly debility and decline. Christian historians conventionally divided the history of the world into a fixed number of ages, commonly six from the time of Creation to the present. The sixth age which had begun with the Incarnation and would end with the coming of Antichrist and Judgement Day, was equated with the Roman Empire – under which they still considered themselves in some way to be living. In fact Roman civilization had long ceased to exist, in all but name – a necessary intellectual contruct. It was this imperial world to which the barbarian kings believed themselves heir, adopting its material insignia and ceremony (see above, p. 3). Alcuin and others would speak of the 'renovation' rather than the 'imitation' of Rome,[34] flattering Germanic emperors with the thought that they were the direct successors of Constantine and Augustus. English sovereigns would eventually trace their lineage through Brutus to those who fought at Troy (see below, p. 175), but motivated more by historical sentiment than accuracy since chronological distance argued against the probability of continuity. In the meantime it remained undisputed that men were living in what was the last age of the world and could look for no improvement until the coming of the kingdom of God. If the world was falling into decay, this was merely an expected sign that the end of the world was at hand. Small wonder that the visible ruins of the Roman world especially should be linked with millennial expectations; had not Christ himself foretold of just such fine buildings that not one stone would be left upon another – their ruin presaging the kingdom of God (Luke 21. 6)?[35] In the religious imagination, the contemplation of present ruin leads naturally enough to reflection on the wasteland of Doomsday.[36]

But whether or not analysed in such academic terms, the ruin inevitably provokes a penitential response; whether regarded as a specific token of divine wrath or merely an example of mortal vanity, its very dilapidation gives occasion for reflection, its grandeur compelling at once both a sense of our own diminished stature – and a human *curiositas* – wonderment at the technical virtuosity of the lost master-builders:

> . . . lamrindum beag,
> mod monade   myne swiftne gebrægd;
> hwætred in hringas,   hygerof gebond
> weallwalan wirum   wundrum togædre.   (ll. 17–20)

[. . . a plaster circle stimulated the mind and prompted a swift idea; ingenious in making chains, the resolute man wonderfully reinforced the foundations with wire.]

The poignant relationship between present decline and former glory is made by a constant movement between past and present tenses, a controlled chronological plaitwork weaving backwards and forwards in time so that past and present are simultaneously before our eyes, serving to emphasize both the contrast and continuity of decay. The verbal echo *brosnað, brosnade* (ll. 2, 28) points to the fact that buildings have not only fallen in the past, but are still doing so, 'kingdom after kingdom' (l. 10), and presumably will continue to do so 'until a hundred generations will have passed' (ll. 8–9) – perhaps a reference to an apocalyptic future time and if so the only such reference in the entire poem – and therefore significant in a work so intimately concerned with the nature of time. The dream-like juxtaposition of what used to be with what now is, allows us to glimpse glittering activity imaginatively reconstructed within and beyond the rubble:

> Beorht wæron burgræced,   burnsele monige,
> heah horngestreon,   heresweg micel,
> meodoheall monig   mondreama full,
> oþþæt þæt onwende   wyrd seo swiþe.   (ll. 21–24)

[There were splendid city buildings, many bath-houses, an abundance of lofty gables, a great tumult of warriors, many mead-halls filled with human revelry – until mighty fate changed that.]

The echo of *crungon* over lines 25–28 makes explicit the link between the building and builder, and the fact that they succumb to the same fate: both inevitably fall to the earth and are enveloped in its grasp. Fate inexorably shatters (l.1) and changes (l.24) both material and man, bringing a continuous change over all things – and will of course continue to do so until the end of the world.

The contrast that is present in the time-slips is no less present in the physical details, the focus shifting alternately from a large panoramic perspective to pathetic details marked throughout by the sympathetic immediacy of the demonstrative 'this . . . .'. The grey and rusty lichen clinging to *this* decayed wall (ll.9–10) is in marked contrast to the gleaming armour and glittering treasure of those who occupied the 'bright fortress' (ll.34–37), symbols of their active enjoyment of its wealth (cf. *Beowulf*, above, p. 57). The present frost on the towering walls (ll.3–4) is at odds with the warm baths welling hot at its heart (ll.38–41) – curiously reminiscent of the Seafarer-persona, fettered with cold without and surging with heated emotion within (see above, p. 114). The reference to heated baths: 'There the baths used to be . . .' – but are of course no longer – is perhaps more than merely wistful at a time when bath-houses, much like modern massage-parlours, were associated in the public mind with sexual licence. In the same way, when those who formerly enjoyed the cities are described as *wlonc ond wingal* [proud and flushed with wine] (l.34), it might recall similar words traditionally used of others prior to sudden destruction – like the inhabitants of Sodom and Gomorrah (*Genesis A*, l.2581) or the hosts of Assyria (*Judith*, ll.16, 26), (see above, pp. 77f, below, p. 156). In *The Seafarer* (l.29) the same collocation is used to describe those who luxuriate in the 'dead life' of the city-dweller, knowing nothing of the joys of the Lord (see above, p. 120); and it is characteristically used of the carelessness of men on the eve of Judgement Day.[37] But any attempt to foist too narrow a single 'meaning' on to the poem is unrewarding; further meaning is available rather than required. At a time when the divorce between concept and appearance, abstract and particular, had not yet come about, the Old English elegists' natural mode of expression seems to be instinctively figurative, anticipating on the part of the audience a sophisticated appreciation of literal experience, readily accepting the interpenetration of concrete and abstract without the need for active homiletic explanation.

When occasionally the Old English poet does venture into an indisputably allegorical mode, the verbal signals are quite explicit, the explication elaborate and precise. It may not be insignificant that invariably in such cases he is drawing directly on eastern sources. Although the western world seems not yet to have adopted the Hellenistic habit of attributing Christian *sens* to secular literary themes, where for example Orpheus with his lute recalls the musician David, or Odysseus fastened to the mast becomes an equivalent of Christ fastened to the cross,[38] there remained the attractive possibility of extending to other parts of God's handiwork the method by which the Bible's inner truth was revealed, for of course the activity of the *Logos* was also to be seen in his material creation. The same Alexandrian strain of thought in the Church which had sponsored the polysemous approach to scriptural criticism could assume a Platonic view of the world in which religion and nature were inextricably wed. Since all creation was avowedly an expression of its creator, the natural world was charged with significance, and if properly directed we might identify the divine thought of which it was the material emanation.

In the same manuscript as contains *The Wanderer, The Seafarer,* and *The Ruin* are found the remains of a three-part physiologus or moralized bestiary – an originally East Mediterranean genre which became exceptionally popular in later medieval times – in which the significant characteristics of a variety of natural phenomena: animals, birds, and even trees or stones, are briefly described, and their 'moral' significance subsequently expounded. *The Panther* is described as a creature gentle to all save the dragon, his implacable foe; having eaten his fill he retreats to a secret lair where he sleeps for three days before waking with melodious sounds and delicious fragrance. This it is made clear (*Swa is*, 1.55) represents Christ in death, burial, and resurrection. *The Whale*, on the other hand (*Swa bið*, ll.31, 62) represents the devil and hell; lying in wait on the ocean it deceives weary seafarers who mistake it for dry land and are thus plunged into the depths. Its sweet breath allures other fishes – which are promptly swallowed. It is indicative both of the lettered and exotic origins of this material that the monster retains its eastern name, *fastitocalon* (1.7) – a distortion of the Greek *aspidocelon* – the original sea-turtle,[39] abandoned in favour of the more familiar leviathan of northern waters.

A more extended and vastly more elaborate example of this style, from the same manuscript, is found in *The Phoenix*. Again adopted from an ultimately East Mediterranean source, it witnesses a bookish sophistication, occasionally overreaching itself and toppling into obscurity, but a delight to those who prefer aesthetically veiled *sens* at the price of direct correlatives. It would probably have found its most appreciative audience among those in the Aldhelmian schools who were conversant with the more complex Alexandrian modes of thought.

The poet's immediate source is the probably fourth-century *Carmen de ave Phoenice* attributed to the North African rhetorician and imperial tutor Lactantius (*c.* 240–325).[40] Although it is strictly questionable whether the *Carmen* was intended to be read as a Christian allegory – there are no direct verbal signals, and it refers to pagan deities rather than to Christ – Lactantius himself elsewhere approves the Alexandrian tradition of employing pagan myths for the dissemination of Christian doctrine.[41] And indeed the phoenix myth had been used in this way since earliest times – a natural parallel for the resurrection symbolism, and one readily taken up by Western writers like Venantius Fortunatus and others.[42]

Lactantius's poem tells of a terrestrial paradise located far off in the East, a level plateau untouched by the violence of either Deucalion's flood or the fires of Phaeton; nothing harmful, either physical or moral, is to be found there. A single fountain called 'the well of life' flows twelve times a year, irrigating and making fruitful the whole land. A tree bears fruits which never fall. The only creature to inhabit this paradise is the phoenix, a unique bird, which reproduces itself by its own death. Each dawn the bird – an acolyte of Phoebus – plunges into the waters of the fountain twelve times and then sits in the tree to await the beams of the rising sun. It greets the first rays with a song unequalled by the song of the nightingale or the music of the muses. It applauds the sun's advance by flapping its wings three times and is then silent. After a thousand years it leaves the plateau and seeks a grove in Syria (Phoenicia) where, secure in a palm tree, it builds what is to be both a nest and funeral pyre from various exotic scented woods and spices. It anoints itself, and dies. Heat from its body kindles a fire which reduces nest and corpse to ashes. The ashes weld together in the form of a seed from which emerges a worm which in turn changes into a chrysalis. When fully formed the phoenix bursts anew from its shell just like a butterfly. Nourished on nothing save sips of ambrosia, it comes to maturity and flies back to its natural abode. First, however, it encloses the remains of its old body in an ointment of balsam, myrrh, and frankincense, which it carries to the city of the sun (?Heliopolis) offering it on the altar there. The whole of Egypt comes to marvel at the bird and carve its image in marble; the day is given a new title in honour of the event. The phoenix then flies through heaven accompanied by a flock of birds made up from every species, assembled without fear, but they are unable to accompany it the whole way, and it returns to its homeland alone. In conclusion, it is said that the mystical bird is neither male nor female; its only venereal pleasure is death – through which, by the gift of the gods, it gains eternal life.

Like *The Dream of the Rood* or, less directly, *The Seafarer*, the poet breaks his material into two parts, first telling his story – a reworking of Lactantius's poem – and then embarking on a homiletic exposition of its significance following Ambrose and other hexameral commentaries.[43] But rather than delay his employment of allegorical treatment to the later part in the manner of the bestiary, the *Phoenix*-poet adapts and supplements his source material in such a way that the allegory is at least implicit throughout, the later explication serving merely to bring together the various strands of interpretation and unite them in a coherent whole.

The author adapts his material with sympathy although the theme was scarcely one that would respond to Cædmonian 'Germanization'. He begins with the traditional introductory formula *Hæbbe ic gefrugnen* (l.1) but the dominant tone is one of academic reference: *swa us gefreogum gleawe witgan þurh wisdom on gewritum cyþað*, [as in their wisdom sages knowledgeable from their studies inform us in books] (ll.29–30, and cf. ll.313, 332, 424–25, 655). As with biblical adaptations, the Old English poet has discarded a large part – roughly one-third – of his source, while expanding the remainder fourfold and incorporating biblical material so as to make his explication the plainer. He removes the obscuring curtain of classical allusion – omitting all reference to pagan deities, exotic tribes and locations, or lists of unfamiliar oriental spices for which Old English naturally lacked the necessary vocabulary. Otherwise, his description of the terrestrial paradise is much the same, save that it is now made clear that it cannot be found by men, and is set apart from all evil-doers (ll.3–6). This fact, like all credit for its beauty, is emphatically attributed to God:

> Wlitig is se wong eall,    wynnum geblissad
> mid þam fægrestum    foldan stencum.
> Ænlic is þæt iglond,    æþele se Wyrhta,
> modig, meahtum spedig,    se þa moldan gesette.    (ll.7–10)

[The whole plateau is beautiful, blessed with delights, with earth's loveliest perfumes. The island is unique, the Creator who formed that land princely, noble, abounding in power.]

It is God who ordains that the trees should remain for ever green, hung with fruit winter and summer alike (ll.35–38, 79–80); it has survived the Flood – biblical rather than Deucalion's presumably – through the grace of God (ll.44–46), and is watered at the Lord's behest (ll.68–70). It will change only with the judgement of the Lord at Doomsday (ll.47–48). As commonly with those who attempt to depict the joys of paradise, the poet frames his description in largely negative terms – the opposite of all that makes for misery for the Wanderer or Seafarer – in an anaphoric series underscored by rhyme:

> Ne mæg þær ren ne snaw
> ne forstes fnæst    ne fyres blæst
> ne hægles hryre    ne hrimes dryre
> ne sunnan hætu    ne sincaldu
> ne wearm weder    ne winterscur
> wihte gewyrdan.    (ll.14–19)

[There neither rain nor snow, nor breath of frost nor scorch of fire, nor fall of hail nor downpour of sleet, nor heat of the sun nor perpetual cold, nor torrid weather nor winter shower can do any harm at all.]

This physical blandness is necessarily far from picturesque; the noble plateau is quite featureless: there are no hills and dales; no rocky cliffs rear aloft 'as with us' (ll.21–23). The moral dimension is no less anodyne:

Nis þær on þam londe    laðgeniðla
ne wop ne wracu,    weatacen nan,
yldu ne yrmðu    ne se enga deað
ne lifes lyre    ne laþes cyme
ne synn ne sacu    ne sarwracu
ne wædle gewin    ne welan onsyn
ne sorg ne slæp    ne swar leger.    (ll.50–56)

[There is in that land no hateful foe, no weeping nor anxiety, no sign of grief, no senility nor disease, no painful death nor loss of life, no onset of anything hateful, nor sin nor strife, nor anxious misery, not the struggle of poverty nor lack of wealth, not sorrow nor sleep nor dire illness.]

The list – not dissimilar from John's account of the New Jerusalem (Revelation 21. 4) – is rather curious inasmuch as it is specifically denied that any man can live there to discern either good or ill. The frame of reference is inevitably one of human experience. The poet concludes with a collocation reminiscent of *The Wanderer*, l.39 (see above, p. 108), declaring that there is not even any need for sleep to ravel up care – by way of which thought he returns to the perennial concerns of the northern world:

ne wintergeweorp    ne wedra gebregd
hreoh under heofonum,    ne se hearda forst
caldum cylegicelum    cnyseð ænigne;
þær ne hægl ne hrim    hreosað to foldan
ne windig wolcen,    ne þær wæter fealleþ
lyfte gebysgad.    (ll.57–62)

[no winter storm nor fierce, deceiving weather beneath the heavens, no hard frost to afflict anyone with freezing icicles; neither hail nor sleet is there to fall to earth, nor windy cloud, nor any torrent of water driven by the wind.]

Anything positive tends to be seen in terms of the artificial (*wrætlic-e*, ll.63, 75, 294, 307), an eastern marvel, like the gem-like blossoms which never wither and fall and fruits that are perpetually fresh (ll.34–39, 74–77) – exotic concepts acceptable to the oriental habit of mind, but wholly alien to the pragmatic Wanderer-sensibility whose fundamental experience of material reality is its transience.

The description of the mythical bird in this setting is progressively modified in human rather than ornithological terms. The phoenix is not 'unique', Lat. *unica* (*Carmen*, l.31) but like the Wanderer, 'solitary', *anhaga* (perhaps 'resolute', see above, p. 105) and bold in spirit, *deormod* (ll.87–88).

Ultimately in terms more associated with the Lord of *The Dream of the Rood,* than with any bird, however remarkable, it is said to be 'war-brave' *heaþorof,* a 'bold warrior', *guðfreca* (ll. 228, 353), although there is no question of any hostility to be overcome, nor even untoward circumstances which might prove the occasion of boldness. In a wholly more animated picture than that in Lactantius, the bird gazes across the water in eager anticipation of, not Phoebus nor Aurora, but (cf. *Exodus,* above, p. 88), 'God's candle . . . ancient work of the Father, . . . the radiant symbol of God' (ll. 91–96):

> Tungol beoþ ahyded,
> gewiten under waþeman    westdælas on,
> bideglad on dægred    ond seo deorce niht
> won gewiteð.    Þonne waþum strong
> fugel feþrum wlonc    on firgenstream
> under lyft ofter lagu    locað georne
> hwonne up cyme    eastan glidan
> ofer siðne sæ    swegles leoma.    (ll. 96–103)

[The stars are hidden, gone below the waves in the regions of the west, quenched by the dawn, and the dark gloom of night is gone. Then the bird, powerful in flight, proud in its plumage, gazes eagerly at the ocean, across the waters beneath the sky, until the light of the firmament comes gliding up from the east over the broad sea.]

Irrelevant to question that this sea should be when nowhere is it suggested that the phoenix's homeland is an island, or in any way physically associated with the ocean. Sufficient only that, in common with *Exodus* or *The Seafarer,* the sun, bright token of God, should run its course over the sea-ways: 'tossing ocean' and 'salt streams' (ll. 115, 120).

The song with which the phoenix now welcomes the sun is likened neither to the nightingale nor the pagan muses but is said to be, in phrases reminiscent of Cædmon's *Creation-Hymn,* simply the most wonderful song heard since the foundation of the world (ll. 128–31), superior to a variety of named instruments, or the voice of man, or the wings of a swan, 'or any of the joys which the Lord has created for men's cheer in this mournful world' (ll. 138–39).

Eventually – and somewhat curiously in a world not subject to the afflictions of old age – the phoenix grows elderly, having 'endured a thousand years of this life'. No mention is made of the logical necessity for his determination to enter a world where death holds sovereignty. Instead, like a Beowulfian adventurer, he seeks out a spacious realm, a wide kingdom, *side rice* (l. 156) where, anticipating his later acclaim in youthful restoration (ll. 335f), he lives in the world for a time as a prince surrounded by a flourishing comitatus (ll. 163–65). But eventually, since he must go to meet his death alone, 'the pure one' hastens to a deserted spot to make the elaborate preparations for his obsequies (ll.167f). Then:

> Ðonne wind ligeð,    weder bið fæger,
> hluttor heofones gim   halig scineð,
> beoð wolcen towegen,    wætra þryþe
> stille stondað,   biþ storma gehwylc
> aswefed under swegle,   suþan bliceð
> wedercondel wearm,    weorodum lyhteð,
> ðonne on þam telgum   timbran onginneð,
> nest gearwian.   (ll.182–89)

[When the wind drops and the weather is fair and the holy, bright jewel of heaven shines, when the clouds are scattered and the raging of the waters is calmed and every storm beneath the firmament is stilled, when from the south the warm candle of the sky gleams, sheds light on nations, then it begins to build in the branches, to prepare a nest.]

The destruction of the phoenix is modified so as to accommodate the Doomsday convention. Whereas the Lactantian bird dies first and then burns – the corpse mysteriously self-combustible – here death comes with the fire, explicitly kindled by the heat of the sun, a cleansing con-flagration. Unlike Lactantius's phoenix however, the Old English bird does not 'commend its spirit' (Carmen, l.93); the poet chooses to ignore the possibility of a perhaps over-facile reference to the death of Christ (Luke 23. 46), preferring instead the traditional native notion of the 'journey of death', although rather awkwardly in this case, the bird 'settling down' to it as if for an uncomfortable train-journey: Siteð siþes fus (l.208). The description of the pyre is full of phrases reminiscent of the funeral of a Beowulfian hero: 'when fire devours the transient body; its life, the doomed one's hoarded spirit, passes on its way . . . the abode of the war-brave destroyed by flame' (ll.219–21, 227–28).

The description of the bird's regeneration is far from direct. The Old English poet abandons what would have been a familiar butterfly image, the metamorphic sequence of caterpillar, chrysalis, and butterfly (Carmen, ll.102–08) in favour of a scarcely credible progression: apple, worm, fledgling. The worm is said, naturally enough, to emerge from an apple-like mass, splendidly gleaming from the shell, scir of scylle (l.234), but then without any intermediate transition simply grows into something like an eagle's chick – a bizarre process which takes place, not inappropriately, 'in the shade' (ll.234–35).[44] The apple might well relate to that which Adam and Eve ate (cf. l.403) since it was their original sin that led to Christ's coming into the world, but any such link is insufficiently signalled. And the notion that the apple is simultaneously the means by which both evil and the resurrected enter the field requires a more robust intellectual framework than the poem affords. The poet then likens the whole life-from-death process to that in which seed-grain is stored against the spring – a resurrection simile ultimately based on I Corinthians 15. 35–38, but here over-extended, so that the point, when it comes, arrives as something of a surprise:

> Sumes onlice
> swa mon to ondleofne    eorðan wæstmas
> on hærfeste,    ham gelædeð
> wiste wynsume    ær wintres cyme
> on rypes timan,    þy læs hi renes scur
> awyrde under wolcnum;    þær hi wraðe metað,
> fodorþege gefeon    þonne forst ond snaw
> mid ofermægne    eorþan þeccað
> wintergewædum;    of þam wæstmum sceal
> eorla eadwelan    eft alædan
> þurh cornes gecynd,    þe ær clæne bið
> sæd onsawen,    þonne sunnan glæm,
> on lenctenne    lifes tacen
> weceð woruldgestreon    þæt þa wæstmas beoð,
> þurh agne gecynd    eft acende
> foldan frætwe;    swa se fugel weorþeð
> gomel æfter gearum    geong edniwe
> flæsce bifongen.    (ll. 242–59)

[In much the same way as people carry home for food the earth's crops, pleasant nourishment, in autumn at harvest-time, before the arrival of winter, lest a downpour of rain spoil them under the clouds; wherein they find sustenance, the pleasure of feasting, when frost and snow with irresistible power cover the earth in winter clothing; from which crops the prosperity of men shall again spring up through the nature of the corn which is first sown simply as seed, when the brightness of the sun, the symbol of life, in spring awakens the world's wealth, so that by their own nature these crops are reborn, the fruit of the earth; just so this bird, grown old in years, is young and clothed in flesh anew.]

Gathering together the ashes of its former body, 'that plunder of the slain' (l. 273), its heir carries them not circuitously to Heliopolis, but directly and appropriately back to its homeland. Nevertheless there remains a passage through the land of men (unlocated) who now flock from all quarters of the globe to admire it, depicting its marvellous form in literature and in art (ll. 320–35). A flock of birds again gathers to glorify the 'brave, holy, wild' thing (ll. 338–39, 343), acclaiming him king, their dear lord. But although 'the joy of his comitatus', *duguða wyn*, he remains *anhoga* [solitary] (ll. 346–48). However great their devotion, his followers are unable to follow him to his true homeland. As they depart, 'sad at heart', *geomormod*, the resurrected phoenix, like a favoured prince, is said to be 'young in the courts', *giong in geardum* (ll.353–55; cf. *Beowulf*, 1.13). The myth concludes with the comment that God alone knows what sex the bird is, avoiding the Lactantian assertion that it is happy in lacking sexual intercourse (*Carmen*, ll.164–65) – rather curiously in view of the contemporary academic obsession with virginity and the monastic assumption that it was tantamount to a guarantee of eternal life – in favour of the doctrinal comment that 'He is himself both his own dear son and dear father, and likewise the heir of his own old relics' (ll.374–76).

At this point the author's dependence on his Latin source ends, but he concludes the first, narrative, part of his poem with a simple twelve-line explanation of its significance in the bestiary manner. This points not to any parallel with Christ, but with the resurrection of man in general.

> Þisses fugles gecynd    fela gelices
> bi þam gecornum    Cristes þegnum.    (ll.387–88)

> [The nature of this bird is very much like the chosen, the servants of Christ.]

It employs imagery familiar from *The Seafarer*: 'Thus it is that each of the blessed chooses for himself through dark death eternal life after painful exile, the reward of everlasting revelry in the heavenly homeland', (ll.381f).

But the phoenix narrative has been far lengthier and more complex than that of the conventional bestiary, and permits more sophisticated explication. The poet now retraces the allegory, making explicit what was formerly only implicit. While avoiding the abrupt bipartite division of the bestiary form, it remains nevertheless a necessarily repetitive extrapolation affording intellectual rather than aesthetic pleasure. The poet reviews various elements of the story with differing emphasis so as to explore in turn a tropological interpretation in which the good man builds a nest of faith, an allegorical in which the phoenix and its followers represent Christ and the Church, or an anagogical referring to the general resurrection at Judgement Day. Beginning with a new introductory formula: *Habbaþ we geascad . . .* (1.393), he refers briefly to Adam and Eve, whose 'busy teeth' (1.407) led to their expulsion from paradise – identified implicitly with the phoenix's 'holy plateau' (*halga wong*), – firmly closed to them until the advent of Christ should open it once more to the holy (ll.393–423). Then with a repeated formula of explanation: *Is þon gelicast, þæs þe us leorneras weordum secgað ond writu cyþað* [Very similar to this, according to what the scholars tell us in their pronouncements and make known in their writings] (ll.424–25), the migration of the old and weary bird is likened to our forebears' long journey into the world to suffer the persecution of

malignant monsters (ll.424–42). It is now clear, at a symbolic level,
why the inviolate phoenix should have been referred to in warlike
terms, although the phoenix, like Christ, was not expelled from
paradise but undertakes to enter the world voluntarily. The lofty tree
in which the phoenix builds its nest and funeral pyre is now identified
as the place in which the holy have their habitation, secure in the Lord,
unharmed by the ancient enemy despite all perils: a *hea beam* (l.447)
which might well recall the cross of the *Dream*-poet (see above, pp.
93f). There follows a series of strangely mixed metaphors. The nest
that the 'warrior of the Lord' (ll.452, 471) builds is constructed from
good deeds: herbs which make a habitation in the heavenly city
(ll.443–80), until interrupted by the warrior Death, 'greedy for
slaughter, armed with weapons', *wiga wælgifre wæpnum gepryped*
(l.486). At Doomsday 'the true King of victories, the Lord of many a
comitatus, will hold a synod', *sigora Soðcyning seonoþ gehegan, duguða
Dryhten* (ll.493–94). With the cleansing fire of judgement, the bird's
significance (*fugles tacen,* l.510) shall be recognized by all men, whose
earthly remains are gathered up by the ascended Christ and carried into
God's presence where, perfumed with the herbs of their good deeds,
*wlitige gewyrtad* (l.543), they will join the heavenly chorus.

At this point, with a rather abrupt intrusion of the narrative voice,
the author apparently falters, protesting his doctrinal propriety and
appealing to the corroboration of scriptural authority:

> Ne wene þæs ænig    ælda cynnes
> þæt ic lygewordum    leoð somnige,
> write woðcræfte.    Gehyrað witedom,
> Iobes gieddinga.    (ll.546–49)

> [No mortal man should imagine that I am composing a song, writing
> poetry, with lying words. Listen to the wisdom of Job's recital.]

proffering to paraphrase words from Job (29. 18; 19. 25–26) a prophet
who foretold the Resurrection and, as a result of ambiguity in the
Septuagint version, was supposed to refer to the phoenix (ll.552–69).[45]

There follows a further duplication of the common Resurrection,
finishing with an explicit identification of the adored sun, not as
formerly with God, but now with Christ the Saviour, the light of the
world (cf. John 3. 19 *et passim*). 'High above the roofs, shining upon
steadfast souls', it is followed by beautiful birds, flocks of the elect,
*fuglas scyne . . . gastas gecorene* (ll.587–93) into the kingdom of heaven –
again described in the inevitably negative terms of the Book of
Revelation (ll.611–14).

The poet insists on a final affirmation of academic authority: 'These
are matters which books tell us about' (l.655), before concluding with a

seventeen-line coda invoking the praise of God, and toppling into macaronic half-lines alternately English and Latin, which serves merely to confirm its lettered stance.

The received narrative clearly did not readily lend itself to systematic fourfold exposition. Flexible rather than disorganized in the retelling, its intellectual elements do not precipitate but interpenetrate in a complex plaitwork of recurrent images and themes that intertwine and develop, requiring a greater intellectual mobility than poetic sensibilities might allow. The poet's energetic and eclectic imagination crowds the poetic idiom in academic licence. The result is neither bestiary nor allegory, but rather a meditation on the theme of resurrection employing a variety of equations in a more casual network of associations than might normally appeal to precise minds – with few explicit or consistently maintained boundaries to enhance its intellectual appeal.

## Notes

1. Compare *The Fortunes of Men* and *Maxims I, passim,* in *The Exeter Book,* edited by G. P. Krapp and E. v. K. Dobbie, The Anglo-Saxon Poetic Records (London, 1931–53), III, pp. 154–63.

2. Compare F. J. E. Raby, *A History of Secular Latin Poetry in the Middle Ages* (Oxford, 1934), I, *passim;* P. L. Henry, *The Early English and Celtic Lyric* (London, 1966), *passim.*

3. See generally, J. E. Cross, 'Aspects of Microcosm and Macrocosm in Old English Literature', *Comparative Literature,* 14 (1962), 1–22. The concept of the journey of life and death, ultimately biblical (Hebrews ll. 13–16, and compare Matthew 7. 13–14), was thoroughly absorbed by the Old English poet; compare *Guthlac B,* ll.1076–80, *Juliana,* ll.699–703, *Vainglory,* ll.54–56, *Maxims I,* ll.77–78, *Riddles,* XLIII, ll.5–6, etc. (*Exeter Book,* edited by Krapp and Dobbie, pp. 80, 133, 148, 159, 204). Compare generally, G. V. Smithers, 'The Meaning of *The Seafarer* and *The Wanderer*', *Medium Ævum,* 26 (1957), 137–53; 28 (1959), 1–22.

4. Compare the proverbial *Maxims II,* ll.11–12, 'The old man is wisest with the experience of years behind him who has suffered much' (*The Anglo-Saxon Minor Poems,* edited by G. P. Krapp and E. v. K. Dobbie, The Anglo-Saxon Poetic Records (London, 1931–53), VI, p. 56; or its corollary in *Precepts,* l.54, 'Seldom does a wise man rejoice free from sorrow' (*Exeter Book,* edited by Krapp and Dobbie, p. 142).

5. See generally, J. E. Cross, '"Ubi sunt" Passages in Old English – Sources and Relationships', *Vetenskaps-Societetens i Lund Årsbok* (1956), 25–44.

6. Compare Bede, 'the apostle James prohibits us from complaining to our fellows in adversity', *Super Epistolas Catholicas Expositio,* edited by J.-P. Migne, *Patrologia Latina* (Paris, 1844–90), XCIII, cols 38f.

7. *Epistulae et Carmina*, edited by C. Lütjohann, *Monumenta Germaniae Historica, Auctorum Antiquissimorum*, VIII (Berlin, 1887), p. 132.

8. Compare the dismal fate of Cumbra in the events leading up to the *coup d'état* at Merton (*Two of the Saxon Chronicles Parallel*, edited by J. Earle and C. Plummer (Oxford, 1892–99), I, pp. 46–47). For some examples of political exile at this date, see *English Historical Documents, c. 500–1042*, edited by D. Whitelock, second edition (London, 1979), pp. 24–25.

9. Bede, himself a convinced and lifelong monk, expresses himself as uneasy for the security of the State when so many young men were abandoning the practice of arms in favour of the contemplative life (*Bede's Ecclesiastical History of the English People*, edited by B. Colgrave and R. A. B. Mynors (Oxford, 1969), pp. 560–61).

10. For the native background to this movement, see Henry, *Early English and Celtic Lyric*, especially pp. 181–92.

11. Compare Augustine, *De Doctrina Christiana*, edited by W. M. Green, *Corpus Scriptorum Ecclesiasticorum Latinorum*, LXXX (Vienna, 1963), p. 10; see also the references cited by G. Ehrismann, 'Religionsgeschichtliche Beiträge zum germanischen Frühchristentum', *Beiträge zur Geschichte der deutschen Sprache und Literatur*, 35 (1909), 209–39; and Smithers, 'The Meaning of *The Seafarer* and *The Wanderer*', *passim*.

12. *Two Saxon Chron.*, edited by Earle and Plummer, I, p. 82, II, pp. 103–05.

13. Compare D. Whitelock, 'The Interpretation of *The Seafarer*', in *The Early Cultures of North-West Europe*, edited by C. Fox and B. Dickins (Cambridge, 1950), pp. 261–72.

14. Compare pseudo-Bede, *In Matthaei Evangelium Expositio*, edited by J.-P. Migne, *Patrologia Latina* XCII, (Paris, 1844–90), col. 43.

15. See, for example, the Doomsday sermons in *The Blickling Homilies*, edited by R. Morris, Early English Text Society, Original Series, 58, 63, 73 (London, 1874–80), pp. 56–59; or Ælfric, *The Homilies of the Anglo-Saxon Church*, edited by B. Thorpe (London, 1844–46), I, pp. 614–15.

16. Compare *Guthlac A*, l.744, in *Exeter Book*, edited by Krapp and Dobbie, p. 70; Alcuin's *Versus de Cuculo*, in *Monumenta Germaniae Historica, Poetae Latini Aevi Carolini*, I, edited by E. Dümmler (Berlin, 1881), pp. 269–70; and generally, Henry, *Early English and Celtic Lyric*, p. 74.

17. The image is developed elaborately by Cynewulf in the Doomsday conclusion to *Christ II*, which had not employed such terms in the body of the poem: 'the plains shall pass away, the strongholds of men burst asunder in ruins; and the fire shall fare forth to consume all the ancient treasures which men in their pride hoarded on earth. . . . Now it is as if we were travelling in ships upon the flood of cold waters, voyaging in ocean steeds, vessels upon the wide sea. The flood is perilous, the waves very great, the billows windy over the deep road on which we are tossed through this changeful world. Hard was the wayfaring before we won to land over these stormy waters; but help comes to us – God's ghostly Son – who leads us to the haven of salvation. . . . Let us therefore fix our hope in that haven that the sovereign of the skies prepared for us, the holiness of heaven, when he rose to his home' (ll.810–14, 850–66), (*Exeter Book*, edited by Krapp and Dobbie, pp. 25–27).

18. Compare *Beowulf*, ll.26–52, in *Beowulf with the Finnesburg Fragment*, edited by C. L. Wrenn, third edition, revised by W. F. Bolton (London, 1973), pp. 98–99, or the ninth-century Life of St Gildas, III, edited by T. Mommsen in *Monumenta Germaniae Historica, Chronica Minora Saec. IV. V, VI, VII*, III (Berlin, 1898), p. 101. For actual examples, see M. Müller-Wille, 'Bestattung im Boot: Studien zu einer nordeuropäischen Grabsitte', *Offa*, 25–26 (1968–69), 7–203.

19. Augustine mentions evidence for the greater physical proportions of men of former times in the discovery of huge bones in ancient tombs (*De Civitate Dei*, edited by E. Hoffmann, *Corpus Scriptorum Ecclesiasticorum Latinorum*, XL (2) (Vienna, 1900), pp. 75–76); the bones of Hygelac, Beowulf's leader, were said to have been of gigantic size, preserved as a curiosity on an island in the Rhine (*Liber Monstrorum*, in *Opuscula*, edited by M. Haupt (Leipzig, 1876), II, p. 223). As a metaphor, the stature of the men of the past is a natural one, extending from Fredegar in the seventh century to Bernard of Chartres in the twelfth, and beyond: *Fredegarii et Aliorum Chronica*, edited by B. Krusch, *Monumenta Germaniae Historica, Scriptores Rerum Merovingicarum*, II (Hanover, 1888), p. 123; Bernard, cited by John of Salisbury, in *Metalogicon*, edited by C. C. I. Webb (Oxford, 1929), p. 136.

20. Compare the opening of *Maxims II*, 'Cities are seen from far off, the ingenious work of giants', ll.1–2, in *Anglo-Saxon Minor Poems*, edited by Krapp and Dobbie, p. 55.

21. Genesis 6. 4; Job 26. 5 (Vulgate *gigantes*).

22. For example, Augustine, in *De Civitate Dei*, edited by Hoffmann, p. 59.

23. See H. T. Keenan, 'The Ruin as Babylon', *Tennessee Studies in Literature*, 11 (1966), 109–18.

24. *Bede's Eccles. Hist.*, edited by Colgrave and Mynors, pp. 16–17.

25. *Opera Poetica*, edited by F. Leo, *Monumenta Germaniae Historica, Auctorum Antiquissimorum*, IV (1) (Berlin, 1881), pp. 271–75.

26. *The Poetry of Llywarch Hen*, edited by P. K. Ford (Berkeley, California, 1974), pp. 112–17.

27. Alcuin, *The Bishops, Kings, and Saints of York*, edited by P. Godman (Oxford, 1982).

28. *The Anglo-Saxon Minor Poems*, edited by Krapp and Dobbie, p. 27.

29. *Two Lives of Saint Cuthbert*, edited by B. Colgrave (Cambridge, 1940), pp. 242–45.

30. 'You can still see many vestiges of its original grandeur: immense palaces which once had roofs with gilded gables in imitation of Roman splendour, built in the fashion of the Roman rulers of old, and embellished with splendid structures; a gigantic tower, remarkable heated baths, the remains of temples, and sites of theatres, all enclosed within excellent walls, parts of which still stand', *Itinerarium Cambriae*, in *Giraldi Cambrensis Opera*, edited by J. S. Brewer *et al.*, Rolls Series, 21 (London, 1861–91), VI, p. 55.

31. *Epistulae et Acta*, edited by O. Faller, *Corpus Scriptorum Ecclesiasticorum Latinorum*, LXXXII (Vienna, 1968), p. 68.

32. Gildas, edited by T. Mommsen, *Monumenta Germaniae Historica, Auctorum Antiquissimorum*, XIII (Berlin, 1898), pp. 36–39.

33. *Sancti Augustini Sermones post Maurinos Reperti*, edited by D. G. Morin (Rome, 1930), pp. 409–10; and compare *De Civitate Dei*, edited by Hoffmann, *Corpus Scriptorum*, pp. 64–65.

34. See sources cited by M. J. Swanton, *Crisis and Development in Germanic Society, 700–800* (Göppingen, 1982), p. 70.

35. Compare Gregory's commentary in *XL Homiliarum in Evangelia*, edited by J.-P. Migne, *Patrologia Latina* (Paris, 1844–90), LXXVI, col. 1080.

36. Compare *Christ*, ll.881, 973–74, 977, 1141–42, in *Exeter Book*, edited by Krapp and Dobbie, pp. 25, 30, 34.

37. Compare *Judgement Day I*, ll. 77–79, in *Exeter Book*, edited by Krapp and Dobbie, p. 214, and *Judgement Day II*, ll. 232f, in *The Anglo-Saxon Minor Poems*, edited by Krapp and Dobbie, pp. 64–65.

38. See generally, H. Rahner, *Griechische Mythen in Christlicher Deutung* (Zurich, 1945), pp. 365–84; J. Pépin, *Mythe et Allégorie: Les Origines Grecques et les Contestations Judéo-Chrétiennes* (Paris, 1958).

39. Pliny, *Natural History*, edited by H. Rackham *et al.* (London, 1938–62), III, pp. 292–95.

40. L. Caeli Firmiani Lactanti, *Opera Omnia*, edited by S. Brandt and G. Laubmann, *Corpus Scriptorum Ecclesiasticorum Latinorum*, XXVII (1) (Vienna, 1893), II (1), pp. 135–47.

41. *Divinae Institutiones*, edited by S. Brandt and G. Laubmann, *Corpus Scriptorum Ecclesiasticorum Latinorum*, XIX (Vienna, 1890), pp. 144, 400, 413 *et passim*.

42. Venantius Fortunatus, *Opera Poetica*, edited by F. Leo, *Monumenta Germaniae Historica*, IV (1) (Berlin, 1881), p. 17; Gregory of Tours, *De Cursu Stellarum Ratio*, edited by B. Krusch, *Monumenta Germaniae Historica, Scriptores Rerum Merovingicarum*, I (2) (Hanover, 1885), p. 411; Hrabanus Maurus, *De Universo*, edited by J. -P. Migne, *Patrologia Latina* (Paris, 1844–90), CXI, col. 246. A large range of other references are cited by M. C. Fitzpatrick, *Lactanti De Ave Phoenice* (Philadelphia, 1933), pp. 12–15.

43. Ambrose, *Opera*, edited by C. Schenkl, *Corpus Scriptorum Ecclesiasticorum Latinorum*, XXXII (1) (Vienna, 1887), pp. 197–98, and compare R. van d. Broek, *The Myth of the Phoenix according to Classical and Early Christian Traditions* (Leiden, 1972).

44. Possibly this was the result of an academic conflation with the silkworm, linked with the phoenix as a resurrection symbol by Ambrose, *Opera*, edited by Schenkl, pp. 195–96.

45. For this confusion see H. Gaebler, 'Ueber die Autorschaft des angelsaechsischen Gedichtes vom Phoenix', *Anglia*, 3 (1880), 488–526 (pp. 520–21) and sources there cited.

# Chapter 5
# An Assured Heroism

*Guthlac A, Judith, The Battle of Maldon* and Laȝamon's *Brut*

In speaking of the need to undertake brave deeds against the devil, the author of *The Seafarer* drew implicitly on the figure of *miles spiriti* (see above, p. 117). This concept is developed explicitly in *The Phoenix,* where the bird is spoken of as 'the Lord's champion', whose charitable actions serve to defend his nest-refuge from malicious attack, and in terms of the life of men on earth, as the holy soldier who earns joy through valour, until snatched away by the warrior Death (see above, p. 137). The metaphor of spiritual warfare derives from Scripture. Christ himself had said: 'I came not to send peace, but a sword' (Matthew 10. 34). Popularized by the letters of St Paul,[1] the image of the Christian fighting the good fight clothed in 'the whole armour of God' was taken up enthusiastically by the early Church.[2] And in an age unaccustomed to dissect the Platonic metaphor, dividing concept from reality, the notion of religious warfare would be taken as seriously as that of religious exile. The early monastic leader Faustus exhorts his community as though they were an armed camp 'met not for peace and security but for struggle and conflict . . . we have embarked on a war'.[3] Whereas the Mediterranean Church typically produced martyrs and virgins, the northern world is characterized by the warrior-saint. The active ideal of ascetic Christianity was well suited to the heroic temper of the times. This phase in the insular Church was characterized by a lengthy catalogue of British and Saxon princely saints to whom the determination and rigour of the eremetic life seems to have proved especially attractive. At least one story would be told of a former prince who secretly wore next to his skin the rotted remains of his original armour so as to mortify the flesh, and who deliberately chose to live among his erstwhile enemies the Welsh, the better to conduct his 'new warfare'.[4]

By the end of the seventh century monasticism was well established and even regally endorsed among the Anglo-Saxons as a socially acceptable mode of life. Many prominent churchmen formerly served in the war-bands of Anglo-Saxon kings, and seem to have welcomed with no less heroic determination the cleansing discomfort of the social and spiritual readjustment their new life required. The case of the Mercian hermit Guthlac is relatively well documented by his early eighth-century biographer Felix.[5] Born *c*. 673 into a branch of the Mercian royal house, he became the leader of an independent *comitatus* during a particularly turbulent period for this warlike frontier province. But eventually, upon reflection on the unhappy deaths of former kings, on the transience of worldly wealth and the brevity of life, he abruptly determined to abandon his secular career in favour of the contemplative life. At the age of twenty-four he entered the monastery at Repton. Two years later, after a novitiate of notable piety and self-discipline, he sought to further his service to God by withdrawing into the wilderness, establishing a hermitage at Crowland in the Lincolnshire fens, where after fifteen years of singular austerity he died in 714. His saintly reputation spread during his own lifetime, and pilgrims flocked to Crowland in search of healing or spiritual guidance. Guthlac's friendship with the powerful Mercian king Æthelbald served to increase his fame; and the memory of his sanctity was perpetuated long after his death by the many miracles worked at his tomb.

Felix's story-materials are straightforward enough, and he claims to have based his narrative upon the first-hand reports of those who knew the hermit well. But by the time Felix composed his *vita* – probably between the years 730 and 740 – the conventions of hagiography were firmly established. The first forty years of the eighth century witnessed a remarkable growth of interest in native saint's-lives among scholarly circles. The writings of Aldhelm and Bede provide ample evidence for a lively interest in the sufferings of the early martyrs – especially virgin-martyrs. But now a new school of Anglo-Latin hagiographers (perhaps writing for an essentially monastic audience) chose to celebrate contemporary saints – men like Cuthbert or Ceolfrith whose faith had been proved not by direct sacrifice of life like the martyrs of old, but by the willing endurance of daily suffering in asceticism which, since the ending of the persecution, had come to be regarded as a form of martyrdom.[6] The model for this development is found not in the *passio* – which details the physical torments endured by a martyr in defence of the faith, but in the *vita*, which records the holiness of spirit achieved by the contemplative. Evagrius's version of Athanasius's Life of the desert hermit Anthony (*c*. 360) and Sulpicius Severus's account of the Life of St Martin of Tours (397) represent the primary models for this development, while a third work: the *Dialogues* of Gregory the Great (594) fostered an innate interest in the marvellous.[7] Such was the respect accorded to these models, the hagiographer's work at times became a tissue of unacknowledged quotations, as when, for example, the anonymous Whitby monk who recorded the Life of Gregory the Great, incorporates a miracle which Gregory himself had attributed to Leo I.[8] Although Felix claims that his description of Guthlac's death was based on a first-hand account given him by an attendant eye-witness, a good deal of that description, including the conversations said to have taken place, seem to have been drawn directly from Bede's *Life of Cuthbert*.[9] Two episodes Felix employed to illustrate Guthlac's powers of prophecy are closely modelled on two incidents in Gregory's *Dialogues*;[10] and even his prefatory claim to have taken care to confirm the veracity of his information merely repeats lines from the prologues of Bede and Athanasius.[11]

By the early years of the eighth century the hagiographer's protestation of authenticity seems to have become as commonplace as the overt plagiarism it denied. But this discrepancy should not be construed as mere naivety. Rather it is symptomatic of the central purpose of hagiography which, like secular epic but unlike historical biography, has a primarily didactic intent, celebrating the most exalted form of behaviour and aiming to inspire both respect for the protagonist and emulation of his conduct. Such didacticism sought less to commemorate an individual than to present a paradigm for the attainment of glory – whether secular or religious. In selecting his material, therefore, the author would consider most significant those features which might best represent his subject's sanctity, rather than the particularity of circumstances, events or characterization which distinguished the individual. Since all saints must be essentially similar in their devotion and desire to serve God, the central facts of their lives might display a fundamental correspondence in all important respects; and the characteristics of one saint might with equal propriety be assigned to another. The *vita* serves not to document but to exemplify: rather than stress the particularity that marked the merely temporal existence of an individual, it links its subject with the whole communion of saints. Any lingering unease as to the method might be dismissed by reference to St Paul's doctrine of the body of Christ.[12] It is arguable that the interest of a *vita* lies in the skill with which it deploys certain well-established formulae, rather than in the pursuit of literary individuality. But for the modern reader its narrative content is all too often an embarrassing combination of piety and sensationalism; a stereotyped compilation of: portentous birth, precocious piety, exemplary novitiate, ascetic zealousness, miraculous powers, joyful death and posthumous miracles. Considerable stress was laid on the miraculous since this provided evidence for the saint's proximity to heaven, and the continuing intervention of God's grace in the lives of men. The audience might expect to hear an account of the saint's meeting with angels or of his vision of the next world or of the journey of his soul to heaven. No less importance was attached to a description of the saint's last days since, as with the secular hero, the manner of his death would probe most profoundly the nature of his spiritual assertion. And the expectation of death was perhaps the sole element the audience might reasonably experience in common with the saint.

This dual dramatic and thematic focus of the Anglo-Latin *vita*, was clearly recognized by the authors of two independent Old English Guthlac poems. While the authors of poetic *vitae* like *Andreas, Juliana* or *Elene* adhere to the traditional formulae in retailing classical stories of Mediterranean saints, the authors of *Guthlac A* and *B* escape the formal constraints of received material. Highly selective, they abandon the conventional chronological progression, ignore the undoubted attractions of the miraculous, and seek instead to encapsulate the significance of the saint's conduct and existence within a single aspect or episode of his life.

*Guthlac B* deals with the death of the saint. Written perhaps some eighty years after Felix in the early years of the ninth century, it draws directly on Chapter 50 of the Latin *vita*. The poet of *Guthlac A*, on the other hand, may well have been a contemporary of Felix, writing perhaps within a generation of Guthlac's death – say, before 750. He repeatedly claims that the events he describes had occurred within living memory (ll.153–57, 752–54, and cf. 93–94, 400–02); and a relatively early date would certainly be supported by its stylistic and metrical resemblances to poems like *Beowulf, Genesis A* or *Exodus*.[13] Like Felix, the *Guthlac A* poet recognizes the central importance of a demonic assault on the saint, although in other respects, both thematic and structural, his poem was conceived quite independently of the Latin *vita*.

Like the funeral motif which opens and closes *Beowulf, Guthlac A* is framed by reference to the journey of the saint's soul at death. An angel has come to conduct the blessed soul to heaven – 'one spirit greeting the other in the happiest of meetings':

Se bið gefeana fægrast    þonne hy æt frymðe gemetað,
engel ond seo eadge sawl!    Ofgiefeþ hio þas eorþan wynne,
forlæteð þas lænan dreamas,    ond hio wiþ þam lice
gedæleð.    (ll.1–3)

[It is the most beautiful joy when first they meet, the angel and the blessed soul! It relinquishes these earthly pleasures, gives up these ephemeral delights, and parts from the body.]

The saint is finally to be admitted to the haven for which the Seafarer had yearned: 'a timely traveller to the heavenly home' where sorrow never enters nor the affliction of poverty – a city ruled by the King of kings, whose halls never fall into decay (ll.9–18), where life does not dwindle but grows better the longer it lasts – the antithesis of life on earth (ll.19–21). The end of the world is anticipated in familiar terms. The world is troubled, *onhrered* (l.37); and as the prophets foretold, the earth is falling into the sere:

Ealdað eorþan blæd    æþela gehwylcre
ond of wlite wendað    wæstma gecyndu;
bið seo siþre tid    sæda gehwylces
mætræ in mægne.    Forþon se mon ne þearf
to þisse worulde    wyrpe gehycgan.    (ll. 43–47)

[The flower of the earth is ageing in every virtue, and the character of its
fruits is to lose their fine appearance; in a later season every seed is feebler in
vigour. Therefore one need look for no improvement in this world.]

Now within this overall framework the poet constructs neither the
allusive fragment of *Deor* nor the thematic interlace of *The Phoenix* but a
small number of discrete narrative panels – a logical series of tableaux
resembling the Romanesque manuscript illustration of saints' lives *in
codice* or, more pertinently perhaps, the sequence of narrative roundels
depicted in the twelfth-century 'Guthlac Roll'.[14]

Men in many conditions of life might be numbered with the saints
provided they keep God's commandments (ll. 30–34). The urgent need to
seek salvation is everywhere evinced by present transience. But at
Judgement Day few will be chosen, so far do men's deeds fall short of
their words. The conduct of some of those who take up holy orders, the
poet insists, is a mockery of the monastic ideals of poverty and
abstinence. But those who adopt the eremitical life to enter into a solitary
warfare against evil might hope to gain a reward in heaven no less
glorious than that bestowed by a leader on the most faithful member of
his comitatus:

Sume þa wuniað    on westennum,
secað ond gesittað    sylfra willum
hamas on heolstrum.    Hy ðæs heofoncundan
boldes bidað.    Oft him brogan to
laðne gelædeð,    se þe him lifes onfonn . . .
Þæt synd þa gecostan cempan    þa þam cyninge þeowað,
se næfre þa lean alegeð    þam þe his lufan adreogeð.    (ll. 81–85,
                                                              91–92)

[Some dwell in the wilderness, of their own accord seek out and inhabit
obscure places. They await a heavenly mansion. Often he who grudges them
life brings some hateful terror upon them. . . . These are the proven
champions who serve a king who never withholds the reward from those
who endure in his love.]

It is only after the poet has narrowed the focus in this way that he
introduces his protagonist, telescoping the circumstances of the saint's
commitment – the young man's rejection of the world and the hermit's
arrival in his solitary refuge – into a dozen lines (ll. 95–107). What

ensues, however, bears little relation to any conventional *vita*; there is scarcely any reference to Guthlac's routine of prayer and fasting; nor does it contain any of the miracle stories with which the saint's life characteristically abounds. Instead we are presented with an elaborate psychomachia, in which the interior temptations which assail the hermit are physically projected – demonic aggression to be opposed by superior spiritual strength. The tone of tranquillity one might expect of a saintly life is entirely absent, and replaced by a martial note more suited to heroic epic than hagiography. But there is no doubt as to the eventual outcome, since from the beginning of the poem we have been aware of the saint's victory – his joyful soul being carried to heaven without further conflict or any need for purgatorial cleansing, by which the contemporary audience would have recognized the passing of a life of great sanctity.[15]

Behind the poet's unconventional narrative of conflict and vision lay a strongly didactic purpose; repeated interventions by the homiletic voice make it clear that the series of demonic assaults is to be read in terms of gradational opposition – an exemplary spiritual progression which the saint's antagonists intend to impede (e.g. ll.153–69, 328–47, 393–403, 514–29, 748–72). Whereas Felix presents the demons' attack as a single, albeit central, phase in the *vita*, the author of *Guthlac A* more realistically represents the same theme not as a single campaign but a constant state of warfare recurring throughout the hermit's life. The conflict is defined by four separate tableaux, each representing a distinct type of temptation which Guthlac must overcome in order to win the victor's crown of salvation. The initial assaults which the demons launch against the saint test his power to resist the physical temptations of the world and the flesh, while the subsequent torments which he must endure represent a more insidious form of spiritual temptation, whereby the hermit is first prompted to doubt the validity of his vocation and is finally tempted to deny his faith in God's benevolence. This programme observes the same psychological verisimilitude that informs Athanasius's account of St Anthony's battle against the demons of the Egyptian desert. As Anthony explains to his disciples, demons 'approach us in a form corresponding to the condition in which they find us, and adapt their delusions to our state of mind'.[16]

While there is no denying the ultimately spiritual significance of Guthlac's conflict, the saint externalizes his demons, just as Beowulf had done. They have literal as well as abstract levels of existence, thus permitting the action to shift alternately between psychological and topographical locations. The action of the narrative hinges around a struggle for possession of the fenland refuge, the image of which is therefore central to the thematic and dramatic structure of the poem, and is itself capable of a variety of interpretations. It is at once a physical and spiritual position the hermit has adopted, and its representation therefore the most complete integration of the poem's spiritual and literal dimensions. In turning to the wilderness, the saint signifies his renunciation of 'the world'. He enters a wasteland (*westen*, ll.208, 296, etc.) to seek out a secret place (*dygle stow*, l.215) – a frontier zone (*mearclond*, l.174), remote from all human habitation (*bimipen fore monnum*, l.147), uncultivated and uninhabited (*idel ond æmen*, l.216). 'Remote from hereditary jurisdiction', the site is said to 'await the counter-claim of a better tenant' (ll.216–17) – prosaic legal vocabulary, the introduction of which both marks a radical development in English verse[17] and acknowledges the genuine, albeit contested, claim of previous occupants. In point of fact, the picture of utter desolation suggested does not quite correspond with the historical situation on the ground. Despite temporary economic regression, the Lincolnshire fenland was far from being a desolate wilderness; Crowland itself had been the site of an active Romano-British settlement.[18] And in any case, Guthlac was not the first anchorite to have entered this area;[19] his hermitage was not the sole outpost of Christianity but only one of a number of religious communities established in the region during the late seventh and early eighth centuries. The term 'desert' is merely a useful metaphor, part of the standard, technical vocabulary of the eremetical life, referring to any spot chosen for the dwelling of an anchorite irrespective of its precise geographical location. The poet rightly imbues the hermit's landscape setting with an air of desolation; to have done any less would have inevitably diminished the stature of Guthlac's achievement. The poet makes no claim to be writing objective history rather than hagiography. Similarly, the claim that Guthlac dwells 'alone' (*ana*, ll.101, 158, 207), omits to take account of either attendants or the constant stream of visitors. It might simply be that, aristocrat as he was, Guthlac no more considered himself 'in company' than the nineteenth-century middle class did in the presence of household servants. And of course 'those who are constantly visited by mortals cannot be much visited by angels'.[20] Guthlac's avowed solitariness is a sign of internal rather than contextual isolation.

In other respects the wilderness is certainly not deserted of course. It was axiomatic that this was the home of outcasts, physical and spiritual: 'the monster must dwell in the fen, lonely in the land'.[21] The drear and dismal borderland formed a refuge for all such exiles as Grendel and his brood or the family of Cain (see above, p. 56). Guthlac's seventh-century Northumbrian counterpart Cuthbert was only able to establish his hermitage on the remote Farne Island after ridding the place of demons.[22] In seeking out such a place, therefore, Guthlac would be known to have deliberately courted the displeasure of malignant beings:

Wid is þes westen,    wræcsetla fela,
eardas onhæle    earmra gæsta.
Sindon wærlogan    þe þa wic bugað.    (ll. 296–98)

[This wilderness is wide, and the number of fugitive settlements many, the secret abode of wretched spirits. Those who inhabit these dwellings are faithless.]

Whether literal or figurative, they not unnaturally dispute his right to displace them.

Although the poet has located the saint in a tangible and identifiable environment, he does not, unlike Felix, provide any specific description of Guthlac's dwelling-place, relying instead on a series of carefully chosen nouns to convey a variety of permissible levels of interpretation. As the anchorite strengthens his resolve, so his dwelling-place appears to assume a new character, mirroring his progress in the ascetic life. Transcending the limitations of his earthly existence, the site of his dwelling seems transformed from dismal swamp to earthly paradise, 'a sanctuary' (l. 716), and 'the dearest place on earth' (ll. 427–28). No longer a dark and sinister 'secret place', *dygle stow*, but a green and pleasant land of victory, *sigewong* (ll. 215–17, 742–48),[23] it is the type of the eternal paradise which will await the saint in heaven.

The major epithet the poet employs to describe the location of Guthlac's dwelling – *beorg* – is significantly capable of multiple interpretations. In its primary sense *beorg* denotes 'hill'; although topographically irreconcilable with a fenland setting, this may well represent part of an interior, psychological landscape: higher ground above the mire – the mount of holiness which the hermit must endeavour to ascend (*gestigan*, l. 175) in his quest for perfection.[24] In association with the verb *beorgan* [to fortify, defend], however, it may also denote a place of retreat and heroic endeavour in which the saint will defend his spirit from the all too palpable demonic assault. Some hermits we know chose to live in defensible sites like disused fortresses;[25] others might erect a symbolic rampart, *vallum monasterii*, either actually or notionally to exclude the temptations of the world.[26] In purely literal terms the battle for the *beorg* might have appeared the record of a feud waged between a group of outcasts and a solitary, albeit renowned, warrior, fighting to occupy and defend an enemy stronghold on behalf of an all powerful lord. But however tangible the physical location of his context, it is with *gæstlicum wæpnum* [spiritual weapons], that the blessed warrior equips himself (ll. 176–78). Like Beowulf, confronting a no less physical demon, Guthlac fights alone (ll. 245, 450), enhancing his heroic stature; also like Beowulf he will relinquish the aid of a sword – but not to prove his own singular strength, but rather his assurance of God's strong aid:

> 'No ic eow sweord ongean
> mid gebolgne hond    oðberan þence,
> worulde wæpen,    ne sceal þes wong gode
> þurh blodgyte    gebuen weorðan,
> ac ic minum Criste    cweman þence
> leofran lace.'    (ll. 302–07)

['I intend to carry no sword against you, no worldly weapon, with enraged
hand, nor shall this ground be occupied for God through bloodshed, but I
intend to please my Christ by a more precious service.']

However martial the imagery, the conflict is clearly conceived as an
interior struggle taking place within the confines of the hermit's soul,
Guthlac a 'warrior fighting for God in his heart' (ll. 344–45). For the true
*miles Christi* the literal framework is far from incongruous. Such redeployment of the heroic idiom is familiar from, for example, *The Dream of
the Rood* (see above, p. 98).[27] The vocabulary of conflict is equally
appropriate to physical and spiritual feud. The hero is repeatedly depicted in the guise of a warrior, *cempa* (ll. 153, 180, etc.), or *oretta* (ll. 176,
344, etc.): the poet specifically inviting the audience to consider his
protagonist in the same light as a secular hero:

> Hwylc wæs mara þonne se?
> An oretta    ussum tidum
> cempa gecyðeð    þæt him Crist fore
> woruldlicra ma    wundra gecyðde.    (ll. 400–03)

[Who was greater than he? That lone warrior and champion demonstrates
that in our own times, for his sake, Christ has demonstrated further miracles
in the world.]

In founding his hermitage where he does Guthlac threatens to dispos-
sess those outcast wretches, *wræcmæcgas* (ll. 231, 263, 558, etc.) from one
of the few refuges that remain to them. They recommend alternative sites
(ll. 308–9), and when he proves obdurate, accuse him of pride (*wlenc*, l. 208,
*oferhygd*, l. 269–70). The ostensible literal motive for the demons' disquiet
and assault is not for possession of Guthlac's soul but of the *beorg*. It is
only in the closing stages of the poem that this issue is finally resolved
(l. 702).

The physical and spiritual dimension of the conflict overlap in one
further sense of the term *beorg*. As interpreted by the ninth-century
vernacular prose translator of Felix,[28] it also denotes 'burial-mound,
barrow'. An unusual, if not inappropriate place for the anchorite to take
up his dwelling, it would represent a perpetual *memento mori* in the eyes of
one aware of the transience and brevity of this present life. It was not

without precedent, for Anthony and other early Christian recluses had sought seclusion by choosing to live in remote tombs.[29] Perhaps more pertinently, however, such barrows were notoriously associated with heathen cults;[30] and as such, an ancient pagan burial-mound would provide a perfectly appropriate challenge to Christ's warrior. It was standard missionary policy to sanctify heathen temples and turn them to Christian use, as Paulinus did at Yeavering or Augustine at Canterbury;[31] and there are several instances where Christian churches are found adjacent to such barrows.[32] A natural *locus* for militant paganism, this certainly explains the urgency with which its former occupants sought to preserve their stronghold from a famous war-leader like Guthlac, and why the conflict should be couched in legalistic, territorial, as well as military terms. At another level therefore, the saint is fighting for supremacy over the forces of evil represented by local *pagani* in the remote countryside to which conservative elements characteristically retreat.

The demons' initial approach accurately reflects the doubts that might first assail the aspiring anchorite, aggravating the *anhaga's* natural craving for companionship (cf. *The Wanderer*, p. 106f above). Not permitted to harm the saint physically (ll. 226–31), they attempt to undermine Guthlac's determination by means of verbal sophistry (*ligesearwum*, l. 228). They remind him of both the attractions and responsibilities of secular life. How will the ex-leader of a comitatus be able to bear such loneliness and isolation? Is it right for him to abandon all the duties owed to his family? (ll. 192–99). How can he, 'God's starveling', survive in the wilderness with no visible means of support – no one to supply him with food and drink? (ll. 272–77). But as it becomes clear that Guthlac can successfully resist such worldly temptation, the demons turn from their spurious appeals to friereason and good sense to threats of bodily violence:

'Geswic þisses setles!    Ne mæg þec sellan ræd
mon gelæran    þonne þeos mengu eall.
We þe beoð holde    gif ðu us hyran wilt;
oþþe þec ungearo    eft gesecað
maran mægne,    þæt þe mon ne þearf
hondum hrinan    ne þin hra feallan
wæpna wundum.    We þas wic magun
fotum afyllan;    folc in ðriceð
meara þreatum    ond monfarum.
Beoð þa gebolgne,    þa þec breodwiað,
tredað þec ond tergað,    ond hyra torn wrecað,
toberað þec blodgum lastum.    Gif þu ure bidan þencest,
we þec niþa genægað.    Ongin þe generes wilnian,
far þær ðu freonda wene,    gif ðu þines feores recce.'

(ll. 278–91)

['Give up this dwelling-place! No one can give you better advice than this whole gathering. We shall be friendly towards you if you will listen to us; otherwise we shall seek you out again with a greater force when you are unprepared, in such a way that no one need lay hands on you, nor for your corpse to fall from the wounds of weapons. We can raze this homestead with our feet; people will rush in with troops of horses and marching men. They will be enraged then, when they knock you down, trample and rend you and vent their anger, carrying off your bloody remains. If you presume to wait for us, we shall come at you with hostility. If you care for your life begin looking for a refuge, go where you have hope of friends.']

The poet's account of this second phase of Guthlac's battle has survived only in a fragmentary form, since a leaf is missing from the manuscript between lines now numbered 368–69. However, as the narrative resumes it is clear that the demons have in fact carried out their threat, and Guthlac has been tormented with fire (ll.374–76), an event which may perhaps be reconstructed from an incident in Felix's *vita* in which the demons in the guise of a British war-band set fire to Guthlac's hermitage.[33] But the saint heroically disdains bodily suffering. He is confident that, although God may allow them to afflict his body with pain, this will merely serve to bring his soul to a nobler state (ll.377–78).

Once the poet has illustrated Guthlac's ability to transcend both the temptations of the world and the weakness of the flesh, the nature of the demons' assault undergoes a fundamental change. Their ostensible motive – resentfulness at his intrusion and their intent to evict him from their own territory – recedes into the background. Now they seek to question first the hermit's beliefs in the integrity of his vocation, and secondly the efficacy of self-denial in overcoming the magnitude of his sins. They will torment the anchorite with visions intended to subvert his most deeply held beliefs. It is now undeniably Guthlac's soul which is the ultimate target of their aggression (ll.564–68). Having failed to persuade him by other means to leave of his own volition, they are nevertheless permitted to remove the saint bodily from the *locus sacer* for the first time. Raised high into the air, he is compelled to witness the corruption and indiscipline flourishing under the guise of monasticism, an element of social criticism new to Old English literature. It is not now Guthlac's own purity of life which is challenged, but rather his charity of spirit. The facts of monastic corruption – for which historical evidence is plentiful – are undeniable. But Guthlac declines to accept the demons' perverse interpretation of reality, which chooses to believe only the worst and ignores the good in men (ll.505–09). Unlike, for example, the visionary Adamman, who would visit such monastic abuse with punitive hell-fire,[34] Guthlac's response is exceptionally humane. The lapses the demons would have him regard as iniquitous, he accepts as merely the levity which God ordains as proper to youth and which, given time, will develop into the wisdom of maturity. Instead of reciting a psalm or making the sign of the cross, as in Felix, the saint's response to the demons' imputation is one of flat, scornful contradiction:

'Ic eow soð siþþon    secgan wille.
God scop geoguðe    ond gumena dream;
ne magun þa æfteryld    in þam ærestan
blæde geberan,    ac hy blissiað
worulde wynnum,    oððæt wintra rim
gegæð in þa geoguðe,    þæt se gæst lufað
onsyn ond ætwist    yldran hades.'    (ll. 494–500)

['Now I will tell you the truth. God created young people and human happiness; they cannot show maturity with their first breath, but they take delight in the pleasures of the world, until the length of years subdues their youth with the result that the spirit relishes the aspect and substance of a senior status.']

Guthlac's status as martyr is now acknowledged (l. 514), but he is about to be subjected to his final and most severe trial. In an ironic parody of the popular *Visio Pauli*, the demons carry Guthlac to the gates of hell and there terrify him with threats of his own imminent damnation. Unerringly picking out the hermit's fear that his life of self-denial and spiritual devotion may prove inadequate to secure salvation, they tempt him to despair which leads the soul to turn away from God, abandoning faith in his infinite mercy, to believe that he may in the end be forsaken – the ultimate human temptation of Christ on the cross (Matthew 27. 46; Mark 15. 34). However, Guthlac's faith proves superior even to this most insidious threat, a final triumphant speech of steadfast assurance marking the climax of his campaign (ll. 592–684). It is at this point that the angelic guide appears, not as the cause, but the effect, of Guthlac's victory: his role not that of some *deus ex machina* rescuing the saint from insuperable adversity, but the signal consequence of Guthlac's ability to overcome the demons through his own spiritual resources. Nevertheless, although Guthlac is said to have conducted his warfare 'alone', he has not been destitute of help (ll. 240–54). We have constantly been aware of the guiding presence of a guardian angel – first as the agent of Guthlac's initial adoption of the religious life – battling with an evil spirit for control of the young man's mind (ll. 114–16), and remaining thereafter as an instrument of his success (ll. 172–74, 189–91) in the assurance of which Guthlac is able to taunt and defy his persecutors. The angel's greeting recalls – and expands – the opening lines of the poem. His declaration that his brother's suffering has distressed him suggests that the communion of saints is mutual – those in heaven suffering together with their imitators on earth. In declaring the ineffectuality of the demons, he speaks in purely physical terms:

'Ne sy him banes bryce    ne blodig wund,
lices læla    ne laþes wiht
. . .
He sceal þy wong wealdan,    ne magon ge him þa wic
                    forstondan.'    (ll. 698–99, 702)

['There is to be no broken bone nor bloody wound, body-bruise, nor any
whit of injury. . . . He is to have control of that place; you cannot withhold
this homestead from him.']

The demons are commanded to heal each one of Guthlac's injuries with
their own hands, and then to be obedient to him (ll. 703–06). Following
his triumph, we are given a charming picture, familiar from the lives of
Cuthbert[35] and other (especially Celtic) hermits, of man living in pre-
Lapsarian harmony with the natural world; the wild creatures and the
birds of the air, recognize a gentle rather than a martial spirit: the
countryside springs into blossom and cuckoos herald the year (ll. 732–44);
the fertile plain rests in God's protection (l. 746), echoing and contradict-
ing the opening picture of decline (ll. 43–46). But since the poet's aim was
to demonstrate the availability and means of attaining salvation through
the example of, in this case, Guthlac, the poem ends not with the
triumphal entrance of the saint's spirit alone into heaven (ll. 781–87), but
with a general admonition and vision of general triumph, as all men of
the sacrament, and all chosen warriors (ll. 796–97) enter into the kingdom, in a exultant conclusion recalling that of *The Dream of the Rood* (see
above, p. 101).

It is perhaps quite fortuitous that the inhabitants of the fenland refuge
whom Guthlac sought to displace, and in whom he must needs find
malignant spirits, are also identifiable as his former enemies: the surviving rump of unabsorbed British enclaves – rural conservatives bypassed
by both the forces of the new religion, and the colonizing armies of
Mercia, whom he must constantly have encountered as a Mercian war-
leader – representing the 'old enemy' in a dual sense. But it is their role
rather than their race that results in the conflict. Heroic society made no
bones about ethnic differentiation; no enemy was despised merely because of his race. Only perhaps the Huns were hateful, as the offspring of
evil spirits and Gothic witches.[36] Although the battle with evil was
readily conceived in physical terms, these are not yet racial. Whatever
their origin, human enemies could still be considered heroic and worthy –
hostile, naturally, but not necessarily evil therefore. Beowulf's Geats will
praise the Swede, Onela, though having little reason to love him. But the
amorphous open society which formed the unique context for the heroic
ethic was doomed to extinction by the very fact of its success. The
establishment of an imperium stretching beyond the confines of personal

relationships required that the comitatus dissolve in favour of a network of tenurial relationships. That the heroic spirit could persist strongly into the second half of the eighth century is proved by the story of Cynewulf and Cyneheard (see above, pp. 6, 8); and as a recognizable literary fiction it could be recalled as late as *The Battle of Maldon* (see below, pp. 165f). But the heroic fact could scarcely survive the feudal ideology of Alcuin.

It was a new and quite unheroic rationale which framed the new stability of western Europe: an intolerant centralism of which Alcuin was the ideologue and which was institutionally embodied in the restoration of the Empire, which this time the attacks of other barbarians, Saracens from the south and Vikings from the north, merely served to confirm. The proprietorial and territorial coherence of feudal ideology carried as its corollary the alien nature of that which lay beyond its confines. It was no longer possible to ignore national, ethnic, or religious boundaries.

The figure of the spiritual *miles Christi* tends inevitably to the notion of a physical 'holy war'. The sophisticated spiritual insight voiced by St Martin: *Christi miles sum; pugnare mihi non licet*, 'I am Christ's soldier; I'm not allowed to fight',[37] productive of situational paradox in the case of Guthlac, was soon neither accessible nor looked for. Ecclesiastical opposition to 'justifiable' bloodshed was increasingly muted. In the case of a specifically pagan invasion overrunning the country, laying waste churches, ravaging the land, and 'arousing Christian people to war', the penance required of those guilty of homicide might be reduced to as little as seven days' excommunication.[38] The alignment of Church and State places the institution firmly behind the notion of the just war in defence of the land against barbarian assault. Already by the eighth century it was assumed that church income would be used for the benefit of the army in the event of alien attack.[39] But by the ninth century the forces of heathenism posed a direct threat to the whole of western Europe. Whereas the military pagan forces of Penda who fought against the saintly King Oswald beneath the sign of the cross itself at the appropriately named Heavenfield in 634, while arrogant and savage, were in no way identified with the Antichrist, the ninth-century Viking opponents of the no more saintly Edmund are clearly understood to be agents of the devil.[40]

For Ælfric as for others, the apocryphal Book of Judith would provide a good precedent for the just war against a heathen invader, equating physical conflict with moral righteousness.[41] It provides a straightforwardly patriotic account of the circumstances surrounding a temporary Jewish victory prior to the Babylonian exile when an arrogant, superior invading army was put to rout by the faithful people of God. A decidedly secular story, albeit with clear moral implications,[42] It is appropriate that a probably tenth-century poetic treatment of the theme should be found in the *Beowulf* manuscript rather than with the Cædmonian collection of biblical poetry.

The Assyrian general, Holofernes, is engaged in a punitive campaign against those client nations who failed to support Nebuchadnezzar in his war with the Medes, and has besieged the Jewish frontier city of Bethulia, when they are routed following the daring ruse of a patriotic and beautiful Jewish woman who enters the Assyrian camp on a pretext and assassinates their leader. Like *Exodus* (see above, p. 84), *Judith* (at least in the form we have it – for a page and perhaps more is missing from the opening[43]), apparently treats only the climactic episode of the story. Circumstantial details are drastically pared down, and the number of named characters reduced to two: the virtuous Judith and villainous Holofernes, allowing for the presentation of a dramatically heightened physical confrontation between the two leaders, all other actors being gathered around these two protagonists. The opening chapters of the apocryphal source provide a considerable amount of information as to the historical and geographical situation only incidentally relevant to the dramatic confrontation at the gates of Bethulia. Aldhelm's account of the same incident opens with the figure of Judith herself, intercalating such circumstantial information as might be necessary in the body of his story.[44] The missing opening would presumably have dealt with the identity of Judith, her character and patriotic motive, and her decision to enter the enemy camp.

As the extant poem opens, Judith has been a welcome guest in the Assyrian camp for four days and Holofernes has given instructions for a sumptuous banquet to be prepared, after which, blind drunk, incapable and insensible, he will be murdered in his bed by the heroine. It is soon clear that this is more than the conventional set piece of doomed warriors engaged in a mead-hall feast; it lacks all formal Beowulfian ceremonial restraint. It is also something other than the honest drunkenness approved by Tacitus several centuries earlier.[45] Those who participate are degraded: no longer warriors at a feast, but feasters above all else, insensible to virtue and vulnerable to attack, both moral and physical.

> Hie ða to ðam symle    sittan eodon,
> wlance to wingedrince,    ealle his weagesiðas
> bealde byrnwiggende.    Þær wæron bollan steape
> boren æfter bencum gelome,    swylce eac bunan ond orcas
> fulle fletsittendum.    Hie þæt fæge þegon.    (ll. 15–19)

['They went then and settled down to the banquet, arrogant men to the wine-drinking, all his companions in evil, bold mail-coated warriors. Deep bowls were frequently borne along the benches there, also brimming goblets and beakers as well to those seated in the hall. They drank them down as doomed men.]

Uncontrolled, Holofernes bawls and roars all day long: *hloh ond hlydde, hlynede ond dynede* (l.23), an embarrassingly over-generous host who, ironically, renders his comitatus 'dead-drunk':

> Swa se inwidda    ofer ealne dæg
> dryhtguman sine    drencte mid wine,
> swiðmod sinces brytta,    oðþæt hie on swiman lagon,
> oferdrencte his duguðe ealle,    swylce hie wæron deaðe
>                                                   geslegene,
> agotene goda gehwylces.    (ll.28–32)

[So all day long the villain, a strong-minded dispenser of treasure, drenched his retinue with wine until they lay stupefied, all his comitatus drunk as though they had been struck dead, drained of every virtue.]

Holofernes's treacherous nature (*inwidda*, l.28) is inadvertently directed at his own retinue, since it is his own hospitality that induces the moral and physical torpor which will prove his and their downfall, incapable as they are of any kind of alertness or vigour under stress. The Old English poem *The Fortunes of Men* makes clear the suicidal nature of drunkenness as distinct from decent party-going conviviality.[46] It was while they were 'sleeping it off' that the inhabitants of Heorot fell prey to Grendel's depredations (see above, p. 56). It is perhaps significant that, whereas the Apocrypha pictures the heroine eating and drinking with her enemy, flattering, cajoling, encouraging him in his drunkenness to a point where excitement at her presence leads him to a degree of excess unusual even for him (Judith 12. 20), in the Old English poem she is not present at the orgy, her absence making clearer the contrast between heroine and villain. The poet avoids the natural temptation to show Judith fulfilling the obvious ceremonial role in serving wine like a Beowulfian queen; and Holofernes's drunkenness is entirely attributable to his own immorality.

The epithets used make emphatically clear the opposition of good to evil. Holofernes is 'wicked' (*bealofull*, ll.48, 63, 100, etc.), 'a traitor, hated tyrant, a terrible creature' (*wærloga, lað leodhata, atol*, ll.71–75), even 'a kind of devil' (*deofulcund*, l.61), who when he dies will go straight to hell (ll.111–21) like the monster Grendel and the wicked spirits of *Genesis A*. Judith by contrast is: a 'blessed maiden' (*eadigan mægð*, l.35), 'wise lady' (*snoteran ides*, l.55), 'holy woman' (*halige meowle*, l.56), 'prudent wife' (*gleawhydig wif*, l.148), and of course a 'woman of God' (*Scyppendes mægð*, l.78, *Metodes meowle*, l.261). He is 'hateful to the Saviour', she 'the Saviour's handmaiden' (*Nergende lað . . . Nergendes þeowen*, ll.45, 73–74).

In the Apocrypha the drunken orgy takes place not in a Germanic mead-hall but in Holofernes's sleeping-quarters. The Old English poet, however, introduced a dramatic change of scene, as Judith is conducted from the guest-hall to bedchamber by an escort of marching soldiers –

honourably and ironically, for this is the only marching we are to see them do. The *locus* of the action is decidedly exotic. Holofernes's bed is surrounded by a fine gauze mosquito-net. More than merely a symbol of an unfamiliar oriental world, it serves to make clear the lack of faith between Holofernes and his retinue: a clear contrast to the characteristically open friendliness of the early heroic Germanic comitatus:

> Þær wæs eallgylden
> fleohnet fæger    ymbe þæs folctogan
> bed ahongen,    þæt se bealofulla
> mihte wlitan þurh,    wigena baldor,
> on æghwylcne    þe ðær inne com
> hæleða bearna,    ond on hyne nænig
> monna cynnes,    nymðe se modiga hwæne
> niðe rofra    him þe near hete
> rinca to rune gegangan.    (ll. 46–54)

[There was a beautiful all-gold mosquito-net hung around the commander's bed, so that the wicked man, the warriors' ruler, could look through at each of the children of men who came in there, but no mortal man at him, unless the proud man summoned one of his actively evil soldiers to go nearer to him for a confidential talk.]

But if Holofernes is depicted as an inaccessible despot rather than a friendly Germanic war-leader, there is no sign of any close heroic relationship among the Bethulians either.

The dramatic scene as villain and heroine come together is effectively reflected in the metre; gorged, hypermetrically expanded lines follow the fumbling drunken leader as he lurches towards his sleeping-quarters, finally to collapse on his bed in a stupor (ll. 54–68), after which the accompanying detachment of soldiers marches rapidly away in quick time and Judith nervously prepares for no less decisive action, in short, tight verse-lines (ll. 69ff.).[47]

There is no doubt as to the outcome. Earlier Old English poetry had notoriously lacked suspense – ironic anticipation of future disaster for example serving to underline present futilities – but this is quite blatant. True, there are great matters at stake; Judith has much to lose – but we know she cannot fail. There are none of the shocks, setbacks, or surprises of adventure, nor any attempt to provide any: no question that Holofernes might awake and summon help, or that Judith will be apprehended and not make good her escape. Like Guthlac, Judith is assured of victory since God is on her side. The first complete sentence of the poem makes it clear that the all-powerful God in whom she trusts will prove her the victor in the hour of need (ll. 2–5). At the bedside 'heaven's judge, shepherd of glory, lord of hosts' will not allow the heroine's defilement (ll.59–61); the villain is to lose his life that very night (ll.63–64); he has been brought to bed for the last time (ll.72–73).

All this might have led one to suppose some allegorical intent on the part of the poet; and indeed the story of Judith could certainly be viewed thus by the persistently symbol-seeking medieval mind. For example, in a commentary dedicated to the Frankish Empress Judith, Alcuin's Frankish pupil Hrabanus Maurus makes considerable play, albeit somewhat mechanically, with the possibilities, representing Judith as Ecclesia and Holofernes as the Antichrist.[48] But of all such material in Old English, this story seems to have proved least conducive to such interpretation. In the eyes of Aldhelm its significance is primarily exemplary rather than allegorical: a simple straightforward instance of chastity triumphant.[49] However, the Old English poet's emphasis is rather different, unable, or unwilling to avoid the intractably ironic implications of his material. A story of intrigue, deception, and feminine wiles, small wonder it came to be excluded from the canon, Jewish as well as Christian. The Apocrypha depicts a beautiful widow who presents herself to the enemy leader as a dissident, encouraging him in the expectation of victory, and promising to betray her country. Dressing in a deliberately alluring manner, she feigns compliance, carouses with him and then, in an unguarded moment, treacherously assassinates him before making good her escape. Such a story could scarcely be regarded as edifying, unless accepted on the grounds that the end justifies the means. Thus Jael who lures the Canaanite general, Sisera, into her tent, and lulls him to sleep before knocking a tent-peg through his skull, is regarded with approval, while Delilah who treats the Jewish hero Samson in much the same way, is not (Judges 4. 17–21; 16. 19). It is the fact that Judith is clearly presented as a figure of virtue that makes the ethical hiatus so disturbing. The redeployment of so realistic a pre-Christian story would, in Christian terms, place much of the action and characterization in an ironic if not deeply embarrassing light. The specific cause of embarrassment lies in Judith's employment of sexual allure to virtuous ends – the double bind of the female role throughout medieval times – both attractive and dreadful – the cause of both pleasure and pain: the 'Godiva syndrome'.

The early medieval Church was deeply distrustful of the figure of woman. The prime example of Eve – channel of all evil, itself specifically associated with sexual allure – gave them cause to suppose the feminine character fundamentally tainted. Women were unreliable, fickle, and – except for the kind of professional virgin Aldhelm celebrated – likely to get good men into trouble. Aldhelm and Ælfric alike emphasize Judith's chastity or 'loyal widowhood' rather than her beauty. The Old English poet, on the other hand, stresses her beauty and, although speaking of her as wise, prudent, holy even – nowhere mentions her chastity. It might well have been dealt with in the lost opening, of course, but it is curious that some diagnostic epithet should not have recurred given the characteristically formulaic manner of composition. The first description of Judith we are given is one who is *ides ælfscinu* [a woman with an elvish aura] (l.14). Although 'elfin' has come to denote a certain type of gamin attractiveness in modern times, the term had distinctively magical, and thereto dangerous, overtones during the medieval period. The primary sense of the *ælf* element has sinister connotations (cf. *ælfscot, ælfsiden, ælfadl* [fairy-induced disease or nightmare]). For the *Beowulf*-poet elves are evil sprites associated with the kindred of Cain (ll.111f). The only other instance of the term *ælfscinu* is where it is used to describe Sarah's bewitching – and fatal – allure for a foreign prince (*Genesis B*, ll.1827, 2731). Judith's 'brightness' (ll.58, 254, 340), not dissimilar from Eve's 'radiance' which is clearly associated with her provocative role of temptress (*Genesis B*, ll.626–27, 700–01, 821–22), is deliberately enhanced with alluring dress and curled hair. No wonder that Holofernes is totally ensnared – and yet by means that the Christian community might ordinarily think to shun. This ambivalence is expressed in words attributed to Augustine, which speak of Judith as 'going to battle with chaste beauty rather than with iron, the weapons of jewels, always hostile to modesty, having learned to strike the enemy'.[50]

Worse still, she lies. All the woman's actions – and presumably her words on first entering the Assyrian camp – are deliberately deceptive. Playing a double game, ironically it is she, rather than Holofernes who is the 'perjurer' (l.71). Indeed, for Holofernes's bad character we have only hearsay. In the Apocrypha version he is even depicted as a man of some virtue: temperate of habit (until meeting Judith), devoted to his lord, and generous: prepared to take Judith at her word and to treat her well. Even in the Old English poem he is despicable only by reason of being 'the enemy'. Although his character is blackened by a series of epithets of villainy, Holofernes never becomes so villainous as to be incredible – unlike, for example, Juliana's persecutor Eleusias.[51] We do not witness him cruel or treacherous, but simply as a glutton. He is certainly lustful – and naturally enough, given that this is just what Judith had set out to provoke. But his desires are neither extreme nor perverted. In the event, his manner of death when it comes is all the more shocking.

In the Vulgate original, Judith has her maidservant stand watch outside while the deed is done. In the Old English poem she is not overtly present. As with Guthlac's conflict, no minor character is allowed to dissipate the direct opposition between the protagonists of good and evil. But despite the carefully prepared contrast of virtue and villainy, when the deed is finally done it is not achieved with heroic despatch but with cold-blooded deliberation. Drawing Holofernes's own sword from its sheath,[52] Judith invokes the vengeance of God (anachronistically calling on both Son and Trinity). Then, much in the manner of a housewife preparing meat in the kitchen, she arranges the head to her own convenience with both hands – presumably putting the sword down in the meantime:

> Genam ða þone hæðenan mannan
> fæste be feaxe sinum,   teah hyne folmum wið hyre weard
> bysmerlice,   ond þone bealofullan
> listum alede,   laðne mannan,
> swa heo ðæs unlædan   eaðost mihte
> wel gewealdan.   (ll. 98–103)

[She then took the heathen man fast by his hair, shamefully dragged him towards her with her hands and skilfully laid out the wicked one, hateful man, so as she could most easily deal with the wretch efficiently.]

The expression *bysmerlice* [shamefully] (l. 100) cuts both ways; if Holofernes is shamed by being taken thus, a degree of shame is also attached to the action. To take a slumbering enemy by the hair in this way is scarcely a heroic gesture; it recalls the act of another equally alluring, equally deceitful, woman: Delilah, who betrayed the slumbering Samson to death thus (Judges 16. 19). The hair is a persistent image of vulnerability, moral as well as physical.[53]

The killing is a long-drawn-out business. Despite Judith's careful preparations, she fails to despatch him at the first blow, only succeeding at the second attempt:

> Sloh ða wundenlocc
> þone feondsceaðan   fagum mece
> heteþoncolne,   þæt heo healfne forcearf
> þone sweoran him,   þæt he on swiman læg,
> druncen ond dolhwund.   Næs ða dead þa gyt,
> ealles orsawle;   sloh ða eornoste
> ides ellenrof   oþre siðe
> þone hæðenan hund,   þæt him þæt heaford wand
> forð on ða flore.   (ll. 103–11)

[Then the curly-haired woman struck the evil-minded foe with the gleaming blade so that she cut half through his neck, so that he lay stupefied, drunk, and sorely wounded. He still was not dead then; in earnest the courageous woman then struck the heathen dog a second time, so that his head rolled on to the floor.]

There follows a rather bizarre sequel in which the heroine takes the severed head as a trophy and stuffs it unceremoniously, and certainly unheroically, into a shopping-bag. Of course it could scarcely be borne heroically aloft on a spear-point or sword if Judith is to pass through the camp undetected and make good her escape. Despite the occasional martial phrase (she has 'fought a battle', ll.122–23, etc.) it is made quite clear that this is the warfare of a woman – though no less terrible in its fashion, as the *Beowulf*-poet pointed out of Grendel's mother, whose Scandinavian antecedents also slew warriors by night in their sleep, stuffing the pieces into their handbags (ll.1251f.).

The fact that the active protagonist is a woman is underlined by the fact that none of the traditional martial epithets strictly apply (indeed they can be used of Holofernes with greater credibility) and much of the language is frankly prosaic, enduing the events with even greater realism. Judith achieves her end in a specifically female, if decidedly unfeminine, manner, the sordid quality of her actions disturbingly juxtaposed with the attributes of beauty. For a woman to engage in violence of this nature, even if only indirectly, would not meet with Anglo-Saxon approval.[54] It is clear that Judith stands apart both from a martial heroine like Elene, whose actions – as an empress at the head of an army – are in every respect indistinguishable from those of a man, or from a passively suffering virgin martyr like Juliana.[55] Ultimately it is not the act itself which causes disquiet (a not dissimilar feat would be recorded of the patriot Hereward[56]), but the fact that it is undertaken by a woman. Of course a man might not so easily gain such intimate access to Holofernes's person. But Judith's chastity is never seriously threatened, since Holofernes is drunk and incapable; and in the event it appears that she can leave at will. On the contrary, Judith seems to represent a militant feminism, utilizing specifically female attributes to overcome her foe. It is not her chastity but her patriotism that triumphs. Unlike Guthlac or Juliana, Judith achieves her victory not through persuasion or moral superiority, but bodily violence, bloodily executed. But this is not the eyeball-to-eyeball confrontation of the traditional heroic duel; there can be exchange neither of blows nor of words, since Judith's opponent is asleep throughout the encounter. When Holofernes's armour is eventually presented to the heroine, the poet stresses its financial value rather than its heroic significance as the symbol of a defeated foe (ll.334–41).

There were, of course, certain notable strong women leaders in the early medieval world – like Alfred's daughter Æthelflaed, the widowed Lady of the Mercians who won back control of Danish Mercia – a sufficiently apt parallel for some critics to have supposed that Judith may have been composed in her praise.[57] But as Ambrose comments of Judith, 'it is scarcely natural that a single woman should overcome a mighty army which had instilled terror into warriors'.[58] Judith's actions not only usurp the traditional male prerogative of leadership, but serve to cast a poor light on the whole pride of the Bethulian army. At the moment of her manly act Judith's feminine appearance is emphasized: a girl with curly (or braided) hair, *mægð wundenlocc* (ll. 77–78, 103); and it is perhaps significant that the same feminine attribute should occur to the poet subsequently when describing the Bethulian menfolk – perhaps stimulated by the use of the word *mægð*, ambiguously 'girl' and 'nation', as a *mægða mærost . . . wlanc wundenlocc* [most famous of people, . . . proud in curly hair] (ll. 324–25), the alliterative collocation suggesting that their pride lay not in weapons or vigour, but in their beautiful hair. Elsewhere the term *wundenlocc* occurs only in the context of an obscene riddle.[59] The Bethulian war-leader Ozias, who might have been slighted by a woman enacting a part and achieving a deed that might more naturally have been his, is simply not mentioned; his role is subsumed in the throngs of rejoicing citizens, graphically depicted assembling to greet Judith at her return (ll. 161–70) – and perhaps recalling an opening scene of farewell as she set out from the city. Judith now assumes a further manly role of war-leader, in exhorting her fellow citizens to do battle with the Assyrians. The dramatic revelation of Holofernes's head by Judith's maid is the hinge both of Judith's speech and the poem (ll. 171–75). It represents graphic proof of Judith's achievement and assurance of Jewish success. It is the knowledge that the enemy army is now leaderless that stirs the Bethulians to assert their manhood. She addresses the starving and demoralized troops as 'victorious heroes', *sigerofe hæleð* (l. 177) – if not ironically, then in anticipation of the victory to come; it is, after all, a victory of which they can be assured since God has already sentenced their enemies to death (ll. 195–98). Their nerve having been stiffened thus, the Bethulians mount a dawn attack on the Assyrian encampment. A dreadful anticipatory sequence draws on the traditional heroic *topos* of the beasts-of-battle, familiar from, for example, *Finnsburh*, ll. 34–35, *Beowulf*, ll. 3024f, *Genesis A*, ll. 1983f, *Exodus*, ll. 162f, and elsewhere, but handled with fine individuality:

> Dynedan scildas,
> hlude hlummon.   þæs se hlanca gefeah
> wulf in walde,   ond se wanna hrefn,
> wælgifre fugel;   wistan begen
> þæt him ða þeodguman   þohton tilian
> fylle on fægum.   Ac him fleah on last
> earn ætes georn;   urigfeðera,
> salowigpada,   sang hildeleoð
> hyrnednebba.   Stopon heaðorincas. . . .   (ll. 204–12)

[Shields rang, loudly resonated. At that the lean wolf in the wood rejoiced, and the black raven, a bird greedy for corpses; both knew that the men of that nation intended to provide them their fill from those doomed to die.

And in their track flew the eagle, eager to eat; wet-feathered, dark-coated,
hook-beaked, it sang a war-song. The warriors marched on. . . .]

The Assyrians are put to flight. It is rather surprising to find the
Bethulian army instantly transformed from the powerless, ragged troop
on the verge of surrender we have been led to expect, to a bold army of
warlike men who crush their opposition with brutal efficiency:
swyrdgeswing swiðlic [violent sword-blows] (l.240). This development –
not part of the original – is significant. The Assyrians are now in fact
routed before learning of their leader's death. Ironically, Judith's
achievement was technically unnecessary. It served merely to put heart
into despondent men. The poet transforms the very direction and thrust
of the Vulgate narrative to portray a new, realistic, and certainly unheroic, view of battle. It is unheroic – if realistic – to know that one's
enemy is at so considerable a disadvantage before having the nerve to
attack him. We are presented with aspects of battle unacknowledged, and
unexplored, in earlier war-literature.

In depicting the plight of the Assyrians the poet shows himself well
aware of the actualities of warfare: the cowardice and brutal death of
those who, having thrown down their weapons, are nevertheless
mercilessly slaughtered while running away. (The Egyptian host of Exodus, hostile and malignant, were at least determinedly on the attack
when so ruinously overcome by the waves, see above, p. 90.) The
battle-beasts' anticipation is dreadfully fulfilled in a brief but effective
reprise: hacked about by swords, the dead and dying are 'a treat for
wolves and a joy to carrion-greedy fowls' (ll.295–96). Ironically, those
who survive flee not from the swords but the shields of the Bethulians – a
striking notion that what the enemy fear is strong defence rather than
offense (ll.296–97).

The horror of battle has its cruelly comic aspects, however, as eye-
witness anecdotes of warfare in any age readily confirm. The conventional response to the surprise attack at dawn is to regroup defensively
(cf. Finnsburh, above pp. 47–48); but the Assyrians' reaction to the
'morning-terror' (l.245) is not to counter-attack, but to run to the skirts of
their leader's tent. There they stand in a set-piece tableau of
embarrassment waiting in vain for their leader to emerge. Their
hesitation to interrupt Holofernes in what they ironically suppose to be
his pleasure with the lovely Judith is treated almost farcically.[60] None
dares waken the despot to enquire how he has enjoyed the night. They
could not know that in the event the only thing Holofernes has had off is
his head! The veil, which was previously employed as a symbol both of
sumptuous luxury and of oriental suspicion, is now made the instrument
of their humiliation. As the sound of the approaching enemy grows
nearer, they try an apologetic communal coughing; and that failing, fall
to nervously whimpering:

> Beornas stodon
> ymbe hyra þeodnes træf   þearle gebylde,
> sweorcendferhðe.   Hi ða somod ealle
> ongunnon cohhetan,   cirman hlude
> ond gristbitian,   gode orfeorme,
> mid toðon torn þoligende.   (ll. 267–72)

[The men stood around their prince's tent, extremely agitated, growing gloomy in spirit. Then all together they began to cough and loudly make noises and, having no success, to grind their teeth, suffering agonies.]

The same sort of words are used of the devils in *Guthlac B* (l. 903) and of the drowning Egyptians in *Exodus* (l. 462). Unaccustomed to act independently, the Assyrians look for leadership, but in vain. Lacking direction, their rout is inevitable.

Bravery is now defined not by opposing an enemy attack but by summoning sufficient courage to trespass on their leader's privacy (ll. 257–58, 275–77). When one of them finally has the temerity to enter the tent and makes the inevitable discovery, he exhibits all the characteristics of battle-exhaustion; his nerve finally cracks and he falls to the ground out of control, shivering, tearing at his hair and clothing, prophesying total disaster now that 'our keeper lies beheaded' (ll. 275–89). It is doubly ironic that the Assyrian officers, now headless, should have been called 'head-protectors' (*heafod-weardas*, l. 239). Instead of crying out for vengeance at such an outrage, (compare the heroism displayed following the bedchamber death of Cynewulf at Merton, see above, p. 6), the panic-stricken army throws away its weapons and flees ignominiously (contrast the dignified composure with which Beowulf's people received the news of their leader's death, and with it the anticipation of their own destruction, see above, pp. 60–61). Nevertheless, the picture the poet presents is an honest appraisal, engaging factors which, despite his efforts, are not entirely one-sided. His heroine cannot be understood as a totally flawless example of virtue, while the enemy provokes, if not our sympathy, at least a degree of understanding.

The moral issues presented by the author of *The Battle of Maldon* are no less ambiguous – provoking what is perhaps one of the most remarkable pieces of war-literature in the English language. It emerges directly from the conditions that prompted Ælfric to identify the story of Judith as a model precedent: the invasion by a hostile, savage, and incidentally heathen, enemy. In the second half of the tenth century the tide had turned in favour of a fresh wave of Viking invasions – not now the Danes who had seized half of Alfred's kingdom a century earlier, but this time Norsemen who had already colonized parts of Ireland and the western coast of Scotland. In the year 991 a relatively small force under the leadership of Justin and Guthmund Stegitanson sailed up the coast to sack Ipswich. The *Anglo-Saxon Chronicle* states simply: 'In this year Ipswich was ravaged and Byrhtnoth slain at Maldon', nothing more.[61] We know that this was not a particularly significant encounter compared with battles that had taken place in previous years, or were to take place three years later when a much more serious campaign began led by the great Norwegian king, Olaf Tryggvason. The only reason the battle at Maldon seems to have been mentioned in the *Chronicle* at all appears to have been the fact that Ealdorman Byrhtnoth, an important provincial leader, had been killed there. The figure of Byrhtnoth is well attested from historical sources. Ealdorman of Essex himself, he was related by marriage to several of the Anglo-Saxon royal houses. His sister Æthelflæd, for instance, married Æthelstan, 'half-king' of East Anglia. His signature occurs as a ceremonial witness to a number of royal charters between 956 and the year before his death in 991. He was one of the largest landowners in the country, and a generous patron of Ely Minster, where his mutilated body was carried for burial after the battle. His widow presented to Ely a tapestry picture (presumably something like the Bayeux Tapestry), depicting a historical account of the deeds of her late husband.[62]

On 10 or 11 August, then, in the year 991, a group of Vikings sailed up the Blackwater estuary in Essex towards the town of Maldon. They hesitated to attack the town which had recently been fortified, but, following a favoured strategy, encamped instead on an island in the estuary: the island of Northey which was approachable at low tide across a hard causeway which straddles the mudflats. It was across this creek that Ealdorman Byrhtnoth with his East Saxon levies faced the Vikings on 11 August 991. He rejected an offer from the Vikings that they should be bought off with money, and foolishly relinquishing his tactically advantageous position, gave ground so as to get to grips with the enemy – and died as a result. He certainly had them in an awkward position, since it was possible that he might have starved them into submission. All we know is, that he did not. He chose instead to die a courageous death, hacked to pieces, his head carried away as a trophy.

Of course we cannot know the immediate purpose for which the poem was composed. Perhaps, like the tapestry, it was commissioned by Byrhtnoth's widow, to place the record of her husband's last acts in a congenial commemorative context. And yet it admits altogether too many realistic implications to suggest that it was merely intended to eulogize the dead ealdorman. The poet certainly knew many of the details of the battle – some of the incidents and names involved; perhaps he was himself an eye-witness of the events he describes. But poetry with a historical setting is not of necessity history. It seems clear that although the poet is using a basis of historical fact to build his picture, simple historical record is not his primary intention. At first sight we might assume *The Battle of Maldon* to be a chronicle-poem of the kind represented by *The Battle of Brunanburh* in the *Anglo-Saxon Chronicle* under the year 937, or *The Capture of the Five Boroughs*, under 942,[63] quite happily looking for an actual time and place to which the details presented by the poet might be tied down. The fact that the site of the battle can be postulated with some precision,[64] tempts a historical rather than literary response, supposing that the poem was simply a realistic description of the historic incident.[65] But *Maldon* cannot be considered a historical poem in the sense that the poems in the *Anglo-Saxon Chronicle* are historical poems, concerned to record significant events with veracity and a relevant understanding of the larger issues involved. For example, the poet of *The Battle of Brunanburh* makes something very different out of his material. He has chosen a significant incident, worth recording for its own sake, and has placed it in historical perspective. He claims for himself the chronicler's veracity. It is ironic in view of his primarily historical concerns that he is in fact more successful than the *Maldon*-poet in transmitting the traditional poetic style. He is not interested in recording fine speeches or heroic sentiments; there is a minimum of actual battle rapportage, but he supplies the facts in a clear and economical way quite foreign to the temper of *The Battle of Maldon*. In many respects *Maldon* has more in common with *Beowulf* or *Finnsburh* than with the avowedly historical poems such as *Brunanburh* or *The Taking of the Five Boroughs*. The *Maldon*-poem deals with a relatively unimportant skirmish on the Essex coast, the defeat and unnecessary slaughter of a group of local levies, otherwise remembered only because of the death there of Ealdorman Byrhtnoth. There is no sense of historical perspective. While possibly mentioned in the missing opening lines, any names of opposing leaders are certainly omitted from the body of the poem, and the enemy throughout is delineated only in terms of non-particularized disparagement.

Instead a great deal of space is given to stating the apparent motives of those who take part in the action of the poem. We are not intended to concentrate on the action of the battle, nor on its consequences, but on the exact nature of what it is that leads the English party to act in the way it does. It is possible of course that the poem was written as a deliberately nostalgic exercise intended to embarrass the weakness and corruption of Æthelred's court. But if this was the case, then it is curious that the poet should not have chosen a current victory to elaborate the theme of virtue rewarded on the Judith model favoured by Ælfric. It is true that the principle of heroic fortitude is best illustrated in the context of defeat, but an honest consideration of events at Maldon could hardly have been calculated to raise English morale. Perhaps the choice was merely a gesture to antiquarian sentiment, portraying a faded picture of heroic idealism, of which, after all, defeat is more revealing than victory. The poet clearly identifies the motives of the action in the antique terms of Tacitus's Germanic warrior-society of some nine centuries earlier: the conspicuous position of the leader in the van of battle (ll. 100–01, 130–31), the function of the retainer's vow or martial affirmation (*beot, gylp*, ll. 15, 213, 274, 290), the importance of kinship in military organization, and the curiously intimate association between uncle and nephew (*swustersunu*, l. 115).[66] But the Anglo-Saxon period was socially no more static than any other. However conservative military society, it is impossible that such an ethos should have survived intact until almost the end of the millennium. We know only too well how inevitably and irretrievably the 'heroic age' had passed. Yet at Byrhtnoth's death Ælfwine speaks like one of Beowulf's comitatus:

'Gemunaþ þa mæla   þe we oft æt meodo spræcon,
þonne we on bence   beot ahofon,
hæleð on healle,   ymbe heard gewinn.'   (ll. 212–14)

['Remember those occasions when we often spoke over the mead, when along the benches, heroes in hall, we would make vows about tough fighting.']

He recalls his lineage, finds the death of both kinsman and lord 'the greatest of sorrows' and 'is mindful of vengeance' (ll. 223–25). Each warrior exhorts the others just as if they had been members of a Migration Age comitatus. But Byrhtnoth was not at the head of a seventh-century comitatus. The East Saxon levies that were called to the defence of Maldon were very different in kind from the pagan war-bands that had settled Essex five or six centuries earlier, the 'greater *fyrd*' now being made up of local peasants fighting with such weapons as were to hand, under the leadership of the landowners on whose estates they worked.

Although the poet approaches his subject with all the appropriate heroic mannerisms culled from traditional battle writings of the past, it is a subject that close examination shows will not support them, and the consequent effect is one of poetic ironies. Elements of prosaic realism unconditioned by the heroic reflex are allowed to creep in to affect the overall structure as well as the detail of the poem.

The opening lines are obviously to be considered significant. The English forces have to be firmly encouraged to stand their ground, the *folc* verbally ('don't be afraid' l. 21) and the nobility by preventative action (ll. 2–3). One lad approaches the battle with hawk on hand, possibly a sophisticate's gesture of defiance, but more probably indicative of an unheroic frivolity. The implication of *ærest* (l. 5) is to suggest that this was the first time he realized that Byrhtnoth 'was not prepared to put up with cowardice' (l.6).

The actual conflict is not anticipated as an unambiguously heroic encounter, a battle between equally worthy opponents engaged in the love of the sport. The Viking approach is qualified. Their spokesman introduces the mercenary note of Danegeld with a cool, persuasive rationality that seems curiously out of place:

'Ne þurfe we us spillan,    gif ge spedaþ to þam;
we willað wið þam golde    grið fæstnian.
Gyf þu þæt gerædest    þe her ricost eart,
þæt þu þine leoda    lysan wille,
syllan sæmannum    on hyra sylfra dom
feoh wið freode,    and niman frið æt us,
we willaþ mid þam sceattum    us to scype gangan,
on flot feran,    and eow friþes healdan.'    (ll.34–41)

['There's no need for us to destroy each other, if you are fortunate enough; we are willing to arrange a truce in exchange for gold. If you, who are most influential here, decide on this, that you are willing to ransom your people, grant the seamen payment of what they decide in exchange for goodwill, and accept peace from us, we will take ship with the money, set sail and keep the peace with you.']

In return, the aristocratic Byrhtnoth brandishes his spear like a Beowulfian hero and responds with sarcasm, offering them spears and swords in place of tribute: þa heregeatu þe eow æt hilde ne deah (l.48). The employment of the term heriot (the service due from a vassal to a feudal lord expressed in terms of the equipment he had given and was therefore owed) must have seemed heavily ironic when it was not only runaway slaves among the Englishmen who fought in Viking armies; particularly so since in the same year as the battle (and presumably therefore before the poem's composition) the Vikings were in fact bought off by Æthelred with an enormous sum, as a matter of national policy.[67] In the meantime, however:

'her stynt unforcuð    eorl mid his werode,
þe wile gealgean    eþel þysne,
Æþelredes eard,    ealdres mines
folc and foldan.    Feallan sceolon
hæþene æt hilde.    To heanlic me þinceð
þæt ge mid urum sceattum    to scype gangon
unbefohtene,    nu ge þus feor hider
on urne eard    in becomon.
Ne sceole ge swa softe    sinc gegangan;
us sceal ord and ecg    ær geseman,
grim guðplega,    ær we gofol syllon.'    (ll.51–61)

['here stands an earl of no ill repute with his troop of men who is willing to defend this homeland, Æthelred's native land, the nation and country of my lord. The heathen shall fall in battle. To me it seems too despicable that you should take ship with our money unopposed, now that you have intruded this far here into our native land. You won't get treasure so easily; first of all, point and edge shall arbitrate between us, fierce battle-play, before we pay tribute.']

Byrhtnoth's death-or-glory defiance ends on a sadly prophetic note, for it is impossible that the audience should not have known the outcome of the event. The posturing then is all on the English side which, having nothing to support it from the Vikings, falls curiously flat.

This verbal irony is reinforced actively by the fact that following these high words of defiance prompt engagement is impossible: 'Because of the water, neither side could get at the other' (l.64). Heroism is frustrated; the 'flower of the East-Saxons' and the 'ship-host' confront each other in all their pompous array (*mid prasse*, l.68) but are temporarily impotent; they are impatient to join battle, but 'Not one of them could injure another unless it be through the flight of an arrow' (ll.70–71).

It is quite plain that Wulfstan, Ælfere, and Maccus can successfully hold the sole 'bridge' between the two armies (ll.74–85), but for some reason Byrhtnoth allows the Vikings to cross unharmed. The poet bluntly ascribes this to his *ofermod* (l.89), less recklessness than simple pride.[68] The poet comments sadly that the English leader has given 'too much land' (*lands to fela*, l.90). If Byrhtnoth chooses to make a sporting fight on level terms, he does so at the expense of other men's lives.[69]

As a direct consequence of his action, bitter slaughter was made. 'Bows', it is said simply, and ominously, 'were busy' (l.110). Bows are realistic but not, one might suspect, conventionally heroic weapons; in the world of Beowulf the bow was used for hunting not fighting.[70] The missile, whether the longbow at Agincourt or the sniper's rifle at Spion Kop, is a democratizing weapon; death rains anonymously out of the sky; you don't necessarily know or even see your attacker – or your victim. Thus 'young men fell', among the first to die being Byrhtnoth's own nephew (ll.113–15). Then the first actively offensive engagement of the leader is described as 'earl approached churl' (l.132). The significance of this action is pointed by internal rhyme within the half-line, emphasizing the brutal realism of actual warfare, where aristocrat no longer faced aristocrat, but the low-born; and within the context of the battle they meet on equal terms (l.133). Whether or not we assume two meanings for the word *ceorl* [churl] in the poem – disparaging when applied to the Viking, yet commendable when later applied to the courageous Dunnere (l.256) – one use inevitably counterpoints the other. It is used first of the Viking who engages Byrhtnoth, and might well be considered at this stage demeritorious. But when the word is later used of the doughty peasant Dunnere, brandishing his spear as he speaks just like his master (l.255), we must recognize that both are *ceorlisc* and that both play the same role – one worthy of some recognition. In this manner a disruptive statement is made without the need to delineate the individual enemy and thus shift attention from the main burden of the poem. In a poem of the earlier heroic era it would have been inconceivable for the peasant mass that made up the body of the armies to have protruded in this way beyond the aristocratic forefront of daring deeds. Here it is recognized that the courageous actions of battle are not the privilege of nobility alone, and an admission that, on the contrary, the nobility themselves, like the sons of Odda, might be prone to inglorious deeds on occasion.

Unlike Waldere or Hengest, Byrhtnoth does not face a notable enemy known by name, defied, and apostrophied. Although slain in turn, it is the Viking 'churl' who first wounds Byrhtnoth, not face to face sword in hand, but discharging a distant yet no less deadly javelin with a cunning blow. When Byrhtnoth is immediately afterwards laid low by a second missile, the young Wulfmær wrenches the bloody dart from his master's wound in order to avenge him – a truly grand, almost melodramatically heroic action, but at the same time a rather irresponsible one so far as his lord's safety was concerned.

At the point of death Byrhtnoth is depicted uttering a formal prayer thanking God for all the joys he has had in the world, and begging that his soul might pass in peace into the keeping of the Lord of angels unassailed by demons (ll.173–80). This is not inappropriate from a man known to be a faithful and God-fearing son of the Church,[71] and since he was slain by heathens in an arguably heathen cause he possibly assumes something of the character of a martyr, although it is clearly important to distinguish between a Christian saint like Guthlac, and a hero who is a Christian like Byrhtnoth.[72] Unlike Guthlac's opponents, Byrhtnoth's enemies may be heathens but they are not devils. Since the end of the ninth century the *Anglo-Saxon Chronicle* occasionally spoke of the English simply as 'the Christians' in contrast to the heathen Vikings;[73] but even the commonplace notion that the fury of the Viking attack was unleashed as a direct result of the people's sins as the millennium approached,[74] did not provoke direct identification of the invader as Antichrist.[75] The confrontation at Maldon is patriotic rather than religious; within the poem at least, Byrhtnoth is first Æthelred's thegn (ll.53, 151, 203) and only secondarily a Christian. His attitude is very different from that of, for example, the Christ-like, royal, saint Edmund who cast down his weapons in order to suffer passive martyrdom at the hands of the Danes in 869.[76] Byrhtnoth goes down fighting. His story is no less secular than Judith's; it is simply given religious tone by prayer at a critical moment. It is interesting that Byrhtnoth prays for himself rather than for his men or his cause. Unlike, say, Hnæf, the heroic commander at Finnsburh (see above, p. 49), he does not ask after the progress of his men, nor even say a word to those loyal retainers who fall at his side. Thereafter follows the description of Byrhtnoth's terrible fate; his body plundered of its valuables and mutilated as it lies.

At this point the poet states baldly, 'those who were not minded to be there retired from the battle' (l.185). The sons of Odda are first to flee; one of them, Godric, ironically stealing the horse of his master 'who had given him many a horse before' (l.188). Many others, quite believing that it was Byrhtnoth himself in flight, also took to their heels. And it is repeated that many men fled, a large part of the army (ll.195, 243). Now while it is natural for an eye-witness like Offa to scorn this easy retreat (ll.237f), it would be naïve for the larger audience to dismiss this simply as cowardice within the narrative structure. Their action, not simply that of anonymous weaklings but of individual nobles defined by name, serves both to underline the stark realities of battle, and also to question implicitly the code which motivates the actions of the heroic protagonists.

The ignominious flight of so many comes as no surprise to Offa, who long before the battle had warned Byrhtnoth that the hall-boasts he had heard were insincere:

> þæt þær modelice    manega spræcon
> þe eft æt þærfe    þolian noldon.    (ll.200–1)

[that many there who spoke bodly would later be unwilling to suffer when need arose.]

Neither had Byrhtnoth himself expected unalloyed heroism at Maldon. At the very beginning of the poem he had commanded the mounted nobility to drive away their horses – a well-known device to prevent flight in the face of the enemy. This action shows him well aware of how at least part of his army might react. It was this that first convinced the young man that Byrhtnoth was not minded to suffer cowardice. Cowards may well exist, but the heroic convention would not have admitted as much before the event. At any rate, the poet has let slip a hint that he was really very well aware of the actual nature of late-tenth-century society. It is, however, the possibility of cowardice that validates the courage of those who remain, even if theirs is no longer an individual heroic defiance – the indomitable integrity of the old heroes (see above, pp. 65–66) – but a stand made out of love for and obedience to a feudal overlord.

The early death of Byrhtnoth and the implicit questioning of the action marks the turning-point of the poem. The first half of the poem points the ironically unnecessary waste of the second half, which is concerned less with actions than with speechifying – the pompous words which lead so regularly and promptly to death, the horrifying rapidity of which is only emphasized by the monotonous repetition of personal names towards the end. The inevitability of their warrior deaths had been anticipated throughout, being capable of brave acts only 'for as long as', *þa hwile*, they might hold their weapons (ll.14–15, 83, 235–36, 272), and 'until', *oðþæt*, they fall (ll.278–79, 300, 324). Only two persons speak of the glory of war – the poet (*tir*, l.104) and the dead leader (*dom*, l.129). Those who die, however, centre each of their speeches on the same theme, recurring to the simple antique notion of loyalty to the lord who has left them in this situation. They see no alternative to the slaughter that has already been twice questioned in the poem, once verbally by the Viking spokesman, and once actively by members of their own party.

Closely associated with, and emphatic of, the prosaic details of the action is the overall style of the piece. In fact a detailed examination of the words and phraseology available to the poet shows material very different in kind from that which went to make up classic heroic verse. The brief urgency of the style of *Maldon* is in marked contrast to the 'grand style' of earlier war poetry like *Beowulf* or *Finnsburh*.[77] The poet seems deliberately to have rejected the prolix style, avoiding ornament and elegant variation in favour of an austere economy of language, preferring simple words rather than compounds, and employing frequent pronouns, prepositions, conjunctions, and articles. Like *Guthlac* and *Judith*, *The Battle of Maldon* admits prosaic vocabulary relatively freely, in conformity with its 'realistic' approach.[78] While poetic compounds like *æscholt* or *wælspere* do occur occasionally, they are swamped by a mass of simple forms, some of them borrowed from the Vikings themselves.[79] Traditional delight in the verbal elaboration of arms and armour is replaced by a view of them simply as so much plunder. There appear to be no verbal archaisms or consciously 'poetic' words, while the kennings which had formerly produced brilliantly imaginative compounds had now for the most part faded into prose usage as simply unrecognized metaphors. Terms like *wælstow* [killing-ground], or *æschere* [spear-host], form part of the common register of the Chronicler, for instance. Similarly, the old names for chieftains and princes are replaced by phrases like 'Byrhthelm's child' or 'Offa's kinsman', indicating a simple relationship or patronymic, against which the traditional compound used just once of Byrhtnoth: *beahgifa*, [ring-giver] (l.290), sounds oddly irrelevant. There are none of the involved parallelisms, parenthetic remarks, or poetic allusions which lent the older battle descriptions the dignity of formal utterance, and against this prosaic matrix the over-lengthy, balanced rhetoric of the warrior-speeches of the second half sound pompous rather than realistic.

Heroic material in the absence of heroic style inevitably falls flat. *The Battle of Maldon* strikes all the old attitudes without the traditional vocabulary which made the earlier heroic verse emotionally valid. It has all the appearance of a subject executed in the wrong materials: a poem composed in a heroic vein in an age that was no longer heroic. Whether or not we ascribe ambivalent social attitudes to the poet himself, his poem itself expresses a disturbing ambivalence. But the equivocation of the poet's view does not preclude the noble and courageous sentiment. His subject is war, and the pity of war.

English sentiment characteristically dwells on the glories of defeat – Balaclava, Gallipoli, Dunkirk – and presents mere reticence in the face of victory, generally embarrassed by any emphasis on the defeated foe. The war memorials of the cities and villages of England celebrate not victory but the remembered dead. The poet's three dozen named individuals – and possibly very many more in the missing ending – are drawn from all social ranks, aristocrat and peasant alike, young and old. Those who fall represent a cross-section of English society. The poem is unlike any other in including so many named individuals – a mounting roll-call towards the end, tolling in almost strophic sacrifice. It comes to form a celebration of the dead, who did not question why they died. Despite the socially anachronistic implications, despite our residual anger at the folly and arrogance displayed, the sentiments expressed often remain deeply moving, allowing us to recognize and respond to acts of individual courage, irrespective of concomitant circumstances, which we may simultaneously deprecate and admire. At the end of all, there come ringing down the centuries what are perhaps the most frequently quoted words of all Old English literature – the old retainer Byrhtwold's defiant definition of man's indomitable will:

> 'Hige sceal þe heardra,    heorte þe cenre,
> mod sceal þe mare,    þe ure mægen lytlað.'    (ll. 312–13)

> ['Thought shall be the sterner, heart the keener, courage shall be the greater, as our strength lessens.']

All too soon Byrhtwold's England was drained of both wealth and the capacity to resist. Within a year or two of the battle Byrhtnoth's disastrous patron, Æthelred, whose kingdom he died to defend, was in disgrace and exile, and the contemptible Viking accepted as lawful overlord. Archbishop Wulfstan, who framed the laws for Æthelred, would do so no less enthusiastically for Æthelred's Scandinavian successors to the throne, affirming the feudal rights of a now Christian Viking sovereign.[80] Within a few decades the hazard of 1066 resulted in suzerainty passing to yet another alien invader – the Norman – no less enthusiastic patrons of religion; and all, it would be argued, in consequence of the sins and degeneration of the people. But whether or not interpreted as the scourge of God, the merest acquaintance with the history of the nation would recognize it as merely part of a lengthy cyclic pattern.[81] Native authors with national concerns who now found themselves unable to execrate the foreign invader, or to speak of contemporary events, in an acceptably public form, might turn with greater safety and circumspection to the glories of the nation's remoter past.

The first and perhaps most impressive vernacular *essai* of this kind was Laȝamon's *Brut* – a large-scale, ambitious survey of national history – significantly in the language of a subject race. Laȝamon's theme is stated clearly in the opening lines:

> Hit com him on mode, ond on his mern þonke,
> þet he wold on Engle þa æðelæn tellen,
> wat heo ihoten weoren ond wonene heo comen
> þa Englene londe ærest ahten.    (ll.6–9)

[It came into his mind, and into his fine imagination, that he would tell of the noble origins of the English – what they were called and whence they came who first possessed England.]

Choosing a larger and more heterogeneous canvas than the single incidents dealt with in *Judith* or *Maldon* and a more complex theme than that which engaged the author of *Guthlac A*, he set out to construct a genuinely national epic: the most sweeping and detailed history of the island that had ever been attempted in the English language, plotting the rise and fall of the British people from their arrival under their eponymous founder Brutus to their final dispersal in the face of the Saxon colonization. The shape of his work was determined largely by the Anglo-Norman *Romanz de Brut* which the Jerseyman Robert Wace dedicated to Eleanor of Aquitaine and which was in turn adapted from the immensely successful *Historia Regum Britanniae* by Geoffrey of Monmouth.[82] Laȝamon's *Brut* represents a substantial literary achievement, although somewhat difficult of access, partly because of its size (at some sixteen thousand lines five times the length of *Beowulf*, embracing an enormous sweep of history, and involving an exceptionally comprehensive cast-list), and partly because the verse chronicle is an unfamiliar and uncertain literary category, although it has much in common with modern historical romance in which the dividing line between historical fact and historical fiction is unreal and unimportant.

Laȝamon's epic falls into three, unequal parts. The first nine thousand lines or so begin with the legendary foundation of the nation by the descendants of Aeneas who fled from the fall of Troy eventually to discover a giant-infested Albion, and continues through the various vicissitudes of Roman times until the disastrous rule of the treacherous Vortigern and the arrival of the Saxons under Hengest (see above, pp. 1–2). The central part may properly be regarded as an Arthuriad, beginning with the 'prophecies of Merlin' (omitted by Wace but available in

Geoffrey), and the begetting of Arthur by Uther Pendragon on Ygerne through the machinations of Merlin; going on to chronicle the events of Arthur's reign which represent the height of British achievements – first the successful rout of the Saxons, and then further conquests which lead to suzerainty over the whole of Europe – and culminating in the submission of Rome itself, at which point the treachery of Arthur's nephew Mordred leads to the slaughter of the knights of the Round Table and the death of Arthur himself (ll. 9229–14297). There follows a substantial coda of some two thousand lines dealing with the sad fate of Arthur's successors, until the final dispersal of the native British tribes with the death of Cadwallon in 689 – and consolidation of English power under Æthelstan (ll. 14298–16095).

Far less episodic than at first it might seem, the shape of history Laȝamon perceives is a recurrent pattern of land and people subject to continual conquest, through which the unique personality of Britain survives time and time again. His is a national and not a racial history; *jus sol ni sanguinus*, the story is not of the Britons but of the land of Britain. Just as the typical 'Englishman' is content to include among his forebears Boudicea, William the Conqueror, William of Orange, or a host of Hanoverian sovereigns, very soon the colonial Normans would speak of themselves as 'English', even before they spoke the language.[83] The terms 'England' and 'the English' are semantically tolerant, frequently considered synonymous with 'Britain' and 'the British', often to the distress of racially conscious Celts. For Laȝamon the terms 'English' and 'British' are interchangeable. Although the historical circumstances cannot avoid the fact that they seem to be major opponents, they are opponents only as part of a provisional pattern of transient fortune. The inescapable facts of Germano-Celtic hostilities in the land, and of their eventual outcome, have large implications which are not lost on Laȝamon as the representative of a recently conquered race, which had now to come to terms with a new set of alien masters, absorbing and eventually submerging them in their own 'nationality'. Although Laȝamon's story is of the past, he will naturally dress it in terms which are meaningful to his age. The landscape, both physical and emotional is a twelfth-century feudal one, of castles, siege-works and jealously guarded deer-preserves (ll. 713f); sub-Roman Winchester is offered its 'freedom' as if it were an early medieval borough (l. 14171).

The traditional theme of earthly mutability persists strongly, although the image of the ruin is no longer viable since by the twelfth century so many ancient towns were either lost from view altogether, or totally rebuilt, with their past affirmed only by historians. Unlike the Wanderer's affective nostalgia therefore, Laȝamon's sentiment is an antiquarian one, symptomized by his constant concern to explain the origins of topographical names together with the events associated with them.

Onomastic precision, albeit often technically inaccurate, lends a convincing air of concrete corroboration quite different from either the imagined world of *Beowulf* or the topographical exactitude of *Maldon*. More than a mere gazetteer, it serves to develop a complete personality of Britain. His summary of the history of London in this respect characterizes his theme (ll. 3528f). The name of the town constantly changes as a result of successive waves of new conquerors; it is called first 'New Troy', then Kaer-Lud – which its greatest developer named after himself so that he might be remembered, but such is the transience of human wishes that:

> Seoðð en her com uncuð folc faren in þessere þeode
> ond nemneden þa burh Lundin an heore leode-wisen.
> Seoðð en comen Sæxisce men ond Lundene heo cleopeden,
> þe nome ileste longe inne þisse londe.   (ll. 3543–46)

[Afterwards there came foreign people into this realm and named the town Lundin in their native language. Afterwards Saxon men came and called it Lundene, a name which lasted for a long time in this land.]

The recurrent phrase *Seoðð en her com* marks the rhythm of successive change until Laȝamon's own times when, revealing partisan sentiment:

> Seoðð en comen Normans mid heore nið-craften
> and nemneden heo Lundres; þeos leodes heo amærden.
>                                         (ll. 3547–48)

[Afterwards came the Normans with their evil power and named it Lundres; they harmed this nation.]

But this is merely an expected part of the regular development of the pattern:

> Swa is al þis lond ivaren, for uncuðe leoden
> þeo þis londe hæbbeð bi-wunnen and eft beoð idriven hennene.
> And eft hit bi-ȝetten oðeræ þe uncuðe weoren,
> ond falden þene ælden nomen æfter heore wille
> of gode þe burȝen ond wenden heore nomen
> swa þat his her burh nan in þissere Bruttene
> þat habbe hire nome æld þe me arst hire on-stalde.   (ll. 3549–55)

[So has all this land fared as a result of foreign nations who have conquered this land but were later driven away. And later others who were foreigners gained it, and suppressed the old names of fine towns as they wanted, and changed their names, so that there is here in Britain no town that has its old name that men gave it first of all.]

The realm of Albion has been held in turn by successive waves of invaders: giants, Britons, Saxons in turn, and now in the writer's own time by Normans. But the implication is clear, that all conquerors are themselves eventually conquered – or absorbed – and it is implicitly understood that the Norman yoke is unlikely to prove permanent. As Merlin says, speaking prophetically of the dragons whose conflict shakes the foundations of Vortigern's fortress – with first the white and then the red dragon wounded in turn and retiring into their holes beneath the foundations so that 'no man saw them afterwards' – what should this betoken, but 'kings that are to come, and their fight and their adventure – and their fated folk' (ll. 7999–8000). There is no doubt as to the eventual outcome. Whatever the result of a momentary contest, it is clear that there are always kings to come, and equally that their people are doomed to fall. Both theme and sentiment are traditional – the lesson of *Deor*, *Wanderer* and *The Ruin* writ large. Whatever the personal achievement of these kings – in an awesome roll-call of a hundred or so rulers, great and small, virtuous or immoral – their end must be the same. All achievements of even the best or most authoritarian of rulers are impermanent. The whole cycle had begun with a reversal of fortune, with refugees fleeing from a once-great and impregnable city now in ruins. Thereafter the larger shape of the rise and fall of nations merely reflects the fate of individuals as king after king is raised to power only to be brought low by treachery, folly, or merely old age. Individuals like King Lear tossed by fortune from power to poverty and back to riches again, experience constant reversal. It offers plentiful scope for irony. The Saxon leader, Childeric, so recently master of the land, now disastrously defeated by Arthur, remarks:

> 'Oft hit ilimpeð a veole cunne þeoden
> þer gode cnihtes cumeð to sturne fihte
> þat heo aerest biȝiteð after heo hit leoseð –
> ond al swa us to-ȝere is ilumpen here
> ond æft us bet ilimppeð ȝif we moten livien.'   (ll. 10364–68)

['It will often happen among many races of people where fine knights come to a fierce fight, that they who first win afterwards lose – and that is just what has happened to us here now, and again better may befall us, if we live.']

Brought finally to bay at Mount Badon, the Saxons are mocked by Arthur as 'yesterday's men' in a cumulative incantation of reversion:

> 'Yesterday Colgrim was the bravest of all men.
>                Now . . .'   (ll. 10628–29)
> 'Yesterday Badulf was the boldest of all knights.
>                Now . . .'   (ll. 10638–39)
> 'Yesterday the Emperor (Childeric) was the bravest
>                of all kings. Now . . .'   (ll. 10646–47)

The anarchic circumstances against which the violent and power-hungry nobles jostled one another in pursuit of their ambitions must have seemed no more capricious than the recent history of Laȝamon's own times from Conquest to Anarchy. The Christian warrior like Arthur may occasionally acknowledge that the outcome of a battle lies in the hands of the Lord of Hosts. But it seems an unconvincing piety – the pattern of history motivated more by the caprice of inscrutable fate than a benevolent providence. Nevertheless, Laȝamon the country priest will end his epic on a pietistic note: 'whatever may be hereafter, happen what may, may it be God's will. Amen'. (ll. 16094–96).

Whereas the stories of many kings are passed over summarily – Hudibras, Lear, Gorboduc, Lud, 'Old King' Cole, Cymbeline – the circumstances leading up to the accession of Arthur are treated in full. In this the figure of Vortigern (see above, pp. 1–2), his career very much enlarged from Wace, plays the role of chief villain: wicked steward and tyrannical ruler by turns, perverting the good order of the realm by the introduction of alien mercenaries – first Picts and then Saxons – pursuing merely personal rather than national advancement and displaying a treacherous disregard for the welfare of his own people. The disapprobation expressed by the narrative voice is emphatic. Whereas Geoffrey or Wace do not allow their personal preferences markedly to obtrude on the narrative, we are left in no doubt of where Laȝamon's sympathies lie, conveying an absolute sense of right and wrong. Of Vortigern's rise to power he remarks by way of anticipation: 'the beginning was unpleasant – and so was the end' (l. 6621). Vortigern plots the downfall of the pious King Constance with a degree of Machiavellian openness.

> Þa isæh Vortiger – *of muclen ufele he wes wær* –
> þat Constanz þe king ne cuðe of londe na-þing
> for he nefde ileorned naver nane lare
> buten in his munstre þat munec scolde drigen;
> Vortiger þat isæh – þe Wurse him wes ful neh –
> ofte he hine bi-ðohte wæht he don mahte,
> hu he mihte mid læsinge i-quemen þan kinge.
> Nu þu miht iheren hu þes swiken him gon varen.
> Weoren of Brutlonde þa bezste alle dæde.    (ll. 6626–34)

[Then Vortigern – he was familiar with great wickedness – saw that Constance the king knew nothing about the world because he had never learned about anything except what a monk performs in his monastery; Vortigern saw that – the Devil was very close to him – and he often wondered, incited by power, how he could flatter the king with lies. Now you can hear what this deceit did for him. The best men of Britain were then all dead.]

The italicized phrase, or variants of it, is associated with the name of Vortigern so regularly that as an expected collocation it can be employed to special rhetorical effect. When the name Vortigern first appears, it is accompanied by the narrative aside, *ȝæp mon ond swiðe war* [a crafty man and very wary] (l.6487), repeated with variations thereafter (ll.6536, 6569, 6588, 6593) until it forms an expected formulaic collocation, merely confirmed by a significant variant to stress Vortigern's decidedly Machiavellian character – *of ufele he wes wel iwar* [he was well aware of (familiar with) evil] (ll.6615, 6626, 6669, 6691, 6899, 6929, etc.) – until finally deceived by the Saxon mercenary leader Hengest, the betrayer betrayed, the poet remarks laconically with an ironic recall of the same formula: *her he wes to un-war*, [here he wasn't wary enough!] (l.7601).

Having perverted the Pictish mercenaries to his own peculiar service:

> 'ȝe scullen habbe seolver ond gold, þe bezste hors of þis lond,
> claðes ond fæire wif; eore wille ich wulle drigen;
> ȝe sculleð beon me leofve, for þa Bruttes me beoð laðe;
> lude ond stille ich wulle don eore wille
> ȝif ȝe wulleð in londe halden me for laverd.'   (ll.6683–87)

[‘You shall have silver and gold, the best horses in the land, clothes and beautiful women; I will perform your will; you shall be dear to me, for the Britons are hateful to me; loud and soft I will do your will if you will maintain me as lord in the land.’]

Vortigern contrives that they shall slay the monk-king, Constance, on the paltry excuse that he has provided insufficient beer-money. Then when the Picts come to present Vortigern with the head of Constance, he falls to the ground in a pretence of despair, thus inciting the British to assault the Pictish community in a wholesale pogrom, taking no captives but slaying even their chamber-servants, cooks, and boys (ll.6842–45). Vortigern reigns supreme for a time but the Picts of the North remain vengeful, becoming increasingly dangerous:

> He wes wod he wes wild, he wes ræh he wes bald;
> of alle þinge he hæfde his iwille – but þa Peohtes neoren nævere
> stille   (ll.6857–58)

[He was mad, he was wild, he was cruel, he was bold; he had his way in every respect – except the Picts were never peaceful.]

added to which there is talk of an attack by the monk-king's surviving brothers, Aurelius Ambrosius and Uther Pendragon. And thus it is that, ever an opportunist, hearing of the arrival of Saxon ships in the Thames, Vortigern invites Hengest's men to intervene. Although heathen, the Saxons are explicitly acknowledged to be 'the finest men that ever came here' (ll.6885–86). They are clearly superior physically, better equipped, better clothed, than Vortigern's retinue, and by implication morally superior: 'Vortigern's court was held in contempt; the Britons were sorry for such a sight' (ll.6980–81). Although heathen, Hengest represents a moral agent, working as it were under the old rather than the new law: 'the most courteous of all knights who lived under heathen law in those days' (ll.7209–10). The formulaic collocation associated with the name of Hengest is one of clear approval: 'finest of all knights' (ll.6933, 6955, 6967, etc.). Despite their heathen nature, which Vortigern himself declares is an abhorrence, he urgently needs their protection against both his former friends the Picts, and increasingly his own alienated people, who now favour the accession of Constance's kin. Hengest contrives that his beautiful daughter Rowenna should come forcibly to the notice of the king – who finally apostatizes in marrying her according to heathen custom; and 'when he had disgraced himself on her, gave her London and Kent' (l.7184).

As the Britons begin to desert Vortigern, Laȝamon creates an almost sympathetic picture of the king's embarrassment, awkwardly caught between two worlds and the conflicting demands of personal and national pride. After all, he *has* invited the Saxons, he *has* contracted a marriage alliance; now 'How, for shame, could I shun them so soon, and drive my dear companions from the land?' (ll.7289–90). Laȝamon's use of direct speech is particularly effective, informing his received materials with a dramatic, almost Shakespearian access to historical events. What it loses in genuine historical perspective, it gains enormously in concrete and dramatic immediacy, allowing us to glimpse the faces of important men – the history-makers – at critical moments in their lives, focusing on scenes of stress or exhilaration so as to identify the all too human element in decisions effecting the fate of nations. Yet despite this human insight, the characters Laȝamon portrays – even those who figure prominently like Vortigern or Arthur – do not develop fully realized personalities but remain two-dimensional Platonically conceived Romanesque personae engaged in a series of situations which display only unmixed motives or emotions, where the connecting strand is narrative rather than psychological.

Very soon Vortigern's land is so full of heathen foreigners (ll.7255–57) that the British cause can be identified with Christendom in the starkly racial terms of crusading times. Laȝamon refers to the Saxon idols – indiscriminately – and of course anachronistically – simply as 'Mahomet', (ll.7279,. 14583), much as a century later the author of *Arthur and Merlin* would term the Briton's pagan enemies not Saxons but 'Saracens'.[84] This simplistic black-and-white framework conveys an absolute sense of right and wrong, which permits the ferocious intolerance characteristic of the era in which Laȝamon lived, compared with which the actions of Judith or Byrhtnoth, Assyrian or Viking, pale into decent defensiveness.

The *Brut* reflects the stark realities of wholesale warfare at a time when in the torture-chambers of twelfth-century baronial castles the devils of Guthlac had become in reality indistinguishable from men, and it was openly said that Christ and his saints slept (see above, pp. 15–16). Having sacked and burned the city of Cirencester, the Saxon leader executes savage reprisals:

> Gurmund falde þa munstres and an-heng alle þa munkes;
> of cnihten he carf þe lippes, of madenen þa tittes;
> preostes he blend; al þis folc he scende;
> ælcne bilefved mon he lette bi-limien;
> and þus he gon to taken on, and fordude al þisne Cristindom.
>
> (ll. 14651–55)

[Gurmund pulled down the monasteries and hanged all the monks; from knights he cut off the lips, and from girls the breasts; priests he blinded; he injured the whole people; each man left behind he deprived of his limbs; and he carried on in this fashion and destroyed all this Christendom.]

But such ferocity is by no means confined to the heathen protagonist. Laȝamon's Christians are never in doubt as to their Christian duty: it is to slay 'heathen hounds'. Wishing to serve Christ the better, the governor, Lucius, at whose request missionaries had first come to Britain, simply has slain all those who refuse baptism, converting by force as if they were twelfth-century captive Saracens or Jews (l.5073). Self-righteous intolerance would readily extend to gratuitous cruelty. Adolf of Gloucester urges Aurelius to let his lads use the captive Hengest as target practice in their games of archery (ll.8261–62); but Bishop Aeldadus demands to have him cut to pieces in the market-place, throwing the pieces about the streets, citing an obscure Old Testament precedent in justification (ll.8289f). If Hengest's remains are eventually buried according to pagan custom, it is not so much to honour a worthy if mistaken opponent, but to ensure – as they explicitly pray – that his soul should go to hell (ll.8344–46).[85] In general the religious sentiment now expressed seems to be fundamentally one of dutiful service in return for divine patronage. The *miles Christi* is no longer the loving and faithful member of Christ's *comitatus*, but a feudal retainer. Aurelius vows to worship God *provided* he enables him to defeat Hengest – striking a pragmatist's bargain (ll.8121–29).

If in some respects Laȝamon falls into simple epic amplification, so that armies of many thousands are said to take the field, to be slaughtered in as great numbers, he realistically depicts scenes of horror unknown – or at least unadmitted – in earlier battle-poetry. In one battle six thousand are said to be trodden to death by horses alone – unseated knights wandering dazed through fields that are so full of blood no one can see where to strike, until it is decided to move to a fresh site (ll. 13703–21). Since the victor of a conflict can now deem his foe unquestionably

vicious, impulsive, savage mockery which serves to degrade and de-
humanize a defeated enemy is apparently acceptable. When Uther
Pendragon, having knocked down Vortigern's son, drives a sword through
his mouth and into the ground, the narrator remarks coolly 'such food was
unfamiliar to him' (l.9028). Arthur will address dead or dying foes with
'gameful words' (l.10693). In such a world the traditional beasts of battle
anticipating carnage are forgotten; instead, it is the men who are pictured as
bestial – a natural development of action and image. The early Britons hide
like badgers, leap like deer out of the woods (ll.6395–402), whither at the end
they return to live like wild animals in the wastelands where, hostile and
suspicious, Guthlac finds them (see above, pp. 148f). Warriors are urged to
have the heart of a boar, the cunning of a raven (l.15169). Arthur rushes on
the Saxon:

> swa þe runie wulf
> þenne he cumeð of holte, bihonged mid snawe;
> ond þencheð to biten swulc deor swa him likeð.    (ll.10041–43)

[like the fleet wolf when he comes out of the forest, hung about with snow,
intent on devouring whatever animals he wishes.]

This extended network of images recurs throughout, but most effectively
in a closely packed sequence serving to heighten the excitement of
Arthur's final rout of the Saxons with startling force. After seven
thousand are slain in the waters of the River Dunglas, the remnant wander
through the fen like noble but faltering heron caught between hawks in
the air and hounds in the reeds (ll.10061–67). Childeric is hunted down
like a fox through the wood of Calidon in a graphic simile sustained
through some sixteen lines (ll.10398–413). During the culminating battle
thousands of Saxons have been cut down crossing the Avon. Looking
down on the river from Mount Badon the Saxon leader Badulf sees:

> hu ligeð i þan stræme stelene fisces
> mid sweorde bi-georede; heore sund is awemmed;
> heore scalen wleoteð swulc gold-faʒe sceldes,
> þer fleoteð heore spiten swulc hit spæren weoren.    (ll.10640–43)

[how in the stream there lie steel fish, girt with swords; their ability to swim
is impaired; their scales are gleaming just like gold-plated shields, their fins
are floating as if they were spears.]

We might have expected another simile; instead, the logic of the equation
is presented in a shocking and effective order. What Badulf sees from his
vantage-point are merely so many fish that happen to look like dead
warriors. We, of course, know all too well the dreadful reality. Well
might the poet add:

þis bið seolcuðe þing isizen to þissen londe:
swulche deor an hulle, swulche fisces in wælle!    (ll. 10644–45)

[This is a remarkable thing come to pass in this land: such a beast on the hill, such fish in the water!]

In the end remarks Lazamon, the Saxon hunter flees from the beast he was accustomed to hunt (ll. 10647–50).

A gamut of human motives are realistically acknowledged. Deceit and cowardice, merely hinted at in *Judith* or *Maldon*, are now fully expounded. A Christian king and *swiðe goud cniht* who has sent thousands of heathen hounds to hell (ll. 14572–74), does not hesitate to abandon his defeated retinue to death at the hands of the enemy, creeping away on all fours as though wounded (ll. 14629–30). Another can apparently admit to having stolen away from his army by night to sleep with his wife (and incidentally because his enemy has such a large force), urging her to bed quickly with the lame excuse that it will improve national morale (ll. 9495–501). The softer side of reality is also admitted. The possibility of manly tears is acknowledged, Aurelius's knights weeping at his death, akin to the dignified distress of knightly mourners figured on thirteenth-century English sculptured tombs (l. 8884). In a well-observed human picture, two reconciled brothers impulsively throw away their weapons and fall to tears like the children they are, as their mother urges them to kiss and make up: 'You are my dear sons . . . both of you brave knights' (ll. 2532–43). The emotional effect of such stories on the contemporary audience is known.[86]

In an unstable world where violence and treachery are commonplace, the virtue of strong, even ruthless, kingship is clear. Lazamon's summary of Arthur's rule: 'pleasant enough where he had his will, but exceedingly stern with those who went against it' (ll. 11235–36), is strongly reminiscent of the Chronicler's view of William the Conqueror.[87] To be an effective king, it seems that one must be not merely loved but feared (ll. 13526–27). Arthur's knights are of course brave and good; they are also threatened and coerced; those summoned to join his army render their service not out of love or loyalty but on pain of death or loss of limbs, or of being burned alive (ll. 11131, 14231–32). Lazamon's leaders – Arthur not excepted – are even less considerate of their men than Byrhtnoth, consigning thousands to death. Like William, or any contemporary feudal ruler, Arthur is quite prepared to harry his own land to bring a disobedient people violently to heel – reducing Winchester to blood-stained rubble for having given a fugitive enemy temporary shelter (ll. 14195–99). Arthur's ferocity is not confined to potential enemies; his retribution against those who break his peace is terrible – whoever they may be. His horrendous response when a drunken Christmas party degenerates from throwing bread rolls to end in knife-play, is to have the knight responsible for starting it promptly dragged to a swamp and drowned, his kinsmen beheaded, and their womenfolk mutilated – their noses cut off so as to destroy their beauty. (And these are the circumstances which lead to the institution of the Round Table!) After this prompt and terrifying execution the merriment resumed at Arthur's behest sounds a somewhat hollow note (ll. 11367–420).

Arthur's ferocious reputation ultimately proves a weakness. As excess of proper awe causes men to fear him, the king is distanced, even alienated from those who should serve him, in a manner reminiscent of the eastern despot Holofernes (see above, pp. 164–65). When Arthur is disturbed by a portentous dream, there is no knight who dares ask him how he feels, or dares offer an unacceptable interpretation 'for fear of losing the limbs he loves' (ll. 12792–93). Such isolation renders Arthur not only morally but politically vulnerable. Deprived of necessary counsel at critical moments, he is thus at least partially responsible for his own downfall. Finally, on the eve of his most dreadful reverse, a messenger critically withholds unwelcome news, delaying revelation of his nephew Mordred's treason – his liaison with Guinevere and usurpation of the kingdom – even declaring that there is nothing to worry about in the king's dreams, the significance of which is patently transparent to all except Arthur, who is reluctant to believe its obvious import (ll. 13971ff).

Neither Arthur nor any of his knights (although undeniably presented as strong and virtuous) display any of the chivalric qualities they assumed for Wace – who presumably wished to satisfy the courtly expectations of his patron, Eleanor. The Roman ambassadors who demand historically justifiable tribute from Britain are not treated honourably like the Viking herald at Maldon, but thrown to the ground by Arthur's knights, who tear them by the hair and threaten worse (ll. 12393–98). Laȝamon has neither the vocabulary nor the mind to treat such sentiments as *curtesie*. The idiom of chivalry was as yet semantically and socially inaccessible to an English audience. The romantic fiction of knight-errantry by which the young squires at the Angevin court thought to measure their lives was differently perceived through English eyes; from the point of view of a subject people, the all-too-familiar mounted soldiery were unlikely to have appeared in all respects the *chevalers* of courtly French romance.[88]

Nevertheless there are already clearly present in Laȝamon's portrayal elements of the Arthur of romance: the British hero, appropriated by English and Norman in turn, who would capture the public imagination of all Europe.[89] More than merely the greatest of British kings, Arthur is different in kind from the long roll-call of rulers depicted in the *Brut*. His conception is supernaturally contrived by Merlin, the first and arguably the greatest wizard to figure in English literature. Engendered on a nun by an incubus (ll. 7835f, 8538), Merlin is a somewhat dangerous agent through whom the supernatural approaches the knightly world. When he moves the enormous rocks of Stonehenge, it is significant that the court stands well back outside the magic circle Merlin draws (8697f). But the supernatural potential remains largely undeveloped. At Arthur's birth elves are present, although they bestow virtues: wealth, long life, and generosity, rather than the enchanted rings and magical paraphernalia of fairy romance (ll. 9608–15). Arthur's weapons and armour are of course remarkable, but not more so than Beowulf's. If Beowulf's byrnie was said to have been Weland's work, Arthur's is attributed to the 'elvish smith' Widia (identifiable as Weland's son by Beadohild, see above, p. 40; ll. 10543–45). Remote and dangerous lakes are infested with the same sort of water-monsters we hear of in *Beowulf*, but they are not directly encountered by human agents. The only dragons seen are in dreams; and the giant of Mont-St-Michel, if gross in size and manners, is very corporeal, and even more credible than Grendel.

After Arthur's final disastrous battle against Mordred – the Round Table dispersed, his kingdom destroyed – the mortally wounded king is borne away to the mysterious Isle of Avalon by elvish maidens. The atmosphere of mystery surrounding his ultimate destination is not dissimilar to that surrounding the departure of Scyld Scefing (see above, p. 52). But Arthur believes that the elves can heal him of his wounds, and that he will return to rule the Britons in peace and prosperity (ll. 14277–82). We know of course that this is unreasonable. However great Arthur may be, within or without the fictive structure he is subject to the same inexorable law of mutability as that long roll-call of kings who have been, are, or are to come, and whose achievement, however great, has come to naught. No mere Arthuriad, Laʒamon's history of the Britons significantly does not end with the passing of Arthur but goes on to tell the sad fate of his successors. Arthur's greatness might delay, but cannot avert, the iterated pattern of 'And then . . .'. It is undeniable that belief in Arthur's survival and ultimate return was an article of faith among the Celts (ll. 14290–92) and the cause of nationalist brawls in Cornwall and Brittany.[90] A persistent cause of political disquiet, it is not insignificant that Angevin pressure was brought on the monks of Glastonbury to search for Arthur's grave – the discovery of which was reported in 1190.[91] But although Arthur was now officially 'dead', the Celtic predilection for such 'Trojan fantasies' would persist well into the thirteenth century.[92] Whereas Wace declared himself personally doubtful as to the story of Arthur's survival, Laʒamon is non-committal, acknowledging the tension present between the credible, albeit enlarged, world of history, and the world of romance. At Arthur's birth Merlin had prophesied that he should never die, but poets and minstrels would feed from his body and men be drunk with his blood in a game that should last them until the world's end (ll. 9406f, 11494f). It is clearly Arthur's reputation rather than his person which is in consideration, since it is only in imagination that the inexorable process of mutability may be defied. But the literary amalgam of reality and fiction could not prove stable, and the Arthur of romance precipitates out from the chronicle.

# Notes

1. Romans 13. 4, 12; II Corinthians 10. 4; Ephesians 6. 11–17; I Timothy 1. 18; II Timothy 2. 3–4.

2. Compare generally, Augustine, *De Civitate Dei*, edited by E. Hoffman, *Corpus Scriptorum Ecclesiasticorum Latinorum*, XL (1) (Vienna, 1891), pp. 481–83; or the opening words of *De Agone Christiano*, edited by J. Zycha, *Corpus Scriptorum Ecclesiasticorum Latinorum*, XLI (Vienna, 1900) p. 101; and Bede's account of Eosterwine, *Opera Historica*, edited by C. Plummer (Oxford, 1896), I, pp. 371–72.

3. *Fausti Riensis, Opera*, edited by A. Engelbrecht, *Corpus Scriptorum Ecclesiasticorum Latinorum*, XXI (Vienna, 1891), p. 314.

4. *Vita Haroldi*, edited by W. de G. Birch (London, 1885), pp. 40, 69, 97.

5. *Felix's Life of Saint Guthlac*, edited by B. Colgrave (Cambridge, 1956).

6. Well known to English hagiographers through the discussion included in Gregory's *Dialogi*, edited by J.-P. Migne, *Patrologia Latina*, (Paris, 1844–90), LXXVII, cols 281–84.

7. Athanasius, *Vita Sancti Antonii interprete Evagrio*, edited by J.-P. Migne, *Patrologia Latina* (Paris, 1844–90), LXXIII, cols 125–70; Sulpicius Severus, *Vita Martini*, edited by Migne, *Patrologia Latina*, XX, cols 159–76; Gregory, *Dialogi*, edited by Migne, *Patrologia Latina*, LXXVII, cols 149–430 (book ii being printed separately as LXVI, cols 125–204).

8. *The Earliest Life of Gregory the Great*, edited by B. Colgrave (Lawrence, Kansas, 1968), p. 153.

9. *Felix's Life of Saint Guthlac*, edited by Colgrave, pp. 152f; compare *Two Lives of Saint Cuthbert*, edited by B. Colgrave (Cambridge, 1940), pp. 270ff, 282–85.

10. *Felix's Life of Saint Guthlac*, edited by Colgrave, pp. 132–37; compare Gregory, *Dialogi*, book ii, edited by Migne, *Patrologia Latina*, LXVI, cols 158, 170.

11. *Felix's Life of Saint Guthlac*, edited by Colgrave, pp. 64–65, 92–93, 150–51; compare *Two Lives of Saint Cuthbert*, edited by Colgrave, pp. 143–45, and Athanasius, *Vita Sancti Antonii*, edited by Migne, *Patrologia Latina*, LXIII, cols 125–28.

12. I Corinthians 12. 12–27; compare *The Earliest Life of Gregory the Great*, edited by Colgrave, pp. 131–34.

13. J. Roberts, 'A Metrical Examination of the Poems *Guthlac A* and *Guthlac B*', *Proceedings of the Royal Irish Academy*, 71(C) (1971), 91–137 (p. 116).

14. *The Guthlac Roll*, edited by G. Warner (Oxford, 1928).

15. Compare Gregory, *Dialogi*, edited by Migne, *Patrologia Latina*, LXXVII, col. 357.

16. Athanasius, *Vita Sancti Antonii,* edited by Migne, *Patrologia Latina,* LXXIII, col. 157.

17. Compare E. G. Stanley, 'Studies in the Prosaic Vocabulary of Old English Verse', *Neuphilologische Mitteilungen,* 72 (1971), 385–418 (p. 389).

18. Roman drainage-engineers had succeeded in converting the wetlands of South Lincolnshire into a major region of peasant colonization, in which Crowland itself played a not inconsiderable role – an important trading-centre (surrounded by a pleiade of others within a seven-mile radius), and the focus of a system of artificial waterways. The breakdown of Roman administration would have led to the collapse of the programme of maintenance on which the drainage system was dependent, with subsequent reswamping of much former pastureland, making for difficult terrain, awkward of access, and a natural refuge for the native inhabitants of Celtic Britain, no less than for post-Conquest guerrilla-fighters like Hereward the Wake. Nevertheless, areas of higher ground (the 'islands') must have remained attractive to settlement, and there is good evidence for a degree of native survival, on to which Germanic newcomers had begun to impinge by the seventh century. Compare *The Fenland in Roman Times,* edited by C. W. Phillips (London, 1970), pp. 274–78; H. E. Hallam, *The New Lands of Elloe* (Leicester, 1954), pp. 4–6, 40, 73, 75, 81; see also, O. K. Schram, 'Fenland Place-names', in *The Early Cultures of North-West Europe, H. M. Chadwick Memorial Studies,* edited by C. Fox and B. Dickins (Cambridge, 1950), pp. 427–41. The region was soon occupied by small, but not totally insignificant groups of English settlers, such as the Spalda, Wigesta, and Gyrwe; compare W. T. W. Potts, 'The pre-Danish Estate of Peterborough Abbey', *Proceedings of the Cambridge Antiquarian Society,* 65 (1974), 13–27. Bede describes the Isle of Ely, for example, as capable of supporting 600 families, exactly comparable in this respect to the densely settled Isle of Thanet in East Kent; *Bede's Ecclesiastical History of the English People,* edited by B. Colgrave and R. A. B. Mynors (Oxford, 1969), pp. 72–73, 396–97.

19. The poetic fiction ignores the proximity of Guthlac's cell to important monastic centres such as Peterborough, sponsored by early East Anglian and Mercian kings. Some forty years before Guthlac established himself at Crowland, a number of monks had left Peterborough to take up the solitary life on islands such as Thorney (formerly Ancarig, 'the anchorites' island'), only four miles away from Crowland; *Two of the Saxon Chronicles Parallel,* edited by J. Earle and C. Plummer (Oxford, 1892–99), I, p. 31.

20. *Felix's Life of Saint Guthlac,* edited by Colgrave, pp. 122–23.

21. *Maxims II,* ll. 42–43, *The Anglo-Saxon Minor Poems,* edited by G. P. Krapp and E. v. K. Dobbie, *The Anglo-Saxon Poetic Records* (London, 1931–53), VI, p. 56.

22. *Two Lives of Saint Cuthbert,* edited by Colgrave, pp. 96–97, 214–15, 276–79.

23. Compare A. P. Campbell, 'Physical Signs of Spiritual Cleansing in Old English Poetry', *Revue de l'Université d'Ottawa,* 45 (1975), 382–91.

24. Compare P. F. Reichardt, '*Guthlac A* and the Landscape of Spiritual Perfection', *Neophilologus,* 58 (1974), 331–38.

25. For example Fursa (*Bede's Eccles. Hist.,* edited by Colgrave and Mynors, pp. 270–71).

26. For example, Cuthbert on Farne Island, ibid., pp. 436–37.

27. Compare generally, J. Hill, 'The Soldier of Christ in Old English Prose and Poetry', *Leeds Studies in English,* New Series, 12 (1980), 57–80 (especially pp. 65–69 for *Guthlac A*).

28. *Das angelsächsische Prosa-Leben des hl. Guthlac*, edited by P. Gonser (Heidelberg, 1909), p. 117.

29. Athanasius, *Vita Sancti Antonii*, edited by Migne, *Patrologia Latina*, LXXIII, col. 132; compare Jerome's *Vitae SS Pauli et Hilarionis*, edited by J.-P. Migne, *Patrologia Latina*, (Paris, 1844–90), XXIII, cols 21, 33.

30. See generally, M. Gelling, 'Place-names and Anglo-Saxon Paganism', *University of Birmingham Historical Journal*, 8 (1962), 7–25; 'Further Thoughts on Pagan Place-names', in *Otium et Negotium: Studies in Onomatology and Library Science Presented to Olof von Felitzen*, edited by F. Sandgren (Stockholm, 1973), pp. 109–28. Also, L. K. Shook, 'The Burial Mound in *Guthlac A*', *Modern Philology*, 58 (1960), 1–10, and K. P. Wentersdorf, '*Guthlac A*: the Battle for the *Beorg*', *Neophilologus*, 62 (1978), 135–42.

31. See above, p. 4; and compare Thomas of Elmham, *Historia Monasterii S. Augustini Cantuariensis*, edited by C. Hardwick, Rolls Series, 8 (London, 1858), pp. 79–81.

32. Compare H. R. E. Davidson and L. Webster, 'The Anglo-Saxon Burial at Coombe (Woodnesborough), Kent', *Medieval Archaeology*, 11 (1967), 1–41 (pp. 8–9).

33. *Felix's Life of Saint Guthlac*, edited by Colgrave, pp. 110–11.

34. *Bede's Eccles. Hist.*, edited by Colgrave and Mynors, pp. 424–27.

35. *Two Lives of Saint Cuthbert*, edited by Colgrave, *passim*.

36. Compare Jordanus, *Getica*, edited by T. Mommsen, *Monumenta Germaniae Historica, Auctorum Antiquissimorum*, v (1), (Berlin, 1882), p. 89.

37. Sulpicius Severus, *Vita Sancti Martini*, edited by C. Halm, *Corpus Scriptorum Ecclesiasticorum Latinorum*, I, (Vienna, 1866), p. 114.

38. *Ancient Laws and Institutes of England*, edited by B. Thorpe (London, 1840), II, pp. 5–6; for a valuable survey of the concept of a 'just war' in early medieval England, see J. E. Cross, 'The Ethic of War in Old English', in *England before the Conquest*, edited by P. Clemoes and K. Hughes (Cambridge, 1971), pp. 269–82.

39. *Die Briefe des heiligen Bonifatius und Lullus*, edited by M. Tangl, *Monumenta Germaniae Historica, Epistolae Selectae*, I, (Berlin, 1955), p. 102.

40. Compare *Bede's Eccles. Hist.*, edited by Colgrave and Mynors, pp. 212–17, and *Ælfric's Lives of Saints*, edited by W. W. Skeat, Early English Text Society, Original Series, 76, 82, 94, 114 (London, 1881–1900), II, pp. 125ff, 315ff.

41. '. . . as an example to you men to defend your native land by armed force against an invading army', in *The Old English Version of the Heptateuch, Ælfric's Treatise on the Old and New Testaments and his Preface to Genesis*, edited by S. J. Crawford, Early English Text Society, Original Series, 160 (London, 1922), p. 48.

42. Compare generally, I. Pringle, '*Judith*: The Homily and the Poem', *Traditio*, 31 (1975), 83–97.

43. A good case for considering that relatively little has been lost from the beginning of the poem was made by R. E. Woolf, 'The Lost Opening to the *Judith*', *Modern Language Review*, 50 (1955), 168–72; for a strong argument that the loss may have been greater, see D. Chamberlain '*Judith*: A Fragmentary and Political Poem', in *Anglo-Saxon Poetry: Essays in Appreciation*, edited by L. E. Nicholson and D. W. Frese (Notre Dame, Indiana, 1975), pp. 135–59.

44. *De Virginitate*, in *Aldhelmi Opera*, edited by R. Ehwald, *Monumenta Germaniae Historica, Auctorum Antiquissimorum*, XV, (Berlin, 1919), pp. 316–17.

45. *Cornelii Taciti, Opera Minora*, edited by M. Winterbottom and R. M. Ogilvie (Oxford, 1975), pp. 48–49.

46. *The Fortunes of Men*, ll. 48–63, 77–79, in *The Exeter Book*, edited by G. P. Krapp and E. v. K. Dobbie, Anglo-Saxon Poetic Records, (London, 1931–53), III, pp. 155–56.

47. Compare B. Raffel, '*Judith*: Hypermetricity and Rhetoric', in *Anglo-Saxon Poetry*, edited by Nicholson and Frese, pp. 124–34.

48. *Expositio in Librum Judith*, edited by J.-P. Migne, *Patrologia Latina*, (Paris, 1844–90), CIX, cols 546, 558.

49. *Aldhelmi Opera*, edited by Ehwald, pp. 316–17.

50. *Sermo XLVIII: De Judith*, edited by J.-P. Migne, *Patrologia Latina*, (Paris, 1844–90), XXXIX, cols 1839–40.

51. *Cynewulf's Juliana*, edited by R. Woolf, second edition (Exeter, 1977).

52. It was perhaps considered especially appropriate that vengeance should be exacted with the offending weapon; compare M. Ashdown, *English and Norse Documents Relating to the Reign of Ethelred the Unready* (Cambridge, 1930), pp. 82–83.

53. Among other strictures, even the servants of early medieval religious women are warned against washing men's hair, *Ancrene Wisse*, edited by J. R. R. Tolkien, Early English Text Society, 249 (London, 1962), p. 218.

54. See comments on Peada's wife, *Bede's Eccles. Hist.*, edited by Colgrave and Mynors, pp. 294–95, or on Offa's wife Thryth, *Beowulf*, ll. 1931–43, in '*Beowulf* with the '*Finnesburg*' *Fragment*, edited by C. L. Wrenn, third edition revised by W. F. Bolton (London, 1973), pp. 168–69.

55. *Cynewulf's Elene*, edited by P. O. E. Gradon, second edition (Exeter, 1977); *Cynewulf's Juliana*, edited by Woolf, second edition (Exeter, 1977).

56. *Lestorie des Engles solum la translacion Maistre Geffrei Gaimar*, edited by T. D. Hardy and C. T. Martin, Rolls Series, 91 (London, 1888–89), I, 385–87.

57. A suggestion originating with T. G. Foster, *Judith: Studies in Metre, Language and Style*, Quellen und Forschungen, 71 (Strasburg, 1892), p. 90, and recently revived by B. F. Huppé, *The Web of Words* (Albany, New York, 1970), p. 147.

58. *Liber de Viduis*, edited by J.-P. Migne, *Patrologia Latina* (Paris, 1844–90), XVI, cols 258–60.

59. *Riddle 25*, l. 11, in *Exeter Book*, edited by Krapp and Dobbie, p. 193.

60. For the burlesque potential in this and other scenes, see F. J. Heinemann, '*Judith* 236–291a: A Mock Heroic Approach-to-battle Type Scene', *Neuphilologische Mitteilungen*, 71 (1970), 83–96.

61. *Two Saxon Chron.*, edited by Earle and Plummer, I, pp. 126–27, II, p. 175.

62. *Liber Eliensis*, edited by E. O. Blake, Royal Historical Society, Camden Third Series, 92 (London, 1962), p. 136.

63. *Two Saxon Chron.*, edited by Earle and Plummer, I, pp. 106–10; *Anglo-Saxon Minor Poems*, edited by Krapp and Dobbie, pp. 16–21.

64. Compare E. D. Laborde, 'The Site of the Battle of Maldon', *English Historical Review*, 40 (1925), 161–73, expanded in *Byrhtnoth and Maldon* (London, 1936), *passim*, and refined by G. R. Petty and S. Petty, 'Geology and the Battle of Maldon', *Speculum*, 51 (1976), 435–46.

65. For a valuable review of opinion, see O. D. Macrae-Gibson, 'How Historical is the Battle of Maldon?', *Medium Ævum*, 39 (1970), 89–107.

66. *Cornelii Taciti, Opera Minora*, edited by Winterbottom and Ogilvie, pp. 41, 44, 47–48.

67. *Two Saxon Chron.*, edited by Earle and Plummer, i, pp. 126–27, ii, p. 175.

68. See generally, H. Gneuss, '*The Battle of Maldon* 89: Byrhtnoð's *Ofermod* Once Again', *Studies in Philology*, 73 (1976), 117–37.

69. Compare J. R. R. Tolkien, 'The Homecoming of Beorhtnoth, Beorhthelm's Son', *Essays and Studies*, New Series, 6 (1953), 1–18 (p. 15).

70. Compare generally, A. T. Hatto, 'Archery and Chivalry: A Noble Prejudice', *Modern Language Review*, 35 (1940), 40–54.

71. Byrhtferth of Ramsey, *Vita Oswaldi*, in *The Historians of the Church of York*, edited by J. Raine, Rolls Series, 71 (London, 1879–94), i, pp. 445, 456; and compare *Liber Eliensis*, edited by Blake, pp. 133–36.

72. See generally, N. F. Blake, '*The Battle of Maldon*', *Neophilologus*, 49 (1965), 332–45; J. E. Cross, 'Oswald and Byrhtnoth', *English Studies*, 46 (1965), 93–109; F. C. Robinson, 'God, Death, and Loyalty in *The Battle of Maldon*', in *J. R. R. Tolkien, Scholar and Storyteller: Essays in Memoriam*, edited by M. Salu and R. T. Farrell (Ithaca, New York, 1979), pp. 76–98.

73. *Two Saxon Chron.*, edited by Earle and Plummer, i, pp. 87, 91 (*s.a.* 894, 897), etc.

74. See for example, Alcuin, *Epistolae*, edited by E. Dümmler, *Monumenta Germaniae Historica, Epistolae*, iv, (Berlin, 1895), pp. 45–47, 155, 181, etc; *Ælfric's Lives*, edited by Skeat, i, p. 352; or Wulfstan, *The Homilies of Wulfstan*, edited by D. Bethurum (Oxford, 1957), pp. 123f, 267f.

75. Although Lupus of Ferrières writing to King Æthelwulf in 852 went so far as to describe the Vikings as 'the foes of Christ . . . enemies of the Christian name', in *Councils and Ecclesiastical Documents Relating to Great Britain and Ireland*, edited by A. W. Haddan and W. Stubbs (London, 1869–71), iii, p. 648.

76. *Ælfric: Lives of Three English Saints*, edited by G. I. Needham, second edition (Exeter, 1976), p. 49.

77. Compare E. D. Laborde, 'The Style of *The Battle of Maldon*', *Modern Language Review*, 19 (1924), 401–17.

78. Stanley, *Neuphilologische Mitteilungen*, 72 (1971), 385–418, *passim*.

79. For example, *ceallian* (l. 91), *dreng* (l. 149), *grið* (l. 35), *wicing* (l. 26). *Eorl* (ll. 6, 51, etc.) of course has shifted its sense under the influence of Old Norse *jarl*. Compare generally B. S. Phillpotts, '*The Battle of Maldon*: Some Danish Affinities', *Modern Language Review*, 24 (1929), 172–90.

80. See generally, *Die 'Institutes of Polity, Civil and Ecclesiastical'*, edited by K. Jost (Berne, 1959).

81. For the web of historiographic interest and shifting perspectives in general, see R. W. Hanning, *The Vision of History in Early Britain from Gildas to Geoffrey of Monmouth* (New York, 1966).

82. *Le Roman de Brut par Wace*, edited by I. Arnold (Paris, 1938–40); *The Historia Regum Britanniae of Geoffrey of Monmouth*, edited by A. Griscom (London, 1929). For an early but still useful account of the use made by Laʒamon of his source, see F. L. Gillespy, 'Layamon's *Brut*: A Comparative Study in Narrative Art', *University of California Publications in Modern Philology*, 3 (1916), 361–510; see further, P. J.

Frankis, 'Laȝamon's English Sources', in *J. R R. Tolkien, Scholar and Storyteller*, edited by Salu and Farrell, pp. 64–75.

83. Ordericus Vitalis, for example, born in Shropshire, the son of a French clerk from Orleans, and who was sent from England to France as a child, constantly refers to himself as *Anglígena*, 'an Englander', *The Ecclesiastical History of Ordericus Vitalis*, edited by M. Chibnall (Oxford, 1969–80), ii, pp. 350–51, iii, pp. 6–7, 168–69, 256–67, iv, pp. 144–45.

84. *Of Arthour and of Merlin*, edited by O. D. Macrae-Gibson, Early English Text Society, 268 (London, 1973), pp. 25, 135, 158–59, 164–65, etc.

85. Interestingly, such unedifying prayers were systematically eliminated by the 'advanced' Otho scribe; for other kinds of deletions, see W. J. Keith, 'Laȝamon's *Brut*: The Literary Differences between the Two Texts', *Medium Ævum*, 29 (1960), 161–72.

86. Compare Aelred of Rievaulx, *Liber de Speculo Caritatis*, in *Aelredi Rievallensis, Opera Ascetica*, edited by A. Hoste and C. H. Talbot, *Corpus Christianorum, Continuatio Mediaevalis*, I, (Turnholt, 1971), p. 90; or Peter of Blois, *Liber de Confessione Sacramentali*, edited by J.-P. Migne, *Patrologia Latina*, (Paris, 1844–90), ccvii, col. 1088.

87. *Two Saxon Chron.*, edited by Earle and Plummer, i, p. 219.

88. Compare D. S. Monroe, 'French Words in Laȝamon', *Modern Philology*, 4 (1907), 559–67.

89. For a valuable introductory survey of the whole complex range of Arthurian romance material, see *Arthurian Literature in the Middle Ages*, edited by R. S. Loomis (Oxford, 1959); *The Development of Arthurian Romance*, by R. S. Loomis (London, 1963).

90. Hermann of Tournai, *De Miraculis S. Mariae Laudunensis*, edited by J.-P. Migne, *Patrologia Latina*, (Paris, 1844–90), clvi, col. 983; pseudo-Alanus de Insulis, *Prophetia Anglicana* (Frankfurt, 1603), p. 17.

91. For the archaeological reality, see generally, C. A. R. Radford and M. J. Swanton, *Arthurian Sites in the West* (Exeter, 1975), pp. 42–44.

92. Compare *Registrum Epistolarum Fratris Johannis Peckham, Archiepiscopi Cantuariensis*, edited by C. T. Martin, Rolls Series, 77 (London, 1882–85), ii, pp. 741–42; *Vita Edwardi Secundi*, in *Chronicles of the Reigns of Edward I and Edward II*, edited by W. Stubbs, Rolls Series, 76 (London, 1882–83,) ii, p. 218.

# Chapter 6
# Things that Falleth to Ribaudrie

*Havelok the Dane, Sir Tristrem, Floris and Blancheflour,*
and *Dame Sirith and the Weeping Bitch*

At several points in its lengthy and complex structure the *Brut* incorporates digressive episodes alluding to or epitomizing stories like those of Cymbeline, or King Lear and his three daughters, revealing a contemporary taste for narrative materials of a less immediately didactic, more entertaining type, often referred to by the generic term romance.[1] 'It isn't all truth – nor all lies – that minstrels sing about King Arthur', says Laȝamon; 'the British loved him greatly and in consequence often lie about him, saying such things that never could be in this world – though the truth itself is marvellous enough' (ll.11455ff). Laȝamon's treatment of, for example, King Arthur's encounter with the giant of Mont-St-Michel, suggests that he can confidently work within romance conventions that are already familiar to his audience. The fiction of knight-errantry is clearly present, albeit by default, when Sir Bedevere, encountering an old woman, bruised, broken, and dazed having suffered multiple rape by the giant – is himself mistaken for a glittering angel of mercy – the archetypal knight in shining armour. We of course know what is expected of him. Indeed, upon being urged by the woman to save himself while he has time, Bedevere insists that 'there was never champion born of lady who would not stoop to help a frail old woman'. But then discretion being the better part of valour, instead of promptly rescuing the old woman – the young princess being already dead – he concludes: 'Now have a very nice day – I'll be on my way' (l.12953) – and goes off to consult Arthur, meanwhile leaving the old woman to suffer further assault. It is significant that whereas in both Geoffrey and Wace Arthur will attempt to take the giant by surprise, Laȝamon's Arthur will reveal sportsmanlike instincts that Beowulf would have approved, by insisting on confronting the giant alone and refusing to attack him while asleep, lest his reputation for fair play should be diminished (ll.12987–94). Tom-and-Jerry-wise, Arthur is chased three times around a tree before catching up the lumbering giant from behind and clouting him (ll.13008–12).

Although naturally undeveloped in the *Brut*, there is good reason to suppose a lively interest in vernacular narrative of all kinds, whether drawing on traditional material, events from national history: the real or imaginary 'matter of Britain' or 'of England', or utilizing newly imported 'courtly' themes introduced by the Norman *maistrie*, or tales from further east, made accessible both physically and imaginatively by crusader or merchant-venturer. Whereas Laʒamon's canvas had allowed merely episodic allusions to such material as part of the wider history of larger communities, the romance proper would concentrate more fully on the circumstances surrounding the tale of a particular hero, in an almost biographical sense. Such stories are concerned only secondarily with the fates of nations or of large armies: their prime concern is with the development of an individual protagonist, explored in action as his character is tested against events – a process of maturation usually achieved by way of a degree of suffering: 'adventure' in terms of, for example, an individual quest or exile. While necessarily purporting to represent reality, such a construct would lay no claim to factual truth; the imprecise boundary between realism and reality could never have been easy – nor useful – to define. The twelfth-century critic Alanus de Insulis speaks of this enhancement of actuality, the literary combination of historical event with imagination, as 'the harmonious joining of diversities which might result in a better story'.[2] This harmony was not always easy to achieve and the dividing line between fact and fiction, always tenuous, is sometimes abandoned. In the years following the Conquest the tales told of the exploits of the resistance-fighter Hereward the Wake have the air of reality, while those told of the later days of Harold Godwinson, are convincing in so far as they represent what so easily *might* have happened, had he survived the Battle of Hastings;[3] but those told of Hereward's West-of-England counterpart Eadric the Wild, although no less presented in terms of the 'true tale', clearly topple into the world of fantasy; he was even said to have married the Queen of the Fairies, Iolanthe-like, and to have brought her to William's court.[4]

For the first hundred years or so following the Conquest, much of the literature produced by and for what was, after all, a depressed race – its language and culture *déclassé* – is simply lost.[5] But from the end of the twelfth century onwards the survival rate is better, perhaps reflecting the new-found cultural self-confidence of an economically and institutionally buoyant citizen class. But whether purveyed publicly in market-place or tavern, or in the more intimate drawing-room context of wealthy mercantile families, and whether or not in fact originating in written form, the early Middle English romance is presented as though the common stock-in-trade of a professional minstrel class.[6] Typical of this urban sponsorship is the romance of *Havelok the Dane*, which must have been of particular interest to the citizens of Lincoln, who would point out to visitors the very stone with which Havelok won the throwing contest, and the chapel where he married Goldbrow[7] – or to those of nearby

Grimsby whose early thirteenth-century town seal, (symbol of corporate independence), proudly depicted the major protagonists of the story: hero and heroine with their friend Grim, eponymous founder of the town.[8]

Like *Hamlet*, the story of *Havelok* must ultimately derive from a period of close connection between Denmark and eastern England during the time of the Viking ascendancy. The historical setting is apparently that immediately preceding Cnut's accession as king of both England and Denmark. But although presented as historically true, the story depicts the inward and outward landscape of a twelfth-century English citizen class, reflecting the concerns of a socially secure but aspirant bourgeoisie, framed in fictive conventions that persist in the romance tradition to the present day: an overall framework of just deserts, virtue eventually rewarded, and infamy punished – the myth of righted wrongs in an ordered society. A handsome prince, noble in both mien and character (Havelok) goes rejected and unrecognized, yet eventually marries a princess (Goldbrow) and comes into his own again. Conversely, the heroine (Goldbrow) forced to marry beneath her (the dispossessed Havelok), finds that in fact she has married a 'frog-prince'. This contrives to incorporate in one fiction both the rags-to-riches wish-fulfilment of the tradesman class and their characteristic belief that breeding will out, signalling both resentment and recognition of their own place in the social hierarchy. It is significant that the sexual interest displayed is in the secure and fruitful relationship of marriage rather than the uncertainties of 'courtly' love. The dispossessed heir achieves maturity not through exploits of chivalric *aventure* but hard work and native courage. His story is located not in some never-never land but in a setting that is physically and emotionally credible.

Despite the obviously popular appeal of much of the poet's story materials, the narrative structure he presents is sufficiently complex and original to suggest an audience that might appreciate a considerable degree of literary artifice concealed behind an unassuming external form. As with Laȝamon, the authorial voice is heard throughout, although here presented through the *figura* of a minstrel recitation. An informal tone is established from the outset with an explicit address to the audience soliciting both attention and goodwill:

> Herkneth to me, gode men,
> wives, maydnes, and alle men,
> of a tale ich you wil telle,
> hwo-so it wile here, and þer-to duelle.   (ll. 1–4)

[Listen to me good fellows, women, girls, and everybody; I'll tell you a tale if anyone wants to stay and hear it.]

The implication of the last line, a conventional enough prefatory formula of the genre at the time,[9] is that the audience was free to move on, suggesting a casual or random venue: market-place or tavern rather than the formal context of guild-hall or solar. Even more than with Laȝamon, we are aware of a distinctive, even forceful personality in the narrative voice, addressing an audience at least notionally his equals – not *lordinges* but 'goodmen', that is ordinary householders, and their wives and daughters. Unlike the contemporary French versions of the tale circulating in the halls of the Anglo-Norman aristocracy,[10] its tone is uncourtly, if convivial; the minstrel calls for ale at the beginning, as he will call for a *pater noster* at the end:

> At þe biginning of ure tale,
> fil me a cuppe of ful god ale;
> and y wile drinken, er y spelle,
> þat Crist us shilde alle fro helle!   (ll. 13–16)

> [At the beginning of our tale fill me a cup of good ale; and before I recite, I'll drink to the hope that Christ may defend us all from hell.]

The minstrel figure is clearly sustained throughout, frequently intervening between his narrative and his audience to voice strongly expressed attitudes towards the personalities and events he portrays – heightening the dramatic effect by personal involvement. He may, for example, invoke a lengthy curse on the traitors Godard and Godrich (e.g. ll. 426–36), or more briefly interrupt the narrative line to interpose an emphatic imprecation (e.g. 'He should be hanged on a hook', l. 1102), or a blessing, as when the poet prays in his own voice that the soul of a virtuous king may dwell with Christ in heaven (ll. 403–07). Such lively engagement with his characters lends them a marked degree of current actuality, as though they exist at the present time, and that the outcome could still lie in the balance: an eventuality to be hoped for, or feared. Present-tense phrases such as: 'May the devil in hell soon take him!' (l. 446) or 'May Christ, who made the lame walk and the dumb speak, avenge you, Havelok, on Godard!' (ll. 542–44), serve to provoke our active concern, which results in a genuine dramatic suspense uncommon in early medieval literature. This authorial contact, made sometimes only in the slightest aside: e.g. 'As I will tell you' or 'As I've already mentioned' – is sustained until the very end, when he asks his audience to offer a silent prayer for the soul of 'him who made the rhyme – and spent so many sleepless nights in its composition' (ll. 2994–3001).

The romance opens with an account of a golden age of peace, justice, and prosperity as it might be conceived from a bourgeois point of view. The firm but fair rule of King Athelwold has ensured an era of law and order – as understood by contemporary jurists like Bracton.[11] Ruling by divine right and social consensus, a friend to widows and orphans, he punishes all wrongdoers irrespective of rank (*were he nevre kniht so strong*, l.80). While providing for the welfare of all classes, he displays a particular concern to secure the rights of property, punish robbers, and ensure the security of commerce (characteristics not dissimilar from the *pax Normanniae* imposed by the Conqueror).[12] *Panne was Engelond at ayse!* (l.59). The societal norm thus established, Athelwold dies, mourned by all. Prior to dying, however, he entrusts his baby girl and sole heir, Goldbrow, to the care of Earl Godrich, who is to act as regent until she comes of age. Godrich takes a sacred oath that the princess will be educated as befits her status (employing the polite French terminology: 'so that she knew the usage of both courtesy and courtship' (*curteysye* and *luve-drurye*), after which he is to see that she marries 'the highest man alive – the best, the handsomest and strongest', that they may rule over England together (ll.192–203). But instead of holding the kingdom in trust, the treacherous Godrich wastes no time in perverting government to his own ends, appointing his own men as judges and sheriffs, until he had all men *at his cri* [beck and call], *at his wille, at his merci* (ll.270–71). Then: *Al Engelond of him stod awe; al Engelond was of him adrad* (ll.277–78).

Determined to see his own child ascend the throne, Godrich has Goldbrow imprisoned at Dover Castle, deprived of her friends, and shabbily dressed. His motivation is expressed in vigorous direct speech – not the courtly terms we might expect of an earl-regent but rather the well-observed material terms of a niggardly burgher:

> 'Hweþer she sholde be
> quen and levedi over me? . . .
> sholde ic yeve a fol, a þerne,
> Engelond, þouh sho it yerne? . . .
> Sho is waxen al to prud,
> for gode metes, and noble shrud,
> þat ic have yoven hire to ofte;
> ic have yemed hire to softe.' (ll.292–93, 298–99, 302–05)

['Why should she be queen and lady over me? . . . Should I give England to a fool, a serving-wench, even if she wants it? . . . She's grown all too proud as a result of the good food and fine clothing that I've too often given her; I've treated her too soft.']

The narrative space permits a sophisticated complexity of motivation to be presented, incidentally revealing a marked increase of interest in individual characterization; figures are no longer depicted as merely symbols of particular traits, good or evil – but a more realistic and credible mixture of both. Godrich, while distinctly villainous, reveals an understandable fatherly concern for his own son's interests, remarking, with loving pride: 'I have a son – a lovely boy' (l.308). Nevertheless, in betraying his feudal oath, his saintly predecessor, and the kingdom itself, the treacherous Godrich is explicitly equated with Judas and dubbed 'worse than Satan' (ll.319, 1100, 1133–34). This usurpation of both moral order and heroine awaits the advent of a hero who can rescue the princess, overthrow the usurper, and restore justice and order to society. The poet concludes this stage of his story by calling for a miraculous intervention to achieve this (ll.331–37).

Now it is that the figure of Havelok – the 'good chap' whose story it is, as announced from the beginning (ll.5ff) – can be introduced. It appears that in Denmark an exactly analogous situation has developed, the rights of the infant Prince Havelok being violently usurped by his treacherous guardian Godard. It is no accident that the two traitors are given closely similar names. The author takes care to develop a symmetrical structure, with a considerable degree of parallelism in incident – extending even to a certain duplication of phraseology, which reinforces the significance of his theme, but avoiding monotony by variation of emphasis. In both cases helpless orphans are stripped of their rights by wicked and powerful adults; but whereas Godrich merely slights his ward, Godard engages in violent assault.

The considerable sympathy evoked for children is characteristic of middle-class aspirant concerns – even the villainous Godrich tries to secure the best future for his child. When the poet describes Godard's ill-treatment of the royal infants ('He didn't clothe them right, nor feed – nor give them decent beds!' (ll.420–21), we are offered a truly pathetic picture clearly intended to touch the goodmen and their wives he addressed. Finding the young children in their castle prison weeping bitterly for hunger and cold (ll.415f), Godard demands testily, 'What's up with you? Why are you crying and yowling now?' (ll.453–54), and the brave Havelok asks like Oliver Twist, for more food: 'Nobody gives us anything to eat or drink! – not half what we could eat! We wish we had never been born' (ll.456–61). At this Godard takes up Havelok's two little sisters – as though he were going to play with them – and slits their throats. Although the two girls – no sooner introduced than dead – play no large part and will not be referred to again, they are provided with individual names: Swanbrow and Elfled the Fair; this ensures their independent identity and adds to the shock of their harsh treatment, thus engaging immediate sympathy. The poet achieves a dramatic spatial effect as Havelok witnesses the dreadful fate, not just of two young girls, but of Swanbrow and Elfled! As in the *Brut* the provision of specific names for quite minor characters lends the credibility of corroborative detail. When the terrified lad drops to his knees and grovels, imploring Godard to let him go and promising to do anything – even to deny his status and identity – even Godard is touched with pity (*rewnesse*, l.502) and lets the bloodstained knife drop. Standing and staring as though crazed, he debates with himself the pros and cons of letting Havelok go. The moment of passion passed, he cannot bring himself to kill the child personally, but instead hands him over to his thrall, a fisherman named Grim, who undertakes to drown the child in return for his own freedom.

In the event, Grim saves the prince's life, ensuring the eventual resolution of the story in a victory of good over evil. But the character of Grim does not fall easily into the stock-figure of folk-tale or romance: the low-life figure with a heart of gold – fisherman/shepherd, dairymaid/prostitute, who comes to the rescue of hero or heroine at the point of their lowest fortunes.[13] The author will not employ any of his characters so simplistically. In the first place Grim is perfectly willing to aquiesce in his master's brutal plan – for a price – holding the audience in continuous suspense. He binds the boy with a cord so tightly as to cause him pain – stuffing an old rag in his mouth so that he can neither speak nor sneeze, and thrusts him in a foul black bag. Grim's wife displays no more matronly qualities, throwing the lad to the ground so hard that he cracks his head against a stone (ll.567–69). They only relent when, stripping the lad of his clothes prior to drowning him, they recognize about his person unmistakable signs of royal birth: a bright aura emanating from his lips and a strange birthmark on his shoulder,[14] which results in their instant transference of allegiance. Grim breaks into tears, (a convention of acknowledged emotion characteristically revealed in romance), and prophesies that the prince will come to rule all Denmark and England, and take vengeance on the usurper. Disarmingly, however, the boy merely returns that he has been half-strangled by the gag, and is hungry. The good woman now brings him a square meal: *bred and chese, butere and milk, pastees and flaunes* . . . 'I know', says the poet, 'he ate a loaf or more!' (ll.643f). Such down-to-earth material references recur throughout the poem, as an index of the hero's advancing fortunes.

Grim might recognize that attachment to popular kingship rather than feudal lordship could better serve his personal advancement, but nevertheless attempts to run with both hare and hounds, declaring falsely that he has done the deed (the boy *eteth he nevre more bred*, l.672), and claiming the reward of his freedom for something he has not in fact done. But there is no honour among thieves, and Grim is pushing his luck. With an arrogant disdain *de haute en bas* that must have been all too familiar to the socially aspirant citizen, Godard reneges on his bargain and dismisses the serf:

> Godard stod, and lokede on him
> þoruh-like, with eyne grim;
> and seyde, 'Wiltu nou ben erl?
> Go hom swiþe, fule drit-cherl!'   (ll.679–82)

[Godard stood and looked at him searchingly with stern eyes, and said: 'Do you want to be an earl now? Get off home quickly, you filthy, dirty peasant!']

The earl even threatens to denounce his accomplice if he causes trouble: 'It wouldn't take much for me to send you to the gallows – for you've done a wicked deed' (ll.686–88). Despite Grim's ambiguous position – the double-dealer actually claiming to have done murder, even if he has not – Godard's outrageous social and moral stance serves both to engage our sympathies for Grim as the genuine underdog, and to advance the plot, for at this point, recognizing that there is only a bleak future in Denmark, Grim decides to take his family, which now includes Havelok, to England, where Goldbrow lies imprisoned.

In England, by dint of hard work, Grim is eventually established as a fishmonger. Meanwhile, with a wealth of sympathetic domestic detail, the career of the growing Havelok is pursued. He displays an innate good breeding rather than chivalric nobility. At the age of twelve, a sense of honour compels him to leave home because he feels a burden to his foster-family: 'I'm not a kid any more; I'm eating more than Grim and his five children put together' (ll.793–94). He determines to earn his living: 'Work's nothing to be ashamed of' (ll.798–99). But unemployment is rife. Whereas the conventional romance hero may frequently masquerade as a beggar, Havelok is genuinely starving, reinforcing the rags-to-riches self-congratulatory mythos of the self-made man throughout the ages: 'Hard work never did me any harm!' His aggressive competitiveness, if distasteful to modern sensibilities, is familiar enough in the context of, for example, nineteenth-century immigrant labour in the United States. When the Earl's cook calls for labourers, Havelok repeatedly shoves others aside or into the mud in order to be first in the queue (ll.868f, 888f); and being employed, pursues advancement with thrusting ambition. An exemplary employee, he displays a positively Stakhanovite energy and enthusiasm for his tasks, sparing 'neither toes nor heels' (l.898), doing more than is expected of him, and asking no other wages than enough to eat (ll.909ff), but all the time continuing to display the qualities of the ideal prince: modesty, generosity, and a ready smile. Popular with all, especially children (ll.945–58), he soon becomes a favourite of the cook, who clothes and feeds him well.

The *Havelok*-author depicts the workaday world with a frank realism rare in romance. Apparently authentic details of market-place and kitchen serve to create a credible and relevant environment in which to explore the interior landscape of the rising bourgeoisie, whose adventures are necessarily closer to real life than the dragons of either Beowulf or Tristrem (see above, pp. 59f, below, pp. 207–8), and require a validating code of sentiment and conduct distinct from that of the merely chivalrous. The noble Horn, although completely destitute, is apparently supplied with a courtly education and never has to earn his living, while Prince

Florentyn, when similarly *déclassé*, seems instinctively to display knightly tastes and an aristocrat's aversion to vulgar trade.[15] Havelok, however, will engage not in the tournament of chivalric romance, but the humbler English fairground sports of wrestling and casting the stone, at which he excels, defeating the barons' champions with ease.

Thus it is that Havelok comes to the attention of Godrich, who happens to have summoned a parliament at Lincoln; and the two strands of the narrative concerning hero and heroine are drawn together. Assuming Havelok to be no more than he seems: *sum cherles sone*, a mere *þral* (ll. 1091–97), Godrich determines to have him married to Goldbrow – thus degrading her status and putting paid to her claim to the throne – humorously declaring that in doing so he is simply fulfilling his oath to have her married to the highest in the land, for after all, doesn't the physically tall Havelok literally stand head and shoulders above anyone present? (ll. 1080–81). But as the audience is of course aware, there is a further level of irony operating. The joke is in fact on Godrich, and evil is thwarted by good, for in the world of romance accidents simply do not happen. With a positively Gilbertian serendipity, Godrich imagines himself to be placing the heroine's claim right out of court by an enforced degradation, whereas in reality he is doing the very reverse, acting unwittingly in his own worst interest. Evil is intended, but the highest good results – only eventually however, for we are still at an early point in the frog-prince play. There is no question of love at first sight; societal rather than sexual interests are paramount. The princess is genuinely distressed at the prospect of a humiliating *mésalliance*. Havelok for his part is no less dismayed. He responds to Godrich's suggestion like the *petit bourgeois* he is, instinctively deferring marital involvement to material establishment: 'What do I want with a wife!'; he cannot feed her, clothe her, or even provide her with shoes; he has neither house nor household goods; even the clothes he stands in belong to the cook, whose assistant he is! (ll. 1137–46). He consents only after beatings and threats to hang him. Fearing Godrich's continuing hatred, the couple flee, eventually coming to Denmark where, after a series of adventures, Havelok is recognized and restored to the throne – subsequently returning to England to oust the usurper and usher in a new golden age of peace and prosperity, as all the named figures live happily ever after.

The tale ends as symmetrically as it began – the two traitors receiving their just, but differentiated, deserts: their hideous deaths described in detail. Neither are allowed the narrative justification of death in battle. Godard is flayed alive (ll. 2488ff) and Godrich by popular demand burned at the stake in Lincoln town (ll. 2820ff). But despite the satisfaction expressed by author and princess, this is not the gratuitous vengeance we might have expected in the *Brut*, but due punishment imposed through the formal process of law – for which the propertied citizenry were always insistent. As the wheel of fortune turns, and even before the two noblemen fall to degrading ignominy, both can be termed 'thrall' and 'filthy churl' (ll.1408, 2533). Thus the moral insight of *Maldon* is writ large: true nobility of character is not a matter of mere rank, and, conversely, even the highest social rank cannot of itself ensure moral superiority.

Havelok's story reflects the social mobility which drew so many ambitious apprentices to the twelfth-century towns, *ouvert aux talents*. His career plots the natural, if enhanced, model of social advancement, progressively rising in turn from pauper to porter and kitchen assistant, and then when married, appearing successively as merchant, knight, and prince – rising from the lowest to the highest in the land – the fulfilled fantasy of the self-made man. Havelok's rise is progressively indexed in terms of the food he eats: at first thinking himself lucky to get bread and cheese, but gradually dining better on: 'crane, swan, venison, salmon, lamprey and good sturgeon', feasted with imaginative anticipation on delicacies 'fit for a king or emperor' (ll.1724–29; cf. 975–78).[16]

The excitement mounts to a pantomimic finale. The beggar-prince has come into his own, and in a sustained wish-fulfilment of the social aspirant, all the *dramatis personae* are given rewards and may be presumed to live happily ever after. Old friends are not forgotten. In a series of improbable social transformations, the fishmonger's sons – homely lads with plain names straight from Hereward's band of outlaws: Roberd the Rede, William Wendut, and Huwe Raven – all more accustomed to wield staves than the knightly sword, are first dubbed knights then made barons – bourgeois sentiment suggesting that their true qualities prove them natural gentlemen. The fishmonger's daughters meanwhile make good marriages: one to the Earl of Chester (who for his part raises no objection to such a *mésalliance*), the other to Havelok's former employer the cook, now made Earl of Cornwall. All live long and produce fine families. Havelok and Goldbrow reign happily for sixty years, producing fifteen offspring, 'whereof the sons were all kings, and the daughters all queens' (ll.2980–82).

The stable marriage is, of course, quintessentially a bourgeois desideratum – an index of social and personal responsibility and security of inheritance. The relationship between Havelok and Goldbrow is presented in terms of social contract rather than amorous connection, passion playing no part. Goldbrow, more concerned at the likelihood of social degradation, does not instantly recognize Havelok's virtues, either physical or moral; while for his part, Havelok is reluctant to marry, both out of material considerations, and because he is no ladies' man (ll.995–98). Once married however, his affection and concern for Goldbrow is undoubted (ll.1189–93, 1668–73); and once together, they stay together. Suffering no stress of separation, Goldbrow is constantly at

Havelok's side, even in exile, to offer sound social and political advice: she is the good woman that reputedly stands behind every successful man. The dual emphasis on hero and heroine, while necessary to the *Havelok*-author's narrative symmetry, merely reflects the increasing emphasis on the role of women in twelfth-century society at large (see above, pp. 17–19). Earlier English authors had not disregarded female existence,[17] but a heroine figure like Judith or Elene tends to stand as a solitary protagonist rather than form part of a cohesive pairing. Relationships between the sexes were either treated in merely socio-economic terms, with the woman, like the queens of *Beowulf*, filling a specifically subordinate peripheral role, or in terms of a morally suspect sexual allure that causes men's downfall; (it is not insignificant that Laȝamon's Rowenna carries her golden phial of poison *bi-neoðen hire titten*, l.7476). Now, emerging *pari passu* the development of courtly love, we will find a narrative model with a dual focus in which hero and heroine play matching, if differentiated, narrative roles, in an articulated whole.

If the *Havelok*-author chose to present his tale in terms of bourgeois values and concerns, this does not mean that the thirteenth-century audience for vernacular fiction was not attracted by the materials and mores of courtly society, even if these are rarely explored with the degree of reflective introspection found in those who, like Hugh de Roteland, found patronage in the Angevin courts.[18] The story of Tristan and Iseult, one of the most popular and persistent of all European love-stories, offers a case in point. Like the Arthurian figures who were destined soon to oust native heroes in the English imagination, distilling racial pride in a new nationality, the Tristan story derived ultimately from the Celtic flux of interior Britain. The figure of what was probably an originally Pictish hero seems to have been brought together in Wales with the half-legendary King Mark of Cornwall, and there attached to an originally Irish story-pattern of a triangular love-relationship – and then finally supplemented with Breton materials.[19] Probably several versions were current in twelfth- and thirteenth-century court circles, but most notably perhaps an Anglo-Norman version apparently composed by a certain Thomas of Britain for the court of Henry II and Eleanor of Aquitaine, some time in the second half of the twelfth century.[20] The story proved exceptionally popular, esteemed, according to one near-contemporary, 'over all that is or was'.[21] Such high esteem is scarcely surprising, for the story was one which explored a theme of considerable contemporary concern: the complex social and moral problem of free love and the relationship between chivalric and passionate love, often difficult to distinguish in real-life situations. There would be an avid audience at all levels for a story which explored what might happen when 'true love' enters 'the real world'; but most especially in a society which had developed a subtle social code of manners to accommodate extra-marital *affaires.*[22] Counterpointing the traditional Church view of sexual love as a fundamentally degrading experience, chivalric idealism had evolved a code in which the love of a lady could be regarded as essentially inspirational and socially enhancing. It sponsored the possibility of a fundamentally virtuous and ennobling love, which was best directed towards an unattainable lady – a thorough programme for which was outlined in extraordinary detail by Andreas Capellanus (see above, pp. 18–19). The Tristan story places an imagined relationship in this context, and tests the framework of the code to the point where it breaks down, since in reality real women are not unapproachable and the 'unattainable' love may well be realized, resulting in a conflict between the self-seeking cult of love and a self-sacrificial duty to society. It approximates a new ethic in which illicit relationships need not have evil consequences, or may simply ignore those that incidentally arise, although in reality chivalric and passionate love prove incompatible.

The Tristan story was sufficiently well known to be alluded to with confidence either verbally or visually. Marie de France, for example, will draw on the story in her *Lay of the Honeysuckle (Chevrefoil),*[23] while it is the most popular secular narrative theme in the realm of medieval decorative arts, appropriately embellishing such costly items as embroidered bed-hangings, comb- and mirror-cases, and less appropriately perhaps, even finding a place in ecclesiastical contexts: hidden in carved misericords at Chester or Lincoln, or more openly in a complete narrative sequence of decorative tiling at Chertsey Abbey.[24]

The early Middle English *Sir Tristrem* has all the appearance of being addressed to an audience to whom the story was already very familiar. The author plays not only with narrative conventions in general, but with narrative details – deeply conscious of the potential humour of the situation and the ironies present in individual events. The plot is compressed and allusive rather than fully expounded; some incidents, like Brengwain's *þouȝt* that she will take Ysoude's place on her wedding night to conceal her mistress's loss of virginity, or the sudden appearance of a dwarf, are not adequately explained at a primary narrative level. The poet's choice of stanzaic form merely compounds this; avoiding continuous logical narrative and promoting a laconic and occasionally enigmatic mode, it lends itself to ballad-like irony and allusion.[25]

The audience addressed (*listneþ lordinges dere*, l.402) although clearly not Thomas's French-speaking *seigneurs*, are prepared to be flattered by an authorial air of deference quite different from the *Havelok*-poet's assumption of equality. His tale has a distinctly courtly setting; despite its popular stanzaic form, its French vocabulary signals an aristocratic tone. The story is the fashionable one currently being 'told about town' by a certain Thomas (ll.10, 412), a tale of *aventour* (l.11) set in the context of castle society, of knights and maidens and tournaments. We will hear of honour and love, *bonair* and *belamye* (ll.311, 530). A far cry from Havelok's market-place and kitchen, the world of *Sir Tristrem* is a leisured society of dalliance, where we might well expect to meet love-potions, enchanted rings, or dragons slain by brave knights. The conflicts depicted are not the massed slaughters of Laȝamon but the single combat of knight-errant and champion (ll.191–210). High passions will be portrayed (l.272). The courtesy of high society is assumed (an etiquette of polite dining-table conversation and washed hands, l.541; the service of porters and ushers is taken for granted). Unlike *Havelok*, the *Tristrem*-author can afford to ignore the descriptive potential of a royal wedding-feast (ll.1706–07). The hero is a well-educated young gentleman, accomplished in all the arts of Angevin high society. His story cannot of itself be one of material or personal advancement, nor depict a process of maturation in any normal sense. Instead it will explore the complexity of human relationships.

Although the social setting of *Sir Tristrem* is precise enough, its geographical and temporal location is only the vaguest. The scene is set not in Grimsby or Lincoln, but merely England, Ireland or 'Ermonie' (?Armenia). The poet opens his story with a 'once upon a time' formula commenting that, as we all know, the world is not now what once it was. Just as the green of 'this lovely summer's day' will pass into the greyness of winter:

> Þe gode ben al oway
> þat our elders have bene.   (ll.18–19)

[The great men who were our predecessors have all gone.]

Like Arthur, Tristrem is conceived out of passion and out of wedlock. During an interval in his war with Duke Morgan, Roland the Lord of Ermonie visits the court of King Mark in England, where his prowess in the tournament-field wins the heart of Mark's sister, the Princess Blancheflour, who openly expresses her feelings in the language of *fin' amor*:

> 'Bot ȝive it be þurch ginne,
> a selly man is he;
> þurch min hert wiþ inne
> ywounded haþ he me
> so sone:
> of bale bot he me blinne,
> mine liif days ben al done.'   (ll.82–88)

['Unless it was done by enchantment, he is a remarkable man; he has instantly wounded me through the heart inside me: unless he saves me from the calamity the days of my life are at an end.']

When Roland is badly wounded in the field, Blancheflour immediately rushes to comfort him as best she may – and promptly (it is baldly stated) conceives. The child that results will be known as '*Tristrem þe trewe*' (ll.107–10). This collocation recurs repeatedly thereafter whenever the name Tristrem is mentioned – often in the most ironic circumstances, for while Tristrem may prove a true lover perhaps, he will prove consistently false in every other respect. There exists throughout the poem a constant counterpoint of truth and falsehood, appearance and reality (*treupe* and *tresoun*): the potential ambiguity present in life-situations, which was to remain a persistent theme of English romance narrative.[26] Learning that the truce with Morgan is broken, Roland returns to the defence of his country, taking the princess whom in due course he marries. Despite prodigies of valour, Roland is betrayed and slain, the shock of which induces Tristrem's birth, and Blancheflour's death. The faithful noble-man to whom the child is entrusted, fearing the malice of Duke Morgan, passes the child off as his own under the name Tramtrist (*þo tram bifor þe trist*, l.253), scarcely a disguise but a significant inversion of the truth, foreshadowing much that is to come. From birth, it seems, the hero is forced to adopt stratagems of deception rather than concealment that will form a recurrent theme to the end of the poem, and the end of his life.

After a variety of misadventures Tristrem comes by chance to England where his skill in aristocratic pastimes secures him a place in the affections of King Mark, which is merely confirmed by the eventual recognition of their uncle–nephew relationship. A handsome and proficient knight, his superiority will be displayed in effortlessly vanquishing champions, giants, and dragons in single combat. Interestingly, however, the conventional piety of *Havelok* is missing; none of the characters involved refer to any kind of religious framework for their actions, which are socially autonomous. Knighted by Mark, Tristrem returns to Ermonie to confront the usurper Morgan in his hall, at first dissembling with true but untrue words:

'As y þe love and an
and þou hast served to me!'   (ll.839–40)

['As I love and cherish you, and you have served me!']

but then demanding amends for a slain father, and his inheritance, Ermonie. In turn Morgan denounces Tristrem's mother as a covert whore, and him as a traitor, and (since they happen to be at table) gives Tristrem a bloody nose with a bread roll (ll.861–71)! Needless to say, Tristrem wins back his kingdom, which he entrusts to his faithful foster-father as regent, and returns to England.

The lengthy prologue over and the theme of dissemblance firmly established, the scene returns to Mark's court where the body of the story will be enacted. Finding his uncle's kingdom the victim of Irish terrorism, Tristrem undertakes to defend its freedom by single judicial combat with the Irish champion Moraunt. At this point the author cannot for once restrain personal comment: *God help Tristrem þe kniȝt; he fauȝt for Ingland!* (ll. 1033–34). Although badly wounded himself, Tristrem slays Moraunt – a fragment of his sword lodging in the Irishman's brain. As the saviour of the kingdom, Tristrem is assured an even greater place in Mark's affections, and is now appointed Mark's heir. Later, seeking to be cured of a wound and finding himself in Ireland, he again dissembles, adopting the name Tramtris and the guise of a merchant, becoming the tutor of Princess Ysoude, instructing her in music and games, since, ambiguously:

> In Yrlond nas no kniȝt
> wiþ Ysoude durst play.    (ll. 1264–65)

[There was no knight in Ireland dared play games with Ysoude.]

Homesick, not for Ermonie but England, *Tramtris þe trewe* (l. 1275) returns home, where chameleon-like, *Now hat he Tristrem trewe* (l. 1303).

Mark reaffirms that Tristrem shall become his heir to the throne, if he will consent to undertake the journey to Ireland to conduct the beautiful Princess Ysoude to England as Mark's wife. In the 'standard' received version Mark's attention had been drawn to Ysoude's existence by one of her hairs being dropped by a passing swallow – an improbable detail which the contemporary German author Gottfried described as patently absurd.[27] It is characteristic of the English author's playful allusion to a known story-line that, when Tristrem is asked to fetch Ysoude, he remarks simply, but apparently apropos of nothing: 'No hassle; I heard a swallow sing!' (ll. 1365–66).

Tristrem's party arrives in Ireland to find the country terrorized by a dragon. This serves to provide an additional complexity in the possible relationship between hero and heroine. The King of Ireland has promised the hand of Ysoude to whomever slays the dragon. Tristrem suggests the adventure to his accompanying knights, potentially losing her; but when they decline, himself undertakes the adventure, potentially winning her. Thus we have a potentially happy ending: brave knight marries fair princess. But the audience, knowing the story, must recognize that this is a mere feint at the convention. Having slain the dragon, Tristrem tears out its tongue but irrationally feels the need to conceal it: an unnecessary act at any primary level, but allowing for the intervention of a false claimant (a familiar romance figure), and providing for an element of broad humour. Instead of concealing it in his bosom, as in for example Gottfried's version of the story, he chooses to stuff it down his tights –

rather grotesquely, and certainly ironically since the envenomed tongue poisons him there!

> When Tristrem speke may,
> þis tale he bi gan
> and redyli gan to say
> hou he þe dragon wan:
> 'Þe tong y bar oway,
> þus venimed he me þan.'
> Þai loke.
> Þe quen þat michel can
> out of his hose it toke.    (ll. 1521–29)

[When Tristrem could speak, he embarked on this tale and readily described how he beat the dragon: 'I carried off the tongue, whereupon it poisoned me.' They looked. The queen, who knew a lot, took it out of his tights.]

Once more wounded, once more claiming to be the merchant Tramtris, the hero remains curiously unrecognized, until Ysoude, admiring his sword, matches a notch with the fragment taken from her uncle Moraunt's brain and immediately identifies him. Seizing the sword, Ysoude rushes instantly to slay the 'traitor . . . this thief' (ll. 1577, 1584). The scene is at once humorous and titillating: the hero caught naked in the bath confronted by an angry, armed, and beautiful girl. But all the while Tristrem smiles (l. 1596) and James Bond-like smooth-talks his way out of the situation; he, and the audience, know that this is not the way romance heroes end their lives. Tristrem eventually persuades the court of his own good intentions, and that Mark intends to make Ysoude Queen of England. So the contract is undertaken.

Ysoude's mother has prepared a love-potion for Mark and Ysoude to be drunk on their wedding-night since the social pact might clearly benefit from some chemical confirmation, but during the voyage back to England it is inadvertently and unwittingly drunk by Ysoude and Tristrem. This at once triggers the tragi-comedy of the main plot. Their deception of Mark, although excusable within the fiction since the couple are subject to enchantment, remains a socially and politically unpardonable betrayal of husband, uncle, and feudal overlord. Nevertheless the poet cannot avoid adding a material gloss, setting the incident in a humorous perspective. He introduces the detail of their dog Hodain licking out the drugged cup, undercutting the lovers' *grande passion* in a thoroughly English way by equating canine with human sentiment and concluding the stanza which describes how the lovers spent the remainder of the voyage, night and day in passionate 'play', with the one-line comment that the dog did too! (ll. 1684–94).

The story of Tristrem and Ysoude is one of a love which, because it is unlawful, must end in tears, if not tragedy. The story unfolds the lovers' mounting ecstasy and mounting suffering, those involved falling by turns from shame to social degradation, physical separation, and bitter-sweet recrimination, frustration, and consequent psychological distortion resolved only by death. Although Tristrem usurps his uncle's bed rather than his throne, his love is fundamentally anarchic, at odds with the established institutions of both Church and State, a necessary threat to the social harmony of the kingdom. Those who question the lovers' actions, albeit unsympathetic (for everyone loves a lover – or ought to!), are acting not merely in accordance with conventional religious disapprobation, but out of proper feudal loyalty and concern for the security of the State and good order of the kingdom. Tristrem's love, however true, for his attractive young aunt, can result in neither legal offspring nor social commendation. Instead of the social rewards of involvement in a fashionable game of *fin' amor*, Tristrem's love brings him only disgrace and exile. Oblivious of all social and moral expectations, the tyranny of their obsession leads them to commit one dishonourable act after another. It is no ordinary love that requires them to stoop to personal and political treachery, bringing Ysoude to plot the murder of her faithful companion, and both into treason against their sovereign and perjury before God. Yet the joker in the pack is the fact that the situation is not of their making, for they are enchanted; they are subject to a magic potion – i.e. passionate love – which abnegates all the rules, or would if it could. Love-sickness was understood to be a genuine illness, akin to madness in that it distorted the normal perception of the world,[28] (an idea reflected, albeit palely, in the distinction we might make between 'to love' and 'to be *in* love'). Are we then justified in concluding that the fault lies not in them but elsewhere? Those who fall in love might lack control of, but not therefore responsibility for, their actions. If the couple's actions are inevitable, so is the tragic consequence. Real life does not allow for the existence of love-potions; nor, by implication, does it make allowance for passionate love.

The couple's deception soon begins to have wretched consequences, as Tristrem drops into the role of languishing lover, and Ysoude that of *belle dame sans merci*:

> Þai wende have joie anouȝ,
> certes, it nas nouȝt so.
> Her wening was al wouȝ
> untroweand til hem to;
> aiþer in langour drouȝ,
> and token rede to go;
> and seþþen Ysoude louȝ
> when Tristrem was in wo.    (ll. 1728–35)

[They expected to have bliss in abundance, but it certainly was not so. Their expectation was quite wrong, playing false to them both; each of them resolved to go on, languishing in sorrow; and then Ysoude laughed when Tristrem was distressed.]

Suspicious that her maid Brengwain may reveal the truth ('*Tristrem and y boape bep schent for our playing*', ll.1743–44), Ysoude treacherously arranges to have her killed until the faithful maid lies verbally as well as physically, exclaiming that she had merely provided her mistress with a clean smock for her wedding-night, since her own was soiled – a familiar half-truth which prompts Ysoude to an impetuous volte-face exclaiming: 'Where is that true maiden!' (l.1793). The poet characteristically uses a stanza end to make a telling point. Here Ysoude's words are diagnostic of the levels of ambiguity present in the situation. Brengwain is certainly no longer a 'maiden' of course; but the real ambiguity lies in her 'truth': she may be false to the facts, but loyal to the lovers, a true and faithful servant. The terms truth and falsehood are turned on their heads. The truth is a societal norm which the lovers merely invert. So it is that the lying Brengwain is a 'true girl', and the loyal Meriadok 'false'. Ultimately Tristrem's disordered mind can even imagine King Mark to be guilty of 'treason' in going to his wife (ll.2689–90).

The theme of the interdependence of truth and falsehood in the perceived situation is effectively illustrated in the figure of Meriadok. Introduced as a man Tristrem always trusted (ll.1926–27), his ultimate loyalty is, as it should be, to the king, to whom he quite properly reveals his suspicions as to the couple's treachery. Yet spying and telling tales is at best distasteful; and since our sympathies now lie, albeit ambiguously, with the lovers, treacherous. In the end the priggish, if socially correct, Meriadok serves only to humiliate the king further. Such deceit proves infectious, as ruse is succeeded by counter-ruse. Eventually Mark is himself persuaded to dissemble, pretending to leave on a pilgrimage in order to spy in secret on the lovers. In what is perhaps the best-known scene of the whole story, he is even induced to climb a tree in order to witness a woodland tryst beneath: an undignified, shameful act of voyeurism (ll.2047ff). In a final act of degradation we are offered the grotesque sight of the king running after a dwarf in an attempt to catch the lovers *in flagrante delicto* – but too late, for Tristrem has fled (l.2586). Meriadok's best intentions have reduced his sovereign from an open-hearted and generous man whose greatest satisfactions lie in the knightly exploits of his nephew and the love of his beautiful young wife, to a cuckolded pantomime buffoon. Small wonder that when Ysoude's ultimate gamble, risking the terrible ordeal of hot iron, finally convinces Mark as to her chastity, the stanza concludes:

Meriadok held þai
for fole in his falshede.    (ll. 2287–88)

[They considered Meriadok a fool for his treachery.]

The world is now topsy-turvy indeed.

The lovers experience genuine misery at separation; Ysoude is so lovesick she wants to kill herself (l. 2029); on hearing Tristrem sing a love-song, she is moved to such 'love-longing' that her heart well-nigh breaks in two (ll. 1862–63). Their passion leads them into squalid subterfuges scarcely commensurate with the romantic ideal; during stolen, nocturnal assignations Tristrem removes a plank in the wall of Ysoude's bower to gain entry and, since it is snowing, wears sieves on his feet to disguise his footprints between bower and hall (ll. 1930ff). As we know, Tristrem is already adept in the art of disguise, but few romance heroes would willingly stoop to don the disguise of a leper in order just to come by the walls where his mistress lies (ll. 3173–77); the contemporary identification of leprosy with venereal disease[29] making it an ironically appropriate form of self-abasement in the circumstances. Or worse still perhaps, what romance lover could bring himself, in the guise of a beggar, deliberately to dishonour his mistress the queen by uncovering her sexual parts, albeit in order to secure their mutual ends:

And on þe quen fel he
next her naked side,
þat mani man miȝt y se
san schewe.
Her queynt aboven hir kne
naked þe kniȝtes knewe.    (ll. 2250–55)

[And he tumbled on to the queen next to her naked flank, so that many a man could see quite easily. The knights realized that, beyond her knees, her cunt was naked.]

The situation is explored in continuous terms of half-truths, which are intended to dissipate suspicion, and for the most part succeed in doing so. The circumstantial lie or *double entendre* is invariably emphatically located at a stanza-end. At Mark's pretended absence, Ysoude demands Tristrem as a guardian: 'I love him the more, because he is your kinsman' (ll. 1978–80). Again, when confronted with outright accusation, she may brazen it out: 'At heart I never loved any man except him who took my virginity' (ll. 2133–34). Or again accused shortly after being carried by Tristrem in the guise of a beggar, she swears that:

'Bot on to schip me bare, –
þe kniʒtes seiʒe wele þan –
what so his wille ware,
ferli neiʒe he wan,
soþe þing;
so neiʒe com never man
bot mi lord þe king!'    (ll. 2271–77)

['Except for the man who carried me on board ship – the knights witnessed that – whatever he may have wanted, he got remarkably near the very thing; no man has ever come nearer except for my lord the king.']

She speaks of course more like a bawdy fishwife than an avowedly chaste queen. But the couple have become outrageously daring in their success, and the uxorious King Mark once more relents.

Superficially humorous they may be, but in for example *Havelok* or the *Brut* such half-truths are always the signs of true villainy. The theme is one of disguise and deceit, lies and treachery – albeit in the name of love. Without apologia or even reflective circumstances which might make it emotionally and philosophically tenable, the bare facts of courtly love become mere adultery. The deception sometimes turns in on itself. When Brengwain advises Ysoude to pretend hatred for Tristrem, this also is a half-truth, since she genuinely hates the scandal surrounding their names (ll. 2003–13). The risks the lovers run are truly appalling. The imminent danger that 'sweet' Ysoude's skin may be mutilated by red-hot iron is only the very least of several dreadful possibilities (ll. 2278–85).

The love of Tristrem and Ysoude is transcendent, however. Banished for a period to the forest, in what ought to have been reduced circumstances, they find an idyllic setting. Living in a grotto made by giants in olden days, *þer hadde þai joie ynouʒ* (ll. 2479–81), love supplying all their needs; they may have had no wine or old ale, but they had all they wanted: their fill of each other (ll. 2491–97). Unlike the Wanderer or Seafarer, still less Cain or Grendel, exile from society causes them no distress – rather the reverse. Tristrem may have lost his *chevalrie* and Ysoude her queenly status, but their love may be openly expressed, freedom from societal constraint transforming the wilderness into an Arcadian landscape. At one with Nature, they need no deception to survive. Their love transforms even the weather; in affective perception the winters are warm and the summers cool (ll. 2487–88). These circumstances affect even external perception. While hunting, Mark finds the couple asleep with a naked sword lying on the ground between them – no ruse, but mere chance. Being a true romantic, Mark chooses to believe that the sword symbolizes something other than it is – a sign of genuine chastity (ll. 2545–52) – and the couple are once more restored to favour, and to court, where they continue to play out their deception. The scene encapsulates the powerful, if ambiguous nature of courtly love. Ironically it is Mark who is the true proponent of courtly love (which after all presupposes the existence of an accommodating husband), the true idealist who interprets the scene as it could ideally be. And yet as we, and the lovers, know, he is mistaken, for it is necessarily a flawed picture. Mark's unwillingness to recognize the facts is understandable at a human level. His constant love for both wife and nephew is nothing but commendable. But his naïvety constantly entraps him in postures which are at best undignified and at worst humiliating.

Any criticism of the situation is merely implied. Unlike the Anglo-Norman Beroul, whose sympathy for the lovers is made clear, the English author stands on the side-lines. There is neither direct authorial statement of values, nor yet, unlike *Havelok*, any convincing indication that the poet's sympathies lie with any of the characters involved in his story. Indeed, in contrast with *Havelok*, any intrusion of the authorial voice is minimal, confined to such minstrel formulas as: 'Listen now, if you will' (e.g. ll.199, 1429, 2573–74). By focusing attention less on the thoughts and feelings of the lovers than on their social setting, our interest lies largely in how the situation is perceived by King Mark's court. The poet does not trace the progress of Tristrem and Ysoude's *affaire* as such, but rather its reception by a society that remains unconvinced of the young couple's guilt. Courtly love is dependent upon the possibility of equivocation. Only those who are openly hostile to the lovers, the unsympathetic figures of Meriadok and the dwarf, recognize the truth for what it is. Mark, who represents both deceived husband and betrayed sovereign, is potentially both plaintiff and judge. Necessarily, however, he demands proof of physical contact, diagnosable in legal and feudal terms, rather than merely the alienation of affection. Although it is invariably through Mark's eyes that the lovers are witnessed at the critical moments, he constantly fails to analyse the most compromising of scenes. The relationship between illusion and reality has legal and psychological as well as artistic implications.

When finally surprised *in flagrante delicto*, Tristrem flees for his life. Ironically it is now the court who, having cried wolf so many times, persuade Mark that contrary to appearances, he must be mistaken in what he saw (ll.2610–11), and Ysoude remains at court. Tristrem's flight takes him to Britanny. There the theme of self-deception will be carried to extreme, even exotic lengths, by way of the further complication of Tristrem's marriage to Ysoude of the White Hands. This development serves not merely to delay the denouement of the plot and add to its symmetry, but allows an additional exploration of Tristrem's dilemma in the light of the courtly code. Tristrem attempts to escape his sexual frustration and forgo his true, i.e. passionate, love for Ysoude – only to marry her mirror-image, the Breton princess Ysoude of the White Hands, whom he seeks out specifically because of her name (ll. 2672–73). The Breton Ysoude overhearing a love-song addressed merely to 'Ysoude' naturally assumes that it is addressed to her – emphasizing the relationship between appearance and reality (ll. 2654–57). It is this act of marriage, rather than his former behaviour towards Mark, which Tristrem now in himself recognizes as 'treasonable' (ll. 2694–95). Tristrem proves ironically impotent in this courtly, available but artificial relationship, and falls to psychological disorder: fantasizing in respect of his true but now genuinely unapproachable love. In a grotesque exaggeration of self-delusion, being as much in love with the image as the reality, he constructs a mysterious chapel of love containing full-size lifelike statues of all the characters in his story – a blasphemous parody of contemporary images of saints – a shrine to the cult of sexual love, like that the monks of Frithelstock were to erect to Diana in the forests of Devon.[30] The statue of Brengwain proves so lifelike that a visiting knight instantly falls in love – or lust – and wishes to lie with her – a masturbatory *Playboy*-like fantasy (ll. 2839f, 2971ff),[31] expressed in the courtly convention of losing one's heart to an image 'lovely beneath her shift' (*luffsum under line*, l. 2816).

More so than most Middle English romances, the plot of *Sir Tristrem* progresses by way of an extraordinary number of episodes: a sequence of separations and reunions, of journeys to and from court, to and from England. The poet employs a narrative mode (perhaps developed in, and certainly well suited to, romances of knight-errantry) in which one incident after another in turn serves as, and in turn requires, a sequel. Like much contemporary art – and most pertinently the narrative sequence of floor-tiles from Chertsey Abbey depicting the Tristrem story[32] – it is a mode of composition that is controlled but infinitely extensible: a pattern in which separate units cohere, but without organic subordination.[33] Nevertheless, like *Havelok*, the story is constantly pulled in the direction of narrative symmetry – a characteristic of romance convention. The three giants whom Tristrem slays on different occasions in different countries, are specifically said to be related (l. 2725). He marries another Ysoude, and meets his death going to the aid of another Tristrem – an *alter ego*. Wounded three times, he is twice healed by Ysoude, but the third time is deceived of such help. Thus the poem ends as it had begun, with passion and death; and of course with deception, for although the final page of the manuscript is missing, we may assume that, as in the 'received version', the Breton Ysoude lies about the death of Tristrem's mistress Ysoude, and so causes his heart to break.

The Tristrem romance incorporates certain narrative motifs – especially those in which verbal or visual equivocation enables adulterous wives to avoid discovery – which seem to derive at one or another remove, ultimately from eastern sources. Most notable of these are the incident of the tryst beneath the tree, in which two lovers have recourse to an impromptu charade to convince the deluded husband of their innocence, and the motif embodied in the 'two Ysoudes', where a second wife resembles the first either in name or appearance, whom the man then neglects, with consequent mental anguish.[34] Another motif in which a young hero cast up on a foreign shore gains an entrée to the court and the love of a princess by display of physical and musical skill, seems to have drawn on the Byzantine romance of *Apollonius of Tyre*, which was translated into English in a relatively pristine form as early as the eleventh century.[35] The channels through which this 'matter of Araby' was transmitted to England are not difficult to visualize, whether direct from Byzantium or through Arab intermediaries in the Mediterranean lands. The numbers of English scholars to make fruitful contact with Arab culture is well documented. The Norman conquest of Saracen Sicily only six years after their conquest of Saxon England, and the whole history of the Crusades, enhanced direct contact with eastern culture. Presumably the western assimilation of Arabic story-materials proceeded *pari passu* the systematic transmission of Arab science and philosophy (see above, p. 25).[36]

The Crusades with their dogmatic cruelty introduced an ambivalent attitude towards eastern culture – the mysterious allure of the East undercut by a deep fear of the unknown – so that the image of the Arab world as purveyed by English writers is a curious mixture of imaginative misunderstanding and authentic detail. If Laȝamon will occasionally equate Saracens with Saxons (see above, p. 181), he is sufficiently knowledgeable to use certain remarkably accurate titles. For example, among the various eastern adherents of Mahoun confronted by Arthur is listed *on admirail* (i.e. emir) *of Babiloine* (l.13810), i.e. the Fatamid Commander of the Faithful in Cairo, to whom the power of the Baghdad caliphate had shifted in the tenth century. The Crusades offered firsthand experience of Arab society in its native lands, and the range of response to alien cultures, as always among colonial troops in the East, was inevitably wide. Both extremes were reflected in contemporary literature. At the lowest level, fostered by the Church, there was an implacable hatred of the Saracen which encouraged physical cruelty and intellectual bigotry. This vicious, propagandistic image of the feared Saracen as an enemy of Christendom whose legendary cruelty would provoke retaliation in kind, was portrayed in for example, the romances of *Beves of Hampton* or *Richard the Lionheart*,[37] where horrific details merely reflect historical barbarisms. The humour of caricature was one method of coping with the apprehension of a threat, real or imaginary. Fat young Saracen, well spiced, is described as a good substitute for pork (ll.3080f); Richard is said to eat Saracen heads 'all hot', and to force his prisoners to do the same (ll.3412f).

There were others, however, who would present the Levant in a far more sympathetic light: a land not only of squalor, disease, and famine, but of fairy-tale romance. Aristocratic Arab society caught the poetic imagination. In contrast with the melodramatic excess of the suspicious outsider's view represented by *Richard the Lionheart*, the author of *Floris and Blancheflour* objectively retails a genuine oriental romance as seen from the inside, presenting a sentimental picture in which the allure of the mysterious East, with all its artificial wonders, is given a credible domestic setting, and the Emir of Babylon is portrayed with humane tolerance and moderation. Retold in a dozen different languages (the thirteenth-century Middle English version apparently following a twelfth-century French intermediary[38]), the love-story of the childhood sweethearts Floris and Blancheflour became almost as popular as that of Tristrem and Ysoude.[39] One fourteenth-century writer describes a finely embroidered robe decorated with the stories of famous lovers in which Floris and Blancheflour appear on a par with Tristrem and Ysoude.[40] Yet the romance of Floris breathes a totally different sentiment from that of Tristrem. Lacking all bitterness and moral dilemma and, it has to be said, psychological realism, *Floris and Blancheflour* is altogether winsome both in plot and characterization. Unlike the story of adult love, tears are incidental and transient; all will end happily ever after in the best fairy-tale tradition.

The children, Floris, son of the Arab King of Spain, and Blancheflour, the daughter of a captive Christian slave-girl, are brought up together. Despite disparity of rank and religion, the two become passionately devoted to one another. 'Nothing so sweet as their love, neither liquorice nor chewing-gum!' (ll. E118–19). The author has a good ear for childhood imagery and for the repetitive, whining cadences of childish importunity. When the king decides to send his son to school:

> Florys answerd with wepyng
> as he stood byfore þe kyng;
> al wepyng seide he:
> 'Ne schal not Blancheflour lerne with me?
> Ne kan Y noȝt to scole goon
> without Blanchefloure', he seide þan.
> 'Ne can Y in no scole syng ne rede
> without Blancheflour', he seide.     (ll. E15–22)

[Floris answered by weeping as he stood in front of the king; weeping continually he said: 'Won't Blancheflour learn with me?' Then he said: 'I can't go to school without Blancheflour. I can't read or sing in any school without Blancheflour', he said.]

Fearing *mésalliance* if the childhood attachment should develop further, the parents determine on their separation. Whereas the king is quite prepared to have the girl cold-bloodedly killed (ll. E46, 140–41), his soft-hearted queen counsels less violent measures. Sending their son to visit his aunt, they sell Blancheflour to travelling merchants from Babylon (Cairo). Ironically the price they receive includes a precious cup engraved with a picture of the abduction of Helen of Troy (ll. E163–68). It is a cruel deception they play. Floris had been assured that Blancheflour would join him within a fortnight, and when she does not, returns only to be told that she has died in his absence – a lie in which the girl's mother colludes. He is shown a false tomb with Blancheflour's name on it: the epitaph a heartless play on the child's devotion:

> 'Here lyth swete Blanchefloure
> þat Florys lovyd *par amoure*.'   (ll. E217–18, 265–66)

[Here lies sweet Blancheflour, whom Floris loved passionately.]

The depth of their passion is not denied; it is readily acknowledged that one might die of heartbreak; the girl's mother tells him that 'she died of love for him' (l. E244), and in turn Floris is 'like to die for sorrow and love' (l. E260). For his part, the distraught child, unable to contemplate life without her, attempts suicide: it is only proper that just as they were born on the same day, so they should have met death together (ll. E277f). But even at the very height of this tragic passion, we are not allowed to forget that Floris is little more than a petulant child, confronted by indulgent parents:

> His knyf he braide out of his sheth;
> himself he wolde have doo to deth.
> And to hert he had it smeten,
> ne had his moder it underȝeten.
> Þen þe queene fel him uppon,
> and þe knyf fro him noom.
> She reft him of his lytel knyf,
> and savyd þere þe childes lyf.   (ll. E289–96)

(He pulled his knife out of its sheath; he wanted to kill himself. And he would have driven it into his heart and done himself to death, if his mother had not realized what was happening. Then the queen fell on him and took the knife away from him. She deprived him of his little knife, and thus saved the child's life.]

The queen pleads with the king. Of twelve offspring Floris is their sole surviving child: it were better he should mate with Blancheflour than die for her sake (ll. E299ff). The king shrewdly consents; Floris is told the truth and promptly sets out in search of Blancheflour, taking with him the cup with which to redeem his beloved. Eventually he learns from merchants in an inn that Blancheflour has been sold into the harem of the Emir of Babylon. He gains access to the tower where she is held by concealing himself in a basket of flowers. The lovers are discovered, but again their selfless display of love discountenances opposition and brings pardon and release. The theme is one of fairy-tale wish-fulfilment: demonstrating the power of innocent love to overcome all obstacles, and without recourse to magic potions or such-like devices.

Although there is no direct Arabic analogue to *Floris and Blancheflour*, the story is a patchwork of narrative motifs for which Eastern parallels may readily be found:[41] a boy and a girl with significantly linked names are brought up together and fall in love; a false tomb is built to persuade a lover that his favourite slave-girl is dead; a prince searching for his lost love learns of her whereabouts from merchants in an inn; a lover gains access to a harem hidden in a chest; young lovers surprised in a harem vie with each other to be slain first – but are saved; and many more.[42]

Both setting and sentiment seem to have intrigued the author. There was no question of adaptation to a western location or attributing more familiar western motivation to the characters, so that in consequence we are presented with a totally distinctive kind of story, avoiding many contemporary narrative clichés, and making a different kind of statement. The only accommodation to a western audience is that the slave-girl is now made a Christian, although somewhat improbably, since brought up in a Saracen context. Sublimely ignoring the brutal realities of dogmatic hostility, young love apparently bridges every gap; and at the conclusion the young couple are married in church with the emir's blessing (ll. E1064–65). The English author omits the French conclusion in which Floris, himself converted, violently imposes baptism on his father's kingdom, having those who object beheaded, burned, or flayed alive. Nevertheless both Floris (perhaps understandably, ll. E828–29), and his Saracen father (improbably) instinctively invoke the name of Christ: e.g. 'May Jesu free thee from thy sorrow' (l. E338). And there is a clearly perceived religious dimension to true love: Floris declares that it would be a great sin to deter him from his quest (l. E334); any man who might enter the emir's harem could wish no more of paradise (l. C254); as the couple are brought to bed Floris thanks 'God's sweet son that I am come to my love' (ll. C541–42); and Blancheflour wishes for no other heaven than to live in love with Floris (ll. C553–54). In concluding, the narrator prays that our love for God may prove as strong as the young sweethearts' for each other, and lead us in turn to heaven (ll. C822–24). Fundamental aspects of the story were readily assimilated, since in many respects the two cultures shared common ground. The structure of Saracen society could be interpreted as merely the eastern counterpart of feudal Christendom. The conventions of *fin' amor* were already well understood. As in *Sir*

*Tristrem*, the author employs an Anglo-Norman vocabulary of refined sentiment: *honour, amour*, and *anguisse, beauté* and *belami*; the lovesickness experienced by Floris at separation, his sleepless nights, loss of appetite, and wasted physical condition are all familiar from the Tristrem experience. But whereas the Tristrem story reflects the fundamental irony and paradox present in self-conscious programmatic love as presented by Andreas Capellanus, the story *Floris and Blancheflour* retails is witness to its more thoroughgoing Islamic counterpart, as represented by the eleventh-century Hispano-Arab treatise of Ibn Hazm,[43] who had himself fallen in love with a youthful playmate with whom he had been brought up. His is a more profoundly philosophical analysis of the relationship between physical and spiritual love in which sex is considered an unquestionably laudable gift of God.

The framing theme of *Floris and Blancheflour*: that of the loss and recovery of the beloved, is a familiar one. But it is presented as a tale of sentiment rather than exploit, a tale of idyllic *amour* rather than chivalric *aventour*.[44] True, the mechanism requires conventional obstacles in the path of true love: disparity of social status, unsympathetic parents, a socially superior rival, and, in the case of the emir, legal claimant, physical, geographical separation, or incarceration in an impregnable tower. But we are not led to believe that any of these will prove serious impediments. Floris's quest is scarcely combative in any sense; he encounters no dragons, giants, or hostility of any kind to hamper his path to reunion. There needs no display of knightly prowess to win his love. (A later French version which includes a scene of judicial combat in which Floris fights for Blancheflour as her champion, strikes a grotesquely virile note in view of the child's age.[45]) Except for the charade of the false tomb, his parents are unfailingly indulgent; thereafter he meets with nothing but kindness from a series of helpful adults: innkeeper, merchants, or porters, all of whom uniformly treat Floris like the lost child he is. Everyone goes out of their way to assist in the process of recovery. There is no struggle for recognition. He experiences no hunger or other material deprivation – except for the company of Blancheflour. He embarks on his quest not as a destitute exile, but with a retinue of servants accompanied by seven fine palfreys laden with treasure, fine clothes, and money *for to spenden by þe way* (ll. E345–46). Small wonder that his half-hearted disguise is instantly penetrated; his manner and mien are clearly those of a prince rather than the merchant he pretends to be. He has funds enough to command heaps of good food despite loss of appetite (a realistic insight into boyish character), or to provide whatever lavish bribes may be necessary. Neither is there any moral tension in the tale, since neither Floris nor Blancheflour can bear any responsibility for their circumstances. Compared with Goldbrow or Ysoude, Blancheflour remains a totally passive moppet, the inactive element of an androgynous union, incomplete without her partner. There is no development in terms of either figure *en route* to reunion. Their adventures, such as they are, bring no maturation, neither do they reveal moral or psychological qualities other than the sole virtue of unflagging fidelity.

It is this very quality of undeveloped youth which allows them to lead an apparently charmed life: the babes-in-the-wood syndrome of fragile innocence in a wicked world. At the dramatic climax of the story when the lovers are discovered to have violated the emir's harem, an offence which, had they been other than they are, should have resulted in death or mutilation:

> Þere was noon so sterne man
> þat þe children loked oon,
> þat þey ne wolde al wel fawe
> her jugement have wythdrawe,
> and wyth grete catel hem bygge,
> ȝif þey durste speke or sygge.
> For Flores was so feire a ȝonglyng,
> and Blaunchefloure so swete a þing.   (ll. E984–91)

[There was no man so stern that saw the children who would not gladly have withheld their sentence and redeemed them with a high price, if they only spoke or talked. Because Floris was so lovely a youth, and Blancheflour so sweet a thing.]

Throughout the two sweethearts are presented with a degree of affectionate humour with which innocent precosity is customarily viewed by the adult world, although it is never quite allowed to lapse into the sickly mawkishness often present in the French version. Unlike the French author who tells for example how the young couple kiss and cuddle out of school, there is little explicit reference to physical attraction, although when finally reunited, there is said to be 'miles of kissing' – an appropriately childish conceit (l. A504). But adult innuendo is inevitably present. A friendly burgess having described how the Emir's tower harem is guarded by eunuchs, no man being allowed to enter 'who bears in his breeches the engine to serve them day and night' (ll. E592–93), nevertheless explains that Floris might gain access if he presents himself as 'a good engineer' (i.e. architect, l. E654), and finally win the fair girl 'with some engine' (i.e. device, l. E717). The core of the tale is, of course, full of the materials of adolescent sexual fantasy and scarcely covert symbolism. A perpetual supply of four-and-twenty virgins who serve the needs of a potent ruler, are imprisoned in a tall tower reached by a bridge; the girls are chosen in an enclosed orchard containing an enchanted spring which turns to blood if an unchaste girl should enter. Above the spring stands an enchanted 'tree of love' from which a flower-petal drops to identify the emir's current paramour – a titillating motif of sexual arbitrariness approximating to the rape-fantasy associated with the 'sheikh of Araby' myth. It seems that in practice the 'magic' of the tree is controlled by the emir, who can arrange to have the petal fall on whomsoever he wants (ll. E629–40). This at once emphasizes the desirability and danger of the heroine, for *ever he herkeneþ after Blancheflour* (l. E642). Much of the description of tower and garden reflects the mechanical ingenuity of contemporary eastern courts, and the Byzantine taste for sophisticated automata was naturally much used by romance writers to impart the full wonder of the East. [46]

The author makes constant play with the humorous potential of his material. It is clear that there is something more to the impossibly heavy basket of flowers (*floris*) the girls struggle to hoist up the outside of the tower. Giggling, they are said to be 'keen to look at and handle the flowers' (ll. E752, 770). But this undeniable innuendo, never less than courtly, is audience- rather than participant-perceived, since it would be inappropriate to such innocent protagonists. Even when Floris and Blancheflour finally come together between the sheets, it is stated quite specifically – and of course ambiguously:

> Þer was no man that myȝt radde
> þe joye þat þey twoo madde.   (ll. E825–26)

[There was no man that could understand the bliss that those two experienced.]

The possibility of explicit physical union is ignored, or left to the reader. Even when the author chooses to play with a conventional narrative *topos*, (the 'good game' of *Havelok*, ll. 2132–36, in which hero and heroine are observed asleep in each other's arms by a superior), instead of the expected titillation, the real situation is far from clear. When the love-birds are discovered 'bill to bill and mouth to mouth', the bedclothes have to be drawn down beneath the breast before it is plain that one is a woman, the other a man (ll. E898–901); even then the question of physical union is left unanswered, the violation of the harem alone being sufficient to bring the threat of instant death. Unlike the real, albeit tragi-comic, adult relationship of Tristrem and Ysoude, the extreme youth of the protagonists – 'just twelve years old' – projects a calf-love closely corresponding to the courtly ideal because physically and socially in-nocent, and in consequence vulnerable to adult mockery or mawkishness: the Bugsy Malone factor. (It may not be insignificant that a similar story of *young* love in the French romance of Aucassin and Nicolette also derives from an Arabic original, as indicated by the name of the hero: al-Qasim. [47])

The androgynous character of Floris is made clearer in the French version: 'no maiden fairer' (the emir at first mistaking Floris for Blancheflour's companion Clarice, ll.2381f, 2438f). And indeed, the very name 'Flower' is scarcely suited to virile achievement of any kind: a mere complement rather than counterpart to the feminine 'Bright-Flower'. Considerable play is made with the potential humour of the hero's name: most notably when he has himself carried into the tower concealed in a basket as one bloom among many.[48] The story then descends to pure visual slapstick as Floris, leaping out of the basket like a jack-in-the-box manikin, finds himself confronting the wrong girl – and promptly creeps back under again (ll.E751–58). The girl, Blancheflour's confidante Clarice, reflecting the indulgent complaisance of an adult observation of children's games, gives a little start and declares she has been frightened by a butterfly alighting on her breast (ll.E771–74). When Floris jumps out for the second time, this time to surprise the right girl, the game, for the now-colluding audience at least, holds no surprise; the situation has fallen to French bedroom-farce, albeit on an infant scale. The flower imagery is pursued at length in the conversation between Blancheflour and Clarice. First her friend pleads with her to come and see the 'flower' she has found:

> 'Suete Blauncheflur,
> wiltu seo a wel fair flur?
> Hit ne greu noȝt on þis londe,
> þat flur þat ihc bringe þe to honde.'    (ll.C481–84)

['Blancheflour, sweet, do you want to see a beautiful flower? It didn't grow around here, the flower that I'm bringing to your hand.']

but it is clear that Blancheflour is aware of the play that is being made and considers she is cruelly mocked. 'One that loves *par amour* and is happy in her love, may love flowers', whereas she for her part lives in sorrow in this tower, and knows that the emir will have her for sure – although she will never forget Floris (ll.C485f). When Clarice observes the couple in a lasting embrace, she teasingly insists on pressing the point, remarking:

> 'Knowestu oȝt ȝete þis flur?
> A litel er þu noldest hit se;
> nu ne miȝte hit lete fram þe.'    (ll.C518–20)

['What do you know about this flower now? A little earlier you wouldn't look at it; now you won't let it go.']

Although there is no ultimate suspense, since we know that the lovers must inevitably be discovered (ll.C555–56), the story introduces an element of sympathetic and humane drama in the manner in which their discovery comes about through the defensive protection of their well-meaning confidante. It happens that the morning after Floris's arrival it is the turn of Blancheflour and Clarice to bring the emir his washing materials: water, towels, comb, and mirror. Clarice calls Blancheflour who merely mumbles a response and turns over sleepily in her lover's arms.

> Quaþ Blauncheflur: 'Ihc am cominge';
> ac heo hit sede al slepinge.    (ll. C573–74)

['I'm coming', said Blancheflour; but she said it still asleep.]

Clarice excuses Blancheflour's absence with the impromptu schoolgirl lie that her friend had spent a sleepless night praying for the emir's well-being, a well-intentioned stratagem which simply serves to make matters worse, since it serves to confirm the emir's affection for Blancheflour (ll. C577f). When the same thing happens the following morning:

> 'Aris', heo sede, 'and go we ifere.'
> Quaþ Blauncheflur: 'Ihc come anon.'
> Ac Floriz cleppen hire bigon,
> and he him also unwise,
> and feolle aslepe one þis wise.    (ll. C592–96)

['Get up', she said, 'and let's go together.' Blancheflour said: 'I'm coming straight away.' But Floris began to embrace her, and he was imprudent too, so they fell asleep like that.]

Again Clarice lies but this time the emir is angry and sends a eunuch to investigate. By all rights this clandestine meeting should have ended in disaster; but instead of striking fear into the pair, their mutual danger merely serves to reveal the selfless quality of their love.

As they are taken out to be burned at the stake Floris passes to Blancheflour a magic ring which renders the wearer invulnerable to fire, water, or steel (ll. E375–78) and can thus save her life; but she will have none of it without him. In a well-observed childish scene:

> Florice þe ring here arauȝt,
> and hi him aȝein hit bitauȝt.
> On hire ne haþ þe ring iþrast,
> and hi hit haveȝ awai ikast.
> A duk hit seȝ and beȝgh to grounde,
> and was glad þat ring he founde.    (ll. A715–19)

[Floris held out the ring to her, and she handed it back to him again. He thrust the ring at her, and she threw it away. A duke saw it, stooped to the ground, and was pleased to find the ring.]

The magic ring is a conventional enough romance motif at this date.[49] It is perhaps surprising at first sight that no recourse should be made to this easy way through the impasse, when so many other problems merely dissipate. But the author is merely playing with the convention. The ring which is apparently rejected with such childish petulance does in fact serve its purpose, but in an unexpectedly negative way. Paradoxically it is their very renunciation of the ring which serves to reveal to the emir (and the audience too) the true quality of their devotion; and this proves enchanting enough in itself to secure forgiveness and release. The author relinquishes the possibility of a brief but dramatic moment of pantomime magic in favour of a more subtle and satisfying employment of the supernatural as a measure of human virtue.[50] The fire is avoided – for unstated reasons – but only to allow a further display of puppy-love, as Floris and Blancheflour childishly vie physically with each other as to who should die first, pushing each other out of the way of the emir's drawn sword:

> Blaunchefloure put forþ hur swire,
> and Florys did her agayn to tyre,
> and seide: 'I am man; I shall byfore.
> With wrong hast þow þy lyf loore.'
> Florys forth his swere putte,
> and Blaucheflour agayn him tytte.   (ll. E1016–21)

[Blancheflour stretched out her neck, and Floris pulled her back again, and said: 'I'm a man; I shall go first. It would be wrong if you were to lose your life.' Floris stretched out his neck, and Blaucheflour tugged him back.]

Moved by such a display of selfless sacrifice, the emir is moved to pity, and lets his sword fall to the ground. The duke who had picked up the ring persuades the emir to forgive the pair in return for finding out how the harem came to be breached. This done, the whole court falls to cleansing, loving laughter (now with, rather than at, the children), which signals forgiveness. The couple's love extends its benign influence over all those with whom they come into contact. In a Gilbertian finale, not only are the young lovers forgiven, but the Saracen emir goes so far as to knight his young rival in love and, relinquishing his proprietorial rights (he had, after all, paid seven times the girl's weight in gold for her), he has them married in church. Racial and religious considerations are not so much harmonized, as blithely ignored, presumably in the spirit of keeping politics out of entertainment! However, the emir is apparently so far persuaded of the virtues of a loyal and true love, as to abandon his promiscuous life-style in favour of contracting a conventional marriage with Clarice. There is no happy ending quite like this elsewhere in medieval romance.

The developing humanism of the twelfth-century schools seems to have corresponded with an increasing emphasis on the objective, human and therefore necessarily humorous, rather than transcendent, dimension of sexual relationships. As witnessed through the eyes of romance authors, sex, which is fundamental to the game of *fin' amor*, however played, is almost invariably a humorous affair, tending to ridicule, either in the eyes of a third party or the participants. The key to the situation is that one or other party is blinded by love, unaware of the hiatus between illusion and reality: whether the childhood sweethearts Floris and Blancheflour, blissfully unaware of adult levels of perception, or the all-too-adult zest with which Tristrem and Ysoude play on verbal and visual *double entendres* to reveal grosser sentiments lying just beneath the courtly mien (see above, pp. 211f). The situation frequently topples into broad humour, as when the Breton Ysoude, splashed beneath her skirt when her horse treads in a puddle, giggles and, when asked the cause of her laughter, remarks that the water lying in her saddle has come closer than any man has ever done (ll.2885–89), thus revealing in public the present impotence of the great lover Tristrem who, not unnaturally, flounces out in embarrassment at this revelation of a matrimonial secret (ll.2916–24).

Humour of this kind is most characteristically exploited in the long-standing tradition of shorter works which seem to have existed alongside the more serious romances: anecdotes or fabliaux, which by their very nature persist more readily in oral than written form. Such frivolous short stories seem to have circulated orally throughout medieval times although repeatedly denounced by ecclesiastical and academic authorities.[51] The ale-house anecdote is essentially an ephemeral genre unlikely to be dignified by a written status, although many of the more innocuous tales would find a place in the late-twelfth- or early-thirteenth-century Latin collections of Walter Map, Odo of Cheriton, or Gervase of Tilbury.[52] Accessible to all English-speaking classes, it is difficult to define the audience at which the anecdote as a genre is aimed; it would be unrealistic to suppose that any one class of society might find the anecdote of itself too unsophisticated a genre to appreciate. While some anecdotes poke fun at courtly assumptions and others mock the smugness of bourgeois conventions, all seek to probe and ridicule moral inadequacy. The manner of telling rarely provokes sympathy of any kind. The kind of events described happen to other people rather than oneself – or so we fondly imagine. That many such tales will have been the product of student circles is suggested by a statute of 1292 warning the students of Oxford against 'songs and stories of lovers or lechers which celebrate lust',[53] and by the prominent and unscathed role in such tales commonly played by a free-wheeling 'clerk'. Perhaps typical is the tale of *Dame Sirith and the Weeping Bitch*. Like *Floris and Blancheflour*, the tale of *Dame Sirith* may ultimately derive from Arabic sources,[54] transmitted to the West either directly or via some intermediary general collection like the Sephardic *Disciplina Clericalis* of Peter Alfonsus.[55] It may not be insignificant that the Middle English version opens with a Norman-French rubric: *Ci commence le fablel e la cointise de dame Siriz*, suggesting a direct association with the well-defined Old French genre of fabliaux: brief and frequently scurrilous tales, known by the diminutive form of 'little fables'.[56]

The 'plot', such as it is, simply concerns the trick by which a procuress (Dame Sirith) persuades an unwilling, but foolish woman (Margery) to accept the amorous advances of a clerk (Wilekin, i.e. Little Willy). As at all times, the recurrent anecdotal subjects are sex or stupidity, or both together. An air of informal immediacy is established by the narrator from the very beginning; it is a tale he has picked up 'on the way' (ll. 1–2): a familiar opening which we might imagine to be a stock verbal signal of the kind traditionally employed by the stand-up comic down the ages – 'A funny thing happened on the way here tonight . . .', or 'Have you heard this one?' – which immediately has the effect of preparing us to anticipate laughter. The teller embarks on this tale without more ado, immediately introducing his subject in the opening few lines. It seems (stanza 1) that there is a spirited fellow, well educated, well dressed, and well set up beneath his clothes who (stanza 2) falls passionately in love with a married woman. This, says the poet in a rare authorial aside (surely a mock-serious note in view of the scurrilous tale he goes on to tell), was not proper (l.9). Racking his brains as to how he might 'get at her' *in ani cunnes wise*, (with an obvious *double entendre* in *cunnes*, where *cunn* is both 'sort', 'kind', and 'cunt', l.15), he takes advantage of the absence of her husband on a business trip, and goes to the hall (*in parenthesis*: 'She was a rich-un'! l.21), where she lives. The opening stanzas have supplied the barest outline necessary to establish the situation; we are provided with no circumstantial details, no localization, geographical or chronological setting, nor any characterization except such as might be imparted by a bare name. The stock characters have no existence prior to the incident in question, and will undergo no evolution during the brief course of the tale. It is an extremely economic narrative mode in which nothing is allowed to detract from the direct humour of the situation presented; no self-identification or audience sympathy will be allowed to dissipate its effect. The anecdote is pure narrative at its simplest and barest, stripped of all psychological, situational or symbolic complexity: the story-teller's art that belies art. The plot itself is reduced to a single incident, requiring no more motivation than merest probability, and no

long-term consequences, moral or otherwise. Its success depends entirely
on the degree to which stock characters fulfil recurrent anecdotal expectations; the myths of persistently libidinous travelling salesmen and
the desirability and availability of farmer's daughters.

*Dame Sirith* has a characteristically narrow field of vision: a strictly
limited group of characters all presented at once: merely wife, lover and
go-between, with no neighbours, children, or other onlookers to distract
attention from the situation. After the brief narrative introduction, the
situation is developed almost wholly in the form of dialogue: the plain,
colloquial speech which contemporary critics approved for comic
material.[57] It is dialogue which supplies the 'realistic' corroboration of
names and location and which, more importantly, gradually discloses
expected postures. The lusty young man opens his address with a
single-line clerical greeting: 'God Almighty be in this house' (1.25). All
the characters invoke religious oaths from first to last, emphasizing the
gap between empty words and deeds. The wife responds with an effusive
welcome, calling him 'my dear', urging him to come and sit down, and
assuring him 'by our Lord' that he will find her more than willing to do
whatever she can for him (ll.26–36) – an unintentional irony available
only to clerk and audience. The clerk replies in a further stanza, beginning with words of flattery: 'Lady, may God reward you!', but hints at
his ulterior motive in hesitation: he will say what is on his mind only if she
promises not to tell or be angry (ll.37–42). Her response is now one of
garrulous, flirtatious innuendo, reflecting the covert attraction clerics
seem to have had for bored housewives and frustrated females down the
centuries. She employs his pet name, Little Willy, assuring him that she
would never be 'uncourteous' about anything she might have that he may
long for; she never has been mean, and doesn't intend to begin now. She
will sit still and listen to whatever he has to say. He isn't to be afraid; she
won't blame him, even if he should suggest something shameful
(ll.43–57). She has clearly led him on verbally. Yet when he comes
directly to the point – he has heard that her husband is away at Boston
Fair, and proposes a pleasant liaison – she instantly and lengthily protests that she's not that kind of woman! Her love for her husband is 'true
as steel': she would never be so foolish as to play the whore, 'neither on
the bed nor on the floor' (ll.88–102); adding, on a rather equivocal note,
and with diminishing emphasis that she would not think of taking a lover
while her husband is alive – not if he were a hundred miles beyond Rome
– before he came home (ll.103–08). Her character is revealed both in
what she says (her husband is *curteis* – and rich, ll.119–20), and how she
says it: a nagging, repetitive protestation of wifely loyalty:

And Ich am wif boþe god and trewe;
trewer womon ne mai no mon cnowe
þen Ich am.   (ll. 121–23)

['And I am a good and faithful wife; no man could know a more faithful
woman than I am.']

She proves obdurate to all Wilekin's special pleading: his blasphemous
prayer that she might change her mind for Christ's sake (ll. 112–13, 146–
47), since after all:

'Swete lemmon, merci!
Same ne vilani
ne bede I þe non;
bote derne love I þe bede,
as mon þat wolde of love spede,
and finde won.'   (ll. 127–32)

['Sweet mistress, have pity! I'm not asking you anything shameful or
dishonourable; I'm only asking you for a secret love, as one who wants to
succeed in love.']

She replies in increasingly frank and colloquial terms: 'Do you take me
for a fool? Sure as Christmas you're silly!' (ll. 115–17), finally abandoning
the leisurely stanzaic exchange for a rapid sequence of rhyming couplets
in a final harangue before breaking off of the conversation (ll. 133–48).
    Two narrative stanzas tell how Wilekin leaves disconsolate and is
advised by a friend to consult a certain Dame Sirith whom he approaches
obliquely with words that are 'mild and also sly' (l. 159). Although it must
be clear that she is a professional procuress, a face-saving game is played
on either side. Wilekin projects his desire not in terms of cold-blooded
self-indulgence, but of conventional love-sickness; the distracted lover, he
will go mad for sorrow, or commit suicide, unless he can get the *swete wif*,
whose name we now learn is Margery, to change her mind (ll. 181–84).
Dame Sirith's own approach is no less oblique. At first she denies her
reputation, protesting that it is a shocking suggestion to make to a poor
sick old woman, who only lives on donations from good men for whom in
return she prays that God may help them when they need it. However,
when he presses the point: a friend who recommended her services knows
differently – 'Give over!', and she will be well paid for her trouble
(ll. 217–25), she has recourse to the procuress's ethic, and asks:

'Liʒ me nout, Wilekin, bi þi leute:
is hit þin hernest þou tellest me?
Lovest þou wel dame Margeri?'   (ll. 228–31)

['Don't lie to me, Little Will. On your honour now, are you sincere in what you're telling me? Do you really love Dame Margery?']

by implication – does he really love Margery, or is it merely lust, to which he replies rather ambiguously:

> 'Ʒe, nelde, witerli
> Ich hire love! Hit mot me spille
> bot Ich gete hire to mi wille.'    (ll. 232–34)

['Oh yes, gammer, of course I love her! It may kill me unless I can get her as I want.']

Professional integrity thus ensured, Dame Sirith promptly agrees to help provided he will keep quiet about it, for fear she will be convicted of bawdry by ecclesiastical courts and condemned to a skimmity ride (ll. 243–48). Promises given, with an oath by the holy rood (l. 254), Dame Sirith reveals her tricks of the trade. She turns abruptly, and somewhat to Wilekin's surprise, to address her little bitch:

> 'Pepir nou shalt þou eten;
> þis mustart shal ben þi mete,
> and gar þin eien to rene.
> I shal make a lesing
> of þin heie renning–
> Ich wot wel wer and wenne.'    (ll. 279–84)

['Now you must eat pepper; this mustard must be your food, so as to make your eyes run. I shall make up a lie about your eyes running – I know very well where and when.']

Her 'double game', *juperti*, is played out when, pretending to come across Margery by chance, she presents her weeping bitch as her own married daughter who has been metamorphosed by wizardry, having foolishly refused the amorous advances of a clerk during the absence of her husband, whom she loved *al to wel* (l. 343. The gullible Margery, recognizing a remarkable parallel to her own story, instantly panics, fearing for her own safety, and regrets her former prudishness irrespective of any protestations of loyalty: 'If only he'd lain with me just once before he went away!' (ll. 380–81). She even goes so far as to offer the old woman money if she will go out and bring the clerk back; to which Dame Sirith kindly consents: 'If I can do it without incurring blame' (l. 392). In a self-deluding parody of her lover's 'plight', she declares that she will be unable to laugh, sing, or be glad, until receiving her beloved (ll. 400–2). She has in fact changed her mind out of fear rather than attraction, and at

Wilekin's surprisingly prompt reappearance, she now dissembles in turn
– offering an effusive and loving welcome:

> 'Welcome, Wilekin, swete þing!
> Þou art welcomore þen þe king.
> Wilekin þe swete,
> mi love I þe bihete,
> to don al þine wille!
> Turnd Ich have mi þout,
> for I ne wolde nout
> þat þou þe shuldest spille.'   (ll. 425–32)

['Welcome Little Will, you sweet thing! You're more welcome than the
king. Sweet Little Will, I promise you my love, and to do anything you
want. I've changed my mind, because I wouldn't want you to hurt yourself
on any account.']

Wilekin dismisses the procuress in lordly and clerical terms (*par mai fai*
[by my faith], l. 436), which underlines the true nature of his avowed
religion; and Dame Sirith leaves the couple together with a few words of
explicit encouragement, the absence of polite euphemism revealing her
own true nature.

> 'And loke þat þou hire tille
> and strek out hire þes.'   (ll. 440–41)

['And see that you plough her and stretch her thighs wide.']

There is little more to add. The tale does not return to the narrative voice
for additional comment, but ends merely with a brief advertising aside by
Dame Sirith who, with professional pride in a job well done, points out to
an audience manoevred into voyeurism, that her services are available to
anyone who needs them – for a price!

The tale is more dramatic than narrative in style, and would perhaps
respond well to different voices in performance. After the first 24 lines of
introduction, there are only 33 narrative lines out of 426, the transitions
marked in the margins of the manuscript by letters: T (Teller), C
(Clerk), V (Wife), and F (Femme). It is not insignificant that the earliest,
indeed almost sole surviving fragment of secular medieval English
drama, the small, two-scene scroll *Interludium, De Clerico et Puella*, which
apparently utilized a very similar plot, in which a clerk addresses himself
to a girl while her parents are away from home, includes much
phraseology, and even whole verse lines, in common with *Dame Sirith*.[58]
Similar plots also occur in twelfth- and thirteenth-century Anglo-Latin
comedies, one of which portrays a closely similar relationship between

cleric and housewife, although their go-between does not resort to the weeping-bitch trick.[59] Possibly the story of *Dame Sirith* as we have it was based on a lost dramatic original, adapted for performance by a single entertainer. Whether or not drama *per se* survived from the classical world into the earlier Middle Ages, there are continuous references to semi-dramatic performances by scurrilous, satirical entertainers – the *mimi* who sang and danced in the market-places of, for example, tenth-century England.[60]

One might have thought *Dame Sirith* a straightforward enough tale of unedifying bawdry. Nevertheless a certain medieval habit of mind was prepared to recognize the hand of God in all things. Since nothing in the world was incapable of revealing some aspect of God's purpose, the most frivolous stories might be utilized in the *exemplum* tradition (a parable mode of teaching), popularized especially by the preaching friars.[61] Supplied with an often bizarre *sens*, such tales would find a place in various collections of moralized fables intended to convey effective religious instruction. There are moralized versions of the Dame Sirith tale in the twelfth-century *Destructorium Vitiorum* attributed to Alexander of Hales,[62] in the thirteenth-century Anglo-Norman *Contes Moralisés* collected by Nicholas Bozon (several of whose tales derive from English originals, as indicated by the presence of English personal names, proverbs, and verbal tags),[63] and in some versions of the widely circulated *Gesta Romanorum*.[64] Here, given a distinctly bizarre interpretation, the wife signifies the Christian soul, the absent husband Christ, the lover worldly vanity, the go-between Satan, and the weeping bitch the hope of long life which frequently afflicts the soul.[65] It was not only sanitized versions of such tales which circulated in religious circles. Enclosed female religious communities seem, not unnaturally, to have formed an avid audience for such gossipy tales. The twelfth-century Cistercian Aelred of Rievaulx warns his sister to beware of old women who tell dirty stories, for when the lips break into a smile or laughter, one imbibes poison with the sweetness which spreads to all the members.[66]

The unadorned anecdote lacks both the psychological perspective and moral potential of the romance. *Dame Sirith* in particular is a tale of unrelieved scurrility; antagonistic to contemporary ecclesiastical and societal conventions alike, it is a celebration of unalloyed vice, serving merely to confirm the cynic's poor opinion of humanity. Not one of the characters engages our sympathy, neither the cold-bloodedly self-indulgent clerk, nor the fickle wife, by turns smug and timid, pretentious and gullible, still less the cynical procuress. There is no expectation that the absent husband will return to discountenance the illicit coupling. Yet although morally unredeemed, with the pretended integrity of all parties undermined, at one level everything ends satisfactorily; everyone gets (if not their 'just' deserts), just what they want:

the lusty clerk physical satisfaction, the procuress ample payment, and the fearful lady at least freedom from perceived threat, if not more. Authorial judgement, largely disallowed by the predominance of dialogue, is presented only in mock-serious terms. We are required to feel no sense of superiority over the characters or action, merely enjoyment of comic imperfections harmlessly displayed. The anecdote, albeit scurrilous at one level, presents avowedly real aspects of humanity rarely afforded by 'serious' literature. It documents the negative. In this sense the tale is not ultimately irredeemable. Its reductive parodic mode, fundamentally egalitarian, cuts all elements down to size, satisfying the innate desire to see everyone as 'only human after all'. None of the characters escapes with their dignity unimpaired – and neither should they. *Dame Sirith* simply explores the stuff of courtly romance applied to an everyday domestic situation: what *might* happen if the beau of the women's magazine actually confronted the suburban housewife. The smug, posturing, bourgeois wife who tumbles on to her back at the first real push is in reality timid as well as gullible, and all too easily bought; the integrity of 'distraught lover', chaste wife, and poor, sick old woman dependent on men's charity, is all opportunistic pretence. If we do not laugh, we must surely weep.

## Notes

1. See generally, W. R. J. Barron, *English Medieval Romance* (London, 1987).

2. *Liber de Planctu Naturæ*, in *The Anglo-Latin Satirical Poets and Epigrammatists of the Twelfth Century*, edited by T. Wright, Rolls Series, 59 (London, 1872), II, pp. 465–66.

3. *Gesta Herwardi Incliti Exulis et Militis*, in *Lestorie des Engles solum la translacion Maistre Geffrei Gaimar*, edited by T. D. Hardy and C. T. Martin, Rolls Series, 91 (London, 1888–89), I, pp. 339–404; *Vita Haroldi*, edited by W. de G. Birch (London, 1885).

4. Walter Map, *De Nugis Curialium: Courtiers' Trifles*, edited by M. R. James, second edition, revised by C. N. L. Brooke and R. A. B. Mynors (Oxford, 1983), pp. 154–59.

5. See generally, R. M. Wilson, *The Lost Literature of Medieval England*, second edition (London, 1970).

6. Compare A. C. Baugh, 'The Middle English Romance: Some Questions of Creation, Presentation, and Preservation', *Speculum*, 42 (1967), 1–31.

7. *Peter Langtoft's Chronicles as Illustrated and Improved by Robert of Brunne*, edited by T. Hearne (Oxford, 1725), I, p. 26.

8. Conveniently illustrated in *The Lay of Havelok the Dane*, edited by W. W. Skeat, second edition, revised by K. Sisam (Oxford, 1915), frontispiece. For a review of

evidence suggesting a date for the romance some time between the late twelfth century and the third quarter of the thirteenth, see G. B. Jack, 'The Date of *Havelok*', *Anglia*, 95 (1977), 20–33.

9.  See *The Romance of Sir Beves of Hamptoun*, edited by E. Kölbing, Early English Text Society, Extra Series, 46, 48, 65 (London, 1885–94), p. 1; *The Romance of Emaré*, edited by E. Rickert, Early English Text Society, Extra Series, 99 (London, 1906), p. 1; or *Otuel*, in *The Taill of Rauf Coilyear*, edited by S. J. H. Herrtage, Early English Text Society, Extra Series, 39 (London, 1882), p. 65.

10. Compare *Le Lai dHaveloc li Danois*, in *Lestorie des Engles*, edited by T. D. Hardy and C. T. Martin, Rolls Series, 91 (London, 1888–89), ɪ, pp. 290–327, ɪɪ, pp. 216–46.

11. *Bracton, De Legibus et Consuetudinibus Angliae: Bracton on the Laws and Customs of England,* edited by S. E. Thorne (Cambridge, Massachusetts, 1968–77), ɪɪ, pp. 18f.

12. *Two of the Saxon Chronicles Parallel*, edited by J. Earle and C. Plummer (Oxford, 1892–99), ɪ, p. 220.

13. Compare M. Mills, 'Havelok and the Brutal Fisherman', *Medium Ævum*, 36 (1967), 219–30.

14. Apparently a conventional sign of regal birth; see the thirteenth-century French romance *Richars li Biaus*, edited by W. Förster (Vienna, 1874), p. 19.

15. *King Horn*, edited by J. Hall (Oxford, 1901), pp. 14–15; *Octovian Imperator*, edited by F. McSparron (Heidelberg, 1979), pp. 72f.

16. For a possible religious significance of this theme, see D. Haskin, 'Food, Clothing and Kingship in *Havlok the Dane*', *American Benedictine Review* (1973), 204–13.

17. See generally, E. T. Hansen, 'Women in Old English Poetry Reconsidered', *The Michigan Academician*, 9 (1976), 109–17.

18. For a useful survey, see M. D. Legge, *Anglo-Norman Literature and its Background* (Oxford, 1963).

19. For a magisterial survey of the origin and growth of the Tristan legend, see H. Newstead *et al.*, in *Arthurian Literature in the Middle Ages*, edited by R. S. Loomis (Oxford, 1959), pp. 122f; and more recently, S. Eisner, *The Tristan Legend: A Study in Sources* (Evanston, Illinois, 1969). For the likely intermediary role played by trilingual interpreters in the West Country and along the Welsh Marches, see generally C. Bullock-Davies, *Professional Interpreters and the Matter of Britain* (Cardiff, 1966). For the archaeological background, see C. A. R. Radford and M. J. Swanton, *Arthurian Sites in the West* (Exeter, 1975), pp. 25–34.

20. *Les Fragments du Tristan de Thomas*, edited by B. H. Wind (Geneva, 1960).

21. Robert Mannyng, in *Peter Langtoft's Chronicles*, edited by Hearne, ɪ, pp. xcix–c.

22. For a refreshingly close criticism of the phenomenon of *fin' amor* as a literary mechanism rather than social document, see B. Bowden, 'The Art of Courtly Copulation', *Medievalia et Humanistica*, 9 (1979), 67–85.

23. *Lais*, edited by A. Ewert (Oxford, 1944), pp. 123–26.

24. R. S. Loomis and L. H. Loomis, *Arthurian Legends in Medieval Art* (New York, 1938), pp. 42–69, figs 19–135.

25. Compare generally, U. Dürmüller, *Narrative Possibilities of the Tail-Rime Romance* (Berne, 1975).

26. For a well-explored fourteenth-century case, see W. R. J. Barron, *Trawthe and Treason* (Manchester, 1980).

27. Gottfried von Strassburg, *Tristan und Îsolt*, edited by A. Closs (Oxford, 1947), p. 83.

28. Compare generally, D. L. Heiple, 'The "Accidens Amoris" in Lyric Poetry', *Neophilologus*, 67 (1983), 55–64.

29. C. Singer, 'A Thirteenth-century Clinical Description of Leprosy', *Journal of the History of Medicine*, 4 (1949), 237–39.

30. *The Register of John de Grandisson, Bishop of Exeter 1327–1369*, edited by F. C. Hingeston-Randolph (London, 1894–99), ii, pp. 1110–11.

31. *Fragments de Tristan*, edited by Wind, pp. 98ff.

32. R. S. Loomis, *Illustrations of Medieval Romance on Tiles from Chertsey Abbey* (Urbana, Illinois, 1916).

33. Compare E. Vinaver, *Form and Meaning in Medieval Romance* (Cambridge, 1966), and 'The Questing Knight', in *The Binding of Proteus: Perspectives on Myth and the Literary Process*, edited by M. W. McCune and T. T. Orbison (Lewisburg, Pennsylvania, 1978), pp. 126–40.

34. Compare H. Newstead, 'The Tryst beneath the Tree: An Episode in the Tristan Legend', *Romance Philology*, 9 (1955), 269–84.

35. *The Old English Apollonius of Tyre*, edited by P. Goolden (Oxford, 1958).

36. Compare D. Metlitzki, *The Matter of Araby in Medieval England* (New Haven, Connecticut, 1977), *passim*.

37. *Romance of Sir Beves of Hamptoun*, edited by Kölbing; *Der mittelenglische Versroman über Richard Löwenherz*, edited by K. Brunner (Vienna, 1913).

38. *Floire et Blancheflor*, edited by M. M. Pelan (Paris, 1956).

39. See generally H. Herzog, 'Die beiden Sagenkreise von Flore und Blanscheflur', *Germania*, 17 (1884), 137–228; compare L. A. Hibbard, *Mediaeval Romance in England*, second edition (New York, 1960), pp. 184–89.

40. *Romance of Emaré*, edited by Rickert, p. 5.

41. G. Huet, 'Sur l'origine de *Floire et Blanchefleur*', *Romania*, 28 (1899), 348–59; 'Encore *Floire et Blanchefleur*', *Romania*, 35 (1906), 95–100.

42. *The Arabian Knights Entertainments*, edited and translated by R. F. Burton (Benares, 1885–88), i, p. 283; ii, pp. 45f, iv, pp. 1–2; vii, p. 256.

43. Ibn Hazm (Ali ibn Ahmad), *The Ring of the Dove* (Tauk al-hamāmah), translated by A. J. Arberry (London, 1953).

44. Compare M. Lot-Borodine, *Le Roman Idyllique au Moyen Age* (Paris, 1913), pp. 9–74.

45. *Li Romanz de Floire et Blancheflor*, edited by F. Krüger (Berlin, 1938).

46. M. Sherwood, 'Magic and Mechanics in Medieval Fiction', *Studies in Philology*, 44 (1947), 567–92.

47. *Aucassin et Nicolette*, edited by F. W. Bourdillon (Manchester, 1919).

48. See generally W. C. Calin, 'Flower Imagery in *Floire et Blancheflor*', *French Studies*, 18 (1964), 103–11.

49. Compare *King Horn*, edited by Hall, pp. 32–33; *Mittelenglische Versroman*, edited by Brunner, pp. 165–66.

50. Not dissimilar to the use of the enchanted girdle in the fourteenth-century romance *Sir Gawain and the Green Knight*, edited by M. Andrew and R. Waldron, *The Poems of the Pearl Manuscript* (London, 1978), pp. 274f.

51. On this subject, see generally, B. White 'Medieval Mirth', *Anglia*, 78 (1960), 284–301.

52. Walter Map, *De Nugis Curialium*, edited by James; Odo of Cheriton, *Fabulae et Parabolae*, in *Les Fabulistes Latins*, edited by L. Hervieux (Paris, 1884–99), iv; Gervase of Tilbury, *Otia Imperialia*, in *Scriptores Rerum Brunsvicensium*, edited by G. W. von Leibnitz (Hanover, 1707–11), i, pp. 884–1004; ii, pp. 751–84.

53. *Munimenta Academica*, edited by H. Anstey, Rolls Series, 50 (London, 1868), i, p. 60.

54. Compare especially F. Falconer, in *The Book of Sindibad*, edited by W. A. Clouston (London, 1884), pp. 61–62, 162–66.

55. *Die Disciplina Clericalis des Petrus Alfonsi*, edited by A. Hilka and W. Söderhjelm (Heidelberg, 1911), pp. 18–19. See further, W. Elsner, *Untersuchungen zu dem mittelenglischen Fabliau Dame Siriz* (Berlin, 1887).

56. *The Humor of the Fabliaux: A Collection of Critical Essays*, edited by T. D. Cooke and B. L. Honeycutt (Columbia, Missouri, 1974).

57. (Geoffrey de Vinsauf), E. Gallo, *The Poetria Nova and its Sources in Early Rhetorical Doctrine* (The Hague, 1971), pp. 116–17.

58. Compare W. Heuser, 'Das *Interludium de Clerico et Puella* und das Fabliau von *Dame Siriz*', *Anglia*, 30 (1907), 306–19.

59. *Early Mysteries and other Latin Poems of the Twelfth and Thirteenth Centuries*, edited by T. Wright (London, 1838), pp. 65f.

60. Compare *Sacrorum Conciliorum Collectio*, edited by J. D. Mansi (Florence, 1759–98), xviiiA, col. 527; and see generally, J. D. A. Ogilvy, 'Mimi, Scurrae, Histriones: Entertainers of the Early Middle Ages', *Speculum,* 39 (1963), 603–19.

61. See generally, G. R. Owst, *Preaching in Medieval England* (Cambridge, 1926), and *Literature and Pulpit in Medieval England* (Cambridge, 1933).

62. Alexander 'Anglus' (or possibly a later compilation by one Alexander 'Carpenter'), *Destructorium Vitiorum* (Cologne, 1485), iii, X c.

63. *Les Contes Moralisés*, edited by L. T. Smith and P. Meyer (Paris, 1889), e.g. pp. 12, 20, 23, 24, 78, 110, 117, 137, 145, 151, 166, 180.

64. For example, *Gesta Romanorum*, edited by A. Keller (Stuttgart, 1842), pp. 52–54; *Le Violier des Histoires Romaines*, edited by M. G. Brunet (Paris, 1858), pp. 78–83; *Gesta Romanorum*, edited by H. Österley (Berlin, 1872), pp. 325–27.

65. One early nineteenth-century translator found even this insufficiently edifying and felt obliged to supply a new ending in which the husband returns during the night and puts the whole party to a shameful death: *Gesta Romanorum*, edited by the Rev. C. Swan (London, 1824), i, p. 124.

66. *Institutio Inclusarum*, in *Aelredi Rievallensis, Opera Ascetica*, edited by A. Hoste and C. H. Talbot, *Corpus Christianorum, Continuatio Medievalis*, I (Turnholt, 1971), p. 638. The thirteenth-century anchorage was often a notorious exchange for gossipy tales of all kinds; compare *Ancrene Wisse*, edited by J. R. R. Tolkien, Early English Text Society, 249 (London, 1962), p. 48. At a more literary level

it is interesting to speculate on the possible nature of the, now lost, *versus ridiculi* composed by the thirteenth-century Abbess of Lacock, Beatrice of Kent: J. C. Russell, *Dictionary of Writers of Thirteenth-Century England*, Bulletin of the Institute of Historical Research, Special Supplement, 3 (London, 1936), p. 23.

# Chapter 7
# The Singer and the Song

*I Walk with Sorrow, Lenten is Come with Love to Town, The Fair Maid of Ribblesdale,* Thomas of Hales's *Love-Song, Gabriel's Greeting to The Virgin Mary, Ubi Sount Qui Ante Nos Fueround, The Follies of Fashion, A Song of Lewes, The Thrush and the Nightingale,* and *The Owl and the Nightingale.*

From *Beowulf* to *Havelok* the conventional expression for the performance of literature is 'to sing', and the object of performance, irrespective of form, 'a song'.[1] Like Cædmon, Tristrem presents his poetry to the accompaniment of a harp,[2] presumably rhythmically delivered in a chanting manner, although no doubt an alternative form of more plainly spoken un-accompanied 'telling' was possible.[3] But if romances might also occasionally be silently read *in codice* by those literate enough, the song is primarily performance literature. Although the term 'lyric' is often loosely applied to the personal voice of poems like *The Wanderer* or *The Seafarer*, no genuine vernacular lyric, that is to say melodic, poetry survives from pre- Conquest England. (The gloss *swin-sung, -sweg = melodium* is insufficiently descriptive, and the term *melodie* was apparently introduced only in the thirteenth-century,[4] by which time the appearance of the stanzaic form together with the union of music and text in one manuscript is well in evidence.) But that there did exist a substantial and relatively sophisticated earlier tradition is indicated by the fact that Hereward the Wake is described singing to the harp in a variety of styles, sometimes singing solo, at other times in a trio with his friends 'in the manner of the Fenland people'.[5]

The earliest fragment of English lyric (if the reference is reliable), is attributed by the twelfth-century historian Thomas of Ely to the Viking King Cnut who, attracted perhaps by the singing of boatmen, perhaps by the chanting of monks, is stimulated to compose a song of his own, of which Thomas cites the first four lines:

> Merie sungen ðe muneches binnen Ely
> ða Cnut ching reu ðer by.
> 'Roweð, cnites, noer the land
> and here we þes muneches sæng.'

[The monks were singing joyfully within Ely as King Cnut rowed past.
'Knights, row closer inshore, and let's hear the monks' song.']

Thomas refers to further verses which were still in his day 'sung publicly in dances'.[6] We are told that the deeds of Hereward were similarly remembered in the dance-songs of country women,[7] and perhaps the 'old songs', *cantilenae,* from which other twelfth-century historians like Henry of Huntingdon or William of Malmesbury culled some of their information as to earlier England,[8] survived in the same way. The 'ring-dance' or *carole,* which seems to have been a popular pastime during the earlier Middle Ages, took the form of a ring or chain of dancers moving to the accompaniment of a directing voice: the leader singing the stanza, the whole company responding with the refrain in unison.[9] An essentially popular form, it probably originated with work-songs. But as the later use of the term 'carol' implies, it eventually entered the ecclesiastical field, where it coalesced with the form of the processional hymn.

By the eleventh century, according to Gerald of Wales, the English lyric had reached a relatively elaborate degree of sophistication, characterized, at least in the North-country, by two-part harmony.[10] The earliest musical scores that survive – albeit often accompanying the most apparently naïve texts – are elaborate enough to suggest an already long-established history.[11] The fact that some collections of lyrics, such as that in MS. Harley 2253, are presented without musical notation suggests that the lyric text may possibly have come to be regarded as a self-sufficient literary genre – unless of course the tunes were sufficiently well known to need no notation; (at least two of the Harley lyrics are accompanied by musical settings in other manuscripts.) But in principle, however, the text is necessarily dominated by the organization of the melody both in general and in detail; and like the tail-rhyme stanza it may prove merely loose unless handled decisively. We may assume that the music, which was in any case less readily documented than words, maintained an existence independent of any given lyric, and might be arbitrarily applied irrespective of the suitability of the accompanying words. One far from optimistic thirteenth-century lyric dealing with the imminence of death (beginning: 'You might think you're going to live for a long time, but . . .') was set to what might be thought a singularly inappropriate catchy dance-tune, counterpointing rather than complementing the sense.[12]

More characteristic, however, is the brief five-line lyric *I Walk with Sorrow,* written out in the sole-surviving copy as a two-part song for upper and lower voices (alto and baritone) in descant:[13]

Fo — we – les    in þe    frith,

þe    fi – sses    in    þe    flod;

and    I    mon wa – xe    wod.

Mulch    sorw    I    wal – ke    with

for    beste    of    bon    and    blod.

[Birds in the woodland, fish in the stream, and I, man (or must) go mad. I toss about in great distress for a beast (or the best) of bone and blood.]

The lyric consists merely of five short lines rhyming abbab, with a metrically regular pattern of two stresses to the line, each line consisting of a self-contained phrase ending in a terminal juncture. It is deceptively simple. Close analysis of this apparently naïve and direct little piece reveals an exceptionally high degree of organization: a complex series of interrelations in a compact sequence of phrases tightly controlled by metre, alliteration, syntax, and sense.[14]

Economical in the extreme, the lyric opens with two structurally parallel lines, linked by alliteration (not an uncommon feature of thirteenth-century lyrics[15]): *foweles, frith, fisses, flod*. Elliptical, omitting the understood verb 'to be', they present a familiar statement of gnomic appropriateness: 'there are birds in the wood, there are fish in the stream'. The next two lines are similarly linked by alliterative metre (*waxe, wod, walke, with*), syntax, and sense, describing similar states of the narrative voice: 'I grow mad; I move restlessly'. The ambiguity in line 3 where *mon* is both a verb, 'shall, must', or, parallel to the subject I, the noun 'man' ('a man' or 'mankind') is stressed in the musical setting. The slower, accented syllabic notation from *flod* to *waxe* alters the emphasis of the text, since the setting normally groups between two and five notes to a syllable; no less than five embroider the unimportant article *þe*, for example. In the emphatic opening of line 3 however, the rhythm and stress clearly changes, slowing down and holding a single note to mark the personal voice; *and I mon* emphasizes the anguish of man – the single narrator, or mankind as a whole – isolated from the rest of creation.[16] Unlike the birds and the fish who are in their own element with others of their kind, he walks in sorrow, mad and alone: alliteration associating *walke* with *waxe wod*. It is ironic that the emphatic final word of each line in turn represents natural habitat: wood, stream, and insanity. Modifying the normal prose order of line 4 and placing the words 'Much sorrow' at the beginning rather than its end, gives prominence to the speaker's distress and bewilderment.

The final line stands apart from the pattern of what has gone before, providing something of a conclusion in rhythm and sense, resolving the implied question as to why the situation should be as it is. Although linked with the previous lines in terms of stress and rhyme, it is grammatically and alliteratively different: a prepositional phrase in which the triple alliteration spreads over two lines but concentrates poetic strength: *beste, bon, blod*. The resolution contains three layers of sense dependent on ambiguities in *for* and *beste*. The complainant may express anguish because his sorrowful state seems unfair 'considering' he is merely a 'beast of bone and blood' and no different in this respect from the birds of the air and fish in the water; or secondarily, his condition is the worse since as a man he is the 'best', or highest representative, of the animal creation. Or at a third level, it may well be that his disordered state (not dissimilar from Tristrem's for example, see above, p. 209) is the result of love-sickness. He grows mad 'for the sake of' a 'creature of blood and bone' – an expression commonly used of women in contemporary lyrics (see below, p. 243).[17] But we do not feel that the layered sense is contrived rather than instinctive.

As an intensely personal expression of feeling, this poem closely reflects that stress on personal experience which was the diagnostic, fundamental tenet of the twelfth-century schools. The main protagonist of the poem is the poet himself, as the individual, subjective point of view acquires intrinsic significance. In marked difference from the Wanderer-persona (see above, p. 107), the genuinely lyric voice is in no way representative. The author is not concerned to point a moral of any kind, nor to make any universally valid statement about the human condition. He merely feels at odds with his environment. The initial evocation of a pastoral setting suggests that we might anticipate a straightforward love-song, albeit reduced to the utmost brevity, yet the expected correlation of mood with season is disappointed. He is out of sorts!

This theme is treated explicitly, and at greater length, in the three-stanza *reverdie*, or spring-song, *Lenten is Come with Love to Town*.[18] Organized in much the same way as the previous lyric, the spring-theme is announced in the opening line and then fully developed through an extended description of the season before the speaker's malaise is revealed. Of course it is perfectly possible for the *reverdie* to exist in its own right. *Sumer is icumen in* is perhaps the best-known example: an exclamatory celebration of the return of spring, listing natural phenomena that might be expected to awaken a joyful response in the listener.[19] The burgeoning of the earth with warmth and rain, provokes not the Seafarer's profound meditation on earthly mutability (see above, p. 119), but is directly associated with the welling up of human desires:

> Lenten ys come wiþ love to toune,
> wiþ blosmen and wiþ briddes roune,
> þat al þis blisse bryngeþ;
> dayeseȝes in þis dales,
> notes suete of nytegales.   (ll. 1–5)

[Spring has come to town with love, with flowers and birdsong, bringing all this happiness; there are daisies in the valley, the sweet note of nightingales.]

The season of blossom and birdsong is associated specifically with renewed sexual activity on the part of all natural beings. The expectation was no less true of man since, in medieval times especially – as in parts of the world at the present day, where normal domestic arrangements preclude privacy – most sexual encounters characteristically took place in open country, the fields and woods which warmer weather made once more amenable to such activities. Both the conventional setting and seasonal frame of reference of love-poetry is firmly mounted in pragmatic considerations; there is nothing intrinsically erotic about birds and bees, although they may be poetically recalled by way of sympathetic reaction to the environment. But whereas we might reasonably expect the revival of the world in spring to be accompanied by a correspondingly joyful mood in the speaker, the reverse is frequently the case, since the natural human instinct for coupling is subject to external factors of choice and delay, and thus inevitable frustration. The speaker therefore not uncharacteristically expresses a love-longing ironically at odds with the season.

The three stanzas represent an emotional progression, gradually revealing the speaker's state of mind. It opens with what is apparently a simple *reverdie*, when after 'winter's woe' (l.8) all plant and bird-life quickens: daisies and woodroff, nightingale and song-thrush, so that by the final line 'the whole wood is ringing' (l.12). The poet's reference to details of the natural world is no longer in the lapidary terms of the Old English elegist, hinting at the Platonic relationship between the finite and infinite world (see above, pp. 128–29), but simply as objects of sensual delight in themselves. The second stanza furthers the sense of burgeoning life: lily, fennel, and thyme all grow with a will; but now we learn that they are seen by the light of the moon (l.16). A line or two later we hear of the mating of wildfowl, and the coupling of all creatures, which, like a softly flowing stream (a familiar sexual simile[20]), serves to make their mates joyful. The stanza ends abruptly, however, with a passionate complaint that the wretched, lovesick speaker is out of tune with nature:

> 'Ichot ycham on of þo,
> for love þat likes ille.'   (ll. 23–24)

['I know that I'm one of them – sick for love.']

Since the speaker is frustrated and unable to participate in this natural activity, it is now clear that the apparently innocent *reverdie* which he began to sing serves merely to aggravate his condition: a masochistic self-mockery. We might have cause to recall a degree of ambiguity in the very opening line. 'Lent' was no empty synonym for 'spring', but already carried religious overtones of seasonable sorrow and denial, so that we have been half-prepared for this element of deprivation from the very beginning. The final stanza develops the speaker's sexual frustration to a climactic degree. It opens with a significant repetition of our earlier hint as to his plight: 'The moon spreads her light' (l.25), followed by a further wet image of 'dew sprinkling the hills' as animals make love (ll. 28–30), extending in bizarre imagination to what cannot even be seen except by the tormented mind: the subterranean courtship of worms, which is in turn bitterly linked in alliteration with women:

> Wormes woweþ under cloude,
> wymmen waxeþ wounder proude.   (ll. 31–32)

[Worms are wooing under the soil, women are growing remarkably proud.]

Whether the pride 'which suits women so well' (l. 33), refers to their seasonal wantonness or merely to their conventional disdain in response to pursuit, is immaterial. In a final tormented gesture, the speaker declares that if he cannot get what he wants from one of these women, he will flee from joy and run wild in the forest (ll. 34–36). A conventional habit of distraught lovers,[21] it is a psychologically convincing reflection of frustrated sexuality – an obsessive extension of the opening *reverdie*, ironically to plunge into close association with constant reminders of what torments him most. To become a wild man of the woods, specifically marks alienation from society, since the anticipated norm is one of urbane courtship: the season of love has come to *toun*.

The posture adopted by the amorous lyricist was by no means invariably one of anguish. The singer of *The Fair Maid of Ribblesdale*,[22] employing the same alliterative twelve-line stanza (rhyming: aabccbddbeeb) no less skilfully than the previous poet, embarks on his quest with a far more light-hearted air, despite striking all the conventional postures of courtly amorous languor. In describing the girl he has in mind, the poet plays with the conventions *con brio*, wittily asserting his own blend of sexual frankness and blasphemous bravado. For the fair object of his desire is no shrinking, untouchable *belle-dame* as the opening lines make clear:

> Mosti ryden by Rybbesdale,
> wilde wymmen forte wale,
> ant welde whuch ich wolde,
> founde were þe feyrest on
> þat ever wes mad of blod ant bon.   (ll. 1–5)

[If I could ride Ribblesdale way in order to pick up wild women, and have whichever one I wanted, there would be found the most beautiful thing that was ever made of blood and bone.]

A paragon of conventional medieval beauty,[23] her features are enthusiastically and systematically catalogued from head to toe. The poet employs a highly ironic range of reference. The lady is repeatedly said to be as white as the lily and as red as the rose (ll. 10–11, 35–36, 50), familiar symbols of chastity not uncommonly applied to the Virgin Mary at this time.[24] And yet her physical charms are unquestionable: her head shines like the sun at noon, the eyes that look laughingly on him are large and grey, the moon is not so bright as her forehead; in consequence of which, it seems, in the final two lines of the second stanza, the speaker 'mourns his life away', and is likely to 'die for love' (ll.23–24). The third stanza continues to enumerate her features (curved eyebrows, not too close together, cute nose), interrupted only by the brief exclamation, 'I die! I'm doomed to death!' (l.29), a comically conventional aside, promptly forgotten as the list continues: her locks (spread loose in undress!) are long: she has a fine chin and pink cheeks. The fourth stanza develops the comic potential further. She has a pleasant mouth and true red lips with which to read out tales of romance. Her ivory-white teeth are straight and even – courtly men might take note! (l.42); and she has a swan-like neck – indeed a span longer than any he has found elsewhere (ll.43–44). No wonder then that the stanza might conclude with a ribald declaration, reminiscent of the opening line of the poem, that he would rather wait for her to come along and then to mount in Ribblesdale than ride as pope in Rome (ll.46–48). (The sexual metaphor is a familiar one (see below, p. 269) and well established by the twelfth century.[25]) One is forcibly reminded of a contemporary goliard's assertion that he would rather sit in the pub with his girlfriend than sit at the right hand of God.[26] The specific localization, (rare in contemporary lyric), together with clearly signalled, albeit blasphemous, clerical reference, strongly suggest a precise context for this piece. The remote north-western region of Ribblesdale formed part of the vast Cistercian sheep-rearing estates, worked by lay-brothers and administered by an inspecting 'outrider' visiting isolated monastic granges, the gates of which notoriously attracted throngs of 'wild women'.[27] *The Fair Maid of Ribblesdale* was perhaps the sort of song one might find on the lips of Chaucer's monk: *an outridere, that loved venerie* – and *'a right prikasour'*.[28]

Travelling steadily down the girl's body, we learn that her breasts are like two Paradisal apples (an ironic enough reference, see above, pp. 79–80), and a feature, the poet assures us, that we might easily enough see for ourselves (ll.58–60). Thus the fifth stanza rounds off with a significant sense of the girl's availability. The sixth stanza ends with the same implication. Her jewelled girdle is fastened with a talismanic buckle which can protect men from sorrow – turning water to wine (when loosened for the purpose presumably) 'as those who have experienced it may vouch' (ll.61–72). The language is that of a miracle, but not the biblical wedding-miracle (John 2) which the allusion suggests. The final stanza assures us that indeed, like the phoenix, the girl is peerless (l.75). Her flanks are:

eyþer side soft ase sylk,
whittore þen þe moren-mylk,
wiþ leofly lit on lere.
Al þat ich ou nempne noht
hit is wonder wel ywroht,
ant elles wonder were.   (ll. 76–81)

[both sides as soft as silk, whiter than the morning milk, with a lovely colour to the complexion. That which I've not mentioned to you is amazingly well made – and it would be amazing if it were otherwise!]

The poet ends climactically with the blasphemous assertion that, like those who enter the emir's harem (see above, p. 218), 'anyone who could make love with such a girl, by Christ, would have little need of Paradise!' (ll. 82–84).

It is scarcely surprising that such lyrics seem frequently to have incurred clerical disapprobation, especially when the spring fertility-dances of women seem often to have been as suggestive as the accompanying words.[29] Some lyrics were apparently banned altogether. Gerald of Wales relates an incident in the diocese of Worcester, where as the result of night-long dancing at a churchyard wake, the priest officiating at mass the following morning could not get the words or tune out of his head so that instead of beginning *Dominus vobiscum*, he sang out to the same rhythm: *Swete lamman dhin are* [Sweet lover have mercy]. In consequence of this scandal, although the full words of the *carole* seem harmless enough, the bishop pronounced an anathema on anyone who should sing it in future anywhere in his diocese.[30] Nevertheless, certain ecclesiastics maintained the Aldhelmian tradition of ensuring that the devil did not have a monopoly of the best tunes,[31] and popular preachers, especially among the friars, would readily turn secular songs to religious ends. One early-thirteenth-century sermon-writer takes for his 'text' a snatch of 'trifling song sung by the wild women and wanton men in my part of the country when they go dancing':

Atte wrastlinge mi lemman I ches
and atte ston-kasting I him forles

[I chose my sweetheart for wrestling, and I abandoned him for stone-throwing]

the preacher going on to interpret the words with spiritual significance, for at Judgement Day we will be expected to account for every careless word (Matthew 12. 36). Men are called to wrestle with the world, the flesh, and the devil, thus gaining our love, who is Christ, but losing him again through stony hearts.[32] The ingenious mind that could discover spiritual significance in the tale of *Dame Sirith* (see above, p. 231), would find no problem with *The Fair Maid of Ribblesdale*.[33]

The intimate relationship between songs which spoke of physical and spiritual love is well exemplified in the juxtaposition in a single manuscript of parallel lyrics: *The Way of Woman's Love* and *The Way of Christ's Love*.[34] The potential contingency of the love of man and the love of God is well developed in a mid-thirteenth-century love-song which, according to a Latin rubric heading the sole-surviving manuscript, was written by Brother Thomas of Hales of the Order of the Friars Minor, at the urgent request of 'a certain girl dedicated to God'.[35] The circumstances are referred to in the opening stanza:

> A mayde Cristes me bit yorne
> þat ich hire wurche a luve-ron,
> for whan heo myhte best ileorne
> to taken onoþer soþ lefmon,
> þat treowest were of alle berne
> and best wyte cuþe a freo wymmon.
> Ich hire nule nowiht werne,
> ich hire wule teche as ic con.   (ll. 1–8)

[One of Christ's virgins ardently begged me to compose for her a love-song, from which she might best learn to take another true-love, who would be the most faithful of all men and best understand how to defend a noblewoman. I can't refuse her anything; I'll teach her what I can.]

It is perhaps not surprising that Thomas should have been approached in this way; he was the author of an elegant Anglo-Norman sermon addressed to a community of nuns, which takes the form of a mystical meditation on Christ as the lover of the soul, emphasizing the role played by Mary and other women in the life of Christ, kissing his feet and so forth.[36] Moreover, as a member of the new Order of Mendicant Friars (see above, p. 23), his attitude towards contemporary secular song and dance would be markedly different from that of conservative churchmen who frequently found occasion to denounce such activities.[37] Whereas by the end of the twelfth century penitential orders like the Cistercians were actively discouraged from using the lyric, presumably because of its dangerous associations,[38] the Franciscans had been explicitly instructed by their founder to adopt the role of 'God's minstrels', consciously exploiting vernacular language and customs to further their mission.[39] It is easy enough to understand the popularity of these *joculatores Dei*. In contrast with the traditional presentation of Christianity, they purveyed a broad social sense of the religious life, and an exuberant spirit of fun which is perhaps reflected in the bold extravaganza *The Land of Cockayne*; a rumbustious mockery of the luxury and laxity prevalent in certain 'enclosed' orders, it describes how ready-roasted geese fly to the table crying, 'Geese, all hot! all hot!', postulants are required to wade neck-high through pig-dung and an abbot summons attention by using his girl-friend's backside as a drum.[40]

In the two dozen stanzas of his *Love-Song* Thomas develops and links the two familiar themes of 'contempt for the world' and the love of Christ. He opens in terms that would have been familiar to his Anglo-Saxon predecessors by pointing to the transitoriness of all earthly things:

> Þeos þeines þat her weren bolde
> beoþ aglyden so wyndes bles,
> under molde hi liggeþ colde
> and faleweþ so doþ medewe gres.   (ll. 13–16)

[Those barons who formerly were brave have passed away like a gust of wind; they lie cold under the earth and decay like the grass in the field.]

Everything in this world glides away like a shadow and drops like leaves from the bough, whether gold and silver, fine furs, or the fickle love of men that causes so much woe (ll. 25–48).

> Monnes luve nys buten o stunde:
> nu he luveþ, nu he is sad,
> nu he cumeþ, nu wile he funde,
> nu he is wroþ, nu he is gled.
> His luve is her and ek a-lunde   (ll. 49–53)

[Man's love lasts for only a while: now he is in love, now he is sated; now he comes, now he wants to go; now he is angry, now he is happy. His love is here, and also elsewhere.]

Not even the most romantic earthly love lasts for ever, not that of Paris and Helen, nor Tristrem, Ysoude, 'and all those' (ll. 65–68). The first half of the song concludes by promising to direct the girl to a true lover (ll. 87–88).

The controlling images of the second half rise naturally out of what has gone before; they are well established as images before their spiritual dimension is revealed.[41] Christ, in parallel with an earthly lover, will offer the lady his castle, and will send gifts of jewels. The association of gems with sexual purity is a traditional one, conventional to the cult of virginity from the time of Aldhelm onwards;[42] while the castle image was made especially popular by the influential Anglo-Norman *Chasteau d'Amour*[43] of Robert Grosseteste, Franciscan lecturer at Oxford and subsequently Bishop of Lincoln. The imagery is thus couched in worldly terms, but the danger of a merely mechanical tone is skilfully avoided by the lively rhetorical style Thomas adopts: 'What's that you're saying about some castle? . . . What's that you're saying about some jewel?' (ll.113, 169). The castle offered is well founded, standing on a sound motte which cannot be undermined; within its joyful courts no one friend flees from another, no one loses their rights (ll.121–32). The jewel that he sends is a hundredfold better than all worldly jewels, more precious than any of those from which the city of heaven is constructed (ll.170–76, 179) (cf. Matthew 19. 29; Revelation 21. 19–20).[44] Whereas the worldly lover, whether Tristrem or Wilekin, lives in a state of constant apprehension, fearing inadequacy or non-requital, those who love God are assured of being loved in return.

Like all Franciscan devotional poetry, Thomas's plea is direct and unintellectual, unhampered by strict theological constraint. Drawing on the concrete immediacy of social values, it develops a characteristically vernacular reaction against the Latinate scholasticism of traditional devotional literature.[45] Thomas's utilization of the secular love-lyric convention usefully blurs the distinctions appropriate to courtly and religious love. *Eros* and *agape* are more readily distinguished intellectually than emotionally, and sexual desire provides a powerful and natural metaphor for the impulse to spiritual union; the ecstatic experience of the religious mystic and that of physical love exhibit not dissimilar external phenomena. And the Bernardine conception of carnal love as merely a provisional stage on the road to the spiritual, differing only in the object of its desire, permits and even encourages an ambiguous exchange in the vocabulary of love. Thus it is that sexual attraction, in a courtly context, endows the beloved lady with a degree of devotion properly belonging to the divine – seen in its most exotic manifestation in Tristrem's sacrilegious chapel of love (see above, p. 214), or at its most instinctive where the embrace of Miss Ribblesdale is equated with the bliss of heaven itself. Thus it is that Andreas Capellanus can add, not a recantation, but a supplement to his treatise on sexual love recommending the superior love of God (see above, p. 18).

The second half of Thomas's *Love-Song* explores the concept of Christ as a knightly lover in the courtly terms of contemporary devotional tracts, such as *An Anchoresses Guide* or *The Wooing of Our Lord*, which were expressly developed to meet the needs of women and drew ultimately on the bride-imagery of the Song of Songs.[46] Since the person of Christ is not only God but truly man, he displays all the desirable qualities of perfect humanity, and may be responded to as a true lover and the worthiest of suitors. 'Ah, sweet lady, if you only knew the fine virtues of this youth!' (ll.89–90). He is handsome and good-natured, open-hearted and exceptionally wise; she need never regret anything she might do while under his protection (ll.89–96). He is well known to be the most powerful man in the land – more powerful even than King Henry of England (ll. 97–102). He offers the maid his suit, and if only she will consent to accept his love, he will present her with clothing better than king or emperor can, and a dwelling-place finer than King Solomon's palace (ll. 103–20). Well might Thomas exclaim: 'Wouldn't a girl be happy who could live with such a knight!' (ll. 143–44).

> He haveþ bi-tauht þe o tresur
> þat is betere þan gold oþer pel,
> and bit þe luke þine bur,
> and wilneþ þat þu hit wyte wel
> wyþ þeoves, wiþ reveres, wiþ lechurs.
> Þu most beo waker and snel;
> þu art swetture þane eny flur
> hwile þu witest þene kastel.   (ll. 145–52)

[He has entrusted you with one treasure that is more precious than gold or rich clothing, and bids you look to your bower, and wants you to defend it well against thieves, against robbers, against lechers. You must be vigilant and alert; you are sweeter than any flower as long as you defend your castle.]

The name of the gem that her lover has entrusted to her is Virginity – the most valuable of all jewels that will not only bring her to paradise (ll. 161–66) but

> Þe hwile þu hyne witest under þine hemme,
> þu ert swetture þan eny spis.   (ll. 167–68)

[as long as you defend it under your petticoat, you are sweeter than any spice.]

It is a stone *ful of fyn amur* (l. 182).

Thomas draws his lyric missive to a close with a two-stanza *envoi* in which he leaves his metaphorical discourse to return to practical circumstances. He is sending the girl this lyric 'open and unsealed' (ll. 193–94); clearly, unlike a secular communication, this 'love-song' contains nothing confidential. He urges her to unroll the scroll (it is apparently visualized as written on the kind of scroll commonly used by friars in preference to codices for popular teaching) and reveal its contents to the other girls (ll. 195–98). When she finds herself 'yearning', she is to take out the scroll, sing the song with a sweet voice, and do as it bids (ll. 201–04), presumably in anticipation of that 'new song' which in the heavenly city only the virgins can sing (Revelation 14. 3–4). Thomas concludes with an Annunciatory reference, Almighty God greeting the girl with an invitation to participate in a wedding in heaven (ll. 205–08), thus implicitly linking his subject with the person of the Virgin Mary.[47]

The Annunciation theme is taken up and exploited at length in the lyric *Gabriel's Greeting to The Virgin Mary*,[48] a free but skilful version of the popular Latin hymn *Angelus ad Virginem*.[49] Written out in one manuscript below the Latin text as a *contrafactum*, it was clearly intended to be sung to the same tune.[50]

An — ge — lus    ad    vir — gi — nem
Ga — bri — el,    fram    e — vene—king

sub — in — trans in    con — cla — ve,
sent    to    þe    mai — de    swe — te,

vir — gi — nis    for — mi — di — nem
brou — te þire    blis — ful    ti — ding

de — mul — cens, in — quit    "A — ve!
and    faire    he gan    hire    gre — te:

A — ve    re — gi — na    vir — gi — num!
"Heil    be    þu    ful    of    grace    a — rith!

Cæ — li    ter — ræ — que    do — mi — num
for    Go — des    sone,    þis    e — vene lith,

con — ci — pi — es
for    man — nes    loven

et    pa — ri — es
wile    man    bi — comen,

in — ta — cta
and    ta — ken

sa – lu – tem ho – mi – num,
fles of þe, mai – den brith,

tu, por – ta cæ – li fa – cta,
man – ken fre for to ma – ken

me – de – la cri – mi – num."
of senne and dev – les mith."

[Gabriel, sent from the King of heaven to the sweet virgin, brought her this joyful news and courteously addressed her: 'Hail to you, full of grace indeed, for the son of God, this heavenly light, for love of man will become man and take flesh from you, bright virgin, to free mankind from sin and the devil's power.']

The difficulties involved in constructing a lyric on a given theme to an existing tune are obvious. Nevertheless the poet managed not merely to fulfil the metrical desiderata of matching the Latin stress and syllable- count, but even to preserve the intricate original rhyme-scheme (ababccddecec). The result is not only a considerable technical achievement, but a no less substantial lyric, lively and fluent in its own right.

The poet skilfully weaves together rhyme and melody to complement the verbal and intellectual movement of his stanza. The opening quatrain introduces the theme: a self-contained narrative statement accompanied by a repeated melodic line, perfectly reflecting the rhyme-scheme abab. The topic of the stanza thus announced is then developed in direct speech over its remaining lines; the following couplet, cc, is tricked out with a brief melodic inversion, echoed over lines 5 and 6, followed by a second, longer melodic inversion from lines 7 to 10, ddee, halting over the three notes of the short line 9 (which therefore forms something of a musical and verbal bob) before repeating in the last two lines of the stanza, 11–12. Lines 10 and 12, rhyming ee, are musically identical, making the last three lines a concluding unit – the melodic structure closely reflecting the verbal statement. This points the ultimate significance of what has gone before: the 'blissful news' of Christ's redemptive mission viewed not dramatically but with theological hindsight.

The overall structure of the whole lyric mirrors that of the individual stanza, its sophisticated external form complementing a no less controlled intellectual sequence of thought and imagery. The first three stanzas relate the dramatic event, the theological significance of which is explained in the last two.[51] Its scheme of thought reflects the Marian cult which, developing *pari passu* both the enhanced position of women and the neo-Aristotelian stress on Christ's humanity, became particularly prominent in the thirteenth century; and it is quite possible that this lyric may have been stimulated by the fashionable devotional exercise of 'the Angelic Salutation' ('Hail Mary'), which was fostered by the Church at this time.[52] Emphatically Marian, the poem explores the theme of virgin motherhood. The term *maiden* is used no less than six times, three times in the first fourteen lines, and usually prominently in the opening lines of each stanza. The poet departs from the strict Gospel account (Luke 1. 26–38), in that Mary is not disturbed by the sudden and dramatic appearance of the angel, but comes immediately to the point: how is it that she is going to bear a child when she thought she was a virgin; thus stressing the feminine (and incidentally, theological) rather than dramatic aspects of the story (ll. 15–16). It will be a 'sweet childbirth' (l. 23), not subject to 'the law of motherhood' (ll. 35–36) which is the punishment of Eve who had responded all too readily to a former angelic salutation, with dire results: that womankind should bring forth their children in pain and sorrow (Genesis 3. 15–16). Mary, a second Eve, as Christ is a second Adam, will give birth to the Saviour:

> Hire wombe arise gan
> þurw þoligastes mithe;
> in hire was Crist biloken anon,
> suth God, soth man ine fleas and bon.   (ll. 39–42)

[Her belly began to swell through the power of the Holy Spirit; forthwith Christ was enclosed within her, true God, true man in flesh and bone.]

It is not Mary's son, however, but her act of giving birth that will redeem mankind and release them from torment (ll. 22–24). Reference to Christ's passion naturally forms no part of the dialogue, although it is introduced at the conclusion of the penultimate stanza, with a verbal echo over lines 22–24 to 47, when the ultimate significance of Gabriel's announcement is made clear. The final stanza shifts the focus decidedly from the historic past of the body of the narrative to the present moment, in an ecstatic sequence which finally breaks the established mould of the previous stanzas, joyfully running over each of the formal units and divisions, to address a direct eulogy to the *Maiden, moder makeless* [Virgin, mother without peer – *or* mate] (l. 49), imploring that she will use her special relationship to intercede for us with her son.

The *contemptus mundi* theme which framed the opening argument of Thomas of Hales's *Love-Song*, is forcibly explored in a fine ten-stanza lyric, *Ubi Sount Qui Ante Nos Fuerount*,[53] possibly composed as a poetic coda to the so-called 'Sayings of St Bernard' with which it is associated in certain manuscript sources.[54] But despite the Latin title, it is no mere scholastic *topos*, but a familiar theme in English literature from the time of *The Wanderer* (see

above, pp. 111–12) onwards,[55] expressing man's fundamental
sense of social and personal insecurity in the world. Here, instead of
Thomas's overt references to the transient glories of well-known personalities from history or literature, the poet refers directly to the familiar
pleasantness of human life he sees about him:

> Were beþ þey biforen us weren,
> houndes ladden and havekes beren
> and hadden feld and wode?
> þe riche levedies in hoere bour,
> þat wereden gold in hoere tressour
> wiþ hoere briȝtte rode.   (ll. 1–6)

[What has become of our predecessors, who led hounds and carried hawks,
and had possession of field and wood – the noble ladies in their bowers, who
wore gold in their hair-dos, with their radiant complexions?]

The lengthy penitential tradition makes it clear that this is more than
merely nostalgic reflection on the glories of former days, whether in general
or personally recollected, although that is necessarily the primary level at
which the audience must receive these fresh and factual references to the
noble life. Its religious significance is made clear with the second stanza,
which is bracketed by two biblical allusions. While apparently continuing
the description of the courtly life, it opens with an ominous reference:
'They ate, drank and made merry', l. 7 (cf. Luke 12. 19–20) and ends: 'And
in a twinkling of an eye they lost their souls', ll. 11–12. Although the *memento
mori* implication is clearly present, they are not yet said to be specifically
dead, but rather to have prejudiced their hope of heaven, when at
Judgement Day 'we shall all be changed in the twinkling of an eye' (i
Corinthians 15. 52). The third stanza develops the point of the biblical
references: that all is turned to vanity. But instead of the Wanderer's
reflective regret, the poet refers back to his previous images of the noble life,
with a more intimidating gesture: 'Who's laughing now!':

> Were is þat lawing and þat song,
> þat trayling and þat proude ȝong,
> þo havekes and þo houndes?
> Al þat joye is went away,
> þat wele is comen te weylaway,
> to manie harde stoundes.   (ll. 13–18)

[What has become of the laughter and the singing, the trailing dresses and the
proud gait, those hawks and those hounds? All that bliss has passed away, that
prosperity has come to 'Woe is me', to many a hard time.]

The next stanza makes the consequences explicitly clear. Those who seized their heaven here on earth, now lie in the fires of hell (ll. 19–21), the perpetual nature of which is emphasized in repetitive monosyllabic exclamation:

> Long is ay and long is ho,
> long is wy and long is wo!    (ll. 22–23)

[Long is 'alas' and long is 'oh', long is 'lack-a-day' and long is 'woe!']

It is a dire warning to the extravagant paradisal longings of the earthly lover (see above, p. 245). Further stanzas exhort the Christian to take on the role of *miles spiriti* to avenge Christ against the 'fiend, that foul thing' (l. 31). 'Up and be a good champion' (l. 34); bearing the cross as your staff and the shield of true faith (ll. 37, 43), take the field against that thief and traitor (ll. 42, 47), so as to win 'that merry land' (l. 48) where there is not only everlasting light and peace, but 'vengeance on every foe' (l. 51). The concluding stanza, as in Thomas of Hales's *Love-Song*, takes the form of a direct address to the 'Virgin mother, queen of heaven', requesting intercession for our sins. A final plea of mounting intensity makes it clear that the shield recommended is not that spoken of by St Paul (see above, p. 142), but the Virgin herself: 'You might, and can, and ought to be, our shield against the devil' (ll. 56–57).

Among the various worldly vanities that the poet urges people to shun, were naturally included the fripperies of fashionable clothing that serve to delude women especially: gold-decked snoods and trailing gowns (ll. 5, 14). *The Follies of Fashion* is a splendidly rumbustious denunciation of women who will go to any lengths to ape the latest styles.[56] A five- stanza lyric of simple structure, each stanza opens with a rhyming quatrain in long lines, aaaa, introducing the stated example of folly to be denounced, followed by a short bob and two further lines to form a surging triplet increasing in length and intensity of denunciation, bbb. As the lyric opens, however, stanza 1 is far from revealing the poet's ultimate target. It begins with an address to God, startlingly forceful in its direct *communicatio idiomatum*:

> Lord þat lenest us lyf ant lokest uch-an lede,
> forte cocke wiþ knyf nast þou none nede.    (ll. 1–2)

[Lord who grants us life and watches over every nation, you have no need to fight with a knife.]

It is self-evident that, unlike men, God does not need to defend himself physically, and we might think that the poet is about to denounce casual violence. Both warrior and woman are afraid of God, lest he be angry with their strife and, since they are unshielded from sin, deny them the joys of heaven (ll. 3–7).

The nature of the particular sin is made decidedly clear in the next stanza:

Nou haþ prude þe pris in everuche plawe,
by mony wymmon unwis y sugge mi sawe,
for ȝef a ledy lyne is leid after lawe,
uch a strumpet þat þer is such drahtes wl drawe;
in prude
uch a screwe wol hire shrude
þah he nabbe nout a smok hire foule ers to hude.    (ll. 8–14)

[Pride now takes the prize in every sport – I utter my verdict from the example
of many a foolish woman, for if a lady's clothes set the fashion, every strumpet
there is wants to take up the style; every slut wants to dress herself proudly, even
though she hasn't a smock to hide her filthy backside.]

The three remaining stanzas employ the same denunciatory structure to satirize particular features of contemporary fashion that the poet found objectionable. Every slut will pout unless she can have the padding, first introduced as a distinction to honour fine ladies – but will pay dear for it:

In helle
wiþ develes he shulle duelle,
for þe clogges þat cleveþ by here chelle!    (ll. 19–21)

[They shall dwell with devils in hell because of the caul that clings to their cheek.]

The linen-encased side-buns make a woman look like a tormented pig with its ears hanging down; the devil often sits and holds court in such elaborate head-dresses (ll. 22–28). If there is a love-lock over the ear or eye, and other hair-lotion is lacking she will damp-set it with worse (i.e. urine![57]). The poem ends in a witty crescendo. If the woman only has a false hair-fillet, she'll hold her head high to show off; but all it shows is 'that she is known and acknowledged to be the moll in a gang of rogues' (ll. 32–35).

Although misogynists exist in every age, anti-feminine satire was given additional force at this time in an inevitable reaction against the cult of women as represented in the doctrines of courtly love and the cult of the Virgin.[58] It is not surprising that the period witnessed a revival both of humanistic sensuality and celibate asceticism. Anti-feminine satire animadverts in general upon the conventional female weaknesses: their, admittedly often unwitting, obstinacy, hypocrisy, jealousy, garrulousness, lasciviousness, greed, fickleness of all kinds, but above all, because underlying all other faults, and more immediately vulnerable to humour, their pride and vanity. Although the lyricist's epithets are extreme (strumpet, shrew, slut), they are of general application. The particular vanity he pillories is not fine attire in its right place – on fine ladies – but the common obsession among socially aspirant women of all classes to ape their betters. As such it might as well represent a bourgeois response to the kind of extravagance which the sumptuary laws would eventually be enacted to curb, as represent an ascetic attack on fine clothing *per se* of the kind we find in the *Ubi Sount* lyric.

Just occasionally the lyricist would leave the common themes of wine and women, love and death, turning the telling effect of a well-pointed tune from ribald affection or clerical denunciation to political polemic. Matthew Paris preserves snatches of song sung by mercenaries ravaging the English countryside in the disorder of the mid-twelfth century.[59] One couplet refers to their contempt for the patron saints of the town of St Ives and the nearby Benedictine monastery – having just sacked both. Another apparently represents the chorus of a jubilant *carole*, as the soldiers leap about, singing:

> Hoppe, hoppe Wilekin, hoppe Wilekin,
> Engelond is min ant tin.

> [Jump to it, jump to it Little Will, jump to it Little Will; England belongs to me and you.]

As might be expected, such ditties of political abuse could be cruelly effective. Henry I was so incensed by one scurrilous song composed about him that he drove the lyricist to commit suicide.[60]

The earliest complete political song to survive is *A Song of Lewes*,[61] a stridently contemptuous piece directed against Henry III's unpopular brother Richard. It was probably composed, together with other songs in Latin and Anglo-Norman,[62] shortly after the Battle of Lewes in 1264, where a royal army in which Richard played a significant role, had been trounced, more or less bloodlessly, by the barons led by Simon de Montfort.[63] One of the few occasions on which early civil war achieved the dignity of a just cause, barons, friars, bishops, and citizens had been brought together to stand against tyrannical centralism; and Simon, who died the following year, was popularly regarded as a saint in some quarters.[64] Like much political satire, its scheme of reference is essentially ephemeral, many of the allusions now requiring an informative gloss. The king, who was present at the battle, is not directly mentioned – perhaps out of due deference. Those of the royal party denounced by name, the Earl de Warenne, Sir Hugh de Bigod, and Prince Edward, had all at one time been friendly to the barons' cause but later defected. The song-writer reserves his greatest malevolence, however, for Richard, who is made the subject of a gleeful chorus:

Richard, þah þou be ever trichard,
tricchen shalt þou nevermore!    (ll.6–7, etc.).

[Richard, although you'll always be a trickster, you'll never trick again!]

The second son of King John, Richard had never been popular in England, although on the Continent he had acquired a considerable reputation as a crusader-diplomat and eventually negotiated his elevation to the German crown. In England his negotiating activities seemed to be less those of an honest broker, than of one who tried to play all sides against the middle. And his financial profiteering as regent during the absence of Henry, only further alienated sympathy.

The first stanza opens with the familiar minstrel's plea.[65] Thereafter it deals with the immediate background to the Barons' War: Richard's offer, made just a day or two before, to act as 'honest broker' between the two sides – for a large sum, of course:

Sitteþ alle stille and herkneþ to me!
Þe kyng of Alemaigne, bi mi leaute,
þritti þousent pound askede he
forte make þe pees in þe countre,
ant so he dude more.

Richard, þah þou be ever trichard,
tricchen shalt þou nevermore!    (ll.1–7)

[Sit quietly everybody and listen to me! By my honour, the Emperor of Germany asked for thirty thousand pounds to arrange peace in the land – and wanted more as well. Richard, although you'll always be a trickster, you'll never trick again!]

The second stanza falls to personal abuse. Having depleted his (not inconsiderable) financial resources on fornication, not a farthing can be got from all his estates (ll.8–10). The next two stanzas allude directly to the aftermath of the battle. The Earl de Warenne's stronghold at Lewes having fallen, Richard was captured hiding in a windmill on the Sussex Downs, where he had barricaded himself in with the aid of some German mercenaries: 'many a sorry spirit' (l.23). He shouted through the chink that, as a foreign monarch, he took no part in local skirmishes.[66] But his pose of neutrality was now quite blown.

Þe kyng of Alemaigne wende do ful wel;
he saisede þe mulne for a castel,
wiþ hare sharpe swerdes he grounde þe stel;
he wende þat þe sayles were mangonel
to helpe Wyndesore.

Richard, þah þou be ever trichard,
tricchen shalt þou nevermore!    (ll. 15–21)

[The Emperor of Germany imagined he'd done very well; he seized the mill
for a castle, secured his position with their sharp swords; he imagined that
the sails were seige-engines to assist Windsor's cause. Richard, although
you'll always be a trickster, you'll never trick again!]

The allusion to Windsor in the bob preceding the chorus occurs with
variation in all but the opening and closing stanzas, ('in spite of
Windsor . . ., to help . . ., to strengthen . . ., for love of . . .', and then
twice again, 'to help Windsor'); it is clearly a reference that rankled. It
refers to the strategic royalist stronghold, currently manned by Prince
Edward's foreign mercenaries, from where Richard had ordered the
country to be put on a war-footing, burning bridges and sinking ships,
where Henry had recently summoned an 'armed parliament' of loyalist
barons, and where Simon de Montfort's eldest son was now held hostage.

Further stanzas allude to the presiding figure of Simon de Montfort
himself. 'Lord Simon de Montfort hath sworn by his chin, that if he now
had hold of the Earl de Warenne. . . ! Lord Simon de Montfort hath
sworn by his head, that if he now had hold of Hugh de Bigod . . .!' (ll. 30–
31, 35–36); but of course they had both bolted for the coast and made
good their escape to France. Prince Edward, however, having rejected his
uncle's (i.e. Simon's) advice, will ride, without the dignity of his knight's
spurs, straight to prison at Dover (ll. 40–46).

Political polemic is necessarily ephemeral. The poet has chosen to
focus not on the worth of his cause (which is left to the contemporary
Latinist) but merely to villify his antagonists. *A Song of Lewes* celebrates
what was, after all, one of the most important battles of English history,
but instead of the serious political or philosophical statement it might
have provoked, it offers merely jingoistic mockery; instead of historical
record, merely the trenchant self-righteousness of a (temporary!) victor.
It is an assertive crow, with no sense of perspective, either historical or
emotional. But if we are a long way from *The Battle of Maldon*, we may
recognize in the implacable hatred for both foreigner and war-profiteer
the unmistakable tones of English soldier-peasantry raised round the
camp-fires or in the baggage-trains of Simon's crusading army.

One later thirteenth-century lyric, commonly known as *The Thrush and
the Nightingale*,[67] bears a close relationship to *Lenten is Come with Love to
Town* (see above, pp. 241–43). It has a close verbal resemblance
throughout the first stanza (in one manuscript the opening couplet is
identical) and it employs the same rhyme-scheme. The *mise-en-scène* is the
same: the season is warm, nightingale and thrush are singing in the
woods, and there is dew in the valley – all of which leads us to expect the
familiar *reverdie*. But it is soon made clear that this *locus amoenus* is

ironically not the setting for love, fulfilled or frustrated, but rather for a fierce debate as to the actual worth of women as an object of love:

> Hic herde a strif bitweies two –
> þat on of wele, þat oþer of wo.
> Bitwene two i-fere,
> þat on hereþ wimmen þat hoe beþ hende,
> þat oþer hem wole wiþ miȝte shende.    (ll. 7–11)

[I heard an argument between two parties – the one successful, the other woeful. Between the two of them, the one praises women because they are gracious, the other would shame them outright.]

The thrush, who may have acquired a reputation for quarrelsomeness,[68] adopts a strong anti-feminine stance: women though beautiful are false, the downfall of many a good man. The nightingale, however, who has by now displaced the cuckoo as traditional harbinger of spring (see above, p. 119), and is no less firmly established in the role of minstrel of love,[69] springs to the defence of women in courtly terms:

> Hit is shome to blame levedy,
> for hy beþ hende of corteisy;    (ll. 25–26)

[It is shameful to blame a lady, because they are gracious out of courtesy;]

they are loving, gentle, and able to heal all the ills and misfortunes of men; both high and low, there is nothing so sweet as their companionship.

Once the narrative voice has established the subject at issue, the remainder of the poem is composed of direct speech, as the two parties, thrush and nightingale, exchange stanzas of argument. Apart from two single-line narrative links initiating nightingale stanzas: ('The nightingale was angry', l. 49; 'Then said the nightingale', l. 145), and one divided stanza (ll. 93/94), it is a highly balanced debate, each speech being contained within the stanza, and as such it would have responded well to performance by two voices. The formal nature of the exchange is reinforced by the thrush citing the evidence of historical precedent as proof for his case, the repeated phrase: *I take witnesse of* . . . (ll. 46, 70, 88) imparting a legalistic tone to the proceedings. As proof of his argument he cites stock examples of good men betrayed by wicked women:[70] from history, Alexander the Great and the Emperor Constantine (ll. 43, 115), from the world of romance, Sir Gawain, well known as a ladies' man (l. 88),[71] and from the Bible, Adam and Samson (ll. 70, 139). The nightingale, unable to offer any precise logical defence in any of these specific cases, is content to respond with mere generalities to the effect that the embrace of a woman's arms afford man's highest bliss on earth – carefully stopping short of the courtly blasphemy mocked in *The Fair Maid of Ribblesdale* (see above, p. 245). She seeks instead to lure her opponent into error. In the event, he is provoked into overstatement. The nightingale concludes stanza 5 by commenting that the thrush's viewpoint is merely due to lack of personal experience (l.60). At this the thrush over-reacts, and thus in legal terms prejudices his testimony, by revealing his own immoral stance as a cynical misogynist rather than the upright moralist he pretends. He is well known in ladies' bowers, and has had his will with them; all it takes is some small reward to get them to sin in secret (ll.62–66). In the event, the thrush prepares the way for his own discountenancing. It is the thrush who first refers to the law (ll.87, 113), and the nightingale who takes up the reference, not by logical argument, but by counter-state-ment, asserting that such lying trespass is likely to get him put in prison (ll.127–32). And it is the thrush who introduces religion with reference to the *holi bok* (l.136) and the name of Jesus (ll.89, 143) – which leads ultimately to the means of his crushing, and immediately acknowledged, defeat. The nightingale reserves her sole, but apparently overwhelming, counter-proof until the end, when at the mere mention of the Virgin's name the thrush performs a Gilbertian *volte-face*, immediately admitting that his former position was sheer madness:

> 'Niȝttingale, I wes woed,
> oþer I couþe to luitel goed,
> wiþ þe for to strive.
> I suge þat icham overcome
> þoru hire þat bar þat holi sone,
> þat soffrede wundes five.'   (ll.181–86)

['Nightingale, I was mad, or else I understood too little of virtue, to contend against you. I declare that I have been overcome through her who bore that holy Son who suffered five wounds.']

Of course the citation is inadequate on any logical grounds of evidence, since Mary is nothing if not atypical of women. But in the medieval manner the symbolic force of the reference is unanswerable. The person of Mary is apparently sufficient to exonerate the character of all women just as Christ redeemed the faults of all mankind. The conclusion was already implicitly present. Although the mention of Adam (l.70) may have resulted in a natural reticence on the part of the nightingale to mention Eve, the natural process of thought would arrive at the second Eve, i.e. Mary, readily enough.

In view of this wholesale capitulation on the part of the thrush, there is no necessity to turn elsewhere for judgement, and it is left to the nighting-ale to pronounce the long-threatened punishment of exile from the 'pleasaunce' which rightfully belongs to the nightingale alone (ll.84, 97–99), out into the open where he belongs:

> 'Fowel, for þi false sawe
> for-beddi þe þis wode shawe,
> þou fare into þe filde!'    (ll.178–80)

['Bird, because of your false statement, I banish you from this woodland grove; get off into the open!']

The religious conclusion might have been anticipated. Not only was the female position now intimately linked with the cult of the Virgin Mary (see above, *passim*); but the association of the nightingale with the lover of Christ was well established with the popularity of the devotional hymn *Philomena*, composed by the Franciscan Archbishop of Canterbury, John Peckham (*c.* 1220–92), in which the soul, pictured as the nightingale, sings of Christ's passion, only to die at three of a broken heart.[72]

*The Thrush and the Nightingale* represents an amalgam of two genres, both ultimately deriving from Classical literature: the Aesopian beast-fable and the personified debate. The debate-genre came especially into vogue with the Carolingian Renaissance, when witty Latin academic disquisitions, such as Alcuin's *Dispute between Spring and Winter* or Sedulius Scotus's briefer *Contest between the Rose and the Lily*,[73] are placed in a pastoral setting which clearly owes much to the classical eclogue. Since the use of personification often results in a spirited conflict beyond the merely abstract ideas they represent, it offers to approach the Prudentian psychomachia with the contestants determined to prove their own superiority by whatever means may be available, fair or foul, often spilling over into verbal abuse, or even resorting to physical contention. Once the narrative voice has introduced the theme, it retires to an unseen position, impartial and unobserved, playing only a minimal role, since, even if the conclusion is an inevitable one, the confrontation must appear to be lost or won on the merits of the case presented. The dramatized debate, using set dialogue, was a traditional mode of instruction in the schools, especially valuable as a device for teaching the grammar, vocabulary, and pronunciation of Latin. Ælfric's late-tenth-century *Colloquy*[74] is perhaps among the most charming examples, deceptively artless in its construction, but subsuming a discussion as to the most valuable member of society. The debate mode was given considerable impetus by the development of dialectic in the twelfth century. A fundamental mode of critical enquiry, the scholastic disputation sought not primarily to establish truth by way of logically pursued argument, but rather to reveal the multi-faceted nature of reality by collating conflicting opinions on a question so as to be viewed by the audience in the clearest light; it assumed no necessary solution, but rather the clarification of complexity.

It was actively educational, since the mode of enquiry sought not to impose received opinion, but rather to encourage students in an active enquiry on their own behalf.

The extension of debate from the abstract and philosophical world to the animal world, endowing beasts with human attributes, allowing them to talk and fight like men, is one stage less bizarre than an argument conducted by, say, flowers. It not only touches some native anthropomorphic chord, but informs an otherwise academic discussion with a livelier and more naturally contentious tone. The Aesopian beast-fable, 'in which a picture of life is drawn through the conversation of dumb animals',[75] had a long history stemming from classical times,[76] and achieved particular popularity in England during the twelfth and thirteenth centuries. Latin or Anglo-Norman collections by Odo of Cheriton, Alexander Neckham, Walter Map, or Nicholas Bozon all seem to have drawn from vernacular sources, while Marie de France explicitly asserts that her fables were directly translated from the English of King Alfred.[77] Allusions to the stories employed could be made both in literature and the visual arts, as in, for example, the margins of the Bayeux Tapestry.[78] The use of animals, especially birds, as protagonists, is by no means necessarily indicative of a frivolous tone, as witness Poe's *The Raven*, or the *Crow* sequence by Ted Hughes. The fact that Odo of Cheriton intended his collection for use as illustrative sermon material,[79] indicates the clear didactic potential of the genre.

While the choice of two birds, thrush and nightingale, as natural disputants in a natural setting, is clearly more convincing and entertaining than the confrontation of such personified opponents as Spring and Winter or the Rose and Lily, they remain, as the thrush's assertion of his experiences with woman makes plain, merely avian mouthpieces for purely human attitudes. Apart from their pastoral setting, the poet takes no cognizance of their bird-like character; and as with the contemporary Latin or Anglo-Norman fable, the poet is interested to personify points of view rather than to develop personalities. Neither is there any complexity in the argument developed: it is quite plain which point of view we are intended to favour.

Much more complex in both form, substance, and characterization, is the contemporary bird-debate, *The Owl and the Nightingale*. Its more substantial theme is reflected in its form. Although composed in the similar octosyllabic rhythm popular for oral performance, it avoids the discontinuous and necessarily artificial stanzaic form which promotes unrealistically balanced exchanges and stanza-contained arguments, in favour of a continuous flow of couplets which allows the presentation of a more developed argument in a freer and more colloquial vein. Moreover, its considerably enlarged canvas (1,800 as against 192 lines) permits the development of a much more substantial theme, which is no less than the relationship of literature to life itself.

The poet plunges immediately into his subject, needing no more than to sketch the conventional *locus amoenus*, since the pastoral setting is explicit throughout:

> Ich was in one sumere dale;
> in one suþe diȝele hale
> iherde ich holde grete tale
> an hule and one niȝtingale.   (ll. 1–4)

[I was in a certain valley one summer, in a particularly secluded corner, when I heard an owl and a nightingale hold a great debate.]

Unlike the thrush, the owl represents a convincing antagonist. It is a predatory bird (proud of its association with the hawk tribe, l.271) and known to prey on small song-birds. It is natural that owl and nightingale should be found together; both are creatures of the night, and both favour woodland haunts.[80] Possibly it was a traditional association. In Alanus de Insulis's account of the glades of Fortune in the seminal *Anticlaudianus* (1184), the pleasant song of the nightingale is heard side by side with the ominous cry of the owl.[81] And they are depicted together by the artist of the Psalter of Robert de Lisle (*c.* 1300) perched in the tree of vice, the nightingale by the label 'Fruits of the Flesh' and the owl on a bough that leads to 'Wrath' on the one side and 'Vainglory' on the other.[82] The nature of the owl as a bird of ill-omen, frequenting tombs and prophesying disaster, was familiar enough.[83] But such is the complex, shifting nature of medieval symbolism, that the owl may have other, less unhappy associations *in bono* rather than *in malo*. Contemporary encyclopaedists suggest that on the one hand the owl (*Bubo*) is the unclean bird of Deuteronomy 14. 12–16, its filthy habits, especially that of fouling its nest, signifying all iniquity, which flees from the light of justice, seeking out the darkness to hide its sins; on the other hand the owl (*Nycticorax*) signifies Christ, fleeing from the vainglory of light, and seeking out darkness the better to convert sinners (cf. John 1.5–9; Psalms 102. 6).[84] As a bird of legendary wisdom, the owl might well stand for Christianized science.[85]

Although they may display significant human concerns from which we can learn, the owl and nightingale are also decidedly avian in character. Their immediate entrance is one of squabbling. Puffing out their feathers:

> An aiþer aȝen oþer sval
> and let þat vvole mod ut al;
> and eiþer seide of oþeres custe
> þat alre worste þat hi wuste.   (ll. 7–10)

[Each swelled with rage against the other, and let loose all their foul temper; and each said the very worst things they knew about the other's character.]

Their differences will range over a wide variety of topics, argued with varying degrees of acrimony: their nesting-habits, diet, appearance, how their young are reared, but over and above all the widely differing nature of their songs:

> And hure and hure of oþeres songe
> hi holde plaiding suþe stronge.   (ll. 11–12)

[And above all else, they lodged the strongest complaints about each other's song.]

The protagonists are realistically conceived, quarrelling, interrupting, and abusing each other like the birds they, at one level, clearly are. We are never allowed to forget their true nature for, although the issues they raise are of some moment, their scheme of reference is systematic and coherent, a world of chickens and crows, foxes, and frogs.

Whereas in the limited space available in *The Thrush and the Nightingale* the academic issue must be made clear from the very beginning, announced by the poet before the debate proper opens, the larger scope of *The Owl and the Nightingale* permits the central topic to be approached more realistically and obliquely, although not insignificantly, through an attack on the character of the owl, who defends herself in turn. The natural opposition of the two birds is reinforced by the setting in which they take up their respective stances; the nightingale sings her joyful and musical song from a burgeoning thicket, perched on a bough thick with blossom (ll. 14–18), in marked contrast with the owl who cries out standing on an old tree-stump all overgrown with ivy (ll. 25–27). At first sight we seem clearly intended to concur with the narrative voice in favouring the nightingale, the cheerful underdog, rather than the overbearing and gloomy owl. And yet for those who wish to recognize it, there is already a clear hint that the picture is not totally one-sided. The presentation of the owl is given distinct ecclesiastical overtones. The expression used of her song, 'to sing the hours', clearly associates it with regular church worship; the place where it is sung is a natural *memento mori*, supporting an evergreen symbol of everlasting life.[86] We scarcely need reminding how quickly blossom fades and falls (see above, p. 247).

It is the nightingale who begins, catching sight of the owl and instantly badmouthing her ('quite naturally', intervenes the narrative voice, 'since all men reckon her loathesome and foul', l. 32); the instinctive basis of her lively invective, is that the owl's mere appearance and overbearing presence is frightening and inhibits her own song:

'Unwiȝt!' ho seide, 'awei þu flo!
Me is þe wrs þat ich þe so.
Iwis for þine vule lete
wel oft ich mine song forlete.
Min horte atfliþ and falt mi tonge
wonne þu art to me iþrunge.
Me luste bet speten þane singe
of þine fule ȝoȝelinge.'  (ll. 33–40)

['Monster', she said, 'fly away! I'm the worse for seeing you. In fact I very
often forsake my song because of your foul behaviour. My heart sinks and
my voice fails when you thrust yourself upon me. When I hear your foul
gurgling I'd rather spit than sing.']

The owl, although naturally furious, manages to contain herself until
evening-time when, almost breathless with rage, she gives tongue. She
may know nothing of the small bird's chirruping, but that doesn't mean
she can't sing! (ll. 47–48); the implication is clearly that it is a question of
definition – or preference. But as the owl continues threateningly: 'If only
I held you in my claw, you'd sing a different tune!' (ll. 51–54), it is clear
that she has been taunted into making the mistake of revealing violent
intentions, which allows the nightingale to respond at length on the owl's
bullying nature. She is merciless against those who cannot protect themselves, and preys on little birds wherever she can, for which reason she is
hated by all of them; 'even the very titmouse would gladly tear you to
pieces!' (ll. 69–70). The nightingale goes on to disparage the owl's lumpen
and bizarre personal appearance, her foul diet: frogs, snails, and mice
(perhaps indicative more of human than avian squeamishness, ll. 85f),
and the filthy habits of the owl's young, fouling their own nest, and sitting
up to their necks in droppings (ll. 92f). In furtherance of this last charge,
the nightingale retails a fable, familiar from Marie de France or Nicholas
Bozon,[87] in which a noble falcon repudiates the filthy owl-chick it had
fostered with the comment that though one may rear them, one cannot
change their nature (ll. 101–26). The falcon young readily identify their
inferior by his different shape; he is cast out and rent by magpie and
crow. That this relates to the world of men is made quite explicit:

'Herbi men segget a bispel –
þeȝ hit ne bo fuliche spel.
Also hit is bi þan ungode
þat is icumen of fule brode
and is meind wit fro monne,
ever he cuþ þat he com þonne,
þat he com of þan adel eye
þeȝ he a fro nest leie.'  (ll. 127–34)

['Apropos of this men tell a parable – although it isn't a full-length tale. It is just like the low-born man, who comes from a foul brood; although he mixes with noblemen, he will always betray where he comes from – that, although he lies in a noble nest, he came from an addled egg.']

The debate as to the claims of nature versus nurture was a fundamental concern of the age, as of every age, but of particular interest in the twelfth and thirteenth centuries; its assumptions underlie such widely differing romances as *Havelok* and *Sir Tristrem*.

The owl, not unnaturally put out by this imputation, sits staring at the ground, swollen and bulging 'as if she had swallowed a frog' (l.146); but she has a ready answer. Why won't the nightingale come out into the open and show which is the more beautiful of the two; but the nightingale isn't to be lured into leaving the security of her branch, and falling into the owl's talons: 'You thought – as your kind does – to deceive me with fair words' (ll.157–58). She proposes, instead, that they leave off squabbling, to rehearse their arguments in a formal debate, conducted with due regard to law and reason, and to leave judgement to a certain Master Nicholas of Guildford (ll.177ff). There seems little doubt but that, in the manner of certain contemporary French, Provençal, and Arabic debate-poems,[88] this is intended as a puff to promote the professional advancement of Nicholas. It is significant that the two birds immediately agree on the virtues of the said Nicholas: 'There's no question about it', says the nightingale (l.190); he is wise, prudent, and moral. Moreover:

'He wot insiȝt in eche songe,
wo singet wel, wo singet wronge;
and he can schede vrom þe riȝte
þat woȝe, þat þuster from þe liȝte.'    (ll.195–98)

[He has a profound knowledge of every song – who sings well, who sings badly; and he can distinguish right from wrong, the light from the darkness.]

The owl duly consents for, although Nicholas may have been somewhat wild in his younger days – too fond of nightingales by half – he has now steadied down, is less easily distracted by frivolity, and will make a sound judge (ll.201–14). At the end of the poem the name of Nicholas will recur, as the wren, king of the birds, makes a plea for his promotion, criticizing those in high places for failing to recognize his obvious merits (ll.1745ff). It is easy enough to find him since, much to the shame of those bishops and others in authority who might have promoted this excellent man but chose to pass him over in favour of lesser men, he only has one dwelling – at Portisham in Dorset. The lines were not impossibly penned by Nicholas himself; such over-fulsome self-advertisement was by no means unknown in academic circles, then as now.

Rather than immediately leaving to plead their respective cases before this judge, however, the momentum of their argument leads them to rehearse the dispute. As with *The Thrush and the Nightingale*, the case is not presented in terms of a closely ordered argument, but rather in the manner of contemporary Abelardan disputation by means of a pattern of assertion and counter-assertion. Often points are not taken up immediately or consecutively, but reflecting traditional legal procedure are often rebutted only after an intervening period, the topic apparently recurring *apropos* of something else. The nightingale's charges against the owl's appearance, diet, and the habits of its offspring, for example, are not substantially countered by the owl until lines 575ff. In this manner, through constant cross-reference we are made aware of the complex interrelationship of what might otherwise seem a mere kaleidoscope of topics: love and adultery, astrology, witchcraft, and many more. Focusing and refocusing, the poet maintains all in suspension, referring all to his underlying theme: the nature and value of the disputants' songs. It is taken for granted by both parties that the quality of the song is intimately related to the character of the singer.

The dispute rages fast and furious in a spirited fashion over a whole gallimaufry of topics for 1,500 lines, from 215 to 1717 where the dispute is interrupted and brought to a conclusion, although not to resolution, by the wren. First the nightingale takes the offensive by expanding her initial charge that the owl is monstrous, *unwi3t* (ll.33, 90, 218). She sings only at night shunning the light of day which can't be right; her 'song' takes the form of a terrifying lament: shrieks and yowls that are grisly to hear and seem calculated to make you weep rather than sing (ll.217–52). The owl does not deny the facts, but merely their interpretation, choosing to approximate her role to *Nycticorax* rather than *Bubo*. She acts merely according to the law of Nature, for which no man can blame her; it is because of her natural fierceness (*ri3te cunde*) that low-flying little birds fear her. But the hawk is no less noble because crows cry out against it! Her love of the dark is not only natural, but virtuous. It is in the night that she comforts the bold armies of men. As for her song, the nightingale simply disapproves of any tune that differs from its own thin piping, whereas in fact her own song can claim to be superior. Its note is smooth, harmonious and loud, bold and masterful like a great horn. Furthermore, whereas the indiscriminate nightingale chatters like an Irish priest (l.322), all night long, thus cheapening its discourse by sheer superfluity (for only the everlasting kingdom of God does not pall), the discriminating owl sings merely the canonical hours, at bedtime, midnight, and dawn: 'Thus I do good with my song, warning men to their advantage' (ll.329–30).

The narrative voice admits that the nightingale is somewhat taken aback by this militant apologia on the part of the owl:

> vor ho ne miȝte noȝt alegge
> þat þe hule hadde hire ised,
> vor he spac boþe riȝt an red.   (ll. 394–96)

[because she could not gainsay what the owl had said about her, because she
had spoken both truly and with good sense.]

Nevertheless, she puts on a bold front – advisedly – and returns to the
attack, taking up the implications of the owl's defence. Why then does the
owl – like a hen in a snowdrift! – seem solely to sing of woe, remaining
dumb all summer (ll. 411–16). That must be because she resents others'
happiness; she is like the misanthropist who 'would like to see tears in
every man's eyes' (ll. 417–26). She concludes her attack by affirming the
owl's acknowledged position: 'when snow lies deep both far and wide,
and hardships are the lot of all, then it is that you sing from evening to
dawn' (ll. 430–32). Ironically the nightingale can accept the facts of the
owl's case, but is temperamentally unable to make the same value-
judgement. For by her very nature, the nightingale is a different kind of
bird and belongs to a different season. She contrasts her associations in
this respect strongly with the owl's, emphasizing her role as the symbol of
*reverdie*. Blossoms burst out in woodland and meadows; celebrating the
lily and the rose, hers is not impossibly a spiritual song: joyous
Franciscan-style lyricism, rather than the dull canonical conservatism of
the monk-like owl.

> Þe lilie mid hire faire wlite
> wolcumeþ me – þat þu hit wite! –
> bid me mid hire faire blo
> þat ich shulle to hire flo.
> Þe rose also, mid hire rude
> þat cumeþ ut of þe þornewode,
> bit me þat ich shulle singe
> vor hire luve one skentinge.   (ll. 439–46)

[The lily with her lovely countenance welcomes me – I would have you know
– prays, with her lovely complexion, that I should fly to her. The rose also,
which in her scarlet comes from the briar-bush, prays that I should sing a
recital for love of her.]

In returning to a former point made by the owl, however, she leaves
herself open to attack. She claims that her song is not in fact, too long.
Indeed, once men turn their minds to bringing in the harvest and the
green leaves turn brown, then she takes her leave. When she sees hard
times coming, she migrates; there is, after all, no point in outstaying her
welcome! In contrast with the owl's stolid dependability, she has im-

plicitly admitted that she is a transient, fair-weather friend. In fact, in describing her seasonable arrival, she had already admitted that men were merry before her coming (1.436); her song is a consequence and not the cause of men's pleasure. The owl has no need to take up this point; its double-edged nature is self-evident. But she makes a final defence and comparison. Her interest is not solely in adversity; like all good men, she cherishes her friends, making merry with them on certain special occasions:

> 'and hure and hure to Cristes masse,
> þane riche and poure, more and lasse,
> singeþ cundut niȝt and dai,
> ich hom helpe what ich mai.'    (ll. 481–84)

['and especially so at Christmas; then when rich and poor, great and small, sing carols night and day, I help them all I can.']

Summertime is all too wanton, and apt to lead men's thought astray from purity to lechery; 'for then no creature is restrained, but each rides on the other' (ll. 493–94). The nightingale's song is explicitly associated with its own sexual activity: *for of golnesse* [lechery], *is al þi song* (1.498); it is passionate enough beforehand, but once copulation has taken place, it cannot utter a word, but squeaks hoarsely like a titmouse – a point not in fact observed in nature,[89] but significantly pointed at post-coital lassitude among men. All summer long churls go mad, writhing and bucking, but not for love, for once they've thrust in under the skirt their love dissipates (ll. 509–16). Mere sexual love is ephemeral. It is adversity that reveals the more durable qualities: when the going gets tough, the tough get going. It is in the winter of man's discontent that the owl's song serves to lessen their pain (ll. 523–40). The owl is triumphant at this rebuttal:

> 'Hu þincþ þe? Artu ȝut inume?
> Artu mid riȝte overcume?'    (ll. 541–42)

['What do you think? Now are you cornered? Are you beaten fair and square?']

The nightingale offers to return to the fray with what she claims will prove a final, overwhelming accusation. But the owl insists that that would be illegal. She has replied to the nightingale's charge, but before proceeding to judgement would like to exercise her right to make a counter-accusation. For the next 600 lines, it is the owl's turn to attack, and the nightingale's to defend herself as best she may. The owl's attack again takes up the topic of nature. Apart from the nightingale's 'shrill throat', what use is she? She is quite lacking in substance, and as such, useless to mankind. The owl quotes, as both birds do from time to time, from the Proverbs of Alfred:[90]

> 'Nis no man for is bare song
> lof ne wrþ noȝt suþe longe'. (ll. 571–72)

['No man is praised or honoured long for a mere song.']

She now counters each of the charges the song-bird had made against her by laying similar charges as to her opponent's appearance, diet, and social habits. The nightingale is certainly not beautiful, but dark and filthy in colour, like a 'little dirty ball' (*a lutel soti clowe*, l. 578). It is lacking in all the physical virtues: beauty, strength, and size. And it has filthy habits. It favours thickets where men go to defecate, shunning any cleaner place. When the owl goes hunting for mice in the night-time, she finds the nightingale in the privy, sitting behind the seat where men thrust out their backsides (ll. 583–96); and although it reproaches the owl for her diet, what does the nightingale eat except spiders and filthy flies? The owl insists on her own service to men; she catches mice in their barns, and rids God's house, which she especially loves, of all vermin. Her home is in a strong tree covered with ivy that is always green whatever the season. If her offspring foul the nest, so does the horse its stable and the ox its stall,

> an lutle children in þe cradele –
> boþe chorles an ek aþele –
> doþ al þat is hore ȝoeþe
> þat hi vorletep in hore duȝeþe.
> Wat, can þat ȝongling hit bihede?
> Ȝif hit misdeþ, hit mod nede.
> A vorbisne is of olde ivurne,
> þat node makeþ old wif urne!   (ll. 631–38)

[and little children in the cradle – both peasant and princely alike – do things when they are young that they give up in their manhood. Well, can the infant help it? If it misbehaves, it's of necessity. There's an old-fashioned saying that 'Need makes the old woman trot!']

In any case, the young owls go to the outside of their nest, which is fashioned like the dwellings of men, 'with a privy at the end of the bower, so they don't have too far to go – and my chicks do the same' (ll. 649–54).

As the owl rightly claims, the truth of what she lays to the nightingale's charge cannot be gainsaid. Nevertheless, an answer must be made, and carefully, 'for a word can quickly go astray when what a man says is not what he feels: and a speech can quickly go wrong, when tongue and heart do not agree. Nevertheless, a man's mind is never so keen as when in doubt as to what to do' (ll.673–82). Breaking the owl's apparent monopoly of spiritual interest, she approximates the Franciscan defence. The nightingale's one song is better than all the owl's tribe ever knew. Why, after all, was mankind created in the first place – but to enjoy the bliss of the kingdom of heaven, where there is eternal song and merriment! (ll.716–18). That's why men sing in church, and clerks compose their lyrics, so that men may remember their destiny, and follow the teaching of the Church. Monks and canons in monasteries by night and priests in their parishes by day are all encouraged by her singing; and she prays that they may attain the self-same song eternal. More than affording mere pleasure, it affords a glimpse of eternity, reflecting an ultimately neo-Platonic view that earthly ecstasy is merely an anticipation of heavenly bliss. It is a claim honoured by established literary precedent. From Ambrose to Sedulius Scotus, bird-song was considered the equivalent of congregational hymns of praise,[91] while for Alcuin the nightingale, despite its unprepossessing appearance, specifically sang in praise of God.[92] It was a common enough lyric stance, borne out by the approximation of hymns to secular melodies (see above, p. 246), but not one that will prove acceptable to the conservative owl. Nevertheless, so convinced is the nightingale of the overwhelming strength of her argument, that she declares she is prepared to go for judgement on that to the very Pope of Rome (ll.745–46). She may be slight, but she is skilful. Strength is no substitute for talent; she needs no other power than the craft of song. For the virtue of intelligence over brute strength, the nightingale adduces a whole host of examples from the world of men and of beasts, until the owl cries a halt:

> 'Abid! Abid!' þe ule seide.
> 'Þu gest al to mid swikelede.
> Alle þine wordes þu bileist
> þat hit þincþ soþ, al þat þu seist!'    (ll.837–40)

['Stop! stop!', said the owl. 'You work altogether by treachery. You gloze over all your words so that all you say seems to be true!']

Men cannot be brought to the kingdom of heaven merely by singing; repentance is necessary first – and this the owl's song is designed to achieve. Indeed, if this point is disputed, she will claim that her very weeping is better than the nightingale's song, *Ich wepe bet þane þu singe* (l.876). Moreover the owl puts its talon on the frequently ambiguous nature of the religious lyric; no one could mistake the nightingale's piping for a priest singing in church (ll.894–902). And since she claims a missionary spirit, how is it that her song is never heard in those cold and remote lands, such as Scotland, Norway, Galloway, or Ireland, where the priests could well benefit from a demonstration of how the angels sing (ll.905–16). The owl, of course, exercises her ministry in every land, urging men not only to avoid sin, but to beware of the nightingale's misleading song (ll.921–26).

The nightingale is both angry and somewhat ashamed; but after a pause to regain her equilibrium (for as King Alfred said, 'the angry man seldom pleads well', l.944), returns an argument which aligns her firmly with the courtly party on two counts. Of course she hovers around the privy – it simply happens to be close to the bower where lord and lady lie together in bed; should she forsake her proper place and her duty to follow the highest things just because of a plank with a hole in it (the privy seat)? (ll.957–70). She implicitly denies any more than a casual relationship between carnal love and alimentary functions. As for her restricted habitat, it is merely a matter of courtly discrimination. What should she do in a poor and barren land peopled by irredeemable barbarians who eat raw fish and raw meat, tearing it to pieces like wolves, and knowing nothing of wine or beer; nothing can check their mad behaviour and they 'live, in truth, like wild beasts' (l.1012). (The nightingale has momentarily forgotten her avian identity.) However long she sang, her song would be completely wasted there; it clearly requires a sophisticated environment. She will sing her hymns only in pleasant lands where the people are gentle, for one will only plough where one expects to reap (ll.1039–42).

Once the topic of carnal love has been broached, the protagonists are unable to retain their composure; the dispute rages fast and furiously, the speeches briefer and more urgent with no pause for reflection between – which as we have been warned, is likely to prove dangerous. Indeed the birds now begin to confirm their natures; the owl's violent and the nightingale's irresponsible. The owl angrily responds without delay, insisting on the corrupting nature of courtly love and the role played by the nightingale in the courts of love. She refers to a version of Marie de France's *Laustic* known to Alexander Neckam,[93] in which a nightingale – perched we now know where – encouraged a lady to indulge an illicit and shameful passion, for which cause the enraged husband trapped the song-bird and had it torn apart by wild horses (ll.1049–62). The nightingale for her part responds immediately and angrily that the charge was malicious; she was not to blame; the guilt was in reality that of the overbearing and unreasonably jealous husband; she had merely taken pity on and tried to offer what comfort she could to a lonely and neglected wife. In any case, adds the nightingale, she now enjoys the specific protection of King Henry – presumably referring to the courtly patronage of the arts, and artists, under Henry II and Eleanor (see above, p. 18) (ll.1091–1110).

The owl, on the other hand, has no such friends. People of all kinds, young and old, choose to pelt it with stones. In fact it is more use dead than alive for, hung on a stick as a scarecrow, it can at least protect crops from other birds (ll. 1115–44). Little wonder that it should be so loathed by men, for it only ever seems to portend disaster, the nightingale offering a long incantatory list of examples beginning:

> Oþer of summe frondes rure,
> oþer þu bodes huses brune,
> oþer ferde of manne, oþer þoves rune,
> oþer þu bodest cualm of oreve,
> oþer þat londfolc wurþ idorve,
> oþer þat wif lost hire make,
> oþer þu bodest cheste an sake;
> ever þu singist of manne hareme,
> þurȝ þe hi boþ sori and areme.   (ll. 1154–62)

[Either you bode the downfall of some friend, or a house burning down; either a battle among men, or a hue-and-cry; either you bode a plague among cattle, or that the people in the land will be stricken; you bode either that a wife will lose her husband, or brawling and strife; you always sing about the troubles of men; through you they are both sad and wretched.]

The nightingale concludes with an imprecation: may the wrath of Almighty God – and of all who wear clothes – descend on her! (ll. 1173–74). The owl instantly returns, questioning the nightingale's curse, for it is she who has first claim to alignment with ecclesiastical institutions. She confirms her prophetic role in a rhetorical sequence similar to that of the nightingale's accusation:

> Ich wot of hunger, of hergonge,
> ich wot ȝef men schule libbe longe,
> ich wat ȝef wif luste hire make,
> ich wat þar schal beo niþ and wrake,
> ich wot . . .   (ll. 1191–95)

[I know about famine, about invasion, I know whether men are to have a long life, I know whether a wife will lose her husband, I know where there will be malice and enmity, I know . . .]

and so on for another dozen lines. She attributes this prophetic knowledge directly to her association with the Church and with book-learning, claiming to be familiar with all the symbolic meanings of biblical study (ll. 1208–14). Since all that happens comes about by the will of God, why should the owl be blamed for simply telling the truth; her warning doesn't bring trouble any closer, it merely gives man the opportunity to prepare himself (ll. 1255ff). She again cites the authority of King Alfred for a summary defence: a gnomic sequence on the transience of worldly affections, a traditional religious theme, powerful since the earliest days of the English Church:

> 'Ne truste no mon to his weole
> to swiþe, þah he habbe veole;
> nis nout so hot þat hit nacoleþ,
> ne noȝt so hwit þat hit ne soleþ;
> ne noȝt so leof þat hit ne aloþeþ,
> ne noȝt so glad þat hit ne awroþeþ;
> ah eavere euh þing þat eche nis
> agon schal, and al þis worldes blis.'   (ll. 1273–80)

['Let no man put too much faith in his wealth, however much he's got; there's nothing so hot that it won't cool down, nothing so white that it won't get dirty, nothing so loved that it won't become loathsome, nothing so joyful it won't get angry; for everything that isn't eternal must pass away – including all the pleasure of this world.']

This time the nightingale is unable to offer an immediate rejoinder for, as the owl rightly supposes, this sombre statement of mutability is a sobering one. Yet the owl's claim to interpretative knowledge is at least open to question. The uncanny and disturbing foreknowledge of which the owl boasts is not only fatalistic and therefore heretical, it smacks of witchcraft, and as such is anathema to the Church (ll. 1298–1308). As for her claim to exegetical skills, 'An ape can look at a book, turn over the pages and close it again, but that doesn't mean to say he has a jot of the clerk's scholarship' (ll. 1325–28). Having, to her own satisfaction at least, disposed of the owl's claims to special consideration on religious grounds, the nightingale is once more able to return to the theme of the love-song. This forms the final confrontation between the two birds, and represents in some respects a curious accommodation of each to the other's position. The nightingale begins by making a substantial defence of love-song in human affairs, pleading her own innocence and claiming that any fault lies not in the song itself but in the use men choose to make of it. She makes a stand for refined spiritual rather than self-indulgent love, and could never encourage adultery, 'for a good wife may within marriage love her own husband far better than any outside philanderer' (ll. 1340–42). Why then should she be blamed if a soft-hearted woman allows herself to be seduced:

> Wummon mai pleie under cloþe
> weþer heo wile, wel þe wroþe,
> and heo mai do bi mine songe
> hwaþer heo wule, wel þe wronge;
> for nis a worlde þing so god
> þat ne mai do sum ungod
> ȝif me hit wule turne amis.   (ll. 1359–65)

[A woman may frolic under her petticoat as she wants to, whether for good
or ill, and as for my song, she will do as she wants, right or wrong; for there's
nothing in the world so good that it cannot do some harm, if one wants to
pervert it.]

All love, of whatever kind, between men and women is pure, unless it
is stolen. Carnal lust is hard to crush, for the flesh is weak, but the sinner
(spoken of as a woman rather than man), though fallen, may rise again;
she is not irredeemable. And sins of the flesh are in any case by no means
the same as sins of the spirit – the vainglorious pride that disdains those
who fall; 'many a man, pure of body, is a devil at heart' (ll.1387–1412).
Moreover, one must distinguish between passion in maidens and
matrons. If a young girl falls in love with some lad playing fast and loose
with her affections, and, led astray by her young blood, stumbles by
nature, *icundeliche* (l.1424), no great damage is done since the error can
soon be put right by marriage:

'Hwat mai þat chil þah hit misfonge?
Hit nuste neaver hwat hit was,
forþi hit þohte fondi þas,
an wite iwis hwuch beo þe gome
þat of so wilde makeþ tome.'    (ll.1440–44)

['How can the girl help but go wrong? She never knew what it was like, and
so she thought to experiment and find out for certain about the sport that
tames so wild a creature.']

The nightingale claims positively educational ends in such circumstances.
Her song – its essentially ephemeral nature now explicitly admitted – will
teach such girls that passionate love is short-lived, 'nothing but a little
breath which soon comes, and soon goes' (ll.1461–62). But if the lapses of
young girls are excusable, she cannot condone the adultery of wives.
Now the nightingale adopts a stance that directly questions the received
view of *fin' amor* by examining the social motivation of the lover *vis-à-vis*
the husband in this triangular relationship. How is it that a man can
wrong another's wife when the husband is a man to be feared or otherwise
respected, and is therefore a cause for restraint, either out of genuine
respect or fear of castration. Alternatively, what pleasure could a man
possibly find lying with a woman whose husband was not worthy of
some measure of respect. (The nightingale clearly thinks in terms of the
game of *fin' amor* rather than indulgent lust.)

ʒef hire laverd is forwurde,
an unorne at bedde and at borde,
hu miʒte þar beo eni luve
wanne a swuch cheorles buc hire ley buve?
Hu mai þar eni luve beo
þar swuch man gropeþ hire þeo?   (ll. 1491–96)

[If her husband is feeble, and useless in bed and elsewhere, how can there be any love with such a churl's belly lying on top of her? How can there be any love where such a man gropes her thigh?]

The nightingale has clearly erred in shifting from a moral stance to one of social utility. The owl certainly considers that her opponent's case has come to grief by apparently being concerned solely for maidens while disregarding the distressed matron. The owl, on the other hand, offers consolation to all. It is not unusual for a husband and wife to be at variance, and small wonder that a woman maltreated through neglect, abuse or over-possessive jealousy should turn elsewhere for comfort:

La, Godd hit wot, heo nah iweld,
þah heo hine makie kukeweld!   (ll. 1543–44)

[Well, God knows, she can't help that, even though she makes a cuckold of him!]

It may be that the nightingale's accusation of spiritual pride has struck home. While not explicitly condoning sexual lapses, the owl reveals a singular streak of sympathetic understanding and compassion. Her song is in part a song of mourning; she weeps with them that weep, the mistreated and the lonely, through the long waking nights, giving what help she can (ll. 1565–1602). Nevertheless, the owl has so convinced herself of her own self-sacrificial virtue, that she too now makes a false step. She returns to the scarecrow image, and seeks to turn it to her own advantage by admitting the facts, but slanting their interpretation. It is true that, martyr-like, her blood is shed, but it is a death that benefits mankind (ll. 1615–17). The nightingale chooses to ignore the Christ-like implications of her own earlier mocking phrase (now repeated), that the owl is hung up *on rodde* (ll. 1123, 1646), since any such acknowledgement must render her own opposition invalid. Instead, triumphantly seizing on the literal aspect, she can claim that the owl's admission of its own shame is tantamount to entering a plea of guilty, totally undermining her whole position:

Me þuncþ þat þu forleost þat game:
þu ȝulpest of þire oȝe schame;
me þuncþ þat þu me gest an honde:
þu ȝulpest of þire oȝene schonde.   (ll. 1649–52)

[I think you've lost the game – you're boasting about your own dishonour; I think you're giving in to me – you're boasting about your own disgrace.]

It is at this point that the dawn-chorus breaks in, providing a both natural and dramatic conclusion. We are suddenly aware that the two birds have argued all night long. They thus have more in common than they like to think: the experience and temperament of both being appropriate to sleepless nights, whether prompted by tears or by love – or both. Since the dawn-chorus is made up of song-birds they naturally side with the nightingale. The owl, presumably with the memory of being mobbed by flocks of song-birds (cf. ll. 65–68), as naturally assumes that the nightingale has summoned an army to assist her, and threatens to retaliate by calling on her own friends, the birds of prey. The issue offers to end dramatically; but then the wren, the smallest of birds yet their sovereign, averts the threat of violence, present from the beginning, by warning that they are likely to cause a breach of the king's peace, and reminding the antagonists of their earlier agreement to seek judgement from Nicholas of Guildford. The wren is said to be not only a fine singer, but particularly wise, since she had been brought up among the race of men and derived her wisdom from them – a rather tongue-in-cheek comment at this stage perhaps (ll. 1723–26). These explicit references to the human scale of values, whether of royal displeasure at the breach of the peace or of the wisdom of men in general, strike a decidedly condescending note. For despite the fact that the birds have reflected human values throughout, their correlative world has been so convincingly portrayed, that it is only now that we are made forcibly aware that their stance is unnatural to them as *birds*, and that their stated moral and social values merely parody those of men. The repeated puff for Nicholas of Guildford brings the audience down to earth with a pragmatic note and into the real world. Within the internal terms of the debate there was no real need to turn to the world of men for judgement; the issue might logically and consistently have been settled by the wren. But now the human framework is explicit we must recognize the voices for what they actually are – merely chattering, quarrelsome birds. The patent absurdity of the situation is revealing. The ability to refocus in this way marks the genuine self-awareness of literary genius; and the laughter which accompanies the recognition is an index of both great humanity and fundamental uncertainty.[94] This is not to say that the views explored in the debate with such wit are not of considerable importance. There is every reason to suppose that *The Owl and the Nightingale* was regarded as a fundamentally serious piece of literature; it was intercalated with items of a religious and moral nature, and apparently shelved together with religious and historical materials.[95]

To have permitted an immediate settlement by, for example, the wren, would have suggested the possibility of unambiguous judgement. Deferment affords a dramatic suspension which enables the poet to conclude with intellectual honesty. As the two disputants fly off unaccompanied to Portisham to consult Nicholas, the poet says simply:

> Ah hu heo spedde of heore dome
> ne can ich eu na more telle.
> Her nis na more of þis spelle.    (ll. 1792–94)

[But as to how they succeeded in their judgement, I can tell you nothing more. There's no more to this tale.]

No verdict is given – or even anticipated – because, of course, none is possible. It is not a juridical dispute the birds present, but an academic and human one. Although we might at various stages have been attracted by the position of one or other party, the case is a complex one, and fortunately we are not called upon to make a choice. There is clear merit on either side, and yet neither is sufficient of itself. The contestants rarely dispute the facts, but merely their interpretation, which is, of course, coloured by their respective temperaments. There is thus no logical arbitration that either party can respect, save that which recognizes both to be merely aspects of a whole. If anything, the poem asserts that there is just cause for argument and for differing interpretation, but denies any one position sole or continuous superiority, and ultimately, quite properly, denies the audience any tyrannical judgement. Since the method of procedure, as commonly with, for example, parliamentary debate or legal pleading, is not conducted according to any algebraic system of analysis, but subject rather to the sequential vagaries of run-of-the-mill human disputes, there can be no real attempt to synthesize alternative interpretations by logical thought. Only after a lengthy, and often self-cancelling, series of charges and counter-charges are we aware that the disputants are approaching the issue with radically different assumptions. When the two birds agree to seek judgement – which may as well mean reconciliation as arbitrary decision for one or other side, it is to restore þis pes that reigned before their gripbruche [breach of the peace], lest their quarrel result in public disorder (ll. 1730–34). Although in the spirited heat of their argument the birds have sometimes toppled into invective, this has lacked genuine malice, and during the course of their debate the protagonists have come at least to respect each other's position, while still disagreeing. And at the end they agree to collaborate peacefully in putting their case before Nicholas; the owl is prepared to rehearse the whole argument – subject to correction – on behalf of them both (ll.1784–88). The owl's undisputed offer suggests that there is a potential harmony to be recognized. Unlike the mode of logical, scientific enquiry, which anticipates definitive resolution – an individual solution to a stated problem – the reflective mode of medieval disputation, reflecting contemporary Abelardan or neo-Platonic modes of enquiry, seeks to expose and assemble, possibly reconcile, opposing views, rather than to arrive at any clear-cut decision. The arguments that are propounded in *The Owl and the Nightingale* are no more capable of resolution than the academic debates between Spring and Winter or Rose and Lily. But the human terms in which they are conducted indicate how fiercely such issues may be engaged. The argument moves back and forth in a spirited fashion, either side showing skill in presentation and refutation, all of which leads the audience, like themselves, to suppose that there may be some just but decisive outcome to the debate.

In fact, rejecting the partial, *parti pris*, and partisan, *The Owl and the Nightingale* encourages a philosophic, tolerant, and humane perspective superior to mere choice – and the consequent 'breach of the king's peace' that intolerance brings – and questions man's inhumane allegiance to superficial dichotomies which ultimately deny the possibility of social or cosmic order. The debate is essentially academic, but it raises issues of some substance; and the altogether disarmingly witty literary form into which they are cast should not lead us to dismiss the serious implications of the statements made. As with all good medieval literature, the possible points of entry and levels of argument are various. The debate genre most explicitly externalizes those tensions and conflicts which it is the singer's impulse to explore. At one level, of course, all literary protagonists, Beowulf or Byrhtnoth, Judith or Ysoude, philosophic Wanderer or womanizing Cleric, are depicted within a state of conflict which is the work's *raison d'être*. The telling of the tale invariably contains dramatic movement of some kind, or some shift in perception which serves to satisfy or frustrate, defeat or elevate the protagonist, without necessarily arriving at any ultimate resolution. The fundamental issue that literary form exists to explore: the problem of how man may reconcile his personal experience of inadequacy and disorder with his own tantalizing expectation of an ordered and sustaining framework to life, was never more acute than in the twelfth and thirteenth centuries; then the debate form explicitly acknowledges the possibility of stringent and direct enquiry, and with it the expectation of arriving at some conclusion. But if *The Thrush and the Nightingale* appears to do so, it is because the nightingale cheats. The particular method of debate fostered by the twelfth-century schools developed a vigorous dialectic in which the truth might emerge from controversy. It is a form of demonstrative argument no less valuable than the logical sciences, which provides a worthwhile means of ascertaining or denying probability rather than establishing incontrovertible certainty. Although demonstrative dialectic will not yield absolute truths, it may indicate by sheer plausibility, or even sophistry, a variety of viewpoints which may solicit our allegiance. The method was epitomized in the Abelardan *Sic et Non* mode, in which 'respondent' and 'opponent' addressed themselves to a 'master', who would be expected, much in the manner of the legal procedure which developed *pari passu*, to summarize the position of either party, and then to present his own considered opinion supported by the citation of due 'authorities'.[96] For the audience of *The Owl and the Nightingale*, as of *The Wanderer*, quietude resides in acknowledging the state of conflict which exists, and of which one is, in some way or other, part; recognizing it to be a fundamental quality of the order of things, since the equilibrium of life consists not in monolithic dead-weight, but in balanced tension. The enthusiasm for formal dialectic, however, probes more explicitly the age-old constituents of conflict in society: the tension between faith and reason, between authority and innovation, the contemporaneity of the old and the new, all of which might cast man's belief in himself into doubt.

Virtually all the literature discussed in this book emerges out of a culture intimately familiar with crisis, with assertion and doubt. Individuals, then as now, finding it difficult to live with conflict, sought personal solutions to the tensions inherent in their perception of universal order. The greatest literature, however, corrects this individual and partial perspective; it will not license intolerance and rarely permits an exclusive or uniform point of view. Debate-poetry in particular, while recognizing the need for special solutions to special problems, seeks to modify the doctrinaire critical imbalance characteristic of much literary theory down to the present day.

## Notes

1. The verb Bede uses to describe Cædmon's extensive compositions on biblical themes is *cantare: Bede's Ecclesiastical History of the English People,* edited by B. Colgrave and R. A. B. Mynors (Oxford, 1969), pp. 416–17. Cynewulf speaks of the words of the patriarch Moses, no less than the psalms of David, as being 'sung', *Cynewulf's Elene,* edited by P. O. E. Gradon, second edition (Exeter, 1977), pp. 39–40. The romance *King Horn*, some fifteen hundred lines of rhyming couplets, begins: *Ihc schal ʒou singe*, and finishes *þus him endeþ Hornes song*, edited by J. Hall (Oxford, 1901), pp. 3, 89. The author of *Èmaré* introduces the subject of his romance thus: *Her name was called Emare, as I here synge in songe*, edited by E. Rickert, Early English Text Society, Extra Series, 99 (London, 1906), p. 1. In *Sir Cleges* it is told how *An harpor sange a gest be mowth*, edited by A. Treichel, *Englische Studien*, 22 (1896), 345–89 (p. 386).

2. *Bede's Eccles. Hist.*, edited by Colgrave and Mynors, pp. 416–17; *Sir Tristrem*, edited by G. P. McNeill (Edinburgh, 1886), p. 85.

3. One manuscript version of the romance *Sir Beves of Hamptoun* begins: *Lordinges, herkneþ to me tale . . . þat y schel singe*, while another begins: *Lystonythe, lordinges . . . of a doughty man I wyll you tell,* and ends by referring to it as a *talking,* edited by E. Kölbing, Early English Text Society, Extra Series, 46, 48, 65 (London, 1885–94), pp. 1, 217. Compare the comment with which Marie de France ends her Lai de Guigemar: 'From the story you've just heard the lay Guigemar was composed, which is played on harp and viol; the tune is pleasant to hear', *Lais*, edited by A. Ewert (Oxford, 1944), p. 25.

4. J. Bosworth and T. N. Toller, *An Anglo-Saxon Dictionary*, with revised and enlarged addenda by A. Campbell (Oxford, 1898–1972), i pp. 958–59, ii, p. 718; *Middle English Dictionary*, edited by H. Kurath and S. M. Kuhn (Ann Arbor, Michigan, 1954, in progress), m, pp. 281–82.

5. *Gesta Herwardi*, in *Lestorie des Engles solum la translacion Maistre Geffrei Gaimar*, edited by T. D. Hardy and C. T. Martin, Rolls Series, 91 (London, 1888–89), i, pp. 351–52.

6. *Liber Eliensis*, edited by E. O. Blake, Camden Third Series, xcii (London, 1962), pp. 153–54.

7. *Gesta Herwardi*, in *Lestorie des Engles*, edited by Hardy and Martin, p. 344.

8. Henry of Huntingdon, *Historia Anglorum*, edited by T. Arnold, Rolls Series, 74 (London, 1879), pp. 60, 91, 213; William of Malmesbury, *De Gestis Regum Anglorum*, edited by W. Stubbs, Rolls Series, 90 (London, 1887–89), i, p. 155.

9. See generally, R. L. Greene, *The Early English Carols*, second edition (Oxford, 1977), pp. xliii–lxiv.

10. 'An age-old tradition', *Itinerarium Kambriae*, in *Giraldi Cambrensis Opera*, edited by J. S. Brewer *et al.*, Rolls Series, 21 (London, 1861–91), vi, pp. 189–90.

11. See generally, E. J. Dobson and F. L. Harrison, *Medieval English Songs* (London, 1979).

12. Ibid., p. 242.

13. *English Lyrics of the XIIIth Century*, edited by C. Brown (Oxford, 1932), p. 14. For the music, see Dobson and Harrison, *Medieval English Songs*, pp. 246, 299–300; also H. D. Chickering, 'Foweles in þe frith: A Religious Art-song', *Philological Quarterly*, 50 (1971), 115–20; *Argo Record*, no. RG443, item 2.

14. See R. Sikora, 'The Structural Simplicity of the Early Middle English Lyric: Three Examples', *Kwartalnik Neofilologiczny*, 11 (1964), 233–36.

15. See M. Fifield, 'Thirteenth-century Lyrics and the Alliterative Tradition', *Journal of English and Germanic Philology*, 62 (1963), 111–18.

16. See Sikora, *Kwartalnik Neofilologiczny*, 11 (1964), 236; and E. Reiss, 'A Critical Approach to the Middle English Lyric', *College English*, 27 (1966), 376–77.

17. See also the lyrics *Blow, northerne wynd*, l. 10, in *English Lyrics of the XIIIth Century*, edited by Brown, p. 148; and *Lollai, lollai litil child*, l. 8, in *Religious Lyrics of the XIVth Century*, edited by C. Brown, second edition, revised by G. V. Smithers (Oxford, 1957), p. 35.

18. *English Lyrics of the XIIIth Century*, edited by Brown, pp. 145–46; *The Harley Lyrics*, edited by G. L. Brook, fourth edition (Manchester, 1968), pp. 43–44.

19. *English Lyrics of the XIIIth Century*, edited by Brown, p. 13; and see P. Heidtmann, 'The Reverdie Convention and *Lenten is Come with Love to Toune*', *Annuale Medievale*, 12 (1971), 78–89 (especially, p. 79).

20. See Heidtmann, Ibid., p. 87.

21. A notion found as early as the eleventh century in the Latin love-lyric *Iam, Dulcis Amore*, included in an anthology from St Augustine's, Canterbury, *Carmina Cantabrigiensa: Die Cambridger Lieder*, edited by K. Strecker, *Monumenta Germaniae Historica, Scriptores Rerum Germanicarum, Separati Editi*, XL, second edition (Berlin, 1955), p. 71. Compare the words of the thirteenth-century lyric *De Clerico et Puella*, in which an amorous clerk protests: *ych have poled for þy love woundes fele sore, fer from bour and eke from men, under þe wodegore*, in *English Lyrics of the XIIIth Century*, edited by Brown, p. 153.

22. *Harley Lyrics*, edited by Brook, pp. 37–39.

23. Compare D. S. Brewer, 'The Ideal of Feminine beauty in Medieval Literature, especially *Harley Lyrics*, Chaucer, and some Elizabethans', *Modern Language Review*, 50 (1955), 257–69.

24. Compare *On god ureison of ure lefdi*, l. 53, in *English Lyrics of the XIIIth Century*, edited by Brown, p. 4; or 'An Autumn Song', ll. 1f, *Harley Lyrics,* edited by Brook, p. 60. See also contemporary commentaries on The Song of Solomon, 2. 1, by, for example, Thomas 'the Cistercian', *Commentarium in Cantica Canticorum*, edited by J.-P. Migne, *Patrologia Latina* (Paris, 1844–90), CCVI, col. 189, or Alanus de Insulis, *Elucidatio in Cantica Canticorum*, edited by Migne, *Patrologia Latina*, CCX, cols 64–65.

25. Compare J.-C. Payen, *Le Prince d'Aquitaine: Essai sur Guillaume IX, son Œvre et son Erotique* (Paris, 1980), pp. 74–77. And compare the lyric *De Clerico et Puella*, in *English Lyrics of the XIIIth Century*, edited by Brown, p. 152, or Robert Mannyng, *Handlyng Synne*, edited by I. Sullens (Binghamton, New York, 1983), pp. 200–01.

26. *Le Credo au Ribaut*, ll. 157–60, in *Parodies de Thèmes Pieux dans la Poésie Française du Moyen Age*, edited by E. Ilvonen (Helsinki, 1914), pp. 123–33 (pp. 130–31).

27. See further, M. Glasscoe, '*The Fair Maid of Ribblesdale*: Content and Context', *Neuphilologische Mitteilungen*, 87 (1986), and references there cited.

28. *The Canterbury Tales, Prologue*, ll. 166, 189, in *The Complete Works of Geoffrey Chaucer*, edited by F. N. Robinson, second edition (London, 1957), pp. 18–19.

29. See *Chronicon de Lanercost*, edited by J. Stevenson (Edinburgh, 1839), p. 109. That the 'sinful' associations of the *carole* were already familiar as early as the eleventh century is clear from Goscelin of Canterbury's deployment of the 'cursed carollers of Colbeck' story, edited by A. Wilmart, 'La légende de Ste Edith en prose et vers par le moine Goscelin', *Analecta Bollandiana*, 56 (1938), 5–10, 265–307 (pp. 287–91).

30. *Giraldi Cambrensis Opera*, edited by Brewer *et al.*, II, pp. 119–20.

31. For example, Thomas of Bayeux, Archbishop of York (*ob.* 1100), an accomplished musician who made a habit of setting sacred words to popular tunes: William of Malmesbury, *De Gestis Pontificum Anglorum*, edited by N. E. S. A. Hamilton, Rolls Series, 52 (London, 1970), p. 258.

32. 'Kleinere mittelenglische Texte', edited by M. Förster, *Anglia*, 42 (1918), 152–54. See the sermon attributed to Stephen Langton, Archbishop of Canterbury (*ob.* 1207), which takes as its text the popular dance-song *Bele Alis*, offering an ingenious spiritual interpretation without directly advocating its performance, in *Religiöse Dichtung im englischen Hochmittelalter*, edited by K. Reichl (Munich, 1973), pp. 379–88.

33. See D. Jauss, 'The Ironic Use of Medieval Poetic Conventions in *The Fair Maid of Ribblesdale*', *Neophilologus*, 67 (1983), 293–304.

34. *English Lyrics of the XIIIth Century*, edited by Brown, pp. 161–63; *Harley Lyrics*, edited by Brook, pp. 70–72.

35. *English Lyrics of the XIIIth Century*, edited by Brown, pp. 68–74. For a detailed consideration of the context and circumstances of composition, see B. Hill, 'The Luve-Ron and Thomas de Hales', *Modern Language Review*, 59 (1964), 321–30.

36. M. D. Legge, 'The Anglo-Norman Sermon of Thomas of Hales', *Modern Language Review*, 30 (1935), 212–28.

37. See Greene, *Early English Carols*, pp. cxlff, and references there cited.

38. See S. *Bernardi, Clarae-Vallensis Abbatis Primi, Opera Omnia*, III, edited by J. Mabillon, in *Patrologia Latina*, edited by J.-P. Migne (Paris, 1844–90), CLXXXIV, cols 1307–08; and see generally Aelred of Rievaulx, *Liber de Speculo Caritatis*, in *Aelredi Rievallensis, Opera Ascetica*, edited by A. Hoste and C. H. Talbot, *Corpus Christianorum, Continuatio Medievalis*, I (Turnholt, 1971), p. 98.

39. *Le Speculum Perfectionis*, edited by P. Sabatier, British Society of Franciscan Studies, XIII, XVII (Manchester, 1928–31), I, p. 290. See generally, D. L. Jeffrey, *The Early English Lyric and Franciscan Spirituality* (Lincoln, Nebraska, 1975).

40. Conveniently printed in *Early Middle English Prose and Verse*, edited by J. A. W. Bennett and G. V. Smithers, second edition (Oxford, 1968), pp. 136–44. See further, T. J. Garbaty, 'Studies in the Franciscan *The Land of Cokaygne* in the Kildare MS.', *Franziskanische Studien*, 45 (1963), 139–53.

41. Compare *Þe Wohunge of Ure Laverd*, edited by W. M. Thompson, Early English Text Society, 241 (London, 1958), pp. 20–38; *Ancrene Wisse*, edited by J. R. R. Tolkien, Early English Text Society, 249 (London, 1962), pp. 202–03. And see further, W. E. Rogers, *Image and Abstraction* (Copenhagen, 1972), pp. 28–40.

42. *De Virginitate*, l. 153 *et passim*, in *Aldhelmi Opera*, edited by R. Ehwald, *Monumenta Germaniae Historica, Auctores Antiquissimorum*, XV (Berlin, 1919), pp. 359f.

43. *Le Château d'Amour de Robert Grosseteste*, edited by J. Murray (Paris, 1918). The image may be traced to patristic interpretation of the biblical phrase: *intravit in quoddam castellum* (Luke 10. 38; Matthew 21. 2), by, for example, Alcuin, *Liber Sacramentorum*, edited by J.-P. Migne, *Patrologia Latina* (Paris, 1844–90), CI, cols 455–56, Anselm, *Homiliae et Exhortationes*, edited by Migne, *Patrologia Latina*, CLVIII, col. 645, or Alanus de Insulis, *Sermones Octo*, edited by Migne, *Patrologia Latina*, CCX, cols 201–2. See generally, R. Cornelius, *The Figurative Castle* (Bryn Mawr, Pennsylvania, 1930), especially pp. 37–46.

44. For the moralization of the apocalyptic stones, see generally, *English Mediaeval Lapidaries*, edited by J. Evans and M. S. Serjeantson, Early English Text Society, Original Series, 190 (London, 1933), pp. 13ff; *Anglo-Norman Lapidaries*, edited by P. Studer and J. Evans (Paris, 1924), p. 260. And compare Rogers, *Image and Abstraction*, pp. 28–40, and references there cited.

45. Compare S. Manning, *Wisdom and Number: Toward a Critical Appraisal of the Middle English Religious Lyric* (Lincoln, Nebraska, 1962), p. 107 *et passim*.

46. Cf *Þe Wohunge of Ure Laverd*, edited by Thompson, and *Ancrene Wisse*, edited by Tolkien.

47. Manning, *Wisdom and Number*, p. 123.

48. *English Lyrics of the XIIIth Century*, edited by Brown, pp. 75–76.

49. Sung by the courteous clerk Nicholas in Chaucer's *Miller's Tale* (l. 3216), in *Complete Works*, edited by Robinson, p. 48.

50. For the music, see Dobson and Harrison, *Medieval English Songs*, pp. 261–62, 303–05; *Argo Record,* no. RG443, item 7. The Latin hymn is found accompanied by alternative music in three other, later, manuscripts, so that Dobson and Harrison are able to reconstruct no less than four further settings (pp. 263–68). See also J. Stevens, 'Angelus ad virginem: The History of a Medieval Song', in *Medieval Studies for J. A. W. Bennett,* edited by P. L. Heyworth (Oxford, 1981), pp. 297–328.

51. See further S. A. Weber, *Theology and Poetry in the Middle English Lyric: A Study of Sacred History and Aesthetic Form* (Columbus, Ohio, 1969), pp. 32–46.

52. English clergy were specifically encouraged in its use by councils meeting at Norwich in 1257 and Exeter in 1287: *Sacrorum Conciliorum Collectio*, edited by J. D. Mansi (Florence, 1759–98), xxiii, col. 967; xxiv, col. 846.

53. *English Lyrics of the XIIIth Century*, edited by Brown, pp. 85–87.

54. *The Minor Poems of the Vernon MS.,* edited by C. Horstmann and F. J. Furnivall, Early English Text Society, Original Series, 98, 117 (London, 1892–1901), ii, pp. 757–63; compare J. E. Cross, 'The Sayings of St Bernard and Ubi Sount Qui Ante Nos Fuerount', *Review of English Studies*, 9 (1958), 1–7.

55. J. E. Cross, '"Ubi Sunt" Passages in Old English – Sources and Relationships', *Vetenskaps-Societetens i Lund Årsbok* (1956), 30–33.

56. *English Lyrics of the XIIIth Century*, edited by Brown, pp. 133–34.

57. R. J. Menner, 'Notes on Middle English Lyrics', *Modern Language Notes*, 55 (1940), 244–45.

58. See generally, F. L. Utley, *The Crooked Rib* (Columbus, Ohio, 1944), *passim*, still the best account of the motive force behind medieval satire of women.

59. *Historia Anglorum*, edited by F. Madden, Rolls Series, 44 (London, 1866–69), i, pp. 271, 381.

60. *The Ecclesiastical History of Ordericus Vitalis*, edited by M. Chibnall (Oxford, 1969–80), vi, pp. 354–55.

61. *English Lyrics of the XIIIth Century*, edited by Brown, pp. 131–32.

62. *The Political Songs of England from the Reign of John to that of Edward II,* edited by T. Wright (London, 1839), pp. 59–68, 72–121.

63. For the historical circumstances of the battle, see generally, M. Powicke *et al.*, *The Battle of Lewes, 1264: Its Place in English History* (Lewes, 1964); a full-length biography of Richard is provided by N. Denholm-Young, *Richard of Cornwall* (Oxford, 1947), especially pp. 118–30.

64. For a prayer written in his honour, see *Political Songs*, edited by Wright, pp. 124–25.

65. C. Brown and R. H. Robbins, *The Index of Middle English Verse* (New York, 1943), list some six dozen such openings.

66. *The Chronicle of Melrose*, edited by A. O. Anderson *et al.* (London, 1936), p. 128.

67. *English Lyrics of the XIIIth Century*, edited by Brown, pp. 101–07, who prints the poem in six-line rather than twelve-line stanzas; but see the Auchinleck MS. version edited by H. Varnhagen, 'Zu den Streitgedichte zwischen Drossel und Nachtigall', *Anglia*, 4 (1881), 207–10.

68. See B. Rowland, 'Chaucer's Throstil Old and other Birds', *Mediaeval Studies*, 24 (1962), 381–84 (p. 382).

69. See *Carmina Cantabrigiensa*, edited by Strecker, p. 71, n. 30.

70. Compare *King Alisaunder*, ll. 7703–09, edited by G. V. Smithers, Early English Text Society, Original Series, 227 (London, 1952), pp. 417–19, or *Sir Gawain and the Green Knight*, ll. 2416–19, in *The Poems of the Pearl Manuscript*, edited by M. Andrew and R. Waldron (London, 1978), p. 295.

71. See B. J. Whiting, 'Gawain; His Reputation, his Courtesy and his Appearance in Chaucer's *Squire's Tale*', in *Twentieth-Century Interpretations of Sir Gawain and the Green Knight*, edited by D. Fox (Englewood Cliffs, New Jersey, 1968), p. 74.

72. *Lateinische Hymnendichter des Mittelalters*, ii, edited by G. M. Dreves, *Analecta Hymnica Medii Aevi*, (Leipzig, 1907), pp. 602ff.

73. *Monumenta Germaniae Historica, Poetae Latini Aevi Carolini*, i, edited by E. Dümmler (Berlin, 1881), pp. 270–72; iii, edited by L. Traube (Berlin, 1896), pp. 230–31.

74. *Ælfric's Colloquy*, edited by G. N. Garmonsway, second edition (Exeter, 1978).

75. *Isidori Hispalensis Episcopi, Etymologiarum sive Originum*, edited by W. M. Lindsay (Oxford, 1911), Lib. i, xl. 2.

76. See generally, L. Hervieux, *Les Fabulistes Latins depuis le Siècle d'Auguste jusqu'à la Fin du Moyen Age* (Paris, 1884–99).

77. *Die Fabeln der Marie de France*, edited by K. Warnke (Halle, 1898), p. 328.

78. H. Chefneux, 'Les fables dans la Tapisserie de Bayeux', *Romania*, 60 (1934), 1–35, 153–94.

79. *Eudes de Cheriton et ses Dérivés*, in *Fabulistes Latins*, edited by Hervieux, iv, pp. 173f.

80. The present author saw – and heard – an owl and a nightingale in the same tree on the edge of the Mersey in a Manchester suburb one warm summer night in 1965; it may not be insignificant that he was on his honeymoon at the time.

81. *The Anglo-Latin Satirical Poets and Epigrammatists of the Twelfth Century*, edited by T. Wright, Rolls Series, 59 (London, 1872), ii, p. 397.

82. *The Psalter of Robert de Lisle*, edited by L. F. Sandler (London, 1983), pl. 8.

83. Compare Alanus de Insulis, *Liber de Planctu Naturæ*, in *Anglo-Latin Satirical Poets*, edited by Wright, p. 438; and see generally M. J. Donovan, 'The Owl as Religious Altruist in *The Owl and the Nightingale*', *Mediaeval Studies*, 18 (1956), 207–14.

84. For example the pseudo-Hugh of St Victor, *De Bestiis et Aliis Rebus, Libri Quatuor*, edited by J.-P. Migne, *Patrologia Latina*, (Paris, 1844–90), clxxvii, cols 30–31, 45; and compare Augustine, *Ennarrationes in Psalmos*, edited by E. Dekkers and J. Fraipont, *Corpus Christianorum, Series Latina*, xxxviii–xl (Turnholt, 1956), pp. 1430–31.

85. See generally, A. C. Cawley, 'Astrology in *The Owl and the Nightingale*', *Modern Langugage Review*, 46 (1962), 161–74.

86. See Greene, *Early English Carols*, pp. cxxvii, 83–84.

87. *Fabeln der Marie de France*, edited by Warnke, pp. 264–66; Nicholas Bozon, *Les Contes Moralisés*, edited by L. T. Smith and P. Meyer, Société des Anciens Textes Français, 28 (Paris, 1889), pp. 23, 205–06. For a closely similar tale in which a buzzard takes the role of the owl, see Odo of Cheriton, in *Fabulistes Latins*, edited by Hervieux, iv, pp. 181, 437–38.

88. Compare H. Knobloch, *Die Streitgedichte im provenzalischen und altfranzösischen* (Breslau, 1886), p. 48; L. Selbach, *Das Streitgedicht in der altprovenzalischen Lyrik* (Marburg, 1886), p. 177; H. Ethé, 'Ueber persische Tenzonen', in *Verhandlungen der 5teh Inter-Nationalen Orientalisten Congresse* (Berlin, 1881), II (1), 48–135.

89. In fact the cock nightingale continues to sing until after the eggs are hatched; but it might have been supposed otherwise by contemporary commentators, see H. B. Hinckley, 'Science and Folklore in *The Owl and the Nightingale*', *Publications of the Modern Language Association*, 47 (1932), 303–14 (p. 309), and references there cited.

90. Possibly only a conventional ascription; by no means all the citations can be traced, see *The Proverbs of Alfred*, edited by O. Arngart (Lund, 1942–55).

91. Ambrose, *Opera*, edited by C. Schenkl, *Corpus Scriptorum Ecclesiasticorum Latinorum*, XXXII (1) (Vienna, 1887), pp. 171–72; Sedulius Scotus, in *Monumenta Germaniae Historica, Poetae Latini Aevi Carolini*, III, edited by L. Traube (Berlin, 1896), pp. 219, 233.

92. *De Luscinia*, in *Monumenta Germaniae Historica, Poetae Latini Aevi Carolini*, I, edited by E. Dümmler (Berlin, 1881), p. 274.

93. Marie de France, *Lais*, edited by Ewert, pp. 97–101; *Alexandri Neckam, De Naturis Rerum, Libri Duo*, edited by T. Wright, Rolls Series, 34 (London, 1863), pp. 102–03.

94. For the suggestion that the whole poem might be considered in terms of self-parody, see further, J. Gardner, '*The Owl and the Nightingale*: A Burlesque', *Papers in Language and Literature*, 2 (1966), 3–12, or C. Hieatt, 'The Subject of the Mock-debate between the Owl and the Nightingale', *Studia Neophilologica*, 40 (1968), 155–60.

95. If an entry contained in one contemporary library catalogue is correctly identified with this work; see R. M. Wilson, 'The Medieval Library of Titchfield Abbey', *Proceedings of the Leeds Philosophical and Literary Society*, 5 (1938–43), 150–77, 252–76 (p. 159).

96. See generally, *La Littérature Quodlibétique de 1260 à 1320*, edited by P. Glorieux (Paris, 1925–35); and E. Reiss, 'Conflict and its Resolution in Medieval Dialogues', in *Arts Libéraux et Philosophie au Moyen Age: Actes du Quatrième Congrès International de Philosophie Médiévale, 1967* (Montreal, 1969), pp. 863–72.

# Epilogue: The Equal Hour

It would be tempting to conclude simply at this point in the fashion of the *Owl and Nightingale* narrator: *Her nis na more of þis spelle* [There's nothing more to say!] But of course that could not be true; the warp and weft of literary history continued unbroken. But if many of the threads survive, the pattern certainly changed – slowly but inevitably. The network of circumstances which permitted, even provoked, open debate, could not long remain. So multifaceted an interpretation of reality as that sponsored by the new wave of learning would prove too deeply disturbing to be accepted by the established institutions. Teachers of conservative temperament, as always a majority, having a vested interest in the intellectual status quo, staunchly resisted what they saw as impetuous innovation. As always the label 'progressive' was sufficient denunciation. Eventually the Church would find it necessary not merely to denounce, but have burned alive those who persistently questioned received opinion. Meanwhile, however, although English schools were un-hampered by the papal ban imposed on Aristotelian teaching throughout the Continent in 1277, the groundswell of the new philosophy, the ex-pansive, all-pervading world-view which thrust into every channel of intellectual life from the twelfth century onwards, had spent itself by the fourteenth. Scholasticism, the dynamic tool which once facilitated the pioneer achievements of English scholars in the fields of mathematics and the natural sciences, fell into mere constipated sophistry – self-perpetuating and pedantic rather than innovative and creative. It was no longer clear that the instrument of logic would prove uniformly efficient in every sphere of human enquiry, particularly, of course, in respect of theology. Duns Scotus (*fl.* 1300) was probably the last major thinker to accommodate religion with philosophy in a coherent in-tellectual system. The followers of Ockham (*fl.* 1325) would abandon any attempt to reconcile faith with reason. Nevertheless there had been clear gains in the field of literature. Now that reality was known to consist of the minutiae of perception, the new science confirmed the literary trend towards individuation, with a growing interest in physical and psychological actuality, so that Platonically conceived personae such as the Wanderer-figure, however powerful, were henceforth inconceivable, except as artificial allegories. Similarly, the traditional images associated with the age-old theme of mutability were ousted by a morbid fascination with the macabre details of death and dissolution *per se* – and little wonder perhaps as bubonic plague revisited England no less than thirty times between 1348 and 1485.

In religious circles, as the nature and range of what could be known with certainty diminished and faith without reason threatened to slide into superstition, the emergence of the phenomena of vernacular mysticism on the one hand and Protestant Lollard idealism on the other, both implicitly and explicitly repudiated the tradition of corporate orthodoxy. *Pari passu* the separation of reason and faith there developed the notion of a self-sufficient sovereign state, and with it the increasing secularization of all aspects of law and government. Henceforth society would be regarded less as a fragment of Christendom and more as a potentially turbulent rabble upon whom law and order was to be enforced by a competent and necessarily ruthless prince. With the roots of potential disorder countered and, theoretically at least, banished at a philosophical level, it would be possible to face otherwise horrendous difficulties with greater equanimity. It is a superb confidence that is reflected in the opulent ornamental development of Gothic art in fourteenth-century England, which now overwhelmed the puritan, elegant simplicity of Early English Gothicism: sheer decorative exuberance, overflowing the margins of books or the sculptured surfaces of buildings – ornament applied apparently regardless of function or structure – the decorative niche often forming as great a focus of interest as the statue it framed. The same decorative impulse in the realm of song would lead to a growing divergence between words and music, resulting in the development of, on the one hand the decidedly 'literary' lyric which, while written in stanzaic form, seems verbally too complex ever to have been sung, and on the other hand a musical line of such elaboration as to swamp any semantic content.

Learned poets were now committed either to the orthodoxies of the Church or to the service of noble patrons, and rarely responded to the popular demands of the market-place and tavern. In the face of repressive policies both civil and ecclesiastical, the satirical voice faltered and fell silent. Anonymity would no longer provide a secure cloak for the dissident clerk. The greater frequency with which authors were identified by name and the increasingly personal tone of their works would be inconsistent with controversial content. The newer mode of irony ultimately depended on a secure supposition of fundamental order in the world.

In any case the market-place no longer provided quite the free context for *vagantes* that once it had. The character of urban life had begun steadily to change. The city was now dominated by the sound of bells from the clock-tower. The mechanical clock now regulated the life of the citizen, synchronizing the activities of an ordered society. A mechanical analysis dissociated from experience, it marked the final divorce from the rhythms of nature which continued to characterize the peasant life of the countryside where throughout the year the days were of uneven duration and the relationship of day and night steadily subject to seasonal variation. Men had taken for granted the necessity of adjusting their lives pragmatically to such exigencies. But now the rhythms of nature gradually ceased to serve as the measure of human activities. The unequal hour had irrevocably passed. Regular time-keeping brought an ungentlemanly uniformity to the life of the workplace. In any case, what with recurrent pestilence and soaring inflation, urban life was proving markedly less attractive to the more successful citizen. The birth-rate fell; fewer sons chose to follow their father's trade, more seeking socially advantageous marriages with the daughters of feudal landowners. The commercially successful citizen began to consider himself a gentleman, investing in property in the shires, bearing arms like the nobility and claiming the burial-rites of a baron – increasingly scorning personal involvement in trade in favour of the fashionable occupations of landed gentry. The expulsion of the Jews from England in 1290 – as much a xenophobic as an anti-Semitic impulse – brought the merchant class more decidedly into the field of investment; and as investor rather than tradesman, the businessman was unlikely to devote his life as well as his fortune to an enterprise, whether risky or merely arduous. The separation of labour and capital (now that the cause of aggravation between citizen and nobleman was increasingly blurred), served merely to shift the focus of class antagonism down the social scale, and charges of oppression and misconduct are more frequently brought against the ruling urban élite. But rural retreats would not remain quiescent for long. The shortgage of labour consequent on the Black Death of 1348 which annihilated one-third of the population, encouraged the demands of a discontented proletariat, coming to a head in the large-scale and widespread Peasants' Revolt of 1381.

Meanwhile, Plantagenet England, increasingly conscious of a national identity, conveyed its hostility beyond its own frontiers with wars, more or less successful, against Welsh, Scots, and French in turn. Anti-French feeling, culminating in the Hundred Years War beginning in 1337, hastened the end of French as the natural language of the establishment. As aristocratic territorial links with former Continental estates were decisively broken, citizen-English continued inexorably to rise in the social scale. French might be preserved in a static, fossilized form in the technical professions of law and government, but it was soon no longer native to the upper classes as a whole. Of the major protagonists at the Battle of Lewes, for example (see above, p. 256), it seems that at least Earl

Richard and Prince Edward habitually spoke English; and French was certainly a foreign language to their offspring. Attempts made to arrest the decline of French by authorities in monasteries and universities – and even by Act of Parliament in 1332 – were to no avail. It is evident that by the early fourteenth century there were many among the nobility who spoke no French at all, while English was once more known to everyone in the land 'both learned and lewd'; no longer merely the unregarded language of a subject race, it was undeniably a medium of social refinement and sensibility.

Paradoxically the re-established universality of the English language served to accelerate the social fragmentation of English literature. English literature could no longer be considered a continuous web, a unified literary culture with a common meaning for all members of society: a coherent audience with broadly similar concerns and perceptions. The decline of French as a viable literary language among the Anglo-Norman aristocracy led to an upper-class market for coterie-literature of refinement – Anglicized versions of Continental poetic forms. English thus assumes a role as a natural aristocratic medium; and for the first time it is genuinely possible to distinguish between 'popular' and 'courtly' categories of literature in English. By this stage, however, the really vital period of French romance-writing had passed, giving way to a mere catalogue of sensational adventures. The English chivalric romances which took their place in the affections of the Plantagenet nobility, while often exceedingly complex structures and profoundly sophisticated in sentiment, were nevertheless increasingly dissociated from reality. By the end of the thirteenth century the last of the crusader knights had been expelled from the Holy Land, the prestigious order of Templars about to be disgraced and dissolved, their religious idealism dissipated by high finance, their master burned at the stake for heresy. Lacking major external validation, the chivalric impulse turned in on itself – a decadent, self-indulgent narcissism nourished by its own myth. Fashionable chivalric orders continued to proliferate, but devoted to the re-enactment of an idealized past. The tournament, no longer a preparation for war, became an end in itself, a static social occasion, the violent *mêlée* of former times replaced by an ornamental pageant, promoting an artificial etiquette. Fantasy-tourneys sponsored by Edward III purported to be the Round Table reconvened with Arthur at its head. On the battlefield, however, the knight was virtually obsolete. The deadly accurate machine cross-bow, or arbalest, despite early ecclesiastical attempts to prohibit its use, resulted in the development of yet more expensive plate-armour, rendering the ranks of knighthood even less accessible. The days of knight-errantry were past, albeit preserved in the myth of the extravagant quest. Divorced from military reality, the figure of the knight survived as a refined function of literature rather than life; and the characteristic chivalric *locus* shifted from battlefield to bedchamber. Henceforth chivalry would be intimately linked with the game of *fin' amor*, while the figure of Arthur himself would degenerate into a ridiculous *roi fainéant*. But if future romance-literature was less immediately constrained by economic or political determinants, it would certainly provide a convenient avenue of escape from the rising tide of mercantilism which must have seemed likely to swamp even the most noble houses. 'Once upon a time' is not necessarily a formula for irrelevance, but fiction becomes increasingly distant, offering less immediate point of contact with everyday life; it will illustrate moral truths in a manner either oblique or ironic. The new literature would reflect the assumptions and aspirations of a new world.

# Appendix: Early English Prosody

The earliest English verse is accentual rather than quantitative. Lacking both end-rhyme and stanza-division, its sequence must have been perceived as a continuous stichic flow. For the great majority of the audience throughout the period under review, such verse must have been apprehended not by the eye but by the ear – an aural rather than visual impact; this is reflected in the manner in which it was set out, written continuously like prose, by contemporary scribes. The modern editorial division of verse into separate lines is thus somewhat misleading.

Analysis reveals that the medium consists of a succession of rhythmic phrasal units with a basically two-stress structure (speech-patterns natural to the English language irrespective of date), a mode of composition reflecting the requirements of performance, eminently suited to memorization and oral transmission. Each rhythmic unit (which usually also represents a grammatical unit or 'thought-moment') consists of two stressed and at least two unstressed syllables. The half-dozen possible types of speech-pattern are:

| | | |
|---|---|---|
| A | &#124; – &#124; – | *where &#124; denotes major, and – minor stress* |
| B | – &#124; –&#124; | |
| C | – &#124;&#124; – | |
| D1 | &#124;&#124; \ – | *where \ denotes medium stress* |
| D2 | &#124;&#124; – \ | |
| E | &#124; – – &#124; | |

Stressed elements are generally those of greatest lexical importance: the initial syllables of nouns and adjectives, or the root-syllables of verbs. Expanded (*hypermetric*) units may also occur, containing three rather than the usual two major stresses; and patterns normally opening with a stressed element may sometimes be preceded by one or more unstressed syllables (*anacrusis*).

It is these rhythmic units, linked in pairs by alliteration, and divided normally by a brief pause (*caesura*) but sometimes by a larger syntactic break, which form the 'normal' Old English verse line set out in modern editions. Alliteration falls on either or both the stressed elements of the first half-line (*hemistich*) and the first stressed element of the second. These patterns of stress, made emphatic by alliteration, impart an incantatory quality to recitation, which we know was at least occasionally, and perhaps customarily, accompanied by a harp or lyre. All rhythmic units, irrespective of syllable-count, probably occupied musically equal intervals – perhaps a chant in 4 : 8 time, which might be reconstructed as two down-beats coinciding with the stressed elements, accentuated by the rhythmic striking of a chord.

This single prosodic mode characterizes all the earliest English verse whether orally transmitted, as we must assume *Widsith* to have been, or more 'literary' creations such as *Exodus*. Conservative authors were clearly capable of reproducing this 'classical' style well into the end of the eleventh century and beyond, as witness the *encomium urbis, Durham*, 1104–09; but the general body of prosody inevitably reflects developmental linguistic trends. While the gross rhythmic patterns of English remained broadly stable, subtle changes in the language took place, although not immediately revealed in its written form, any more than the pronunciation of Modern English is accurately reflected by its written appearance. The gradual breakdown of the synthetic nature of the language was marked by a levelling and eventual loss of inflectional endings and the increased deployment of function-words; as the syntax became more diffuse and the line consequently 'fuller', the prosodic effect was to diminish the force of classical metre. Whereas in the oldest poetry it was nouns which characteristically occupied stressed positions, increasingly words from almost any part of speech are found to be stressed, or not, according to sense. This disturbance of the accentual system was further complicated towards the end of our period by the absorption of a mounting volume of French vocabulary having a quite different rhythmic structure.

Already by the tenth century it is evident from poems like *The Battle of Maldon* that a considerable loosening of former prosodic conventions could be countenanced – possibly *pari passu* the incorporation of 'prosaic' vocabulary. Occasionally, for example, it is the second rather than the first stress of the second hemistich that bears alliteration, or the alliteration is born by an element carrying secondary rather than primary stress, such as parts of the verb 'to be'. Alliteration will now often fall on verbs or adverbs at the expense of nouns, especially in the second hemistich. Anacrusis and hypermetricism are increasingly frequent. The mid-line caesura is less emphatic, with verbal phrases frequently spanning the two half-lines, and a larger number of lines end-stopped. Overall there is less versatility of rhythmic patterns, with a higher proportion of A-types and very few of the asymmetrical D- or E-types; and sometimes merely repetitive sequences of one type only.

From earlier times alliteration was occasionally supplemented by internal rhyme or assonance for special effect to heighten or fortify the sense, athough this was sporadic and had never displaced alliteration as the connecting element. But by the eleventh century in some poems incorporated into the *Anglo-Saxon Chronicle*, such as *The Death of Alfred (s.a.* 1036) or *The Rime of King William (s.a.* 1086), it was evidently considered possible to employ rhyme or assonance as the sole, rather than as the supplementary, means of linking half-line units, although not yet regarded as sufficiently emphatic a marker of unit-division as to affect the layout of the poem on the page, which is still written out continuously like prose.

The free range of prosodic convention at the end of the Old English period is such that with an author like Ælfric it has been a matter of dispute whether sometimes he is best regarded as writing irregular verse or a particularly rhythmic prose. The verse-form employed by Laȝamon (*fl.* 1200) represents an advanced and assured stage of this latest Old English development: a flow of long lines, each basically consisting of four major accented elements, and often divided into two syntactically integral halves by a slight pause; these are not infrequently linked by both alliteration and rhyme – or by neither. Henceforth, since the alliterative link may now be replaced in principle by internal rhyme or assonance, alliteration may be reduced to collocative doublets confined to one or other half-line. Alliterative collocations remain a persistent feature of early English verse, employed even in stanzaic or couplet structures which otherwise exhibit little that is traditional. These belong rhythmically as well as formally to a different tradition and, in the absence of any evidence for insular generic development, must be presumed to derive from French or Provençal forms. In any case, where alliteration supplements such rhyming structures it is increasingly drawn to the final (i.e. rhyming) syllable of the line, rather than lying on the penultimate stressed element, thus decisively shifting the balance of the traditional rhythmic line.

End-rhyme, linking pairs or more sophisticated groupings of lines, makes line-division emphatic, and columnar layout more or less inevitable; the manner of setting out manuscript verse now suggests a prosodic mode in which visual apprehension was at least as important as aural. The columnar layout of divided lines in turn promotes a metrical regularity already encouraged by the influence of syllabic verse-forms in fashionable French literature, resulting in a prosodic convention less dependent on the natural rhythms of speech. Nevertheless, despite this tendency, the prosodic medium of, for example, *Havelok the Dane* or *The Owl and the Nightingale,* is better described as a basically four-stressed, rather than irregular octosyllabic, line. Rather curiously the long-standing Latin tradition provoked no emulation, save for the phonetically interesting but exceedingly tedious septenaries of the late twelfth-century *Ormulum*. Genuinely quantitative verse is not native to English and, at least during the period under review, represented only by the wholly exceptional *contrafactum*, *Gabriel's Greeting to the Virgin Mary*.

# Chronology

The following tables itemize historical, literary, and artistic developments, mainly in England, over the period 450–1300. The historical events listed in the third column are neither comprehensive nor systematic, but chosen either because of their diagnostic value, or simply to mark the movement of time. The works of literature listed in the first two columns refer only to works drawn upon in the course of this volume. Column one lists works of English literature, and column two works written, mainly in England, but in languages other than English, notably Welsh, Anglo-Norman, and Latin. It is usually possible to ascribe only very broad or relative dates to early medieval works of art or literature, indicated by their approximate position in the column – a problem exacerbated by the exigencies of the printed page which suggests an unrealistic sequence for works which might be contemporaneous.

| WORKS OF ENGLISH LITERATURE | LITERATURE IN LANGUAGES OTHER THAN ENGLISH | HISTORICAL EVENTS | WORKS OF ART AND ARCHITECTURE |
| --- | --- | --- | --- |
| | Cassiodorus *Institutiones* and *History of the Goths* | 450  The Jutish war-bands of Hengest and Horsa, invited to Britain by Vortigern, drive back the Picts but seize Kent | |
| | Faustus of Riez Semi-Pelagian tracts | 451  Attila defeated and turned back at Chalons-sur-Marne | |
| | | 476  Romulus Augustulus, the last Roman emperor, deposed by the Germanic Odoacer (Eadwacer) | Sub-Roman zoomorphic 'Jutish Style A' |
| Legends of the Migration-Age heroes circulating orally throughout the Anglo-Saxon settlements | | 491  Saxon war-bands under Aelle complete the conquest of Sussex | |
| | | 495  Saxon war-bands under Cerdic and Cynric invade Hampshire | |
| | Boethius *The Consolation of Philosophy* | c. 518  The British, probably led by Arthur, defeat the Saxons at Mount Badon | |
| | | 530s  The Saxon kingdoms of Essex and Middlesex established | |
| | Jordanes *History of the Goths* | 550s  The Anglian kingdoms of Northumbria, East Anglia, and Mercia established | |
| | Gildas *De Excidio et Conquestu Britanniae* | 563  Irish monks under Columba found the monastery at Iona | Disjected zoomorphic 'Salin Style I' |

| Texts | Events | Art and architecture |
|---|---|---|
| Elegies and cross-cult hymns<br>Gregory of Tours<br>*History of the Franks*<br>Gregory the Great<br>*Dialogues* and *Pastoral Care* | the River Severn and defeat the British at Deorham<br><br>595 The Northumbrians defeat the British at Catterick (Catraeth) | The Augustine Gospels brought from Italy |
| The laws of the kingdom of Kent 'recorded in the Roman manner' | 597 The Roman mission begins, and Augustine converts King Æthelbert of Kent | |
| Aneirin<br>*Y Gododdin* | 607 The first St Paul's Church is built in London | Sutton Hoo jewellery made |
| Taliesin<br>Welsh elegies and encomiae | 625 The Roman mission extended to Northumbria, and Paulinus converts King Edwin | Yeavering palace *floruit* |
| Isidore of Seville<br>*Etymologiae* | 630s–50s Northumbrian ascendancy under Kings Oswald (633–41) and Oswy (654–70) | The churches of St Martin and St Pancras built at Canterbury |
| *Widsith* | 635 Monks from Iona under Aidan found the monastery at Lindisfarne | |
| The *Waldere* fragments | 657 Double monastery founded at Whitby under Abbess Hild | |
| The *Fight at Finnsburh* | 664 The Synod of Whitby establishes Roman dominance over the British Church | |
| *Deor* | 668 Theodore of Tarsus elected Archbishop of Canterbury | Bradford-on-Avon, Bradwell-on-Sea, Brixworth and Escomb churches built |
| Cædmon's *Creation-Hymn* | 681 Benedict Biscop founds the monasteries at Monkwearmouth-Jarrow | The Book of Durrow illuminated |
| Cædmon at Whitby, embarks on a programme of biblical poetry | 697 Guthlac establishes a hermitage at Crowland | The Echternach Gospels, Lindisfarne Gospels, and Codex Amiatinus produced in Northumbria |
| Aldhelm at Malmesbury<br>English songs | | |
| Aldhelm at Malmesbury<br>*De Laude Virginitatis*<br>*De Laudibus Virginum*<br>*De Metris* | | |
| Bede at Monkwearmouth-Jarrow<br>Biblical commentaries, hagiographies, scientific tracts; *Historia Ecclesiastica* completed 731 | | |
| *Genesis A* | | |

| WORKS OF ENGLISH LITERATURE | LITERATURE IN LANGUAGES OTHER THAN ENGLISH | HISTORIAL EVENTS | WORKS OF ART AND ARCHITECTURE |
|---|---|---|---|
| The Exeter Book *Riddles* | Hwætberht, Tatwine, and Boniface Riddle-collections | 711 Islamic armies conquer Visigothic Spain | The Ruthwell and Bewcastle crosses erected; Franks Casket carved |
| *The Dream of the Rood* | | 718 Boniface enters the missionfield in Germany | |
| *Exodus* | Felix *Life of St Guthlac* | 732 An invading Islamic army is defeated and turned back at Tours by Franks under Charles Martel | The Chad Gospels and Vespasian Psalter produced in Mercia |
| *Guthlac A* | Alcuin at York and, from 781 Aachen | | The Breedon sculptural friezes carved |
| *Beowulf* | Theological, historical, grammatical, and scientific works; poem on *The Bishops, Kings and Saints of York* | 757 Accession of Offa of Mercia; the silver penny introduced | The Book of Kells illuminated |
| | | 779 Offa's defeat of the West Saxons at Benson establishes Mercian supremacy; Offa claiming the title *Rex Anglorum* | The silver Witham pins, Ormside bowl, and St Ninian's Isle treasure produced |
| The Exeter Book elegies | The *Liber Monstrorum* | 787 The first Viking raids on England | The Gandersheim ivory casket carved at ?Ely and Genoels-Elderen ivory diptych carved in Northumbria |
| *The Wanderer* | Nennius | | |
| *The Seafarer* | The *Historia Brittonum*, | | |
| *The Ruin* | incorporating the earliest account of King Arthur | 790s The Vikings sack the abbeys on Lindisfarne (793) and Iona (795) | |
| Cynewulf | The Llywarch Hen poems composed in Powys | 800 Charlemagne crowned emperor at Rome | |
| *Elene* | | | |
| *Juliana* | | | |
| *Christ II* | | 825 Egbert of Wessex defeats Mercians at Ellandun, establishing West Saxon supremacy | The Easby cross erected |
| *Andreas* | Hrabanus Maurus at Fulda Poetry, biblical commentaries, and *De Universo* | | The Book of Cerne illuminated |
| *Guthlac B* | | 850 The Danish army first takes winter quarters in England | Greensted wooden church built |
| *The Phoenix and Physiologus* | Sedulius Scotus at Liège Biblical commentaries, philosophical tracts, and Latin poetry | 870 The Danes conquer East Anglia | The Strickland and Fuller silver brooches produced |

| | | |
|---|---|---|
| The Alfredan programme of prose translations | 871 Accession of Alfred, King of Wessex | The Trewhiddle silver hoard |
| Bede's *Ecclesiastical History* | 876 Danish kingdom of York established | The Alfred and Minster Lovell jewels produced |
| Orosius's *World History* | 878 The Treaty of Wedmore establishes Danelaw | |
| Boethius's *Consolation of Philosophy* | | The Deerhurst font sculpted |
| Augustine's *Soliloquies* | 890s A further wave of Danish raids begins, and Alfred establishes a naval defence | The Cuerdale silver hoard |
| Gregory the Great's *Dialogues* and *Pastoral Care* | 899 Accession of Edward the Elder, King of Wessex | New Minster, Winchester, abbey consecrated |
| The *Anglo-Saxon Chronicle* systematized | 910 The West Saxons defeat the Danes of York, and advance against Danish armies in East Anglia and Essex | The Reculver cross-shaft sculpted |
| *Genesis B* translated from Old Saxon | | |
| Asser *Life of King Alfred* | *c.* 919 The Welsh princedoms and the kingdoms of Scotland, Strathclyde and York acknowledge Edward as overlord | Embroidered vestments ordered by Queen Ælflæd for Bishop Frithestan of Winchester, presented by Athelstan to the shrine of St Cuthbert at Chester-le-Street (934) |
| *Judith* | 924 Accession of Athelstan, King of England | |
| | 937 Athelstan defeats Scots, Viking and Strathclyde armies at Brunanburh | The Chester-le-Street Gospels and Athelstan Psalter brought to England |
| *The Battle of Brunanburh* | 942 Edmund, King of England, takes possession of the major Viking strongholds in Mercia | |
| *The Capture of the Five Boroughs* | 954 Eric Bloodaxe, Viking King of York, is expelled, and Northumbria returns to English control | |
| | 959 Accession of Edgar, King of England | |

| WORKS OF ENGLISH LITERATURE | LITERATURE IN LANGUAGES OTHER THAN ENGLISH | HISTORICAL EVENTS | WORKS OF ART AND ARCHITECTURE |
| --- | --- | --- | --- |
| The Blickling Homiliary compiled | Æthelwold at Winchester The Regularis Concordia | 960s–70s Benedictine monastic revival; Dunstan Archbishop of Canterbury (960), Æthelwold Bishop of Winchester (963), and Oswald Archbishop of York (972) | The Benedictional of St Æthelwold illuminated at Winchester |
| | | 978 Accession of Æthelred the Unready, King of England | Gosforth cross erected |
| The Battle of Maldon Ælfric at Cerne Abbas The Catholic Homilies Lives of Saints | Ælfric at Cerne Abbas Latin Grammar and Colloquy | 980s Renewed Viking raids | The Exeter Book and Vercelli Book compiled |
| | | 991 Viking raiders defeat the English under Byrhtnoth at Maldon | |
| Wulfstan at York The Sermo Lupi ad Anglos Institutes of Polity | Byrhtferth at Ramsey Life of St Oswald Commentaries on Bede Manual | 994 Olaf Tryggvason and Sweyn Forkbeard besiege London; Danegeld is instituted | The Junius Manuscript written and illuminated at Malmesbury |
| The Apollonius of Tyre story circulating | The 'Cambridge Songbook' compiled at Canterbury | 1013 Sweyn Forkbeard forces Æthelred into exile in Normandy | The Grimbald Gospels and Utrecht Psalter-copies made |
| | | 1016 Accession of the viking Cnut as King of England | Ælfric's Pentateuch illuminated at Canterbury |
| The Death of Alfred | Ibn Hazm at Cordoba Tauk al-Hamama (The Ring of the Dove) | 1030s Rise of Earl Godwine; Æthelred's son Alfred (1036) slays | The Winchester Old Minster 'Sigmund' frieze sculpted |
| The Rectitudines Singularum | | 1042 Edward the Confessor, King of England, returns from Normandy; Robert of Jumièges Bishop of London (1044) and Archbishop of | The Sacramentary of Robert of Jumièges illuminated |

| Literature | Events | Art and Architecture |
|---|---|---|
| the Norman minstrel Taillefer | Normandy, defeats Harold Godwinson at Hastings | Odda's chapel at Deerhurst and the first Westminster Abbey consecrated |
| Leofric's memoir on the Life of Hereward the Wake | 1071 Hereward the Wake submits to William after the Siege of Ely | Lady Gunhild's ivory cross carved and Bayeux Tapestry embroidered |
| Domesday Book compiled<br>Anselm at Canterbury *Cur Deus Homo* and *Dialogues On Truth and On Freewill* | 1096–99 The First Crusade | The Anglo-Norman Romanesque cathedrals planned: Durham, Ely, Hereford, Lincoln, Norwich, Rochester, St Albans, etc |
| *The Rime of King William* | 1098 Stephen Harding founds the Cistercian Order of monks | The Flambard crosier made |
| Earliest record of a miracle-play *A Ludus de Sancta Katerina*, at Dunstable | 1100 Accession of Henry I; his marriage with Matilda unites Norman and Saxon royal interests | The Gloucester candlestick cast |
| Arabic translations by Adelard of Bath, Robert of Chester *et al.* | | The St Albans Psalter illuminated and Chichester bas-reliefs sculpted |
| *The Site of Durham* | c. 1115 Henry I establishes a menagerie at Woodstock | The Bury St Edmunds Bible illuminated |
| Latin histories by Henry of Huntingdon, William of Malmesbury, and Ordericus Vitalis. | 1135–54 Reign of Stephen; civil war with Matilda | Kilpeck Church built, and Kempley wall-paintings executed |
| *The Peterborough Chronicle* begins | 1147–49 The Second Crusade | |
| Geoffrey Gaimar *Estorie des Engles* | 1152 Henry of Anjou marries Eleanor of Aquitaine, and becomes King Henry II of England (1154) | The Great Lambeth and Dover Bibles and Eadwine Psalter illuminated; the Isle of Lewis chessmen carved and the Warwick ciborium and Henry of Blois enamels made |
| Robert Wace *Brut* and *Roman de Rou* | 1164 The Constitutions of Clarendon are issued | |
| *The Proverbs of Alfred*<br>Geoffrey of Monmouth *History of the Kings of Britain* | c. 1167 English students expelled from Paris settle at Oxford | |
| Aelred of Rievaulx *Speculum Caritatis*<br>*De Institutione Inclusarum* | 1170 Thomas Becket assassinated at Canterbury | The rebuilding of Canterbury cathedral begins in Early English Gothic style, followed by Fountains, Rievaulx, and Glastonbury abbeys. |
| John of Salisbury *Policraticus* and *Metalogicon* | 1189 Accession of Richard the Lionheart as King of England | |
| Lagamon *The Brut*<br>Thomas of Britain *Tristan and Ysolt*<br>Marie de France *Lais and Fables*<br>Hugh de Roteland *Ipomedon* | 1190 Richard joins the Third Crusade; Jewish pogrom in York; Henry Fitz-Ailwin becomes first Mayor of London | The St Nicholas ivory crosier and Bury St Edmunds ivory cross carved |

| WORKS OF ENGLISH LITERATURE | LITERATURE IN LANGUAGES OTHER THAN ENGLISH | HISTORIAL EVENTS | WORKS OF ART AND ARCHITECTURE |
|---|---|---|---|
| *The Owl and the Nightingale* | Daniel of Beccles *Urbanus Magnus* | 1199  Accession of John, King of England | The Leningrad Bestiary illuminated |
| | Alexander Neckham *De Naturis Rerum* | 1204  The provinces of Normandy, Maine, Anjou, and Brittany ceded to France | |
| Orm *The Ormulum* | Walter Map *De Nugis Curialium* | 1209  After rioting at Oxford, some students move to Cambridge | The Aberdeen and Ashmole Bestiaries and the Guthlac Roll illuminated |
| | Alanus de Insulis *De Planctu Naturae Anticlaudianus* | 1215  The barons force John to accept Magna Carta | |
| | Geoffrey de Vinsauf *Poetria Nova* | 1216  Accession of Henry III as King of England | |
| | Gervase of Tilbury *Otia Imperialia* | 1217  A French invasion repelled | |
| *King Horn* | Gerald of Wales Historical and topographical works | 1220s  The arrival of friars in England: Dominicans (1221) and Franciscans (1224) | |
| *Havelok the Dane* | | | Stained-glass windows in the corona of Canterbury Cathedral designed |
| An Anchoress's Guide (*Ancrene Riwle,* reworked as *Ancrene Wisse,* c. 1240) | Odo of Cheriton *Parabolae* | | The Early English Gothic style is developed in the building of Wells and Salisbury cathedrals |
| *The Wooing of Our Lord* | Alexander of Hales *Destructorium Vitiorum* | 1236  Henry III marries Eleanor of Provence, the influence of whose relatives proves unpopular in England | The Painted Chamber at Westminster Palace, and the Antioch and Alexander Chambers |
| *The Sayings of St Bernard* and *Ubi Sount Qui Ante Nos Fuerount* | Matthew Paris at St Albans *Chronica Majora Historia Anglorum* | | |
| *The Provisions of Oxford,* 1258 (the first official use of English | Robert Grosseteste at Lincoln | | |

| | | |
|---|---|---|
| | 1264 The barons under Simon de Montfort defeat the royalist army at Lewes | The illuminators William de Brailes and Matthew Paris begin working at Oxford and St Albans respectively |
| | 1265 Prince Edward defeats and slays Simon de Montfort at Evesham | The rebuilding of Westminster Abbey begins |
| | 1271 Accession of Edward I, King of England | The Amesbury, Cuerdon, and Oscott Psalters, and Douce, Trinity and Wilton Apocalypses illuminated |
| | 1277 Edward invades Wales; Llywelyn ap Gruffydd slain (1282) | The Westminster Abbey retable painted |
| | 1278 Edward and his queen, Eleanor of Castile, attend the opening of King Arthur's tomb at Glastonbury | Rebuilding of Exeter Cathedral begins in English Decorated Gothic style |
| | | Important works of *opus Anglicanum*: the Clare chasuble and Syon cope embroidered |
| | 1290 The Jews are expelled from England. Eleanor of Castile dies | The Chertsey Abbey Tristan and Iseult floor-tiles laid |
| | | The Eleanor crosses sculpted |
| | 1296 Edward invades Scotland, incarcerating John Baliol, seizing the coronation stone of Scone, and defeating William Wallace at Falkirk (1298) | The Psalter of Robert de Lisle is illuminated, and the Hereford World Map drawn |

*A Song of Lewes*

Thomas of Hales
*A Love-Song*

*De Clerico et Puella*;
*Dame Sirith and the Weeping Bitch*

Henry de Bracton
*De Legibus et Consuetudinibus Angliae*

William of Sherwood
*Introductiones in Logicum*

John of Peckham
Franciscan tracts and Latin hymns

*The Land of Cockayne*

*The Follies of Fashion*

Duns Scotus
Theological and philosophical tracts

*Lenten is Come with Love to Town*

*The Thrush and the Nightingale*

*The Fair Maid of Ribblesdale*

*Gesta Romanorum* compiled

*Arthur and Merlin*

*Bevis of Hampton*

Nicholas Bozon
*Contes Moralisés*

*Richard the Lionheart*

*Sir Tristrem*

# General Bibliographies

*See also references cited in the end-notes to each chapter.*

## Chapter 1: Anxiety and Assertion

The best general historical survey of the period remains the relevant volumes of the *Oxford History of England*:

Stenton, F. M.,     *Anglo-Saxon England*, 3rd edn. (Oxford, 1971).

Poole, A. L.,     *From Domesday Book to Magna Carta, 1087–1216*, 2nd edn. (Oxford, 1955).

Powicke, M.,     *The Thirteenth Century, 1216–1307*, 2nd edn. (Oxford, 1962).

For the material arts see generally the relevant volumes in the *Pelican History of Art:*

Rickert, M.,     *Painting in Britain: The Middle Ages*, 2nd edn. (Harmondsworth, 1965).

Stone, L.,     *Sculpture in Britain: The Middle Ages*, 2nd edn. (Harmondsworth, 1972).

Webb, G.,     *Architecture in Britain: The Middle Ages*, 2nd edn. (Harmondsworth, 1972).

Important studies of particular sites and objects include:

Bruce-Mitford, R. L. S.,     *The Sutton Hoo Ship-Burial*, 3 vols (London, 1975–83).

Hope-Taylor, B.,     *Yeavering: An Anglo-British Centre of Early Northumbria* (London, 1977).

Wilson, D. M., ed.,     ed. *The Bayeux Tapestry*, (London, 1985).

For major social, economic, and intellectual developments, see also:

Haskins, C. H.,     *Studies in the History of Mediaeval Science* (Cambridge, 1927).

Curtius, E. R.,    *Europäische Literatur und lateinisches Mittelalter* (Berne, 1948), translated as *European Literature and the Latin Middle Ages* (London, 1953). (A rather unwieldy but invaluable collection of essays.)

Laistner, M. L. W.,    *Thought and Letters in Western Europe, AD 500 to 900,* 2nd edn. (London, 1957).

White, L.,    *Medieval Technology and Social Change* (Oxford, 1962).

Bumke, J.,    *Studien zum Ritterbegriff im 12. und 13. Jahrhundert* (Stuttgart, 1963), translated as *The Concept of Knighthood in the Middle Ages* (New York, 1977).

Daiches, D., and A. Thorlby, eds,    *The Mediaeval World* (London, 1973).

Cobban, A. B.,    *The Medieval Universities, their Development and Organization* (London, 1975).

Platt, C.,    *The English Medieval Town* (London, 1976).

Boase, R.,    *The Origin and Meaning of Courtly Love* (Manchester, 1977).

Swanton, M. J.,    *Crisis and Development in Germanic Society, 700–800,* Göppinger Arbeiten zur Germanistik, 333 (1982).

Strayer, J. R., ed.,    *Dictionary of the Middle Ages* (New York, 1982, in progress). (A systematic work of general reference.)

Benson, R. L., and C. Constable, eds,    *Renaissance and Renewal in the Twelfth Century* (Oxford, 1982).

Arnold, C. J.,    *Roman Britain to Saxon England: An Archaeological Study* (London, 1984).

Haren, M.,    *Medieval Thought. The Western Intellectual Tradition from Antiquity to the Thirteenth Century* (London, 1985).

Those requiring an introduction to the language of Old and Middle English literature should consult:

Mitchell, B., and F. C. Robinson,    *A Guide to Old English,* 2nd edn. (Oxford, 1982).

Wardale, E. E.,    *An Introduction to Middle English* (London, 1937). (Frequently reprinted; Old-fashioned but still valuable.)

The standard dictionaries are:

Bosworth, J., and T. N. Toller,    *An Anglo-Saxon Dictionary* (with Addenda and Corrigenda by A. Campbell, Oxford, 1972).

Kurath,  H.,  and  S.  M.    *Middle English Dictionary* (Ann Arbor, Mich., 1954, in
            Kuhn, eds,    progress).

Further general bibliographical information is available in:

Watson, G.,    *The New Cambridge Bibliography of English Literature,
            Volume I, 600–1660* (Cambridge, 1974), supplemented
            by: *Annual Bibliography of English Language and
            Literature*, Modern Humanities Research Association
            (Cambridge, 1921, in progress).

# Chapter 2: Until the Dragon Comes

## Widsith

Chambers, R. W.,    *'Widsith': A Study in Old English Heroic Legend*
            (Cambridge, 1912). (Old but still valuable.)

Malone, K., ed.,    *Widsith*, 2nd edn. (Copenhagen, 1962). (The standard
            edition.)

Recent articles include:

Eliason, N. E.,    'Two Old English Scop Poems', *Publications of the
            Modern Language Association of America*, 81 (1966),
            185–92.

Howlett, D. R.,    'Form and Genre in *Widsith*', *English Studies*, 55 (1974),
            505–11.

Fry, D. K.,    'Two Voices in *Widsith*', *Mediaevalia*, 6 (1980), 37–56.

Rollman, D. A.,    '*Widsith* as an Anglo-Saxon Defense of Poetry',
            *Neophilologus*, 66 (1982), 431–39.

## Deor

Malone, K., ed.,    *Deor*, rev. edn. (Exeter, 1977). (Contains full
            bibliography to 1975.)

More recently see also:

Tuggle, T. T.,    'The Structure of *Deor*', *Studies in Philology*, 74 (1977),
            229–42.

Kiernan, K. S.,    '*Deor*: the Consolation of an Anglo-Saxon Boethius',
            *Neuphilologische Mitteilungen*, 79 (1978), 333–40.

Condren, E. I.,    '*Deor's* Artistic Triumph', in *Eight Anglo-Saxon Studies*,
            ed. by J. Wittig (Chapel Hill, NC, 1981), pp. 60–76.

## Waldere

Schwab, U., ed.,     *Waldere: Testo e Commento* (Messina, 1967). (Definitive but in Italian.)

Zettersten, A., ed.,     *Waldere* (Manchester, 1979).

This poem has as yet attracted little critical appreciation, but see:

Magoun, F. P. and H. M. Smyser.,     *Walter of Aquitaine: Materials for the Study of his Legend* (New London, Conn., 1950). (Translations of comparative materials.)

## The Fight at Finnsburh

Fry, D. K., ed.,     *The Finnsburh Fragment and Episode* (London, 1974). (The standard edition.)

Tolkien, J. R. R.,     *Finn and Hengest: The Fragment and the Episode* (London, 1982). (A glossary and textual commentary published posthumously, ed. by A. Bliss.)

See also various entries cited in the *Beowulf* section below.

## Beowulf

Wrenn, C. L., ed.,     *'Beowulf' with the Finnesburg Fragment*, 3rd edn. rev. by W. F. Bolton (London, 1973). (The most accessible edition for the beginner.)

For a thorough survey of critical work to 1978, see:

Short, D. D.,     *'Beowulf' Scholarship: An Annotated Bibliography* (New York, 1980).

Among the most useful full-length studies are the following:

Whitelock, D.,     *The Audience of 'Beowulf'* (Oxford, 1951).

Brodeur, A. G.,     *The Art of 'Beowulf'* (Berkeley, Calif., 1959).

Chambers, R. W., and C. L. Wrenn,     *'Beowulf': An Introduction to the Study of the Poem with a Discussion of the Stories of Finn and Offa*, 3rd edn. (Cambridge, 1959).

Nicholson, L. E., ed.,     *An Anthology of 'Beowulf' Criticism* (Notre Dame, Ind., 1963).

Sisam, K.,     *The Structure of 'Beowulf'* (Oxford, 1965).

Fry, D. K., ed.,     *The 'Beowulf' Poet: A Collection of Critical Essays* (Englewood Cliffs, NJ, 1968).

Garmonsway, G. N., and J. Simpson,     *'Beowulf' and its Analogues* (London, 1968).

Irving, E. B.,     *A Reading of 'Beowulf'* (New Haven, Conn., 1968).

Goldsmith, M. E.,     *The Mode and Meaning of 'Beowulf'* (London, 1970).

Shippey, T. A.,     *Beowulf* (London, 1978).

# Chapter 3: Verbum de Verbo

Shepherd, G.,     'Scriptural Verse', in *Continuations and Beginnings*, ed. by E. G. Stanley (London, 1966), pp. 1–36.

## Cædmon's *Creation-Hymn*

Smith, A. H., ed.,     *Three Northumbrian Poems*, rev. edn. (Exeter, 1978). (The standard edition, together with *Bede's Death Song* and *The Leiden Riddle*. Contains full bibliography to 1976).

See further:

Huppé, B. F.,     *Doctrine and Poetry: Augustine's Influence on Old English Poetry* (Albany, NY, 1959), Chapter iv.

Fry, D. K.,     'The Memory of Cædmon', in *Oral Traditional Literature,* ed. by J. M. Foley (Columbus, Ohio, 1981), pp. 282–93.

Schwab, U.,     'The Miracles of Cædmon', *English Studies*, 64 (1983), 1–17.

## Genesis A

Doane, A. N., ed.,     *Genesis A: A New Edition* (Madison, Wis., 1978). (The standard edition, containing full bibliography.)

See also:

Huppé, B. F.,     *Doctrine and Poetry: Augustine's Influence on Old English Poetry* (Albany, NY, 1959), Chapter v.

And more recently:

Brockman, B. A.,     '"Heroic" and "Christian" in *Genesis A:* The Evidence of the Cain and Abel Episode', *Modern Language Quarterly*, 35 (1974), 115–28.

Hieatt, C. B.,     'Divisions: Theme and Structure of *Genesis A*', *Neuphilologische Mitteilungen,* 81 (1980), 243–51.

Boyd, N.,     'Doctrine and Criticism: A Revaluation of *Genesis A*', *Neuphilologische Mitteilungen*, 83 (1982), 230–38.

## Exodus

Lucas, P. J., ed., *Exodus* (London, 1977). (The standard edition, containing select bibliography.)

See also:

Wall, C., 'Stylistic Variation in the Old English *Exodus*', *English Language Notes*, 6 (1968), 79–84.

Farrell, R. T., 'A Reading of OE. *Exodus*', *Review of English Studies*, 20 (1969), 401–17.

Earle, J. W., 'Christian Tradition in the Old English *Exodus*', *Neuphilologische Mitteilungen*, 71 (1970), 541–70.

Ames, R. M., 'The Old Testament Christ and the Old English *Exodus*', *Studies in Medieval Culture*, 10 (1977), 33–50.

Luria, M., 'The Old English *Exodus* as a Christian Poem: Notes Towards a Reading', *Neophilologus*, 65 (1981), 600–06.

## The Dream of the Rood

Swanton, M. J., ed., *The Dream of the Rood*, 2nd edn. (Manchester, 1978). (The standard edition, containing full bibliography.)

This poem continues to attract considerable scholarly attention. See for example:

Raw, B., '*The Dream of the Rood* and its Connections with Early Christian Art', *Medium Ævum*, 39 (1970), 239–56.

Lee, N. A., 'The Unity of *The Dream of the Rood*', *Neophilologus*, 56 (1972), 469–86.

Lee, A. A., 'Towards a Critique of *The Dream of the Rood*', in *Anglo-Saxon Poetry: Essays in Appreciation*, ed. by L. E. Nicholson and D. W. Frese (Notre Dame, Ind., 1975), pp. 163–91.

Howlett, D. R., 'The Structure of *The Dream of the Rood*', *Studia Neophilologica*, 48 (1976), 301–06.

Payne, R. C., 'Convention and Originality in the Vision Framework of *The Dream of the Rood*', *Modern Philology*, 73 (1976), 329–41.

# Chapter 4: The Ruin of Time

Green, M., ed., *The Old English Elegies: New Essays in Criticism and Research* (London, 1983).

## The Wanderer

Leslie, R. F., ed.,   *The Wanderer*, rev. edn. (Exeter, 1985). (The most useful edition, containing select bibliography.)

This poem continues to attract considerable critical attention. See for example:

Fowler, R.,   'A Theme in *The Wanderer*', *Medium Ævum*, 36 (1967), 1–14.

Bolton, W. F.,   'The Dimensions of *The Wanderer*', *Leeds Studies in English*, new series, 3 (1969), 7–34.

Kintgen, E. R.,   'Wordplay in *The Wanderer*', *Neophilologus*, 59 (1975), 119–27.

Clark, S. L. and Wasserman, J. N.,   'The Imagery of *The Wanderer*', *Neophilologus*, 63 (1979), 291–96.

Hait, E. A.,   'The Wanderer's Lingering Regret: A Study of Patterns of Imagery', *Neophilologus*, 68 (1984), 278–91.

## The Seafarer

Gordon, I. L., ed.,   *The Seafarer* (London, 1960, repr. Manchester, 1975). (The standard edition, containing select bibliography.)

This poem continues to attract considerable critical interest. See for example:

Calder, D. G.,   'Setting and Mode in *The Seafarer* and *The Wanderer*', *Neuphilologische Mitteilungen*, 72 (1971), 264–75.

Davenport, W. A.,   'The Modern Reader and the Old English *Seafarer*', *Papers on Language and Literature*, 10 (1974), 227–41.

Mandel, J.,   '*The Seafarer*', *Neuphilologische Mitteilungen*, 77 (1976), 538–51.

Osborn, M.,   'Venturing Upon Deep Waters in *The Seafarer*', *Neuphilologische Mitteilungen*, 79 (1978), 1–6.

Vickrey, J. F.,   'Some Hypotheses Concerning *The Seafarer*', *Archiv für das Studium der neueren Sprachen und Literaturen*, 219 (1982), 57–77.

## The Ruin

Leslie, R. F., ed.,    *Three Old English Elegies*, rev. edn. (Exeter, 1986). (The standard edition, together with *The Wife's Lament* and *The Husband's Message*. Contains full bibliography.)

See also:

Calder, D. G.,    'Perspective and Movement in *The Ruin*', *Neuphilologische Mitteilungen*, 72 (1971), 442–45.

Doubleday, J. F.,    '*The Ruin*: Structure and Theme', *Journal of English and Germanic Philology*, 71 (1972), 369–81.

Lee, A. T.,    '*The Ruin*: Bath or Babylon; A Non-archaeological Investigation', *Neuphilologische Mitteilungen*, 74 (1973), 443–55.

Talentino, A. V.,    'Moral Irony in *The Ruin*', *Papers in Language and Literature*, 14 (1978), 3–10.

## The Phoenix

Blake, N. F., ed.,    *The Phoenix* (Manchester, 1964). (The standard edition, containing select bibliography.)

See also:

Kantrowitz, J. S.,    'The Anglo-Saxon *Phoenix* and Tradition', *Philological Quarterly*, 43 (1964), 1–13.

Cross, J. E.,    'The Conception of the Old English *Phoenix*', in *Old English Poetry: Fifteen Essays*, ed. by R. P. Creed (Providence, RI, 1967), pp. 129–52.

Bugge, J.,    'The Virgin Phoenix', *Mediaeval Studies*, 38 (1976), 332–50.

Heffernan, C. F.,    'The Old English *Phoenix*: A Reconsideration', *Neuphilologische Mitteilungen*, 83 (1982), 239–54.

# Chapter 5: An Assured Heroism

## Guthlac A

Roberts, J., ed.,    *The Guthlac Poems of the Exeter Book* (Oxford, 1979). (The standard edition, containing full bibliography to 1978.)

See also:

Calder, D. G.,   *'Guthlac A* and *Guthlac B*: Some Discriminations', in *Anglo-Saxon Poetry: Essays in Appreciation*, ed. by L. E. Nicholson and D. W. Frese (Notre Dame, Ind., 1975), pp. 65–80.

And more recently:

Dubs, K. E.,   'Guthlac *A* and the Acquisition of Wisdom', *Neophilologus*, 65 (1981), 607–13.

Olsen, A. H.,   *Guthlac of Croyland: A Study of Heroic Hagiography* (Washington, D.C., 1981).

Stevick, R. D.,   'The Length of *Guthlac A'*, *Viator*, 13 (1982), 15–48.

Bridges, M. E.,   *Generic Contrast in Old English Hagiographical Poetry*, Anglistica, 22 (Copenhagen, 1984), Chapters i–ii.

## Judith

Timmer, B. J., ed.,   *Judith*, 3rd edn. (Exeter, 1978). (The standard edition, containing full bibliography to 1975.)

See also:

Renoir, A.,   '*Judith* and the Limits of Poetry', *English Studies*, 43 (1962), 145–55.

Huppé, B. F.,   '*Judith*', in *The Web of Words* (Albany, NY, 1970), pp. 113–89.

Campbell, J. J.,   'Schematic Technique in *Judith*', *English Literary History*, 38 (1971), 155–72.

Kaske, R. E.,   'Sapientia et Fortitudo in the Old English *Judith*', in *The Wisdom of Poetry: Essays in Early English Literature in Honor of Morton W. Bloomfield*, ed. by L. D. Benson and S. Wenzel (Kalamazoo, Mich., 1982), pp. 13–29, 264–68.

## The Battle of Maldon

Scragg, D. G., ed.,   *The Battle of Maldon* (Manchester, 1981). (The standard edition, containing full bibliography.)

See also:

Irving, E. B.,   'The Heroic Style in *The Battle of Maldon*', *Studies in Philology*, 58 (1961), 457–67.

Clark, G.,  'The Battle of Maldon: A Heroic Poem', Speculum, 43 (1968), 52–71.

Robinson, F. C.,  'Some Aspects of the Maldon Poet's Artistry', Journal of English and Germanic Philology, 75 (1976), 25–40.

Doane, A. N.,  'Legend, History and Artifice in The Battle of Maldon', Viator, 9 (1978), 39–66.

Stuart, H.,  'The Meaning of Maldon', Neophilologus, 66 (1982), 126–39.

## Laȝamon's Brut

Brook, G. L., and R. F. Leslie, eds,  Laȝamon: Brut, Early English Text Society, 250, 277 (Oxford, 1963–78). (Definitive text; an additional volume containing full apparatus is announced.)

Convenient extracts in a form suitable for the beginner will be found in:

Brook, G. L., ed.,  Selections from Laȝamon's Brut, 2nd edn, rev. by J. Levitt (Exeter, 1983). (Contains lines 7715–11209, 12346–613, and 13971–14297, together with a select bibliography.)

See also:

Schirmer, W. F.,  'Layamon's Brut', Modern Humanities Research Association Annual Bulletin, 1957, 15–27.

Davies, H. S.,  'Laȝamon's Similies', Review of English Studies, 11 (1960), 129–42.

Lewis, C. S.,  'The Genesis of a Medieval Book', in Studies in Medieval and Renaissance Literature (Cambridge, 1966), pp. 18–40.

Swart, J.,  'Laȝamon's Brut', in Studies in Language and Literature in Honour of Margaret Schlauch, ed. by M. Brahmer et al. (Warsaw, 1966), pp. 431–35.

Ringbom, H.,  Studies in the Narrative Technique of 'Beowulf' and Lawman's 'Brut' (Åbo, 1968).

## Chapter 6: Things that Falleth to Ribaudrie

Mehl, D.,    *Die mittelenglischen Romanzen des 13. und 14. Jahrhunderts* (Heidelberg, 1967), translated as *The Middle English Romances of the Thirteenth and Fourteenth Centuries* (London, 1968).

### Havelok the Dane

Skeat, W. W., ed.,    *The Lay of Havelok the Dane*, 2nd edn., rev. by K. Sisam (Oxford, 1956). (The standard separate edition but somewhat in need of revision.)

The text is also available in the following anthologies:

French, W. H., and C. B. Hale, eds,    *Middle English Metrical Romances* (Englewood Cliffs, NJ, 1930, repr. New York, 1964), pp. 71–176.

Sands, D. B., ed.,    *Middle English Verse Romances* (New York, 1966, repr. Exeter, 1986), pp. 55–129.

Schmidt, A. V. C., and N. Jacobs, eds,    *Medieval English Romances* (London, 1980), pp. 37–121.

Useful articles include:

Hanning, R. W.,    '*Havelok the Dane*: Structure, Symbols, Meaning', *Studies in Philology*, 64 (1967), 586–605.

Weiss, J.,    'Structure and Characterisation in *Havelok the Dane*', *Speculum*, 44 (1969), 247–57.

Halverson, J.,    '*Havelok the Dane* and Society', *Chaucer Review*, 6 (1971–72), 142–51.

Staines, D.,    '*Havelok the Dane:* A Thirteenth-century Handbook for Princes', *Speculum*, 51 (1976), 602–23.

### Sir Tristrem

McNeill, G. P., ed.,    *Sir Tristrem*, Scottish Text Society, I, 8. (Edinburgh, 1886). (The sole edition, drastically in need of revision.)

This poem has been sadly undervalued hitherto, the only substantial appreciation being:

Rumble, T. C.,    'The Middle English *Sir Tristrem*: Toward a Reappraisal', *Comparative Literature*, 11 (1959), 221–28.

## Floris and Blancheflour

de Vries, F. C., ed.,     *Floris and Blauncheflur* (Groningen, 1966). (The most recent separate edition, with select bibliography.)

The text is also available in anthologies edited by French and Hale (pp. 823–55), Sands (pp. 279–309). (See bibliographical details cited in the *Havelok* section above.)

This poem has not yet attracted the critical attention it deserves, but see:

Geddes, S. S.,     'The Middle English Poem of *Floriz and Blauncheflur* and the Arabian Nights Tale of *Ni'amah and Naomi*; A Study in Parallels', *Emporia State Research Studies*, 19 (1970), 14–24.

Reiss, E.,     'Symbolic Detail in Medieval Narrative: *Floris and Blancheflour*', *Papers on Language and Literature*, 7 (1971), 339–50.

Barnes, G.,     'Cunning and Ingenuity in the Middle English *Floris and Blauncheflur*', *Medium Ævum*, 53 (1984), 10–25.

## Dame Sirith

McKnight, G. H., ed.,     *Middle English Humorous Tales in Verse* (Boston, Mass., 1913, repr. New York, 1972), pp. 1–24.

The text is also available in the following anthology:

Bennett, J. A., and G. V. Smithers, eds,     *Early Middle English Prose and Verse*, 2nd edn. (Oxford, 1968), pp. 77–95.

This piece has not yet provoked substantial criticism, but for the *fabliau* genre in general, see:

Cooke, T. D., and B. L. Honeycutt, eds,     *The Humor of The Fabliaux; A Collection of Critical Essays* (Columbia, Mo., 1974).

# Chapter 7: The Singer and the Song

## Early Middle English Lyrics

Brown, C., ed.,     *English Lyrics of the XIIIth Century* (Oxford, 1932). (A valuable general collection.)

Brook, G. L., ed.,     *The Harley Lyrics*, 4th edn. (Manchester, 1968). (The standard edition of a single medieval anthology, with select bibliography.)

Useful general studies include:

Stevick, R. D.,     'The Criticism of Middle English Lyrics', *Modern Philology*, 64 (1966), 103–17.

Oliver, R.,     *Poems Without Names: The English Lyric 1200–1500* (London, 1970).

Reiss, E.,     *The Art of the Middle English Lyric* (Athens, Ga., 1972).

Howell, A. J.,     'Reading the Harley Lyrics: A Master Poet and the Language of Conventions', *English Literary History*, 47 (1980), 619–45.

## The Owl and the Nightingale

Stanley, E. G., ed.,     *The Owl and the Nightingale*, 2nd edn (Manchester, 1972). (The most useful separate edition, containing select bibliography.)

Atkins, J. W. H., ed.,     *The Owl and the Nightingale* (Cambridge, 1922). (Old but containing a valuable introduction.)

Still useful are:

Huganir, K.,     *'The Owl and the Nightingale': Sources, Date, Author* (Philadelphia, 1931).

Carson, M. A.,     'Rhetorical Structure in *The Owl and the Nightingale*', *Speculum*, 42 (1967), 92–103.

Schleusener, J.,     *'The Owl and the Nightingale:* A Matter of Judgment', *Modern Philology*, 70 (1973), 185–89.

Hume, K.,     *'The Owl and the Nightingale': The Poem and its Critics* (Toronto, 1975). (A systematic consideration of earlier opinion.)

More recently, see also:

Olsson, K.,     'Character and Truth in *The Owl and the Nightingale*', *Chaucer Review*, 11 (1976), 351–68.

Moran, I.,     'The Owl and the Nightingale: An Interpretation', *Annali Istituto Orientale di Napoli (Filologia Germanica)*, 20 (1977), 151–212.

# Notes on Individual Writers, Works and Sources

## (i) Writers and writings in English

ÆLFRIC (*c*.955–*c*.1020). The most accomplished and prolific prose-writer of his day. A product of the tenth-century monastic revival, he was educated at Winchester under Bishop Æthelwold, and subsequently taught at the restored Benedictine abbey at Cerne Abbas, Dorset, from 987 until 1002 when he was made first abbot of a new foundation at Eynsham, Oxfordshire. His wide-ranging production, the greater part of which was completed before his promotion to Eynsham, includes: Old Testament translations, theological commentaries, two series of homilies, saints' lives, pastoral letters, (some on behalf of Archbishop Wulfstan, *q.v.*), works on monastic customs and various teaching-aids, such as a Latin grammar and glossary, and a school-book dialogue or colloquy. His writings continued to be copied in the West of England well into the twelfth century, and a relatively large number of manuscript sources are extant.

See: Hurt, J., *Ælfric* (New York, 1972).

ALDHELM. See section ii below, pp. 331–32.

ALFRED, KING, (849–901). Succeeded to the throne of Wessex in 871 at a critical moment in the Danish incursions, which remained a persistent problem throughout his reign. In 878 he was able to secure a temporary peace by ceding the northern and eastern parts of England to 'Danelaw', and inevitably acquired a considerable reputation as the popular leader of a beleaguered nation. In an attempt to raise national morale at a particularly low ebb in its fortunes, Alfred promoted an extensive programme of translations from texts previously available only in Latin, including: *The Ecclesiastical History* of Bede; the *Historiae adversum Paganos* of Orosius; the *Consolation of Philosophy* by Boethius; the *Soliloquies* of St Augustine; and the *Dialogues* and *Pastoral Care* of Gregory the Great (all *q.v.*). The king's personal contribution to the programme is debated, but his hand is certainly recognizable in the *Consolations, Soliloquies,* and *Pastoral Care.* The king may also have been responsible for initiating the systematic compilation of the *Anglo-Saxon Chronicle* (*q.v.*).

Alfred's reputation for learning became legendary, and a number of early works of 'wisdom-literature' were attached to his name, probably without foundation, including: a lost collection of Aesopian fables, according to Marie de France (*q.v.*), and the probably twelfth-century *Proverbs of Alfred*; and 'King Alfred's sayings' are constantly quoted by the author of *The Owl and the Nightingale (q.v.).*

See: Loyn, H. R., *Alfred the Great* (London, 1967).

*ANCHORESS'S GUIDE.* An influential devotional manual composed early in the thirteenth century in the West Midlands for three young sisters who had chosen to adopt the life of religious recluses (*Ancrene Riwle*); reworked towards the middle of the century for more general use (*Ancrene Wisse*). Manuscript sources date from *c.* 1230 to the fifteenth century, the best being the mid-thirteenth-century Corpus Christi College, Cambridge, MS. 402 (*Ancrene Wisse*).

*ANDREAS.* An Old English narrative poem of some seventeen hundred lines describing episodes in the legendary mission of St Andrew (*Andreas*) to the cannibal Mermedonians, and drawn from a lost Latin version of the apocryphal Acts of Andrew and Matthew. Written in a style similar to that of Cynewulf (*q.v.*), it probably belongs to the late eighth or early ninth century. The sole manuscript text is found in the Vercelli Book (*q.v.*).

*ANGLO-SAXON CHRONICLE.* A substantial corpus of annals apparently originating in the monastic world which marked the passage of time by re-cording events of national or local significance; systematized probably during the reign of King Alfred (*q.v.*), and thereafter maintained and kept up to date at a variety of centres of learning. Four distinct versions of the *Chronicle* survive in seven different manuscript copies, varying in the nature and amount of local information they incorporate. In one or another recension the *Chronicle* records events of contemporary or retrospective significance from the birth of Christ to the anarchy of the mid twelfth century. Some annals are brief and impersonal – little more than single-line entries; others are much fuller, such as those describing the dramatic events surrounding the deaths of Cynewulf and Cyneheard (*s.a.* 755), the ninth- and tenth-century Viking Wars, or conditions during the Civil War of Stephen's reign (*s.a.* 1137).

> Fac.: Flower, R., and H. Smith, eds, *The Parker Chronicle and Laws*, Early English Text Society, Original Series 208 (London, 1941). (Corpus Christi College, Cambridge, MS. 173; ninth-century Winchester.)
> Whitelock, D., ed., *The Peterborough Chronicle*, Early English Manuscripts in Facsimile, IV (Copenhagen, 1954). (Bodleian Library, Oxford, MS. Laud Misc. 636; twelfth-century Peterborough.)

*APOLLONIUS OF TYRE.* An early Greek romance, originating during the second or third century in Hellenstic Asia Minor, and achieving widespread popularity, translated into almost every language of medieval Europe; the plot was incorporated into the *Gesta Romanorum (q.v.)* and was the ultimate source of Shakespeare's *Pericles*. An Old English translation is found in a mid–eleventh-century Wulfstan (*q.v.*) manuscript, Corpus Christi College, Cambridge, MS. 201B.

*ARTHUR AND MERLIN.* A late thirteenth-century narrative poem of some ten thousand lines in rhyming couplets, composed somewhere in the south-east of England, probably Kent, describing the birth and character of the wizard Merlin and the succession and reign of King Arthur until his marriage with Guinevere. Several manuscript texts are extant; the earliest and best is found in the early-fourteenth-century Auchinleck Manuscript (*q.v.*).

*AUCHINLECK MANUSCRIPT.* National Library of Scotland, Edinburgh, Advocates' MS. 19.2.1. A verse anthology, probably produced in a London workshop *c.* 1330–40. Its varied contents include religious poems like *The Sayings of St Bernard (q.v.)*, the dramatic lyric *The Thrush and the Nightingale (q.v.)*, and many romances such as: *Arthur and Merlin, Beves of Hampton, Floris and Blancheflour, King Alisaunder, Otuel, Richard the Lion-heart,* and *Sir Tristrem* (all *q.v.*).

Fac.:   Pearsall, D., and I. C. Cunningham, introd., *The Auchinleck Manuscript* (London, 1977).

*BATTLE OF BRUNANBURH.*   Mid tenth-century. A seventy-three-line historical poem incorporated into several versions of the *Anglo-Saxon Chronicle (q.v.)* for the year 937, describing in classical Old English terms, a notable victory won by King Athelstan, grandson of King Alfred (*q.v.*), against an allied invading army composed of Vikings, Scots, and Strathclyde Britons. The geographical location of the battle has not been identified with any certainty. See generally above, p. 167.

*BATTLE OF MALDON.*   A late tenth-century narrative poem, some three hundred lines long, composed probably in the south-east of England, describing a disastrous confrontation near Maldon, Essex, in 991, between a group of Viking raiders and local levies led by Ealdorman Byrhtnoth. See generally above, pp. 165–74. The only known manuscript copy of this poem was destroyed in the early eighteenth century, but a reliable transcript had been made a year or two earlier.

BEDE. See section ii below, p. 333.

*BEOWULF.*   Mid late eighth century. A substantial verse epic of some three thousand lines dealing *inter alia* with two major events in the career of its eponymous hero, a sixth-century warrior from Geatland (southern Sweden), first as a young man ridding the Danish court of the depredations of hideous monsters, and later, as an old king in his own homeland, meeting his death confronting a marauding dragon. See generally above, pp. 49–66. The sole extant text, found in British Library MS. Cotton Vitellius Axv, was copied in a late West Saxon literary koine *c.* 1000, but linguistic fossils embedded in the text strongly suggest that an Anglian (i.e. Northumbrian or Mercian) written version existed some time in the eighth century; and the story-materials must have been circulating for some time previously.

Fac.:   Zupitza, J., introd., *Beowulf,* 2nd edn. rev. by N. Davis, Early English Text Society, Original Series 245 (London, 1959).

Malone, K., ed., *The Nowell Codex: British Museum, Cotton Vitellius Axv, Second MS.,* Early English Manuscripts in Facsimile, xii (Copenhagen, 1963).

*BEVES OF HAMPTON (SOUTHAMPTON).*   A late thirteenth-century verse romance of some four and a half thousand lines, partly stanzaic partly rhyming couplets, written in southern England, perhaps at Southampton. Based on an Anglo-Norman romance, it retails a gallimaufry of extraordinary adventures ascribed to the eponymous hero, including fights with Saracens, giants, and dragons, on the way to recovering his lost fortune. Several manuscript copies are extant; the earliest is found in the fourteenth-century Auchinleck Manuscript (*q.v.*).

*BLICKLING HOMILIARY.*   Princeton, New Jersey, Sheide Library MS. 71. A late tenth- or early eleventh-century collection of sermons for Sundays and saints' days, arranged roughly in order of the Church calendar. An internal reference indicates that the Ascension Day sermon at least was composed shortly before the year 971, and perhaps the whole collection belongs to roughly the same date.

The manuscript belonged to the Corporation of Lincoln from at least 1300, although later housed at Blicking Hall, Norfolk – hence its title of convenience.

Fac.: Willard, R., ed., *The Blickling Homilies*, Early English Manuscripts in Facsimile, x (Copenhagen, 1960).

BYRHTFERTH OF RAMSEY. See section (ii) below, p. 334.

CÆDMON (*fl.* 650–70). The first Old English poet known by name, a Yorkshire cowherd, subject to a mystical experience when advanced in years, and thereupon taken into the monastic community at Whitby during the incumbency of Abbess Hild (657–80). His subsequent literary career is outlined by Bede (*q.v.*) who indicates an ambitious programme of composition on biblical themes. Poems such as *Genesis* (*q.v.*) or *Exodus* (*q.v.*), although Cædmonian in concept, are almost certainly by separate hands. The only poem attributable with any certainty to Cædmon is the *Creation-Hymn* quoted by Bede; see generally above, pp. 70–74. The English text is found in the margin of two near-contemporary manuscripts: Leningrad Public Library MS. Q.v.1.18, and Cambridge University Library MS. Kk.5.16 (the Moore Manuscript).

Fac.: Arngart, O., ed., *The Leningrad Bede*, Early English Manuscripts in Facsimile, II (Copenhagen, 1952).
Blair, P. H., ed., *The Moore Bede*, Early English Manuscripts in Facsimile, IX (Copenhagen, 1959).

*CAPTURE OF THE FIVE BOROUGHS*. Mid tenth century. A thirteen-line historical poem composed in traditional style, incorporated in several versions oi the *Anglo-Saxon Chronicle* (*q.v.*) for the year 942, celebrating the West Saxon recapture of five major Midland strongholds formerly under Viking control.

CHAUCER, GEOFFREY (*c.* 1340–1400). The son of a successful London wine-merchant, be became Member of Parliament and held various offices of responsibility under Edward III and Richard II. Master-poet of the fourteenth century, his best-known works include the romance *Troilus and Criseyde* and the unfinished *Canterbury Tales*.

See: Kane, G., *Chaucer* (Oxford, 1984).

*CHRIST II*. Late eighth–early ninth century. A narrative poem of some thirteen hundred lines on the topic of Christ's ascension into heaven, signed by Cynewulf (*q.v.*) and drawing on a Latin ascension sermon by Gregory tne Great (*q.v.*). The sole extant text is found in the tenth-century Exeter Book (*q.v.*).

CYNEWULF (*fl.* 800). The only Old English poet to sign his works: *Christ II* (*q.v.*), *Elene* (*q.v.*), *Juliana* (*q.v.*), and *The Fates of the Apostles*, probably working during the later eighth or earlier ninth century somewhere in midland England. He cannot be identified with any known historical personage, but if a purportedly 'autobiographical' epilogue to *Elene* be taken at face value, the poet may have lived for a time as a warrior in well-to-do circumstances before experiencing a conviction of sin and religious conversion. Certainly the learned character of his writings and his religious preoccupations suggest that he was probably a cleric.

See: Calder, D. G., *Cynewulf* (Boston, 1981).

*DAME SIRITH AND THE WEEPING BITCH*. A thirteenth-century verse *fabliau* of some four hundred and fifty lines recounting the manner in which an amorous cleric seduces a gullible woman. Set in dramatic form with blocks of dialogue and marginal letters indicating the sequence of speakers, it is written in a mixture of tail-rhyme stanza and couplet. See generally above, pp. 226–32. The sole extant text is found in the late thirteenth-century manuscript: Bodleian Library, Oxford, MS. Digby 86.

*DEATH OF ALFRED.*  Mid eleventh century. A brief historical poem written in the developed later Old English style: about twenty-five long lines with liberal internal rhyme and assonance. It describes the imprisonment and murder by Earl Godwine of one of the sons of Æthelred, and was incorporated into two versions of the *Anglo-Saxon Chronicle (q.v.)* for the year 1036.

*DE CLERICO ET PUELLA.*  A thirteenth-century lyric of nine four-line stanzas, dramatically conceived as an exchange between an amorous cleric and a reluctant girl. The sole extant text is found in the early fourteenth-century Harley Manuscript (*q.v.*).

*DEOR.*  An early, possibly seventh-century, poem offering consolation in distress by cataloguing a number of well-known situations from history and legend where misfortune was eventually overcome. The poem's forty-two lines are divided into irregular 'stanzas' punctuated by a one-line refrain. See generally above, pp. 39–43. The sole extant text is found in the tenth-century Exeter Book (*q.v.*).

*DREAM OF THE ROOD.*  A late seventh- or early eighth-century Northumbrian crucifixion poem of some hundred and fifty lines. A composition of considerable theological sophistication and dramatic ingenuity, its core is an account of Christ's crucifixion as remembered by the personified cross. See generally above, pp. 94–101. The full text of the poem is found only in the eleventh-century Vercelli Book (*q.v.*), but extracts from the poem, or an earlier version of it, were carved on the sides of an impressive sculptured stone preaching-cross at Ruthwell, Dumfriesshire, *c.* 700.

*DURHAM.*  Early twelfth century. A twenty-one-line verse encomium on the site of the city of Durham in the north of England and the religious relics preserved there, written 1104–09 but in classical Old English metre. Two manuscript sources are known: one destroyed in the eighteenth century, but printed first; and another in a late twelfth-century Durham collection: Cambridge University Library MS. Ff.i.27.

*ELENE.*  A late eighth- or early ninth-century narrative poem of some thirteen hundred lines, signed by Cynewulf (*q.v.*). Drawing on a Latin version of the Life of St Judas Cyriacus in the *Acta Sanctorum*, it tells of the adoption of the cross-symbol by the fourth-century Roman Emperor Constantine, and the subsequent discovery (*invention*) of the true cross by the emperor's mother, St Helen (*Elene*). The sole extant text is found in the eleventh-century Vercelli Book (*q.v.*).

*EMARÉ.*  A late fourteenth-century stanzaic romance of about a thousand lines, written in the north-east of England. Drawing on a lost Breton original, it retails the conventional 'patient Griselda' theme, describing the adventures of a virtuous but misunderstood and banished heroine, Emaré ('the undefiled'). The sole extant text is found in the fifteenth-century British Library MS. Cotton Caligula Aii.

*EXETER BOOK.* Exeter Cathedral Library MS. 3501. The largest, and arguably the most important, extant anthology of Old English verse, compiled probably at Crediton, Devon, *c.* 980, and bequeathed to Exeter Cathedral library by the first Bishop of Exeter, Leofric, *ob.* 1072. It contains some of the best-known Old English verse, including: *Deor, Christ, Guthlac A* and *B, Juliana, Maxims I, The Phoenix, Physiologus, The Ruin, The Seafarer, The Wanderer,* and *Widsith* (all *q.v.*). Although coloured by the contemporary late West Saxon literary koine, it clearly includes some pieces of considerable antiquity.

Fac.:    Chambers, R. W., *et al.*, introd., *The Exeter Book of Old English Poetry* (London, 1933).

*EXODUS.* Probably composed in eighth-century Northumbria; a narrative poem of some six hundred lines in the manner of Cædmon (*q.v.*) on the theme of the Israelites' crossing of the Red Sea, based on Chapters 13–14 of the biblical Book of Exodus. See generally above, pp. 84–93. The sole extant text is found in the early eleventh-century Junius Manuscript (*q.v.*).

*FAIR MAID OF RIBBLESDALE.* A thirteenth-century lyric of seven twelve-line stanzas, ironically applying the conventions of courtly love-song to a certain 'wild woman' of the poet's acquaintance. See generally above, pp. 243–45. The sole extant text is found in the early fourteenth-century Harley Manuscript (*q.v.*).

*FIGHT AT FINNSBURH.* A forty-eight-line fragment of an early, perhaps seventh-century, heroic verse epic, dealing with the violent circumstances surrounding the visit of a group of Danish warriors to the stronghold of the Frisian war-leader Finn, some time during the fifth century. See generally above, pp. 45–49. The sole manuscript text, a single folio formerly in the library of the Archbishop of Canterbury at Lambeth Palace, London, is lost, and our knowledge is dependent on an early eighteenth-century printed version.

*FLORIS AND BLANCHEFLOUR.* A mid-thirteenth-century verse romance of some thirteen hundred lines in rhyming couplets, composed somewhere in the south-east Midlands. Drawing ultimately on eastern sources, transmitted via French romance, it tells of the separation and eventual reunion of childhood sweethearts: Floris, the son of a Saracen king and Blancheflour, the daughter of a Christian slave. See generally above, pp. 216–25. Four manuscript versions are extant, including one in the fourteenth-century Auchinleck Manuscript (*q.v.*).

*FOLLIES OF FASHION.* A thirteenth-century lyric of five seven-line stanzas, satirizing extravagant dress among women. See generally above, pp. 254–56. The sole extant text is found in the early fourteenth-century Harley Manuscript (*q.v.*).

*FORTUNES OF MEN.* An Old English verse homily of about a hundred lines, emphasizing the need for Christian stoicism in view of the various dire fates that may befall a man during his lifetime. The sole extant text is found in the tenth-century Exeter Book (*q.v.*).

*GABRIEL'S GREETING TO THE VIRGIN MARY.* A thirteenth-century Annunciation-lyric of five twelve-line stanzas, closely following a Latin original: *Angelus ad Virginem.* See generally above, pp. 250–52. The dual text, together with musical notation, is found in the late thirteenth-century British Library MS. Arundel 248.

*GENESIS.* An early Old English narrative poem of almost three thousand lines in the manner of Cædmon (*q.v.*), paraphrasing the first book of the Bible from the story of Creation to the sacrifice of Isaac. See generally above, pp. 77–84. The sole extant text is found, together with illustrations, in the early eleventh-century Junius Manuscript (*q.v.*). The main body of the poem is apparently contemporary with *Beowulf* (*q.v.*) and may possibly originate with Cædmon himself (*Genesis A*). The passage from lines 235–857 is a later interpolation (*Genesis B*), markedly different in style and based on a Continental Old Saxon poem incorporated some time in the mid to late ninth century, perhaps translated by one of the Continental scholars attracted to the court of King Alfred (*q.v.*).

*GESTA ROMANORUM.* See section ii below, p. 336.

*GNOMES.* See *MAXIMS*, below, p. 327.

*GUTHLAC A.* An eighth-century hagiographic poem of some eight hundred lines, describing the life of the Mercian warrior-turned-hermit, St Guthlac (*ob.* 714), at Crowland, Lincolnshire, and the difficulties encountered there. See generally above, pp. 143–54, and cf. Felix, section ii, below, p. 335. The sole extant text is found in the tenth-century Exeter Book (*q.v.*).

*GUTHLAC B.* A late eighth- or early ninth-century narrative poem of some five hundred lines in the manner of Cynewulf (*q.v.*), describing the death of St Guthlac (see previous entry), perhaps based on part of a Latin *Vita* by Felix (*q.v.*). The sole extant text is found in the tenth-century Exeter Book (*q.v.*).

*HARLEY MANUSCRIPT.* British Library MS. Harley 2253. An anthology of Middle English, Anglo-Norman, and Latin prose and poetry, compiled probably in Herefordshire *c.* 1320. It contains a considerable amount of thirteenth-century verse including the romance *King Horn* and the lyrics: *De Clerico et Puella, The Fair Maid of Ribblesdale, The Follies of Fashion, Lenten is Come with Love to Town,* and *A Song of Lewes* (all *q.v.*).

Fac.:   Ker, N. R., introd., *Facsimile of British Museum MS. Harley 2253,* Early English Text Society, 255 (London, 1965).

*HAVELOK THE DANE.*   A thirteenth-century verse romance of some three thousand lines, written in rhyming couplets, composed probably in Lincolnshire where much of the action is located. It describes the adventures of the eponymous hero, heir to the throne of Denmark, who is treacherously dispossessed as a child but eventually recovers his fortunes, coming to the throne of both Denmark and England. See generally above, pp. 194–205. The sole complete text is found, together with *King Horn* (*q.v.*), in the early fourteenth-century Bodleian Library, Oxford MS. Laud Misc. 108.

*HEREWARD, DEEDS OF.* See section ii below, p. 337.

*I WALK WITH SORROW.* A five-line love-lament found, accompanied by musical notation, in the mid thirteenth-century compilation, Bodleian Library, Oxford, MS. Douce 139. See generally above, pp. 238–41.

*JUDITH.* An early tenth-century narrative poem based on the Apocryphal Book of Judith, describing how the leader of an invading Assyrian army, Holofernes, is slain by the Jewish heroine Judith. See generally above, pp. 155–65. The surviving poem is some three hundred and fifty lines long; its opening is lost, but exactly how much is missing is debatable. Written in the late West Saxon literary koine, the sole extant text is found in the late tenth-century British Library MS. Cotton Vitellius Axv, together with *Beowulf (q.v.)*.

*JULIANA*. A late eighth- or early ninth-century narrative poem of some seven hundred lines, signed by Cynewulf (*q.v.*). Drawing on a version of the Latin Life of Juliana in the *Acta Sanctorum*, it describes the martyrdom of its heroine, the fourth-century Byzantine virgin-saint. The sole extant text is found in the tenth- century Exeter Book (*q.v.*).

*JUNIUS MANUSCRIPT*. Bodleian Library, Oxford, MS. Junius 11. Named after a seventeenth-century owner, Francis Junius; a volume of biblical verse paraphrases in the manner of Cædmon (*q.v.*), compiled, and in part illustrated, at Malmesbury, Wiltshire, *c.* 1000. It includes the early poems *Genesis (q.v.)* and *Exodus (q.v.)*.

> Fac.:   Gollancz, I., ed., *The Cædmon Manuscript of Anglo-Saxon Biblical Poetry, Junius XI in the Bodleian Library* (Oxford, 1927).

*KYNG ALISAUNDER*. An early fourteenth-century verse romance of some eight thousand lines in rhyming couplets, written somewhere in the south-east of England – perhaps London. Based on the twelfth-century Anglo-Norman *Roman de Toute Chevalrie* by Thomas of Kent, it describes legendary adventures ascribed to the Macedonian Emperor, Alexander the Great. The text is best preserved in the late fourteenth-century Bodleian Library, Oxford, MS. Laud Misc. 622; and there is a four-hundred-line fragment in the Auchinleck Manuscript (*q.v.*).

*KING HORN*. An early thirteenth-century verse romance of some fifteen hundred lines in rhyming couplets, probably composed in the South, or south Midlands, describing the fictional adventures of its eponymous hero, an Anglo- Scandinavian prince during a period of Saracen incursions, when *inter alia*, he regains his betrothed from hostile suitors. Three early, i.e. late thirteenth- or fourteenth-century copies of the text are extant, including one in the Harley Manuscript (*q.v.*).

*LAȜAMON*. (*fl.* 1175). Parish priest at Areley Kings, Worcestershire, the otherwise unknown author of the *Brut*, an ambitious history of Britain, written in 33,000 lines of rhyming couplets. Drawing immediately on the Anglo-Norman *Brut* of Wace (*q.v.*), and ultimately on the *History* of Geoffrey of Monmouth (*q.v.*), it covers the story of the nation from its foundation by refugees from Troy until the final British dispersal following the death of Cadwalldon in the seventh century, and devotes some space to the events of King Arthur's reign. See generally above, pp. 175–87, 193. Two mid thirteenth-century copies of the text are extant: British Library MS. Cotton Caligula Aix (also containing *The Owl and the Nightingale*), and British Library MS. Cotton Otho Cxiii, the latter presenting a revised and 'modernized' text.

*LAND OF COCKAYNE*. A lively anti-monastic satire in the goliardic manner, consisting of about a hundred lines of rhyming couplets. See generally above, pp. 246–47. The sole extant text is found in an anthology probably compiled at Kildare in Southern Ireland, *c.* 1310–20: British Library MS. Harley 913.

*LENTEN IS COME WITH LOVE TO TOWN*. A thirteenth-century lyrical *reverdie*, or spring-song, in three twelve-line stanzas. See generally above, pp. 241–43. The sole extant text is found in the early fourteenth-century Harley Manuscript (*q.v.*).

LEOFRIC.  See *HEREWARD, DEEDS OF*, section (ii) below, p. 337.

MANNYNG, ROBERT (*c.* 1283–1340). Born, like Hereward the Wake (*q.v.*), at Bourne, Lincolnshire, and later canon and schoolmaster at nearby Sempringham Priory. The author, (before 1303), of the anecdotal religious manual *Handlyng Synne*, some twelve thousand lines of rhyming couplets, based on the Anglo-Norman *Manuel des Péchiez* of William of Waddington, and *c.* 1338, of a substantial verse *Chronicle* of some twenty-five thousand lines of couplets, also drawing extensively on Anglo-Norman sources: the *Chronicle* of Peter Langtoft and the *Brut* of Wace (q.v.). Several manuscript copies are extant of both of Mannyng's works.

*MAXIMS (GNOMES).* Free-ranging sequences of proverbial lore in Old English verse. Two collections exist: I in the tenth-century Exeter Book (*q.v.*) and II in the eleventh-century Abingdon version of the *Anglo-Saxon Chronicle* (q.v.), British Library MS. Cotton Tiberius Bi.

*OCTOVIAN IMPERATOR.* A mid fourteenth-century stanzaic romance describing the adventures of the twin offspring of the Roman Emperor Octavian: Florentyn and young Octavian, maliciously disavowed but eventually restored. Two versions exist: a northern of some seventeen hundred lines in twelve-line tail-rhyme stanzas, and a south-eastern of some two thousand lines in six-line stanzas. Extant manuscript copies are of the fifteenth century.

ORM (*fl.* 1200). An Augustinian canon, living perhaps in Lincolnshire, known only as the author of a collection of verse homilies compiled at the request of his brother Walter, also an Augustinian canon, and 'entitled the *Ormulum* because Orm wrote it'. Incomplete (only 32 of the planned 242 homilies are present), its 20,000 lines are in an unusual metre, similar to the Latin septenarius; it is chiefly interesting as a philological document because of the distinctive mode of phonetic spelling Orm adopted. The unique text, Bodleian Library, Oxford, MS. Junius 1, almost certainly represents the author's autograph.

*OTUEL.* An early fourteenth-century verse romance of some seventeen hundred lines in rhyming couplets, composed somewhere in the east Midlands, describing the adventures of its eponymous hero, a Saracen knight converted to Christianity at the court of Charlemagne. The sole extant text (incomplete at the end) is found in the early fourteenth-century Auchinleck Manuscript (*q.v.*).

*OWL AND THE NIGHTINGALE, THE.* Late twelfth–early thirteenth century. A debate-poem of some eighteen hundred lines in rhyming couplets, composed *c.* 1200 in the south of England, possibly by an ambitious clerk, one Nicholas of Guildford, Surrey. The poem's protagonists are the two birds of the title; their debate ranges over a variety of topics centred on the relationship of literature to life, without reaching any formal conclusion. Two copies of the text are extant: the mid thirteenth-century British Library MS. Cotton Caligula Aix (also containing the earlier version of Laʒamon's *Brut*, *q.v.*), and a 'revised and modernized' text in the late thirteenth-century Jesus College, Oxford, MS. 29 (which also contains Thomas of Hales's *Love-Song, q.v.*, and a version of *The Proverbs of Alfred, q.v.*).

> Fac.:  Ker. N. R., introd., *The Owl and the Nightingale*, Early English Text Society, 251 (London, 1963).

*PANTHER.* See *PHYSIOLOGUS*, below, p. 328.

*PHOENIX*. Probably a ninth-century allegorical poem of some seven hundred lines, based on the Latin *Carmen de Ave Phoenice* attributed to the fourth-century poet Lactantius (*q.v.*), relating the life, death, and resurrection of the legendary bird to the person of Christ and the Church. See generally above, pp. 129–38. The sole extant text is found in the tenth-century Exeter Book (*q.v.*).

*PHYSIOLOGUS*. An Old English verse bestiary in which the appearance and habits of various animals are symbolically interpreted with religious meanings. See generally above, p. 129. How much, if anything, is lost is debatable, but only *Panther*, *Whale*, and *Partridge* are represented in the sole extant text, which is found in the tenth-century Exeter Book (*q.v.*).

*PROVERBS OF ALFRED*. See ALFRED, KING, above, p. 319.

*RECTITUDINES SINGULARUM PERSONARUM*. An early to mid eleventh-century prose treatise on estate management setting out the services expected of various classes of peasantry. The sole extant text is included in a collection of laws copied in the south-east of England, perhaps London, *c*. 1100: Corpus Christi College, Cambridge, MS. 383.

*RICHARD THE LIONHEART*. A late thirteenth-century verse romance of some seven thousand lines in rhyming couplets, composed somewhere in south-west England. Apparently based on a lost Anglo–Norman original, it presents a highly partisan account of adventures ascribed to the crusader king, Richard I. See generally above, pp. 215–16. Copies of the text survive in several manuscripts, the earliest being a substantial fragment in the early fourteenth-century Auchinleck Manuscript (*q.v.*).

*RIME OF KING WILLIAM*. Late eleventh century. A brief historical poem written in the developed later Old English style: about twenty long lines with liberal internal rhyme and assonance. Incorporated into the Peterborough version of the *Anglo-Saxon Chronicle* (*q.v.*) for the year 1086, it presents a summary view of the career and personality of William the Conqueror.

*RUIN, THE*. A forty-nine-line fragment of Old English verse, probably composed in eighth-century Mercia, describing and meditating upon the ruined foundation of a Roman fortress. See generally above, pp. 122–28. The sole extant text is found in the tenth-century Exeter Book (*q.v.*).

*SAYINGS OF ST BERNARD*. A thirteenth-century religious poem of about a hundred lines, cast in lyric form, written probably in the south-east Midlands. Summarizing the admonitions of the twelfth-century monastic reformer Bernard of Clairvaux in respect of the world, the flesh, and the devil, the poem is textually linked with the lyric *Ubi Sount Qui Ante Nos Fuerount* (*q.v.*) in a variety of manuscript copies, including those found in the fourteenth-century Auchinleck and Harley Manuscripts (both *q.v.*).

*SEAFARER, THE*. An eighth-century poem of some hundred and twenty lines cast in the form of a dramatic monologue, associating the hardships of life at sea with the journey of life and death. See generally above, pp. 114–2. The sole extant text is found in the tenth-century Exeter Book (*q.v.*).

*SIR CLEGES*. A late fourteenth-century stanzaic romance of some five hundred and fifty lines, composed in the north Midlands. It tells a humorous tale of a

Christmas Day miracle in which the charitable and impoverished knight of the title receives his due reward at the court of Uther Pendragon. The text is extant in two late fifteenth-century copies: National Library of Scotland, Edinburgh, Advocates' MS. 19.1.11, and Bodleian Library, Oxford, MS. Ashmole 61.

*SIR GAWAIN AND THE GREEN KNIGHT.* A late fourteenth-century stanzaic romance of some two and a half thousand lines, composed in the north-west Midlands by a master-poet who was probably responsible also for three religious poems included in the same manuscript: *Patience, Pearl,* and *Purity.* It describes the testing quest of the eponymous hero Sir Gawain, framed by an exchange of beheading blows with the bizarre Green Knight. The sole extant text is found in British Library MS. Cotton Nero Axv, *c.* 1400.

   Fac.:   Gollancz, I., introd., *Pearl, Cleanness, Patience and Sir Gawain,* Early English Text Society, Original Series 162 (London, 1923).

*SIR TRISTREM.* A late thirteenth-century stanzaic romance of some three thousand three hundred lines, composed perhaps in the south-east Midlands, and recounting in an oblique and ironic fashion the well-known story of the adulterous love between Tristan and Iseult. See generally above, pp. 203–15. The sole extant text is found in the early fourteenth-century Auchinleck Manuscript (*q.v.*).

*SONG OF LEWES, A.* Mid thirteenth century. A fifty-line political song (eight five-line stanzas with refrain) denigrating Richard, Earl of Cornwall, defeated at the Battle of Lewes, Sussex, in 1264. See generally above, pp. 256–58. The sole extant text is found in the early-fourteenth-century Harley Manuscript (*q.v.*).

*SUMMER IS ICUMEN IN.* A fourteen-line lyrical *reverdie* or spring-song, the sole extant text of which is found, together with instructions for performance, in a mid thirteenth-century compilation probably made at Reading Abbey, Berkshire: British Library MS. Harley 978.

THOMAS OF HALES (*fl.* 1250). A Franciscan preacher, perhaps from Hailes, Gloucestershire, the author of one known Anglo-Norman, and possibly several Latin sermons. At the request of a young nun of his acquaintance, he composed a '*Love-Song*', in twenty-six eight-line stanzas, recommending the superiority of Christ's love. See generally above, pp. 246–49. The sole extant text is found, together with versions of *The Owl and the Nightingale, (q.v.)* and *The Proverbs of Alfred (q.v.)* in the late thirteenth-century Jesus College, Oxford, MS. 29.

*THRUSH AND THE NIGHTINGALE, THE.* A late thirteenth-century debate poem, in sixteen twelve-line stanzas, composed somewhere in the west Midlands. Alternate stanzas are exchanged by the protagonists of the title, discussing the merits and demerits of womankind. See generally above, pp. 258–62. Like the lyric *Ubi Sount Qui Ante Nos Fuerount (q.v.),* the text is found in two manuscripts: the late thirteenth-century Bodleian Library, Oxford, MS. Digby 86, and the early fourteenth-century Auchinleck Manuscript (*q.v.*).

*UBI SOUNT QUI ANTE NOS FUEROUNT.* An early thirteenth-century lyric of ten six-line stanzas on the theme of the transience of earthly glories. See generally above, pp. 252–54. Like *The Thrush and the Nightingale (q.v.),* the text is found in two manuscripts: the late thirteenth-century Bodleian Library, Oxford, MS. Digby 86, and the early fourteenth-century Auchinleck Manuscript (*q.v.*).

*VERCELLI BOOK:* Vercelli Cathedral Library MS. CXVII. A late tenth-century compilation of religious verse and prose sermons, written perhaps at Rochester, Kent, and preserved from early times in the cathedral library at Vercelli in north Italy. The poetry includes *Andreas, The Dream of the Rood* and *Elene* (all *q.v.*).

Fac.:    Sisam, C., ed., *The Vercelli Book*, Early English Manuscripts in Facsimile, XIX (Copenhagen, 1976).

*VESPASIAN HOMILIES, THE.* A small collection of four early thirteenth-century sermons, probably written somewhere in the south-west of England, found in British Library MS. Cotton Vespasian Axxii.

*WALDERE.* Two fragments of dialogue (amounting to little more than sixty lines in all), from an early, perhaps eighth-century, verse epic, dealing with the adventures of the fifth-century hero Walter of Aquitaine fleeing from the court of Attila the Hun. See generally above, pp. 43–45. The text is found on two manuscript leaves, written in a late tenth- or early eleventh-century hand, preserved in the Royal Library at Copenhagen: MS Ny kgl. saml. 167b.

*WANDERER, THE.* An eighth-century poem of some hundred and fifteen lines cast in the form of a dramatic monologue, linking the plight of an individual exile with that of mankind at large. See generally above, pp. 105–14. The sole extant text is found in the tenth-century Exeter Book (*q.v.*).

*WAY OF CHRIST'S LOVE, THE,* and *THE WAY OF WOMAN'S LOVE.* Two linked thirteenth-century lyrics, each of five six-line stanzas with refrain, comparing earthly with spiritual loves. The texts are set out adjacent to each other in the early fourteenth-century Harley Manuscript (*q.v.*).

*WHALE, THE.* See *PHYSIOLOGUS,* above, p. 328.

*WIDSITH.* An early, perhaps seventh-century, poetic catalogue, about a hundred and forty lines long, listing the stock-in-trade of topics offered by the wandering minstrel of the title. See generally above, pp. 32–39. The sole extant text is found in the tenth-century Exeter Book (*q.v.*).

*WOOING OF OUR LORD, THE.* An early thirteenth-century mystical prose treatise extolling the person of Christ as lover, probably written somewhere in the south-west of England. The text is found, together with a version of the *Anchoress's Guide (Ancrene Riwle) (q.v.)* in the thirteenth-century British Library MS. Cotton Titus D.xviii.

WULFSTAN (*ob.* 1023). A prominent statesman-cleric; Bishop of London from 996 to 1002 and Archbishop of York from 1002 to 1023, which office he held in plurality with the see of Worcester until 1016. Wulfstan's considerable ability as a preacher is revealed in the forceful style of some two dozen homilies; equally active in affairs of state, he was responsible for much of the legislation of both Æthelred and his Viking successor Cnut, as well as for such legal codes as *The Institutes of Polity* and the so-called *Canons of Edgar.*

Fac.:    Loyn, H. R., ed., *A Wulfstan MS. containing Institutes, Laws and Homilies: BM. Cotton Nero Ai*, Early English Manuscripts in Facsimile, XVII (Copenhagen, 1971).

# (ii) Writers and writings in languages other than English

**ABELARD, PETER** (1079–1142). Born into an aristocratic family at Pallet, Brittany; he won early acclaim as a vigorous student and teacher of theology and dialectic at Paris. Mugged and mutilated by the guardian of Héloïse, a pupil with whom he was having a love-affair, he entered the Benedictine Order, but continued to teach; his views roused the opposition of Bernard of Clairvaux (*q.v.*) and others, and resulted in papal condemnation. His extensive writings include important works on logic, a series of lectures on the Trinity, the influential patristic compilation *Sic et Non* (1123–36), and letters to Héloïse and others.

**ADELARD OF BATH** (*c.* 1070–1145). Apparently a Benedictine from Bath, Wiltshire, educated at Tours, and sometime teacher at Laon. Travelling extensively in Spain, Sicily, Greece, and possibly the Near East, he played an important role in the transmission of Byzanto-Arab learning to the West, translating Arabic textbooks on Euclidian mathematics and Aristotelian empiricism.

**ÆLFRIC.** See section i above, p. 319.

**AELRED OF RIEVAULX** (1110–67). The son of a hereditary priest at Hexham, Northumberland; he was educated at Durham and spent part of his youth at the court of King David of Scotland, before entering the Cistercian monastery at Rievaulx, Yorkshire, in 1134, where he became abbot twelve years later. He was the author of various historical works including a *Life of Edward the Confessor* and a tract on the *Battle of the Standard* (1138) and, more importantly, religious works such as *Speculum Caritatis* (written at the suggestion of Bernard of Clairvaux, *q.v.*), and *De Institutione Inclusarum*, a treatise on the life of an anchoress written at the request of his sister, *c.* 1160, both of which were translated into English in the fourteenth century.

**ALANUS DE INSULIS, OR DE LILLE** (*c.* 1114–1203). A Cistercian savant of unknown origins, teaching at Paris *c.* 1157–70. An influential polymath, he wrote on theological, philosophical, and scientific topics in both prose and verse; his works include *De Planctu Naturae*, and the epic *Anticlaudianus*, treating the relationship of mankind to nature.

**ALCUIN** (*c.* 735–804). The foremost man of letters of Carolingian Europe. Born probably at York, where he was educated and later taught; he was invited in 781 to direct the educational programme of Charlemagne's palace schools. Influential both as administrator and author, he wrote extensively on theological, historical, grammatical, and scientific topics in both prose and verse, and was a prolific correspondent. His verse encomium on *The Bishops, Kings and Saints of York* includes a valuable survey of books available in the York library.

**ALDHELM** (*c.* 640–709). Born into a wealthy West Saxon family; he was educated first at the Celtic school of Maildubh at Malmesbury, Wiltshire, and later under Theodore of Tarsus at Canterbury. He became Abbot of Malmesbury from 675 and Bishop of Sherborne from 705. His writings, in both prose and verse, are marked by a florid Latin style. They include the tracts *De Laude Virginitatis*, in prose, and *De Laudibus Virginum*, in verse, and a treatise of metrics addressed to the scholarly King Aldfrith of Northumbria. His English poetry, admired by King Alfred (*q.v.*), is lost.

ALEXANDER OF HALES (*c.* 1185–1245). Born into a wealthy family at Halesowen, Shropshire; he became Canon of Lichfield and, from 1231, Archdeacon of Coventry, and entered the Franciscan Order in 1236. Sometime teacher of theology at Paris, his considerable scholastic reputation caused a variety of works to be ascribed to him, including the anecdotal *Destructorium Vitiorum*.

ALEXANDER NECKHAM (1157–1217). Born at St Albans, Hertfordshire; he taught at Dunstable and St Albans before studying theology at Oxford. He entered the Augustinian Order *c.* 1200 and became Abbot of Cirencester in 1213. A man of encyclopaedic learning, his writings, in verse and prose, include works on religion and the natural sciences, (*De Naturis Rerum*), and a verse translation of the fables of Aesop.

AMBROSE (*c.* 340–97). The foremost churchman of his day. Born at Trier on the Mosel, son of the governor of the western provinces of the Roman Empire; he studied law and became civil magistrate at Milan. Elected Bishop of Milan by popular demand in 374, he exercised considerable influence, notably on Augustine of Hippo (*q.v.*). He was the author of a considerable body of expository writings on the Old Testament, beginning with the *Hexaemeron*, or commentary on Creation, several sermons or homilies on the theme of virginity, and a number of hymns.

ANDREAS CAPELLANUS (*fl.* 1175). The otherwise unknown author of a Latin treatise on the nature and practice of human love, *De Arte Honeste Amandi*, possibly ironic but reflecting acknowledged conventions. He claims to have been a royal chaplain, and may possibly have been attached to the court of Marie de Champagne at Troyes.

ANEIRIN (*fl.* 600). Welsh bard, known only as the author of *Y Gododdin*, an encomium on the retinue of Mynyddawg Mwynfawr of Edinburgh, annihilated during a raid on the Anglian stronghold of Catterick, Yorkshire, *c.* 595.

ANSELM (1033–1109). Born into an aristocratic Burgundian family at Aosta, Piedmont; he was educated in Normandy under Lanfranc, whom he succeeded first as Prior of the Abbey of Bec, and eventually as Archbishop of Canterbury, to which he was consecrated by Thomas of Bayeux (*q.v.*) in 1093. The author of a considerable body of theological and philosophical writings, including the tract *Cur Deus Homo*, ontological arguments for the existence of God in *Monologion* and *Prosologion*, and dialogues *On Truth* and *On Freewill*.

*ANTHONY, LIFE OF.* Influential *Vita* of one of the founding-fathers of ascetic monasticism, the Egyptian hermit St Anthony, *c.* 250–355, written in Greek *c.* 357 by his friend Athanasius, Bishop of Alexandria, and shortly afterwards translated into Latin by Evagrius, Bishop of Antioch.

*ATLAKVITHA (LAY OF ATTILA(.* An Old Norse poem in the Poetic Edda, a thirteenth-century compilation but clearly containing ancient material. It tells a story of the Burgundian–Hunnish Wars similar to that found in the

*Nibelungenlied (q.v.)*, but here Attila (Atli/Etzel) is the villain, slain by his wife Gudrun (Kriemhild) to avenge the deaths of her brothers Gunnar (Gunther) and Hogni (Hagen).

*AUCASSIN ET NICOLETTE* An early thirteenth-century French *chantefable*, (told in alternate prose and verse): it describes how Aucassin, son of the Count of Beaucarie, falls in love with a captive Saracen girl, Nicolette, thereby incurring official displeasure, but after various vicissitudes is allowed to marry her.

AUGUSTINE, AURELIUS (354–430). Foremost theologian of the early Church. Born into a relatively humble Algerian family; he studied and subsequently taught rhetoric at Carthage; he was associated with a Manichean group who secured for him a position in Milan; there he was strongly influenced by Ambrose (*q.v.*) before returning to North Africa, where he became Bishop of Hippo (Annaba) in 395. The most prolific, learned, and influential theologian of his day, he was the author of numerous biblical commentaries, homilies, and polemical works, including the *Confessions, Soliloquies,* and *The City of God.* He died during the Hunnish Siege of Hippo in 430.

BEATRICE OF KENT (1257–80). Abbess of Lacock, Wiltshire, the author of certain *versus ridiculi*, now alas lost.

BEDE (673–735). The foremost scholar of the early Anglo-Saxon world. Born in County Durham; he was a lifelong monk at the joint foundation of Monkwearmouth-Jarrow. His extensive writings include: expository commentaries on the Old and New Testaments; works on hagiography, grammar, and metrics; scientific tracts, and an important *History of the English Church and People,* translated into English at the time of King Alfred (*q.v.*). He was completing an English translation (now lost) of St John's Gospel when he died.

See:   Thompson, A. H., ed., *Bede: His Life, Times, and Works* (Oxford, 1935).

BERNARD OF CHARTRES (*c.* 1090–1130). An influential Breton who taught logic and grammar at the cathedral school of Chartres. None of his writings survive, but one of his pupils, John of Salisbury (*q.v.*) quotes from them, and speaks of him as 'the most thorough-going Platonist of our Age'.

BERNARD OF CLAIRVAUX (1090–1153). Born into an aristocratic family near Dijon; he early withdrew into the new religious Order of Cistercians, becoming Abbot of Clairvaux in 1115. An influential teacher and administrator, he was given charge of preaching the Second Crusade, 1146–47, and wrote *De Laude Novae Militiae*, commending the Order of Knights Templars. He was the author of a number of theological and mystical writings.

*BJARKAMÁL (LAY OF BJARKI).* A probably tenth-century Old Norse poem, describing the last stand in his hall at Leire (Heorot) of the sixth-century Danish King Hrólfr (Hrothulf). The text survives only in fragments quoted by Snorri Sturluson (*q.v.*).

BOETHIUS, ANICIUS MANLIUS TORQUATUS SEVERINUS (*c.* 475–524). Born into a wealthy family at Rome; he was educated at Athens and Alexandria, wrote a number of textbooks on logic and music, and became tutor to the young Cassiodorus (*q.v.*). He was well known in governmental circles and made consul in 510. He became adviser to the Ostrogothic Emperor Theodoric at Ravenna, but eventually fell into disfavour and was accused of treason. Imprisoned at Pavia and awaiting execution, he composed the stoic *Consolation of Philosophy*; one of the most influential works of medieval times, it was first translated into English by King Alfred (*q.v.*).

BONIFACE (ALIAS WYNFRITH) (*c.* 675–755). Born in Devonshire and educated first locally at Exeter and then at Nursling, Hampshire, he left England in 716 and spent the greater part of his life in missionary work among the pagan German tribes east of the Rhine. A missionary bishop without a see from 723, he was eventually established as Archbishop of Mainz in 742, but was killed preaching to hostile Frisians in 755. He was a prolific correspondent, and also wrote a number of sermons and a collection of Latin riddles.

BYRHTFERTH OF RAMSEY (*fl.* 1000). A Benedictine monk at Ramsey, Huntingdonshire, where he was taught by Abbo of Fleury; he later studied at Canterbury and at Echternach (an early English foundation in the Ardennes). He was the author of several Latin writings, including a *Life of St Oswald*, founder-abbot of Ramsey, commentaries on the scientific works of Bede (*q.v.*), and a *Manual*, composed partly in Latin and partly in English, concerned primarily with astronomy and the computation of the calendar.

CAMBRIDGE SONGS, THE Cambridge University Library MS. Gg.5.35. An important anthology of goliardic and other verse in Latin and German, apparently drawing on a Rhenish source, but compiled at St Augustine's Abbey, Canterbury, *c.* 1000. The manuscript also contains verse by: Aldhelm, Bede, Boniface, Hrabanus Maurus, Hwætberht, Lactantius, Prudentius, Tatwine, and others (all *q.v.*).

CASSIODORUS, FLAVIUS MAGNUS AURELIUS (*c.* 485–580). Born into a noble Italian family at Squillace, Calabria; he became adviser and chief administrator to the Ostrogothic Emperor Theodoric. After the collapse of Theodoric's empire, he retired to monastic seclusion on his Calabrian estate. The author of a variety of historical and religious works, he wrote a *History of the Goths* (now lost), a *World History*, the influential encyclopaedic *Institutiones Divinarum et Humanorum Lectionum*, and a collection of letters under the title *Variae*.

CHRONICLE OF LANERCOST, THE. A general history of England and Scotland, 1201–1346, inaugurated probably during the reign of Edward I, at Lanercost Priory, near Carlisle; it is chiefly interesting for its accounts of contemporary events.

CHRONICLE OF MELROSE, THE. A general history of northern England and Scotland, 731–1275, compiled *c.* 1236 by a monk at Melrose Abbey, Borders, and maintained for a further forty years; it is chiefly interesting for its accounts of contemporary events.

DANIEL OF BECCLES (*fl.* 1180). Author of prose and verse, apparently attached to the court of Henry II; his only surviving work a Latin verse manual of etiquette, entitled *Urbanus Magnus*.

DUNS SCOTUS, JOHN (*c.* 1265–1308). Probably born in south-west Scotland; he was educated among Franciscans at Dumfries, and later taught at Oxford, Paris, and Cologne. The foremost scholastic philosopher of his day, he was the author of a wide variety of theological and philosophical tracts.

FAUSTUS OF RIEZ (c. 410–92). A Briton, or possibly Breton, who entered the Provençal monastery on the Ile de Lérins, c. 426, becoming Abbot in 433, and subsequently Bishop of Riez c. 458. He acquired the reputation of an effective preacher, and was the author of a series of letters, homilies, and semi-Pelagian tracts on *The Holy Spirit* and on *The Grace of God*.

FELIX (*fl.* 730). The otherwise unknown author of a Latin Life of the Mercian hermit Guthlac (*q.v.*), written at the request of the East Anglian King Ælfwald, c. 735; it was subsequently translated into Old English prose, and drawn upon by the authors of the poems *Guthlac A* and *B* (*q.v.*).

FREDEGAR (*fl.* 650). The author, (probably Burgundian but otherwise unknown), of a continuation of the *History of the Franks* by Gregory of Tours (*q.v.*), covering the years 585–642.

GEOFFREY GAIMAR (*fl.* 1140). A member of a Norman family, possibly from Caen, probably living in Lincolnshire. The author of an Anglo–Norman verse *Estorie des Engles*, which, drawing on Geoffrey of Monmouth (*q.v.*), began with an account (now fragmentary) of the foundation of the nation, and continued to the death of William Rufus.

GEOFFREY OF MONMOUTH (c. 1100–1155). The son of a Welsh priest at Monmouth; he was made Archdeacon of Llandaff c. 1140, and Bishop of St Asaph from 1152. He is best known as the author of the *Historia Regum Britanniae*, in which, at the request of Alexander, Bishop of Lincoln, he reduced a mass of ancient Welsh legends to the form of Latin chronicle. It outlines the history of the British nation from its foundation by refugees from Troy, until the final British dispersal following the death of Cadwallader in the seventh century, and devotes some space to the 'Prophecies of Merlin' and the reign of King Arthur. Enormously influential, it was followed in turn by Geoffrey Gaimar, Wace, and Laʒamon (all *q.v.*), and thereafter entered European tradition.

GEOFFREY DE VINSAUF (*fl.* 1205). A member of an Anglo–Norman family, he apparently studied at Paris, and taught for a while at Northampton before being displaced by a certain Robert. He was the author of various Latin works, most notably the *Poetria Nova*, a compendious poem on the art of poetic composition, drawing on Horace and Cicero.

GERALD OF WALES (1147–1223). Born into an aristocratic family at Manorber, Dyfed, the son of a Norman father and a Welsh mother who claimed royal antecedents. He was educated at Paris and became Archdeacon of Brecknock and a royal chaplain to the household of Henry II; but finding his further clerical ambitions frustrated, he turned to scholarship. His considerable body of writings include spirited treatises on government (*De Principis Instructione*), ecclesiastical matters (*Gemma Ecclesiae* and *Speculum Ecclesiae*), topography (the *Itinerarium* and *Descriptio Kambriae* and *Topographia Hiberniae*), as well as a revealing autobiography (*De Rebus a Se Gestis*).

GERVASE OF TILBURY (c. 1140–1220). Probably a native of Tilbury, Essex; he spent much of his life abroad, travelling in Italy and Norman Sicily, studying and teaching for a while at Bologna. He was attached for a period to the court of the Holy Roman Emperor Otto, to whom he dedicated his only surviving work, the encyclopaedic compendium *Otia Imperialia*.

*GESTA ROMANORUM.* A collection of some four-dozen moralized tales, from a variety of sources, probably compiled in England late in the thirteenth century. Highly influential, it was extensively drawn upon by preachers, and translated into most languages of medieval Europe, although the earliest known English translations belong to the fifteenth century.

GILDAS (*c.* 516–70). A British cleric, probably from Strathclyde, who travelled widely, in the manner of the time, through the Western Approaches: Ireland, Wales, and Brittany. The author of the *De Excidio et Conquestu Britanniae*, lamenting the fate of the British at the advent of the Saxons.

*GODODDIN, THE.* See ANEIRIN, above, p. 332.

GOSCELIN OF CANTERBURY (*fl.* 1099). A Lotharingian monk from the Norman Abbey of St Bertin, who came to England in the train of his compatriot Hermann when he was made Bishop of Ramsbury by Edward the Confessor in 1045. Settling eventually at Canterbury, he wrote Lives of the missionary St Augustine and of his successors at Canterbury, which he dedicated to Anselm (*q.v.*).

GOTTFRIED VON STRASSBURG (*fl.* 1210). The otherwise unknown author of a substantial, and uncompleted, Middle High German verse romance, *Tristan and Isolde*, based on the Anglo-Norman version by Thomas of Britain (*q.v.*).

GREGORY (THE GREAT) *c.* 540–604. Born into a wealthy family living in Rome; he studied law and embarked on a governmental career, but withdrew into monastic seclusion *c.* 575, and was elected Bishop of Rome in 590. He was responsible for important administrative and liturgical developments, and was highly regarded in England since it was at his instigation that the Roman mission to the pagan Anglo-Saxons was undertaken in 597. He was the author of various biblical commentaries and homilies, including the so-called *Dialogues* on the lives and miracles of early Italian saints, and the *Pastoral Care*, describing the responsibilities of episcopal office, both of which were translated into English during the reign of King Alfred (*q.v.*).

GREGORY OF TOURS (538–94). Born into an influential clerical family at Clermont-Ferrand in the Auvergne; he early entered the Church, rising rapidly to become Bishop of Tours in 573. He wrote various historical works, including *Lives of the Fathers*, an account of the *Miracles of St Martin of Tours*, and, most notably, a *History of the Franks*, which covered the period from Creation to 591 and was particularly important as a chronicle of contemporary events.

*HAROLD, LIFE OF.* A speculative account of the religious life said to have been taken up by Harold Godwinson (presuming him to have survived the Battle of Hastings), retailed by an anonymous canon of Harold's foundation of Waltham Abbey, Essex, *c.* 1205.

HENRY DE BRACTON (*c.* 1210–68). The most prominent jurist of his day. Born into a wealthy family at Bratton Fleming, Devonshire; he studied law, probably at Oxford, becoming an itinerant justice in the South-west from 1244, and eventually Chancellor of the Diocese of Exeter in 1264. He was the author of the first systematic English law-manual, *De Legibus et Consuetudinibus Angliae*.

**HENRY OF HUNTINGDON** (*c.* 1084–1155). Born into a clerical family in the Diocese of Lincoln, and brought up in the household of the Bishop of Lincoln, he became Archdeacon of Huntingdon in 1100. The author of a substantial Latin *History of England*, drawing on Bede and the *Anglo-Saxon Chronicle* (both *q.v.*), but valuable also as an independent source.

**HEREWARD, DEEDS OF.** A Latin biography of the post–Conquest guerrilla-fighter Hereward the Wake (*fl.* 1070), compiled some time during the earlier twelfth century by a monk of Ely called Richard, drawing on a memoir (now lost) written in English by Hereward's former chaplain Leofric, and supplemented by the personal recollections of some of Hereward's other associates.

**HRABANUS MAURUS** (776–856). Born into a wealthy family at Mainz on the Rhine, educated first at Fulda, an English foundation of Boniface (*q.v.*), and later at Tours under Alcuin (*q.v.*); he returned to Fulda as schoolmaster, becoming abbot in 822, and was made Archbishop of Mainz in 847. An influential figure in the Carolingian renaissance, he was a prolific author, writing poetry, biblical commentaries, and, drawing extensively on Isidore of Seville (*q.v.*), an encyclopaedic dictionary *De Universo*.

**HUGH DE ROTELAND** (*fl.* 1185). An Anglo-Norman poet, born at Rhuddlan, Clwyd, and living at Credenhill near Hereford. The author of a substantial but urbane, knightly love-story, *Ipomedon*, and its sequel, *Protheselaus*.

**HUGH OF ST VICTOR** (1096–1141). A member of a wealthy Flemish or Lotharingian family, he early entered the Augustinian Order, teaching at the Abbey of St Victor, Paris, for the greater part of his life after 1115. He was an influential author of biblical commentaries and religious mystical writings.

**HWÆTBERHT (ALIAS EUSEBIUS).** Abbot of Monkwearmouth-Jarrow from 716 to *c.* 745, a friend of Bede and Boniface (both *q.v.*); the author of a series of Latin riddles in the manner of Tatwine (*q.v.*).

**IBN HAZM** (994–1064). The son of a Moslem vizier at Cordoba, he travelled widely in Arab Spain. An elegant writer in both prose and verse, his works include treatises on biblical textual criticisms, logic and ethics, but he is best known as the author of *Tauk al-Hamāma, The Ring of the Dove*, a systematic enquiry into the nature of human love.

**ISIDORE OF SEVILLE** (*c.* 560–636). Born into a North African family that had moved to Andalusia, he was educated by his elder brother, the Archbishop of Seville, whom he succeeded in that office in 600. One of the most erudite men of his time, he was the author of several philosophical, religious, and historical studies, and most notably of the pioneering encyclopaedia, *Etymologiae*.

**JEROME** (*c.* 345–420). Born in relatively modest circumstances at Stridova in what is now Yugoslavia, he was educated at Rome, and subsequently became acquainted with monasticism at Trier on the Mosel; he travelled widely through Asia Minor and lived for five years as a hermit in the desert of Syria, 374–79, before finally settling at Bethlehem where he founded a monastery. He was a friend of Augustine and opponent of Pelagius (both *q.v.*). Probably the most learned man of his time, he was a prolific author, who wrote biblical commentaries, homilies, and polemical works commending virginity and the eremetical life, but he is best known for his Latin translations of the Greek and Hebrew books of the Bible (the Vulgate).

JOHN OF BASINGSTOKE (*ob.* 1252). Presumably associated in some way with Basingstoke, Hampshire; educated at Oxford and Paris, and one of the first men of his day to have an original knowledge of Greek, which he studied at Athens under the young female teacher Constantia. A friend of Simon de Montfort and Robert Grossteste (*q.v.*), he was Archdeacon of Leicester by 1235, but little more of his career is known. He was the author of works on grammar and mathematics.

JOHN OF PECKHAM (*c.* 1220–92). Born at Patcham, Sussex; he was educated first at nearby Lewes, and subsequently at Oxford and Paris, where he also taught theology. He entered the Franciscan Order *c.* 1250 and was appointed Archbishop of Canterbury in 1279. A Platonist rather than an Aristotelian, he was the author of a number of works on science (optics) and philosophy, homilies, and Franciscan tracts on poverty, and some notable religious poetry including the hymn *Philomena*.

JOHN OF SALISBURY (*c.* 1115–80). Born in relatively humble circumstances at Old Salisbury, Wiltshire; he was educated at Paris, under Abelard (*q.v.*), and later Chartres, where he also taught for a time. He became a valued ecclesiastical administrator under Theobald, Archbishop of Canterbury, and was a friend of Thomas Becket – with him at Canterbury on the day he was assassinated. Towards the end of his life he returned to Chartres as bishop, 1176. The author of various works including Lives of Thomas Becket and of Anselm (*q.v.*), and most importantly the educational treatise *Metalogicon* in defence of the trivium, and the encyclopaedic *Policratus*, or 'Statesman's Guide', a study of political theory.

JORDANES (*fl.* 550). The earliest Gothic historian whose work survives. A member of a leading family, he was for some time secretary to the Alan prince Candac before becoming a cleric. He was the author of a general Latin history (*Romana*) and, more importantly, a history of the Goths (*Getica*), significant in so far as it drew heavily on the lost work of Cassiodorus (*q.v.*).

LACTANTIUS, LUCIUS CAECILIUS FIRMIANUS (*c.* 240–325). Apparently born in North Africa, where he taught rhetoric. Later he was tutor to Crispus, son of the Emperor Constantine, at Trier *c.* 317. An elegant stylist in both prose and verse, he was the author of a number of theological and philosophical works, and poems including the *Carmen de Ave Phoenice*.

*LIBER ELIENSIS (THE ELY BOOK)*. A history of the Church in the eastern counties of England, with particular reference to Ely and its environs, apparently compiled *c.* 1131–74 by a monk of Ely called Richard, who drew extensively on Aelred, Bede, Felix, Henry of Huntingdon, William of Malmesbury, etc., and various vernacular sources, possibly including *The Battle of Maldon* (all *q.v.*). It gives an account of William the Conqueror's Siege of Ely in 1071 similar to that retailed in *The Deeds of Hereward* (*q.v.*).

*LIBER MONSTRORUM (BOOK OF MONSTERS)*. A late eighth- or early ninth-century Anglo-Saxon compilation, presenting brief accounts of strange monsters, beasts, and serpents, drawing extensively on classical sources.

LLYWARCH HEN. A sixth-century British warrior and semi-legendary bard, contemporary with Aneirin and Taliesin (both *q.v.*), possibly ruling in Cumbria before migrating to North Wales. The poems associated with his name: various heroic fragments, laments, and encomia, probably represent the verse elements of lost sagas composed some time in the late eighth or early ninth century in Powys or the Welsh Marches.

MARIE DE FRANCE  (*fl.* 1170). An Anglo-Norman poetess, probably identifiable as the half-sister of Henry II who was Abbess of Shaftesbury, Dorest, 1181–1216. The author of a collection of verse *Lais*, romantic short stories, dedicated to Henry II, and of a collection of Aesopian fables, *Ysopet*, translated from the English of King Alfred (*q.v.*) at the request of a certain Count William, possibly William Longsword, an illegitimate son of Henry II, and thus Marie's 'nephew'.

MATTHEW PARIS  (*c.* 1199–1259). He entered the Benedictine Abbey of St Albans, Hertfordshire, in 1217, and trained as a scribe and illuminator. He was the author and illustrator of several historical works including the *Lives of the Two Offas*, and the substantial *Chronica Majora* (from the Creation until 1259), and the *Historia Anglorum* (from the Norman Conquest until 1253).

NENNIUS  (*fl.* 796). A Welsh historian probably living on the Mercian border, author of the *Historia Brittonum*, a sketch of British history down to the eighth century, drawing on Gildas (*q.v.*) and other early sources; it incorporates an account of *The Campaigns of King Arthur*, a *Life of St Patrick* and a topographical *Wonders of Britain*.

*NIBELUNGENLIED*. A substantial Middle High German verse epic, composed probably somewhere in Austria, *c.* 1200, but utilizing early story-materials from the fifth-century Burgundian–Hunnish Wars. Siegfried, a warrior from the lower Rhine, woos the beautiful Burgundian Princess Kriemhild, but is slain by her brother Gunther and his friend Hagen. Later Kriemhild is married to Etzel (Attila) and avenges Siegfried by contriving the deaths of his slayers.

NICHOLAS BOZON  (*fl.* 1300). A friar, probably from Nottingham, the author of various Anglo-Norman writings: allegorical religious poems, saints' lives and sermons, and, most notably, a collection of *Contes Moralisés*, an anecdotal preaching manual.

ODO OF CHERITON  (*ob.* 1247). Born at Cheriton near Folkestone into a feudal east Kent family claiming descent from Thomas Becket. He was the author of a collection of sermons and 'parables' characteristically illustrated by fables like those of Reynard the Fox, some of which found a place in the English version of the *Gesta Romanorum* (*q.v.*).

ORDERICUS VITALIS  (1075–1143). Born at Atcham, Shropshire, the son of a Norman priest and an English mother; he was educated first at Shrewsbury and then sent to the French Benedictine monastery of Saint-Évroul, but later returned and travelled extensively in his native land. He was the author of an important and wide-ranging *Eccclesiastical History*, which is particularly significant as a chronicle of his own times, 1125–40.

OROSIUS  (*fl.* 415). He was apparently born in Spain *c.* 385, although nothing is known of his early life. He appeared briefly at Hippo in 414 to consult Augustine (*q.v.*), by whom he was sent on an anti-Pelagian mission to Palestine, although he was unsuccessful in persuading the Jerusalem synod to condemn the teachings of Pelagius (*q.v.*). At Augustine's suggestion he wrote the *Historiarum adversos Paganos*, arguing that greater calamaties had befallen the world in pagan times than since the advent of Christianity. Nothing is known of his later life. An English translation of Orosius's *History* was made during the reign of King Alfred (*q.v.*).

PELAGIUS (*fl.* 400). A British theologian and polemicist (the name by which he is known is possibly a classicized version of Mawgan); he appeared in Rome *c.* 375, travelling thence through Asia Minor to Palestine. A vigorous and influential proponent of the ascetic life, he emphasized the importance of will-power and questioned the necessary virtue of celibacy, thus arousing the enmity of orthodox preachers like Augustine and Jerome (both *q.v.*). Most of his writings were systematically destroyed, only a few innocuous tracts surviving, and his arguments are known largely through quotation by his opponents.

PETER ALFONSUS (1062–1140). An Aragonese Jew, born Moises Sefardi, he adopted the name of his godfather, Alfonso I of Aragon, when baptized at the age of forty-four. Physician to Alfonso, and probably also to Henry I, he was in England by 1130. A friend of Adelard of Bath (*q.v.*), he was the author of several works on mathematics and astronomy, as well as a collection of moralized tales under the title *Disciplina Clericalis*, which helped transmit oriental stories to the West.

PETER OF BLOIS (*c.* 1135–1212). Born probably at Blois on the Loire, and educated at Tours; he taught law for a time at Bologna and Paris and was tutor to the Norman Prince of Sicily before taking the post of secretary to Henry II and, on the death of the king, to Queen Eleanor. He was made Archdeacon of Bath in 1175 and of London in 1202. He was a prolific letter-writer, and the author of poems and various sermons, satires, and polemical tracts.

PETER DAMIAN (1007–72). Born at Ravenna, north Italy, in relatively humble circumstances; he was educated at Parma and Modena, before entering a Benedictine monastery at Fonte Avellana in 1035, becoming prior in 1043. An influential reformer, he was the author of a range of polemical tracts, as well as sermons, saints' lives, hymns, and liturgical works.

PRISCUS (*fl.* 450). A native of Thrace in the diplomatic service of Rome, he accompanied Maximinus on important embassies to the court of Attila and elsewhere. He was the author of a history of his own times, which survives only in fragments, but which was known to Jordanes (*q.v.*).

PRUDENTIUS (AURELIUS PRUDENTIUS CLEMENS) (348–*c.* 405). Born into a wealthy Hispano-Roman family, probably at Calahorra in northern Spain; he was educated in rhetoric and law, serving as a civil administrator under the Emperor Theodosius, before taking up the religious life. The first great Christian poet, he composed a considerable amount of religious verse in various metres, most notably hymns and the influential *Psychomachia*, an allegory describing the battle between virtues and vices for control of the soul.

ROBERT OF CHESTER (*fl.* 1143). Born apparently at Ketton, Cambridgeshire, for which 'Chester' was probably an early error. A contemporary of Adelard of Bath and Peter Alfonsus (both *q.v.*), he studied science in Moslem Spain, becoming Archdeacon of Pamplona in 1143. He was the author of various mathematical textbooks, including a translation of the algebra of al Khwarizmi; he supplied the first western translation of the Koran, and wrote a number of anti-Islamic tracts.

ROBERT CROSSETESTE (*c.* 1168–1253). Born in Suffolk in relatively humble circumstances, he studied at Oxford and Paris, and, although not himself a friar, became first rector of the Franciscan students at Oxford in 1224. Acquiring a reputation for high integrity and saintliness, he advanced rapidly in the Church and was elected Bishop of Lincoln – a large and turbulent diocese – in 1235. An influential author, he wrote Latin treatises on theology, physics, and astronomy, commentaries on Aristotle and Boethius, and translations from Greek; and in Anglo-Norman a treatise on estate management for the Countess of Lincoln, and the allegorical religious poem *Chasteau d'Amour.*

*ROLAND, SONG OF.* A substantial Old French verse epic, composed in its present form at the end of the eleventh century, but utilizing earlier materials. It provides a legendary account of a historical event in 778, when Charlemagne's rearguard, led by his nephew Roland, was annihilated in the Pyrenees while returning from an invasion of Saracen Spain. An earlier version of the story was sung before the Battle of Hastings by the Norman minstrel Taillefer. Several manuscript copies are extant, the earliest and best of which was written in England, 1130–50: Bodleian Library, Oxford, MS. Digby 32.

SEDULIUS SCOTUS (*fl.* 848–58). Born presumably somewhere in Ireland during the first half of the ninth century; he appears as the leader of a colony of Irish scholars at Liège *c.* 848, and, moving in governmental circles, he became an influential figure in the Carolingian world. He was the author of a variety of works of biblical exposition and political philosophy, and wrote a quantity of religious poetry in a variety of Latin metres.

SIDONIUS, CAIUS SOLLIUS APPOLLINARIS (431–88). Born at Lyons, the son of a wealthy Gallo-Roman family; appointed prefect and married the emperor's daughter; elected Bishop of Clermont in 471. He was the author of a number of elegant poems and letters of social and historical interest.

SIMON DU FRESNE (*fl.* 1200). A canon of Hereford Cathedral, Anglo-Norman poet, and friend of Gerald of Wales (*q.v.*) to whom he addressed verses recommending the facilities of the Hereford school. He also wrote a *Roman de Philosophie,* a reworking of the *Consolation* of Boethius (*q.v.*), and a *Passion of St George,* perhaps inspired by the Third Crusade.

SNORRI STURLUSON (1178–1241). The foremost Icelandic writer of medieval times. A member of a prominent landowning family in Iceland, he was educated at Oddi and elected 'law-speaker', i.e. the chief officer of the Icelandic republic, in 1213 and again in 1222. He was accused of treason by King Haakon of Norway, and assassinated in 1241. He was the author of substantial Old Icelandic writings, including a collection of sagas of the Norse kings (*Heimskringla*), and the *Prose Edda,* a combined manual of vernacular poetic conventions (*Skáldskaparmál*) and Scandinavian mythology (*Gylfaginning*).

STEPHEN LANGTON (*ob.* 1228). The son of a Lincolnshire squire; he studied at Paris and subsequently taught theology there for twenty years, during which time he made influential friends including the future Pope Innocent III. He was made cardinal in 1206 and Archbishop of Canterbury the following year, although he was prevented from taking up this appointment by the hostility of King John. He later played an influential part with the barons in procuring the Magna Carta. A prolific author, he wrote more than five hundred sermons, historical works on Richard the Lionheart and Mohammed, and some hymns, but he is best known for his biblical commentaries (in which he divided the text into the system of chapters still used).

SULPICIUS SEVERUS (*c*. 355–420). A member of a wealthy Gallo-Roman family in Aquitaine; he practised law until *c*. 392, when he retired from the world under the influence of his friend Martin of Tours. His *Life of St Martin* became an influential model for later hagiographers.

SYMMACHUS, QUINTUS AURELIUS *c*. 345–405. Born into a wealthy Gallo-Roman family; he was educated at Bordeaux and enjoyed a successful governmental career, becoming Proconsul of Africa in 373, Prefect of Rome in 384, and Consul in 391. He was an enthusiastic devotee of the declining pagan cults but managed to remain on good terms with leading Christian opponents such as Ambrose and Prudentius, and was instrumental in appointing Augustine to a teaching post at Milan (all *q.v.*). Symmachus's surviving letters and reports are a valuable historical source for the period.

TACITUS, CORNELIUS (*c*. 55–120). A member of a wealthy Roman family, probably from Narbonne in southern Gaul; he had a successful administrative career, made Consul in 97, and Governor of Asia in 112. A distinguished orator and man of letters, his writings include: a biography of his father-in-law, the general Agricola, two collections of *Annals* and *Histories*, covering the years 14–69, and the *Germania*, an important ethnological survey of the Teutonic tribes living beyond the Rhine.

TALIESIN (*fl*. 600). Welsh bard, probably a younger contemporary of Aneirin (*q.v.*) attached to the retinue of Urien of Rheged during the period of their migration from southern Scotland to Powys. He was the author of various heroic poems (of which only fragments survive), as well as laments and encomiae.

TATWINE (*ob*. 734). A monk from Bredon, Worcestershire, elected Archbishop of Canterbury in 731; he was the author of a series of Latin riddles (*cf*. Hwætberht).

THOMAS OF BAYEUX (*ob*. 1100). The son of a Norman priest at Bayeux, he was brought up in the household of Bishop Odo, whom he accompanied to England at the Conquest. A chaplain to William I, he was made Archbishop of York in 1070. He took an active interest in music, and is said to have composed many hymns, but none is identifiable with any certainty. He also wrote the verse epitaph for William's tomb at Caen.

THOMAS OF BRITAIN (*fl*. 1160). The otherwise unknown author of an Anglo-Norman version of *Tristan and Ysolt* which Gottfried von Strassburg (*q.v.*) professed to have used. He was possibly the same Thomas who composed an Anglo-Norman version of *King Horn* (*q.v.*).

THOMAS THE CISTERCIAN (*fl*. 1200). An otherwise unknown monk from Citeaux who wrote a commentary on the Psalms, dedicated to the Bishop of Clermont-Ferrand.

THOMAS OF ELMHAM (*fl*. 1415). Born probably at Elmham, Norfolk, towards the end of the fourteenth century; he became a military chaplain and was present at the Battle of Agincourt, 1415. Subsequently a monk at Canterbury, he wrote various historical works including a Life of Henry V and a history of his own monastery of St Augustine's, Canterbury.

THOMAS OF ELY (*fl.* 1170). An otherwise unknown monk of Ely, Cambridgeshire; he was the author of a collection of miracles incorporated into the *Liber Eliensis* (*q.v.*).

VENANTIUS FORTUNATUS (*c.* 530–610). Born at Treviso near Venice; he was educated at Ravenna and became court poet in the retinue of the Frankish King Sigibert at Metz, a post he relinquished *c.* 565 to become first steward, then chaplain, to the Thuringian princess-turned-nun, Radegunde, at Poitiers. He was eventually elected Bishop of Poitiers in *c.* 599. He was the author of a number of elegant verse elegies and panegyrics including the *De Excidio Thoringiae*, composed for his patroness, Radegunde, and, prompted by the presentation to Poitiers of relics of the true cross, the cross-cult hymns *Vexilla Regis Prodeunt* and *Pange Lingua*.

*VISIO PAULI.* The Latin version of a Greek or Syriac original, enlarging St Paul's statement about being 'caught up into the third heaven' (II Corinthians 12. 2); it describes the fires of hell and various punishments reserved for sinners, and the activities of St Michael and other angels in guarding souls on their journey from earth to heaven. A persistent influence, it was drawn upon, for example, by the author of one of the Blickling Homilies (*q.v.*).

*VOLUNDARKVITHA (LAY OF WELAND).* An Old Norse poem in the Poetic Edda, a thirteenth-century compilation but clearly containing ancient material. It describes how the legendary smith Weland is captured by the Geatish King Nidúd (Nithad) and forced to work in the king's smithy, but eventually takes his revenge by slaying the king's young sons and raping his daughter Bödvild (Beadohild), before escaping.

WACE, ROBERT (*fl.* 1160). Born in the island of Jersey, he studied at Caen and later became a cleric at Bayeux, Normandy. Among other poetry on religious and historical topics, he composed an Anglo-Norman *Brut*, or history of Britain, dedicated to Eleanor of Aquitaine and drawn upon by Laȝamon (*q.v.*), and the *Roman de Rou*, a history of the Dukes of Normandy, including an account of the Conquest of England by William I.

WALCHER OF MALVERN (*ob.* 1135). A Lotharingian monk, who was in England by 1091 and eventually became Prior of Malvern Abbey, Worcestershire. Mathematician and astronomer, he conducted experiments attempting to fix differential time between England and Italy, and later employed an advanced form of reckoning by degrees, minutes, and seconds, learned from Peter Alfonsus (*q.v.*).

WALTER MAP (*c.* 1140–1210). A cleric of Welsh descent, possibly from Herefordshire; he studied at Paris before joining the secretariat of Henry II, where he enjoyed a considerable reputation as a humorist – reflected in his sole authenticated work, the gossipy, anecdotal compendium, *De Nugis Curialium*, ('Courtiers' Trifles'), 1181–93. He was made a canon of St Paul's, London, in 1192, and Archdeacon of Oxford five years later.

*WALTHARIUS POESIS (THE SONG OF WALTER/WALDERE).* A Germano-Latin verse epic, probably of the ninth century. Set against the background of the fifth-century Burgundian–Hunnish Wars, it describes events contingent upon the escape from Attila's court of the West Germanic hostages Hagena, Walter (Waldere) and his betrothed Hildegund (Hildegyth).

**WILLIAM OF AQUITAINE** (1071–1127). Seventh Count of Poiters and ninth Duke of Aquitaine, he inherited estates greater than those of the King of France. Socially dissolute, he proved a disastrous general during the First Crusade. He was among the earliest known French troubadours; eleven of his poems survive: five of them obscene in the *fabliau* manner, the remainder more courtly in tone.

**WILLIAM OF MALMESBURY** (*c.* 1085–1143). Born in the south-west of England, of mixed Norman and English parentage; he was brought up in the Benedictine abbey at Malmesbury, Wiltshire, where he eventually became librarian. He was the author of various historical works, notably the substantial *Gesta Regum Anglorum*, a political history from Anglo-Saxon times to his own day, the *Gesta Pontificum Anglorum*, a history of the English Church over the same period, and the unfinished *Historia Novella*, dealing with the Civil War of Stephen's reign.

**WILLIAM OF OCKHAM** (*c.* 1285–1349). Probably born in Surrey; he studied at Oxford and, although denounced as a heretic by the chancellor, later taught theology there before moving on to Paris. He took a leading part in defending the Franciscan Order against attacks by the papacy, and urged the freedom of the State from ecclesiastical jurisdiction. An eminent Aristotelian logician, philosopher, and political theorist, his most influential writings include a *Commentary on the Sentences* and *Quodlibeta*.

**WILLIAM OF SHERWOOD** (*ob.* 1279). He presumably came from Nottinghamshire, but little is known of his early life until he became Treasurer of Lincoln Cathedral in 1254. A one-time teacher at Paris, he was among the earliest to introduce Aristotelian logic to the West, and wrote the influential textbook *Introductiones in Logicum*.

# Index

345